Patricia Clarke, a journalist for many [...] ies and *A Colonial Woman*, has uncovered [...] m the first women to publish in Austra [...] r-national acclaim; from the writers o [...] se 'daring' copy brought a raffish touch [...] m crusading reformers to society ladies who wrote the social notes.

Previous books

The Governesses. Letters from the Colonies 1862–1882 (1985)
A Colonial Woman. The life and times of Mary Braidwood Mowle
1827–1857 (1986)

PEN PORTRAITS

*Women writers and journalists in
nineteenth century Australia*

Patricia Clarke

PANDORA

Sydney   London   New York

First published in Australia by Pandora Press, an imprint of the trade
division of Unwin Hyman Limited, in 1988

Set in 10.5/12pt Goudy Old Style by Indah Photosetting Centre Sdn Bhd, Malaysia
and printed in Singapore by Kim Hup Lee Printing

Allen and Unwin Australia Pty Ltd
8 Napier Street, North Sydney, NSW 2059, Australia

Pandora Press
Unwin Hyman Limited
15-17 Broadwick Street, London W1V 1FP, England

Allen and Unwin New Zealand with the Port Nicholson Press
60 Cambridge Terrace, Wellington, New Zealand

National Library of Australia
Cataloguing-in-Publication entry:

Clarke, Patricia.
Pen portraits: women writers and journalists in nineteenth century Australia.
Bibliography.
Includes index.
ISBN 0 04 649044 2.
1. Women authors, Australian — 19th century. 2. Women journalists-Australia.
3. Journalism — Australia — History — 19th century. 4. Australian literature —
19th century. I. Title.
A820.9'9287

Contents

Illustrations   vii

Acknowledgements   x

1 **A Blank Page**   1
   Thérèse Huber; Mary Leman Grimstone

2 **The First to Publish**   11
   *Ann Howe; Anna Maria Bunn; Fidelia Hill; Charlotte Barton; Mary
   Theresa Vidal*

3 **A Degree of Professionalism**   27
   Catherine Helen Spence; Louisa Anne Meredith; Louisa Atkinson

4 **Visitors and Lady Travellers**   45
   *Elizabeth P. Ramsay-Laye ('Isabel Massary') Clara Aspinall; Caroline
   Woolmer Leakey; Celeste de Chabrillan (Mogador); Ellen Clacy;
   Elizabeth A. Murray; Mrs R. E. (Sarah) Lee; Anne Bowman; Isabella
   Lucy Bird; Lady Broome*

5 **Eccentric Entrepreneurs**   64
   Cora Anna Weekes of the Spectator; *Caroline Dexter and Harriet
   Clisby of the* Interpreter

6 **Mostly Moral and Earnest**   85
   *Matilda Jane Evans ('Maud Jean Franc'); Maria Scott ('Mist'); Ellen
   Liston; Henrietta Foott; Eliza (Winstanley) O'Flaherty; Sarah Susannah
   Perry; Caroline Carleton; Mary Eva O'Doherty; Francis R. Hopkins
   and the* Australian Ladies' Annual

7 **Early Journalists and Country Editors**   106
   *Adelaide Eliza Ironside; Anna Blackwell; Emily Manning ('Australie');
   Mrs Carl (Jane) Fischer; Elizabeth Macfaull; Mercy Shenton; Sarah
   Gill; Margaret Falls; Mrs David Griffiths Jones; Marion Leathem; Mary
   (Boyle) Garland; Annie Christie Massy*

8 **Voices from the Bush**   126
   *Katherine Kirkland, Annie Baxter (Dawbin); Harriet W. Daly; Mrs
   Edward Millett; Jessie Lloyd; K. Langloh Parker; Laura Maude Palmer-
   Archer; Barbara Baynton*

9 Renown, Mostly Abroad   142
   *Ada Cambridge; Jessie Catherine Couvreur ('Tasma'); Rosa Caroline
   Campbell Praed; Catherine Martin; Coo-ee—Harriette Anne Martin,
   Kathleen Caffyn ('Iota') and Margaret Thomas; By creek and
   gully—Mary Lucy (Lala) Fisher*

10 New Women in Print   160
   *Louisa Lawson and Dawn; Maybanke Susannah Wolstenholme
   (Anderson) and Woman's Voice; Ellen Augusta Chads; Catherine Hay
   Thomson; Evelyn Gough; Annie Bright*

11 Women's Voices, Very Diverse   183
   *Alice Henry; Bella Guerin; Mary Gaunt; Frances Gillam Holden;
   Grace Jennings Carmichael; Mrs (Bessie) Harrison Lee*

12 Women's Pages, Slightly Fanciful   203
   *Lucinda Gullett; Mary Hannay Foott; Agnes G. Murphy; Ada (Kidgell)
   Holman; Agnes Rose-Soley ('Rose de Bohème'); Stella Allan; Janet
   Nanson; Margaret Baxter; Hummer and 'Lucinda Sharpe'; Mary Ann
   Cameron; Jeannie Lockett; Mary Gilmore*

13 Newspaper Women and Social Ladies   226
   *Alexina Maude Wildman ('Sappho Smith'); Florence Baverstock; Louise
   Mack; Conor O'Brien; Alice Rosman; Eugenia Stone; Isabelle Le
   Patourel; Theodosia Britton; Zara Aronson; Ethel Turner; Mary Grant
   Bruce*

14 Postscript   251

Notes   254

Select Bibliography   270

Index   274

Illustrations

Female writer, *Colonial Advocate* 1828   8
Advertisement for *Woman's Love* 1832   8
Preface of *Woman's Love*   8
Woman's Love Postscript   10
Sydney Gazette 1833   13
Anna Maria Bunn   14
Sampler, Anna Maria Bunn 1824   15
Title page of *The Guardian*   17
Drawing by Anna Maria Bunn   17
Subscribers to Fidelia Hill's *Poems*   19
Charlotte Barton   21
Dedication of *A mother's offering to her children*   22
Advertisement for *A mother's offering*   22
Mary Theresa Vidal   25
Catherine Helen Spence   30
Louisa Anne Meredith   37
Title page of *My home in Tasmania*   37
Title page of *Bush friends in Tasmania*   39
Caroline Louisa Waring Atkinson   41
'Bushfire' in *Gertrude, the emigrant*   42
'New chum' in *Gertrude, the emigrant*   42
Title page *The broad arrow*   48
Celeste de Chabrillan   51
Elizabeth A. Murray   55
Title page *Adventures in Australia*   58
'The kangaroo hunt' *Adventures in Australia*   59
Isabella Bird Bishop   62
Spectator 31 July 1858   66
Spectator 1 September 1858   69
Caroline Dexter   74
'Bloomer' revolution   76
Title page and frontispiece *Ladies Almanack 1858*   78
Title page and page 2 of *Interpreter*   81
Dr Harriet Clisby   83
Title page of *Marian*   88
Ellen Liston   91
Sketch of Darling River, Henrietta Foott   93
Henrietta Foott   94
Eliza Winstanley   96
'Song of Australia'   99
Eva O'Doherty   101

Title page of *Ladies Annual 1878*   103
Adelaide Ironside   107
Anna Blackwell   111
Emily Manning   114
Mrs Carl Fischer   117
Mrs Marion Leathem   120
Annie Christie Massy   124
Jessie Lloyd   129
Illustrated Sydney News 23 December 1882   131
'Norah' in *Retribution*   132
Illustration *Retribution*   132
K. Langloh Parker   135
Laura Palmer-Archer   137
Barbara Baynton as a young woman   139
Barbara Baynton   139
Ada Cambridge   143
Jessie Couvreur   148
Rosa Campbell Praed   153
Lala Fisher   159
Louisa Lawson   161
First issue of *Dawn* 15 May 1888   163
Boycott of *Dawn* 5 October 1889   166
Advertisements in *Dawn*   168
Fashion page in *Dawn*   169
Cover of *Dawn* March 1891   170
Seventeenth anniversary *Dawn*   171
Advertisement from *Australian Woman's Magazine*   173
Maybanke Susannah Wolstenholme (Anderson)   174
First issue of *Woman's Voice*   175
Woman cyclist in *Woman's Voice* 1894   179
Alice Henry and Evelyn Gough   185
Bella Guerin   189
Mary Gaunt   191
Illustration from *Childhood in bud and blossom*   192
Frances Gillam Holden   195
Frances Holden versus doctors *Bulletin* 27 August 1887   195
Mrs Harrison (Bessie) Lee   201
Lucinda Gullett   208
The Lady's Page *Australasian* 16 May 1891   209
Mary Hannay Foott   211
Major General C. H. Foott   214
Lieutenant Arthur Foott   214
'Lady's Letter' *Punch* 2 April 1891   216
Agnes Rose-Soley   218
'Feminine Facts and Fancies' *Age* 10 September 1898   219
'Women's Realm' *Argus* 16 April 1898   221
Stella Allan   221
Janet Nanson   223
'Sappho Smith' *Bulletin* 21 September 1889   229

Florence Baverstock   232
Louise Mack   235
Alice Grant Rosman   239
Isabelle Le Patourel   241
Theodosia Britton   242
Zara Baar Aronson   244
'Ladies' Page' *Sydney Mail*   245
Ethel Turner   247
Mary Grant Bruce   249

Acknowledgements

The aim of this book is to celebrate the lives and achievements of women writers and journalists in nineteenth century Australia. Many of the pioneers in the field — creative writers; writers of serials (the nineteenth century equivalent of today's radio and television 'soap operas'); and journalists, are included but I make no claim to have written about *all* women writers or journalists.

In the case of journalists it is unfortunate that the identities of many will remain unknown. This is not only because of the widespread use of pseudonyms but because at least until the last decade of the century, they were employed mainly as casual contributors. Tracing these women has been a considerable exercise in detection, in the course of which I contacted most major newspapers in Australia. Unfortunately few have retained any sort of staff records from the nineteenth century.

The *Sydney Morning Herald* is an exception, in having an archives section, although many valuable records have been disposed of; I am grateful for the valuable help I received from the archivist Eileen O'Dwyer. A few records of the Melbourne *Argus* and *Age* are held by the Latrobe Library and I acknowledge the help of Tony Marshall, manuscripts librarian in locating these. The *West Australian* through Chief Librarian, David Andrews, also provided some valuable information. Unfortunately, however, the reply of Keith Dixon, archivist at the *Age*, anxious to help but unable to do so, was typical. He wrote, 'there literally are no records'. Paybooks from the last century were found to be in the way and were 'simply dumped' in the 1960s. For women journalists in the country I acknowledge the help and interest of Rod Kirkpatrick, author of *Sworn to no master*, a history of the Queensland country press.

As in the past, I have had wonderful help for which I am very grateful from the staff of the National Library of Australia in the Australian Studies, Newspaper and Microfilm, Manuscripts, Pictorial and Inter-Library Loan sections. I am also indebted to the staffs of the Mitchell Library in Sydney, the Latrobe Library in Melbourne, the John Oxley Library in Brisbane, the Tasmanian State Library and State Archives and from the South Australian State Library, the Battye Library in Perth and the Fawcett Library at the City of London Polytechnic.

I am grateful for help from Jan Blank, Librarian, and Sandra Birchill, English Department, at the Australian Defence Forces Academy, Canberra, particularly for the opportunity to use their literary database. I also wish to thank Geoffrey Serle, Chris Cunneen and Ann Smith of the *Australian Dictionary of Biography* for access to unpublished material and card indexes, particularly Robin Walker's and Jim Gibbney's newspaper indexes.

I have had valuable assistance from many other people, some of them descendants of the women writers/journalists I have written about. I wish to thank them for their very kind interest and help: Dr Terry Bunn, Thirroul, New South Wales; Mr Norm Bloomfield, editor of the *Molong Express*, New South Wales; Mrs Gladys Cooney, Broadbeach Waters, Queensland; Miss Janet Cosh, Bowral, New South Wales; Mrs Audrey Dudley, Toorak, Victoria; Mrs Althea Farr, Double Bay, New South Wales; Mr Richard Goodwin, editor *Warnambool Standard*, Victoria; Mr H. B. Gullett and Mrs Ruth Gullett, Griffith, Australian Capital Territory; Ms Fleur Harmsen, Snug, Tasmania; Ms Eleanor Rice Hays, New York, USA; Mrs Ethel Heward, Rosebery, New South Wales; Mrs Isobel Keep, Hawthorn, Victoria; Mr Ian Macfarlane, Malvern, Victoria; Mrs Joan McKenzie, Coonamble, New South Wales; Mrs Jill Marshall, Kerang, Victoria; Lady Murray, Murrumbateman, New South Wales; Mr Don Norman, Hobart, Tasmania; Mrs Bethia Ogden, Gloucestershire, England; Mr Glenville Pike, Mareeba, North Queensland; Mr David Rutherford, Forster, New South Wales; Mrs Celia Taylor, Rockingham, Western Australia; the late Wilfred Wallace, Summer Hill, New South Wales; Mrs Sheila Wigmore, Hobart, Tasmania; Dr Ailsa Zainu'ddin, Monash University, Victoria; Dr Gerhard Bagan, University of Kiel; Mr Bill Cameron, Bourke and District Historical Society, New South Wales and Mr Maurice Gentry, Kyneton Historical Society, Victoria.

I am also very grateful to some of those mentioned who lent me photographs for copying and to my husband, Hugh for his assistance and for the interest he took in the book. I also thank the people and organisations who have given permission for their photographs to be reproduced.

This book was researched with the assistance of a Special Purpose Grant from the Literature Board of the Australia Council. This helped with travel and research expenses and the acquiring of photographs and I express my appreciation to the Board.

1

A Blank Page

'. . . all the young ladies write Novels . . .'
London *Times*

At the time the first women convicts arrived in Australia, writing novels was a fashionable pursuit among the young ladies of London society. In 1796 the London *Times* in a satirical comment implied that encouraging pupils to write novels was the main aim of fashionable boarding schools: 'Four thousand and seventy-three Novels are now in the Press from the pens of young ladies of Fashion. At Mrs. D . . . s School all the young ladies write Novels . . .'[1] Few of the women who came to Australia were ladies of fashion — the overwhelming majority in the early years were convict and poor, many illiterate. No more than a handful would have heard of the novel-writing fashion.

Those who could write told of life in an alien environment in letters to their families and friends, in their diaries, or in petitions in which they pleaded for a reduction in their sentences or other indulgences from the authorities. It is not surprising therefore that the first novel written by a woman and published in Australia did not appear until fifty years after the first fleet sailed into Botany Bay. (The first novel written by a man and published in Australia, Henry Savery's *Quintus Servinton*, preceded it by only eight years.) When the first novel by a woman did appear in 1838 its author was anonymous, although she is now known to have been Irish-born Anna Maria Bunn. Her book was in the style of the light romantic novels fashionable at the time in Britain. In this she was atypical of women writers in Australia in the nineteenth century.

The women writers who did emerge in Australia were usually not fashionable entertainers but serious women. Many of them wrote to convey a message — often of moral uplift — to their readers. Many also wrote to make money, for although emigration to the new world was often seen as a way to improve one's lot, this was not always the case. Not a few women who arrived as members of middle-class families found themselves searching for ways to supplement faded family fortunes or substitute the earnings of male family members struck down by illness or a turn of fortune.

Many such women had been educated at home in families where there was a respect for learning; some had learned several languages; others had studied natural history. Quite a number had a talent for drawing and painting as well as for writing. The acceptable way for educated women of limited means to earn money in nineteenth century Australia was by becoming a governess or a teacher. Employment as a governess was insecure, subject to the whims and financial stability of the employing family, as was employment as a teacher until government schools became more widespread. Greater still, however, was the insecurity involved in attempting to make money by writing.

Only a small number of women wrote for publication in colonial Australia. It was an unusual occupation for women and by and large the writers themselves were out of the ordinary. Some had literary talent; some found they could make money out of writing; some had a compelling urge to communicate their views on social issues. Because they chose such an uncertain and such a public way of making money (although they often used pseudonyms) and because they had confidence in the belief that their ideas were worth communicating, they were generally strongly individualistic. Difficult though it often was for them, through selling their work in the commercial world they increased the prospects of independence for women.

The first women to write in Australia and to achieve publication were born in England, Ireland or Scotland. Most came from middle-class families—the daughters of clergymen, merchants, doctors, army officers—and they brought with them the ideas acquired from their upbringing. When they wrote it was as women from their home countries. In Anna Maria Bunn's novel *The Guardian* Australia is mentioned rarely and then only in a derogatory way as a strange, uncivilised place. Mary Vidal, a clergyman's wife, expressed English views on the role of servants and the proper structure of society in her *Tales for the bush*. The first change came with Charlotte Barton, a governess of independent mind from London and Australia's first writer for children. Although her technique was far from new, the stories in her *A mother's offering to her children*, published in 1841, were adventures set in Australia, and gave Australian children local heroes to read about for the first time.

Women of greater accomplishment followed, women with vision and talent to convey their experience of Australian life. The first social commentary written from a woman's viewpoint to reach the outside world came from a talented Englishwoman from Birmingham, Louisa Meredith. Catherine Spence, arriving from Scotland as a young girl, was the first woman writer to accept Australia as home and as a place to exercise her talents for social reform. Louisa Atkinson, who wrote true-to-life novels set in the Australian bush and delicate commentaries on natural phenomena, was the first native-born Australian woman writer of note.

Such women were followed later in the century by those whose writing received greater acclaim although their work sometimes lacked an Australian flavour. Ada Cambridge languishing in one country parsonage after another in Victoria, wrote successfully about characters that belonged as much to the English provinces where she had grown up as to Australia. Rosa Campbell Praed, born on a Queensland sheep and cattle station, was also most successful but as an expatriate writer. She left Australia at the age of twenty-five and later wrote over forty novels of which about half had no Australian association. Jessie Couvreur too left Australia before writing the novels that won her acclaim. The best imaginative writing was to come from the enigmatic Barbara Baynton towards the end of the nineteenth century. Her writing was set firmly in the bush but she too was an expatriate for a long period.

By the end of the century there were many strands to women's writing in Australia. Through the second half of the century there had been a number of women writers visiting the country. They had written perceptively of Australia, usually with a sure sense of what readers on the other side of the world wanted to read. There were women, like Catherine Spence, who wrote with reforming zeal, some of them advancing extreme solutions to social problems. 'Maud Jeanne Franc' followed in Mary Vidal's footsteps with book after book pointing her readers to the narrow path of virtue. As women writers became more vocal: Louisa Lawson advocated female suffrage, freedom for women to work at jobs previously closed to them, and freedom from unhappy marriages; Maybanke Wolstenholme advocated, in addition to female suffrage, many other freedoms necessary for female emancipation; Frances Holden sought better education for women and Bessie Lee counselled celibate marriages as a means of stopping the too-frequent births that were crippling the lives of overburdened mothers.

Some of the better-known writers achieved publication in book form without much trouble, more usually through English publishers. The lesser-known discovered that the most accessible outlets for their fiction and poetry were newspapers and periodicals. Some few women had their novels published initially as books, but more often fiction by women writers appeared first in serial form in newspapers. It was the age of serials, in England the next episode of the current Charles Dickens serial always being awaited eagerly. In Australia the situation was accentuated by the scarcity of book publishers. Women who could not get their books accepted by an English publisher — and with the difficulties with mails and the lack of overseas interest in Australian life this was difficult if not impossible — sought serial publication in Australia. When serial-reading was at its height many newspapers and periodicals ran three or four simultaneously.

Through this first contact with newspapers some women writers, offering their novels for publication as serials, were able also to interest editors in series of factual articles. Louisa Atkinson had serials published in the *Sydney Morning Herald* and the *Sydney Mail* and was able in 1861 to interest the editor, James Fairfax, in publishing a series of articles 'A Voice from the country', the first such long-running series of newspaper articles by a woman to be published in Australia. Jessie Lloyd did much the same twenty years later with her series, 'The Silverleaf Papers' published in the *Illustrated Sydney News* which followed the publication of her serial, 'All aboard: A tale for Christmas' in the *Echo*.

These, and many other women like them, were the forerunners of women journalists. The more fortunate were engaged under arrangements with some continuity to do a series of articles, but the majority were casual contributors with no security and were no doubt paid, as many male casual journalists (known as 'penny-a-liners') were, at so much per line. They were followed by a few women in the 1880s who were appointed to full-time positions on newspapers and periodicals.

The first women employed to write for newspapers wrote on general rather than specifically women's topics. This situation changed in the 1880s and 1890s when newspapers and periodicals began to include women's columns and pages. This increased the demand for women writers and led to more gaining permanent employment as journalists, but it was a backward step for their professional development. Soon almost all women journalists were confined to 'the deadly, dreary ruck of long dress reports and the lists of those who "also ran" at miscellaneous functions'.[2] Women journalists were not the only losers in this situation, for what they wrote tended to reinforce complacency in their women readers and to shield them from issues of some significance.

In the nineteenth century some women began publications of their own. Until Louisa Lawson's *Dawn* and, to a lesser extent, Maybanke Susannah Wolstenholme's *Woman's Voice*, however, these were short lived. One, the *Interpreter* was an esoteric curiosity that ran for only two issues, another the *Spectator*, a periodical of professional appearance, was apparently produced by a charlatan. The *Australian Woman's Magazine and Domestic Journal* proved to be a forerunner of the popular twentieth century women's magazines in its aim to provide entertainment rather than enlightenment.

Before the advent of women's writing in Australia, two women—Thérèse Huber and Mary Grimstone—provided a link with the cosmopolitan world of European women's writing and with ideas on the role of women much in advance of Australian attitudes.

Thérèse Huber

Thérèse Huber, one of the first professional woman writers in Germany, never actually visited Australia but she wrote the first novel to use Australia as part of its background. Written in German, *Adventures on a journey to New Holland* was published under the name of her second husband, Ludwig Ferdinand Huber, in 1801. She obtained the information for her book from her first husband, (Johann) Georg Adam Forster, a German writer, traveller and revolutionary who, at the age of eighteen, with his father Johann Reinhold Forster, had accompanied Captain James Cook on his 1772–75 voyage around the world. Georg Forster's account of this voyage, *A voyage round the world in His Brittanic Majesty's sloop, Resolution*, became one of the most popular travel books of the time.[3]

In 1785 Forster married Thérèse Heyne, daughter of the professor of classics at Gottingen University, but the marriage was unhappy and a young diplomat, Ludwig Ferdinand Huber, joined the household at Mainz as Thérèse's lover. After the death of Forster in 1794, Thérèse married Huber and until his death in 1804 published all her writings under his name.

Adventures on a journey to New Holland is a novel written in the form of letters from a character named Rudolph to his friends in Germany from places touched on during his voyage, among them the Cape of Good Hope and the convict settlements at Sydney and Norfolk Island. While Thérèse Huber's book is no more than a curiosity in the history of Australian writing, it is noteworthy that several other women also wrote about Australia without seeing the country.

Thérèse Huber was an outstanding woman. From 1816 to 1823 she was editor of one of the widest-read German newspapers, the Stuttgart *Morgenblatt fur gebildte Stande*, which is said to have exercised a great influence on German cultural and literary life. Between 1795 and 1829 she wrote about sixty stories and novels. When she died in Augsberg in 1829 she was described as 'one of the most remarkable women of the age'.[4]

Mary Leman Grimstone

'Woman has, like Esau, sold her birthright for a mess of potage . . .'

Mary Leman Grimstone was a visitor to Hobart from London for three years from 1826 to 1829. During that time she was not only the author of the first novel written by a woman in Australia but created a sensation among

Hobart's small and insular population with a sensational article she had published in London. At a time when it was very unusual for women's writings to be published in the press, Mary Grimstone was probably the first woman to look at Australian society and to have her views published in a major newspaper.

The circumstances of Mary Grimstone's life when she arrived in Hobart twenty-two years after the establishment of the penal colony, are uncertain. She appeared in the shipping list of the *Cape Packet* as 'Miss Reed' [Rede] but when she left Hobart three years later she left as 'Mrs Grimsone' [Grimstone], although there is no record of her marriage or of a Mr Grimstone in Tasmania. From some of her poetry it seems likely that she was already widowed when she arrived in Hobart. She travelled on the *Cape Packet* with her sister, Lucy Lemon Adey (formerly Rede), wife of Stephen Adey, who had been appointed a managing agent for the Van Diemen's Land Company.[5]

Mary Leman Grimstone was a daughter of Leman Thomas Rede, a lawyer and writer, born in Beccles, Suffolk, who had to leave England to escape from creditors. Mary was born in Hamburg about 1800 and in 1810, after the death of her father, she and her mother, brothers and sisters returned to England to live. Two of Mary's brothers, Leman Thomas Rede (1799–1832) and William Leman Rede (1802–1847) were connected with the theatre. Leman Rede, trained as a lawyer, acted in many melodramas in English provincial cities. William Rede was the author of many plays, his most successful, *The Rake's Progress*, running for a season at the Olympic Theatre in 1833.[6] Mary Grimstone's sister, Lucy Leman, wife of Stephen Adey, was a writer who had had a small book of poems published in London in 1824.

Hobart had few attractions for a woman fresh from such a world. While still only about twenty, Mary Grimstone had had two volumes of poetry published in London under the pseudonym 'Oscar': *Zayda, a Spanish tale, in three cantos, and other poems, stanzas, and canzonets* (1820) and *Cleone, Summer's Sunset Vision, the Confession, with other poems and stanzas* (1821).[7] She had also probably written her novel, *The Beauty of the British Alps; or, Love at first sight*, which she described as a 'first essay', although it was not to be published until her return to England.

Her views on Hobart society were published in London under the title *Extracts from a letter from a lady residing in Hobart Town*:

> ... you could hardly imagine that a country like England could produce such an illiterate cub as this Colony. Who would not have expected to find by this time a Library at least. They had one at South Carolina before it was established twelve months. Saturn is not more remote from the sun than Hobart Town from all science and literature. Variety is a word unknown in its vocabulary, and "the light that surrounds you must be all from within." The mercantile classes are animated by an avaricious, I should rather say, *voracious* spirit of money-getting, which

engenders jealousy and ill-will when there is the least collision of interest or chance of rivalry; there are the democracy of the Colony, proscribed at Government House, and hostile to all the measures that emanate thence; and looking to Murray, the Editor of the *Colonial Times* as their political leader. The Government and law officers &c. &c., form, and are completely in the spirit of the aristocracy; they are dull, reserved, punctiliously jealous of compromising their rank; all etiquette and caution. One reason for all this is, that there are a great many mushrooms among them; and there is no pride so stiff and ungraceful as the pride of upstarts. Entertainments are occasionally given, but, as Madame de Stael says of the Germans, they are rather ceremonies than parties of pleasure; and this remark applies to the first house in this place.

A card for a dinner-party gives me the horrors; its very touch has the effect ascribed to the torpedo. Often, very often, I had much rather stay at home; but, like the poor King of Arragon, "etiquette won't let me." I summon my fortitude and set forth. The servant that opens the door to me says, in his manner, "You may come in; but are to say nothing." I find the chairs set in a row, and the company in as good order as a fine set of teeth, not grinning however; had Lord Chesterfield himself been master of the ceremonies, they could not be more remote than *that*. Some spirit more adventurous than others will, perhaps, make a remark, as you would throw ballast out of a balloon, in order to get above a foggy atmosphere; but caution, like the physician at Sancho's governor's dinner, stands by, and forbids any thing like freedom of discussion or observation . . .

Accustomed, as I have been to a cultivated country, abounding with sources of interest and excitement, and in my own family to a great share of wit, humour, and originality, it is hardly possible to give you an idea how much *I feel the Cimmerian dulness* [sic] of this town . . .

To any one asking me about settling in Hobart Town, Humdrumstadt, I should say, that there were good salaries attached to public offices, and little to do; and, from all I can learn, the returns in business are very fair, and the commerce increasing: but beyond that, unless to eat, drink, and sleep, and mope were sufficient to render their lives endurable, let them not attempt it . . .[8]

When reproduced in the *Colonial Advocate* in Hobart under the heading 'FEMALE WRITER', with some minor alterations, it created a furore.

While she was in Hobart Mary Grimstone wrote a novel *Woman's Love*, published in London in 1832, and several poems which appeared in Hobart papers. After her return to England she sent some poems and articles to Australian papers including 'The Little Prisoner's Expostulation by M. L. G. Author of "Woman's Love" ' which appeared in the *Hobart Town Chronicle* on 5 March 1833 and 'Van Diemen's Land', a poem by M. Leman Grimstone, which appeared in the *Port Phillip Patriot and Morning Advertiser* on 12 June 1845. She was also the author of several other novels including *Louisa*

FEMALE WRITER.

Extract of a Letter from a Lady residing at Hobart Town, Van Diemen's Land, inserted in the Morning Herald, as alluded to in the Colonial Advocate for March.

After an absence of nearly three months, Mr. * * * * returned to Hobart Town. For the last seven or eight weeks, we had no letters from him, he having no means of sending them—and our anxiety became very great, especially as he was coasting, and we knew the coast to be a dangerous one. Mr. * * * * is pleased with the country, in many parts, as far as he has seen, and still more so with the climate, which on that side of the Island, the North-east and North-west, is greatly superior to that of Hobart Town.

While living in Hobart, London author Mary Leman Grimstone sent an article containing her views on Hobart society to the London Morning Herald. *When the article was reprinted in the* Hobart Colonial Advocate *it created a furore.* (Colonial Advocate 1 May 1828)

JUST RECEIVED
And for sale at the Courier Office.
MRS. GRIMSTONE'S new novel in 3 vols, entitled ' Woman's Love.'

JUST RECEIVED PER LAST AR-RIVALS,
And on sale at the Courier Office,
Liverpool-street,
DR. HENDERSON'S new work on these colonies, with plates, price 16s.
Also,—
Alexander's East India Magazine and Colonial and Commercial Journal, 2s. 6d. each number.

SUPERIOR TEAS.

The first novel written by a woman in Australia was Woman's Love. *Soon after it was published in London in 1832 the Hobart Town* Courier *announced that it was for sale in Hobart.* (Hobart Town Courier 5 October 1832)

PREFACE.

THE following pages were written in Van Dieman's Land. A voyage is said to improve Madeira, I would it had the same effect on a manuscript; I should then have less occasion to claim indulgence for the defects and deficiencies of this production.

It may be asked, why did I not look around me for the materials of my story? First, because, to use the language of the eloquent L. E. L., I am " intensely English," and during my absence from home, found one of my greatest enjoyments in giving to it my imagination. Secondly, in the small circle of a Colonial community, I could scarcely have escaped, however unreal might be the characters I drew, the charge of designed personality. But I have not come away without recol-

---

In the Preface to Woman's Love *Mary Leman Grimstone explained the Tasmanian origins of her book. She was in her late twenties when she arrived in Hobart with her sister Lucy Leman Adey and was probably a widow. (W. L. Crowther Library, State Library of Tasmania)*

Egerton, or Castle Herbert, published in 1830.

In the preface to *Woman's Love* she said that the novel was written in Van Dieman's Land but she had decided against using local material, because:

> I am "intensely English," and during my absence from home, found one of my greatest enjoyments in giving to it my imagination. Secondly, in the small circle of a Colonial community, I could scarcely have escaped, however unreal might be the characters I drew, the charge of designed personality.[9]

Woman's Love is a complicated romance set among provincial society in Devonshire. It includes some advanced views on the role of women and has been described as an early feminist novel. There are a few minor references to Tasmania, including transportation and the alleged ugliness of the Tasmanian Aboriginals.[10]

In a postscript to *Woman's Love* Mary Grimstone put her views on woman's position in society. She pleaded for recognition of the equality of men's and women's intellects — 'The depreciation of the female intellect is an evil of no limited extent; it acts and reacts fatally on all the institutions and relations of social life'[11] — and the need for equal education for women:

> Are the women of a country not so important to the well-being of a country as the men? Why then are colleges (with their honours and rewards) endowed for the one; while the other have no refuge from ignorance, but in those miserable asylums, (speaking of the generality), boarding-schools?
>
> The depreciation of woman, and all its consequent evils, have resulted from error and miscalculation on both sides. Man argued that it would procure him more happiness to make woman his slave than his coadjutrix in life; and she saw him take the business, believing that he left her the pleasures of existence . . . Woman has, like Esau, sold her birthright for a mess of potage . . . Extravagant refinement, luxurious idleness, hyberbolical [sic] flattery, these have been the bribes of her abasement.[12]

Mary Grimstone continued to produce novels including *Character, or Jew and Gentile*, a plea for social freedom for Jews, with a plot which includes the transportation of a Jew to Van Dieman's Land. The *Tasmanian and Austral-Asiatic Review* in a review praised the author's 'intimate knowledge of human nature'.[13] In *Cleone: a Tale of Married Life*, published in 1834, the story ends with the return of the hero, a barrister, to Van Dieman's Land where he had been previously a convict.

Soon after her return to England, Mary Grimstone became associated with the circle of women who wrote for *La Belle Assemblée or, Bell's Court and Fashionable Magazine*, one of the forerunners of today's glossy women's magazines, which featured London and Paris fashions and literary articles. She

9

POSTSCRIPT.

Tʜᴇ dramatist has his prologue and epilogue, and, at his *entrée* and exit, speaks for himself. The preface affords to other writers the first advantage, but they have nothing adequate to the latter, unless it be a postcript—an *addenda* never adopted, except, according to current opinion, by a woman : it is also generally believed she *will* have the last word ; both these real, or imputed, privileges I now mean to assert, though few, perhaps, will favour me with further attention.

I feel the present to be a period pregnant with important changes. A liberal spirit is abroad that seems disposed to recognize the interests of humanity upon a broader principle than heretofore. In the midst of this I glow with zeal for the cause of my own sex : this preference may be pardoned, since I am not insensible to the beautiful principle that embraces *universal* interests ; but it is natural that, with such little

In a fifteen-page Postscript to Woman's Love *Mary Leman Grimstone, who held advanced views on the role of women in society, argued for better education and more freedom for women. She continued to write novels after she left Australia and she contributed to* La Belle Assemblée, *a forerunner of today's glossy women's magazines. (W. L. Crowther Library, State Library of Tasmania)*

continued to write poetry and short stories. In *The English Annual for 1836*, a sentimental story 'The Settlers of Van Dieman's Land' was published and in the same publication there was a poem by Mrs Leman Grimstone 'The Betrayed'.[14] It is likely that after a second marriage she was the author Mary Leman Gillies who wrote social articles and short stories, some of which deal with Van Dieman's Land, for the *People's Journal* in the 1840s.

It was to be many years before such feminist views as Mary Grimstone's were to be expressed in Australia. The views she held were also to be submerged in Britain under the overwhelmingly domestic view of women dominant until the latter part of the Victorian era.

2

The First to Publish

... 'the first who has ventured to lay claim to the title of
Authoress ...'

Fidelia Hill

The women writers who followed Mary Grimstone have claims to fame as
pioneers in their fields but their virtues as writers are those of worthy
provincials, not London sophisticates. Anna Maria Bunn wrote in the
romantic tradition common among English women fiction writers using the
well-worn technique of an exchange of letters; Fidelia Hill wrote poetry of
historic rather than literary interest; Charlotte Barton followed a formula well
established in English writing for children; and Mary Vidal wrote moral,
uplifting tales of a type that was to continue to find a market for most of the
nineteenth century.

The credit and fame due to them is in being the first women to achieve
publication in Australia at a time when Sydney was a town of only 20 000 to
25 000 people. The stories of how they managed this give an interesting
picture of the book publishing facilities then available. Anna Maria Bunn,
like many women writers in the nineteenth century, chose to hide her
identity, yet as a thirty-year-old widow she must herself have searched among
the few printers in Sydney for a publisher for her novel, *The Guardian*. She
succeeded in having it printed in 1838 by the publisher of the Sydney
newspaper the *Colonist*. Charlotte Barton's collection of children's stories was
printed at the office of another newspaper, the *Sydney Gazette*, in 1841. Mary
Vidal's stories were published at first in eight parts enclosed in coloured
wrappers selling for sixpence each and then in book form by Daniel Lovett
Welch, a printer in George Street, in 1845. It is not surprising that two of
these books were printed at newspaper offices, as newspaper proprietors owned
the largest printing presses. The printers of these books may have acted as
book publishers, undertaking the expense and the risk of printing, but it is
more likely that they were paid by the authors, perhaps by deferred payment

out of the proceeds of sales. In the case of Fidelia Hill's book of poems, printed in 1840 by Thomas Trood, a printer in King Street, the cost of printing was underwritten by the subscribers the author obtained before the book was printed—an early example of a form of self-publishing.

Ann Howe

The printing of Charlotte Barton's book by the *Sydney Gazette* is of particular interest as for some years that newspaper's proprietor was a woman. Ann Howe was the forerunner of a number of women who were to become associated with newspapers in Australia as publishers and sometimes editors following the deaths of their publisher/editor husbands. Born in Sydney in 1803, Ann Bird in 1821 married Robert Howe, a son of George Howe, Australia's first newspaperman. George Howe, a Creole born in the West Indies where his father was government printer, had worked on the London *Times* before being sentenced to transportation to Sydney in 1800 for shoplifting. His printing experience was very valuable in the colony and on 5 March 1803 he began publication of the first newspaper in Australia, the government-backed *Sydney Gazette and the New South Wales Advertiser*. His son, Robert, born in 1795, was apprenticed to his father at the age of nine and took over the business following his father's death in 1821. Just before his own death by accidental drowning in 1829 Robert Howe appointed a Methodist Minister, Rev. Ralph Mansfield, who had had a great influence on his life, as editor.

On her husband's death Ann Howe became proprietor of the *Sydney Gazette*, but Mansfield continued as editor until 1832 when he was dismissed. (Mansfield's ability was recognised in 1841 when he was engaged as editor of the *Sydney Herald* by John Fairfax.) He was succeeded by two other editors, but in June 1833 Ann Howe took over more direct control of the paper although Edward O'Shaughnessy, an emancipist, remained editor. Ann Howe became the lover of William Watt, a Scottish-born *Gazette* journalist who had obtained a ticket of leave after serving part of a fourteen year sentence for embezzlement. However, after Watt published an attack on the cruelties of landholder James Mudie towards his convict servants, he found his ticket of leave transferred to Port Macquarie. Mrs Howe planned to transfer the *Gazette* newspaper operation to the northern convict outpost, but was prevented from doing so by a creditor. She followed William Watt to Port Macquarie in 1836, severing her connection with the *Gazette*, and they were married. Watt made one unsuccessful attempt to escape and during his second attempt in 1837 was drowned when his boat capsized crossing the harbour bar.[1]

Colonial-born Ann Howe became Australia's first woman newspaper proprietor when she took over the Sydney Gazette after the death of her husband Robert Howe in 1829. At first the paper's editorial policy was controlled by the editor, Rev. Ralph Mansfield (later editor of the Sydney Herald) but from 1833 to 1836 Ann Howe took direct control. (Sydney Gazette 13 April 1833)

Anna Maria Bunn

'New South Wales . . . the last refuge for the wretched.'

The first novel written by a woman and published in Australia was *The Guardian, A Tale* by 'An Australian'. Published in Sydney in 1838, fifty years after white settlement, it was also the first novel published on the mainland of Australia. The authorship of this work remained unknown (it was sometimes attributed to Lady Darling, wife of Governor Sir Ralph Darling) until Gwendoline Wilson, while researching for her book *Murray of Yarralumla* (published in 1968), discovered a note in the library at the Bunn's property, St Omer, near Braidwood, written by William Bunn, son of Anna Maria Bunn. The note stated, 'Mother was the author of *The Guardian*, the first novel ever published in Australia'.[2]

Anna Maria Murray was born into an Irish Catholic family at Balliston, County Limerick in 1808, the only daughter of Terence Murray, paymaster in the 2nd Brigade of Foot Guards and later in the 48th Regiment of Foot, and his wife, formerly Ellen Fitzgerald. Her father was stationed in Portugal during much of her childhood and her mother died when she was six. The relatives

13

This portrait of Anna Maria Bunn was taken from a pencil sketch drawn at her home at Newstead in Sydney when she was in her twenties. She was widowed when she was twenty-six and afterwards wrote the first novel by a woman to be published in Australia. (Dr T. Bunn, Thirroul, New South Wales)

who cared for her carried out her mother's wish that she be sent to the Ursuline Convent in Cork as a boarder. She remained there at least ten years and wrote later that 'the convent, nuns and young ladies, became so dear to me, that I love them still and ever will'.[3] In her novel she used the strong friendships that are a feature of boarding-school life as part of the plot. At a time when penal laws discriminated against Catholics and many had no educational opportunities, Anna Maria, on the evidence of her writing, was well educated and absorbed many of the social attitudes of the ruling class.

Anna Maria came to Australia on the *Elizabeth* with her father who had retired from the army in 1827, and they went to live at Erskine Park near Penrith, west of Sydney, a property leased by Murray from the widow of his former commanding officer, Colonel James Erskine. There she met Captain George Bunn, the agent for the property, and on 5 May 1828 when she was twenty they were married in Sydney. Captain Bunn, reputed to be one of the wealthiest merchants in Sydney, was a master mariner, principal of the merchant firm of Buckle, Buckle, Bagster and Buchanan, and Director of the Bank of Australia. He built a large stone house, Newstead, at Darling Harbour for his bride. In the next few years they had two sons, William and George, and a daughter who died while a baby, but after they had been married less than six years, Captain Bunn died suddenly, leaving Anna Maria with a large debt on his estate.[4] Although she was left with some income, Anna Maria Bunn may have started writing in an effort to pay off the debt.

The Guardian was printed by James Spilsbury, of Jamieson Street, Sydney, printer and publisher of the *Colonist or Journal of politics, commerce,*

As this sampler indicates Anna Maria Bunn was born Anna Maria Murray and educated at the Ursuline Convent in Cork. At a time when penal laws discriminated against Catholics and many had no educational opportunities, Anna Maria Bunn, on the evidence of her authorship, was well educated. (National Library of Australia. Photograph reproduced by permission of Mrs Ethel Heward)

agriculture, literature, science and religion, with which Dr John Dunmore Lang was associated. It is not clear to what extent Spilsbury backed the production financially or how the book was distributed. Early in the same year Spilsbury had published James Maclehose's *The Picture of Sydney and Strangers' Guide in N.S.W. for 1838.* This book was publicised freely in the *Colonist* but a quick search of the paper's columns during 1838 reveals no publicity for Anna Maria Bunn's book. It is not known how many copies of *The Guardian* were printed or sold.

The Guardian is a long, involved and sensational story set among provincial society in south-west Ireland and in England. Told partly in the form of letters between two girls who had been friends at school, it begins as an unremarkable romance but develops into a melodramatic story culminating in a tragedy involving incest. The inventiveness of the plot, and what would have been regarded at the time as its sensational aspects, combine to make it an interesting work and it is easy to imagine that the novel would have been popular when it was released.

New South Wales is mentioned several times but always in a derogatory way, as a place where life is uncivilised and the people stupid. These references, although infrequent, are so pronounced as to make the reader wonder at how unhappy Anna Maria Bunn may have been during her long life in Australia. Perhaps, however, she was merely reporting remarks made about Sydney in the circles in which she moved. She was to live in New South Wales for sixty-two years, fifty-five of them as a widow, before her

15

death at the age of eighty-one. Initially she lived at Newstead, later success-ively with her brothers Terence Aubrey (later Sir) Murray at Yarralumla and with Dr James Murray at Woden, both situated on what was later to be the site of Canberra. She then moved to a property of her own, St Omer at Braidwood, New South Wales. She had planned to return to Ireland to live but the collapse of the Bank of Australia left her with insufficient money.[5]

The first mention of New South Wales in *The Guardian* is by the youthful correspondent of the heroine, who in writing of a suitor says:

> He then told me he could, if he wished, have the Government of New South Wales . . . He said he hated going to a country, where the Governor would be like the old man with his ass, trying to please every one, and sure to please no one . . . He said he became sick when he thought of going to a country, where society was divided into parties, dust blown as well as thrown in your eyes, children ran under your horses' feet, dogs lay about the streets, ladies talked of wool, and dressed like antediluvians; and one beautiful spot of land is styled Pinchgut, and another Longbottom.[6]

Another reference, 170 pages further on, is in a long sequence involving minor characters, one of whom asks:

> 'To New South Wales?' cried Mrs. De la Fare with indignation, 'is it where dey send de villians and de ruffians?'

A further forty pages on another minor character remarks:

> 'He intends going to New South Wales, Mr. Barnwall', said Althorpe, 'the last refuge for the wretched'. . . . 'Sydney must be an extraordinary place, I read an advertisement in one of the papers I received, stating that a *respectable* servant was required in a *respectable* family, residing in a *respectable* neighbourhood, a *respectable* distance from the town of Parramatta . . .'[8]

The novel ends when the heroine, Jessie, is told that her husband, Francis Gambier, is her brother and her child a product of incestuous love. In despair she allows her baby to fall over a cliff into the ocean and then follows herself, both of them drowning in the foaming water. Her husband's:

> . . . wild holla was the last earthly sound Jessie had heard. As he now looked upon her stormy grave, his brain reeled, his senses refused to receive sorrow so severe, and he sunk back upon the earth.[9]

Gambier then travels to the Greek islands, the author commenting 'When such a feeling is one of woe like Gambier's, life cannot long endure'.[10]

Apart from letters to family and friends, many of which are preserved in the National Library, it does not appear that Anna Maria Bunn wrote anything else during her long life. She did not confide to her brothers her

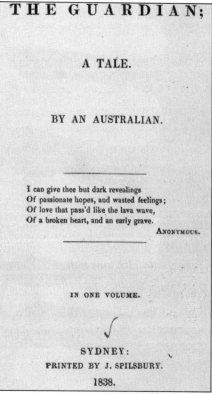

Right: The Guardian *was the first novel to be published in mainland Australia. Anna Maria Bunn dedicated the book to Edward Lytton Bulwer, MP, (later Lord Lytton), a Liberal Member of the House of Commons from 1831–41 and a novelist. Anna Maria Bunn dedicated the book to wife, Rosina, also a novelist, who like herself came from County Limerick. (Title page of* The Guardian*)*

Below: *Anna Maria Bunn wrote nothing more for publication after her one novel in 1838. Later she lived at Woden (now part of Canberra) and at her own property at St Omer, Braidwood. At both places she did hundreds of paintings of the plants and insects in the gardens and the bush. (National Library of Australia. Photograph reproduced by permission of Mrs Ethel Heward)*

THE GUARDIAN;

A TALE.

BY AN AUSTRALIAN.

I can give thee but dark revealings
Of passionate hopes, and wasted feelings;
Of love that pass'd like the lava wave,
Of a broken heart, and an early grave.

ANONYMOUS.

IN ONE VOLUME.

SYDNEY:
PRINTED BY J. SPILSBURY.
1838.

authorship of *The Guardian* although it seems likely that they would have read the book. Terence Murray was a great reader and book collector and was a sponsor of George B. Barton's *Literature in New South Wales*, published in 1866. James Murray was a classical scholar. For the rest of her life Anna Maria Bunn expressed her creative talents by painting the flowers and butterflies she found in the gardens and bush around Woden and Braidwood.

Fidelia S. T. Hill

Born in Yorkshire about 1790, Fidelia Hill was the first woman to have a book of poetry published in Australia. She was not Australia's first woman poet, however, as several poems written by women had appeared in newspapers. They included some written by Mary Leman Grimstone and two by 'Frances' (probably Frances Hannah Gunn), — *Lines, written on the recent visit of the Aborigines to Hobart Town* and *The voice of the Gospel* published in the Hobart Town *Magazine* in 1833–34.[11]

Fidelia Hill arrived in Adelaide on 28 December 1836, a few months after the first white settlers and on the same ship, the *Buffalo*, as the first Governor, Captain John Hindmarsh. Three years later, after apparently suffering personal disasters, she moved to Sydney. In 1840 she published a book of verse, *Poems and recollections of the past*, claiming in the preface that she was 'the *first* who has ventured to lay claim to the title of Authoress, in Sydney'. In a strict sense this is correct, as Anna Maria Bunn had published her work anonymously.

Fidelia Hill dedicated her book to the Dowager Queen Adelaide. She apologised for defects:

> ... the poems having been written during seasons unfavourable to composition, of severe domestic calamity, and bodily suffering. Several of them were suggested by the singular reverses of fortune, which it has of late been the writer's fortune to experience.[12]

She had written poetry in England and claimed to have 'received the most flattering encouragement from one of the first booksellers in London, to publish a Volume of Poems'.

Many of the poems in *Poems and recollections* were written before her arrival in Australia and one, 'My Brother', was written while the *Buffalo* was in harbour at Rio de Janeiro on the voyage to Australia. Her poems on her arrival in Adelaide are of historic interest. In one she claimed to be the first white woman in Adelaide:

> They bore me to the future Capitol,

LIST OF SUBSCRIBERS.

SUBSCRIBERS.

Copies	
1	Bedwell, Mrs. Paterson
1	Browne, Mrs. Cairnesmore, Williams' River
1	Blunden, Miss, South Australia
4	Campbell, Robert, Esq. M.C. George-st.
4	Campbell, Robert. Esq. Cumberland-st.
1	Campbell, Mrs. Napoleon Cottage
2	Cox, Mrs. Hobartville
2	Cox, Mrs. George, Mulgoa
1	Cox, Mrs. Edward, ditto
2	Clarke, Captain
1	Cooper. Mrs. R. Ormonde House
1	Cobb, Mrs. James
1	Chapman. Mrs. Thomas, George-street
1	Cruden, Miss
1	Chambers, C. H. Esq.
1	Crawford,——— Esq. Hill End
1	Crawford, Mrs.
2	Dawes, Mrs. Hunter-street
1	De Mestre, Mrs.
1	Deane, Mrs. Prince's-street
1	East, Mrs. Penrith
2	Forbes, Captain
3	Friend, a
1	Ditto ditto
3	Gipps, Lady
4	Garling, Frederick Esq. Bathurst-street
2	Garling, Frederick, Jun. Esq.
1	Gibbs, Mrs. W.
1	Gibbons, Miss, Prince's-street
1	Gordon Mrs. H.

Copies	
4	Australia, the Lord Bishop of
1	Allwood, Rev. R.
1	Allwood, Mrs.
3	Allen, Mrs. Toxteth Park
1	Allen, John, Esq.
2	Aspinall, Mrs. Edward
1	Baraey, Mrs. Major
1	Browne, Mrs. Brenchly
2	Betts, John, Esq. Glebe
1	Beattie, Miss, Napoleon Cottage
2	Bennett, George, Esq.
1	Bell, Mrs. Belmont
1	Beddek, Mrs. Claremont
2	Brooks, Mrs. Parramatta
1	Blachford, Mrs. Claremont
1	Brown, Mrs. John
1	Birch, Mrs. A.
1	Bridgen, D. A. C. G. Esq.
1	Bodenham, Thomas, Esq.
1	Balsover, Mrs.
4	Bland, William, Esq.
1	Bowden, Mrs.

Fidelia Hill was the first woman to publish a book of poems in Australia. Before having it printed she obtained a list of subscribers headed by such notables as the Bishop of Australia and Lady Gipps to ensure its success. Subscribers took about 200 copies. (First two pages of subscribers' list from Poems and recollections of the past)

Ere yet 'twas more than desart [sic] — a few tents,
Scatter'd at intervals, 'mid forest trees . . .
'Twas then they hail'd me as the *first* white lady
That ever yet had enter'd Adelaide . . .

In another she foretold a large city developing on the site of Adelaide then home to a few hundred people:

I entered the wide spreading streets — me-thought
Of a vast city; all was bustle there: . . .
While many a rising spire, and spacious dome,
Reminded me of London and of home!

A list of subscribers published in her book included the Anglican Bishop of Australia who bought four copies, Lady Gipps who took three, Mrs Hindmarsh of South Australia, and many other well-known people in New South Wales and South Australia. Altogether just over two hundred copies were sold to subscribers. This was Fidelia Hill's only publication in Australia. Later she moved to Launceston where she died in 1854.

Charlotte Barton

'... *the first work written in the Colony expressly for children.*'
Sydney Morning Herald

The first opportunity Australian children had to read stories set in their own country came with the publication of A *mother's offering to her children* in Sydney in 1841. The stories included descriptions of thrilling, frightening and intriguing events that had occurred in Australia's short history, such as the loss of the *Stirling Castle*, the wreck of the *Charles Eaton*, and the settlement at Port Essington, a doomed venture near present-day Darwin. The book also contained information on natural formations, plants and animals and some extraordinary tales concerning Aborigines. A *mother's offering to her children*, by 'a Lady, long resident in New South Wales', was published by Evans, printed at the *Gazette* office and sold for the large sum of six shillings per copy, at a time when a day's wage for even a skilled worker was only seven shillings. Its authorship remained a mystery until recently when Marcie Muir discovered a review in a Sydney paper in which a Mrs Barton was named as the author.[13] Until then it had been assumed that Lady Bremer, wife of Admiral Sir Gordon Bremer, who was in charge of the settlement at Port Essington on the north coast of Australia, was the author, although it is unlikely that Lady Bremer ever visited Australia.

It seems clear that the author was Charlotte Barton, an early settler with a strong-minded, individualistic character and an interesting history. She was described by her daughter, Louisa, as 'particularly handsome and brilliant in appearance, having full black eyes, black hair which curled naturally, and fine features', and as having 'brilliant talents and great courage of mind'.[14] She was the daughter of a London lawyer who was interested in natural history and drawing.

As Charlotte Waring, she arrived in Australia as a 29-year-old governess under arrangement to work at the historic Parramatta property, The Vineyard, for the former Maria King, daughter of Governor King and wife of Hannibal Hawkins Macarthur, pastoralist and businessman and nephew of John Macarthur. She had been recruited by Maria's sister-in-law, Mrs Harriet King, wife of Admiral Phillip Parker King, who wrote to her husband that she was 'highly recommended'. Charlotte Waring sailed on the *Cumberland* from Plymouth on 19 September 1826 with Mrs King and her family. In the Bay of Biscay there was a tremendous gale (described in a story in A *mother's offering to her children*) and the bulwarks were washed away. On board, to the displeasure of Harriet King, who saw a competent governess being lost to the family, Charlotte Waring became friendly with a fellow passenger, James Atkinson, and within three weeks was engaged to marry him. Mrs King

Charlotte Barton gave Australian children their first opportunity to read stories set in their own country. At the time she wrote A mother's offering to her children, *she was supporting four children after leaving her second husband. Her youngest child, Louisa Atkinson, became Australia's first native-born novelist. (Mitchell Library)*

thought this was very bad behaviour but Charlotte Waring was not a woman to be dominated. She told Mrs King she 'must be mistress' of her own actions.[15]

James Atkinson was a well-known and successful farmer in New South Wales. He had arrived in 1820 and received two land grants totalling 2000 acres as a reward for service as principal clerk in the Colonial Secretary's Office. Since 1822 he had been settled at Sutton Forest, in the Berrima district south-west of Sydney on a property called Oldbury where he had built a substantial home.[16] In 1825 he visited England where his book *An account of the state of agriculture and grazing in New South Wales*, a valuable work describing the way of life on the land at the time, was published by J. Cross the following year.[17]

Charlotte Waring and James Atkinson were married at Sutton Forest in September 1827 and they had four children before James Atkinson died, less than seven years after their marriage. Two years later, in 1836, Charlotte married again, her second husband being a friend of Atkinson's, George Bruce Barton, who shortly after the marriage became insane. Forced to leave Barton, the family lived for a while at an outstation on a creek flowing into the Shoalhaven River about twenty miles from Oldbury. Later they lived in Sydney and it is probably during this time that Charlotte wrote *A mother's offering to her children* using her experiences of life in the bush as well as stories of adventures that had been published in the press. The *Sydney Morning*

PREFACE.

—

TO MASTER REGINALD GIPPS,
SON OF HIS EXCELLENCY SIR GEORGE GIPPS,
Governor of New South Wales and its Dependencies,
AND OF LADY GIPPS,

THIS little work is dedicated by permission, and the author hopes the incidents it contains may afford him some little entertainment in the perusal: its principal merit is the *truth* of the subjects narrated; the accounts of the melancholy shipwrecks being drawn from printed sources; and perhaps it may claim some trifling merit also from being the first work written in the Colony expressly for Children.

The Author is fully aware how greatly the value of these little Books will be enhanced by the high and kind patronage of Master REGINALD GIPPS, to whom she begs to subscribe herself his

Truly obliged,
And most obedient humble servant,
And well-wisher,
THE AUTHOR.

Sydney, New South Wales,
29th October, 1841.

CHRISTMAS GIFT.

THIS DAY is published by Evans, price Six Shillings, " A Mother's offering to her Children," by a lady, long resident in New South Wales.

Left: *Fulsome dedications were usual in nineteenth century books. Charlotte Barton, author of* A mother's offering to her children, *the first children's book to be set and published in Australia, used her dedication to ten-year-old Reginald Gipps, son of Governor Sir George Gipps and Lady Gipps, to obtain vice-regal patronage. (Preface from* A mother's offering to her children) *Above: When* A mother's offering to her children *was published in Sydney in December 1841, it was advertised as an ideal Christmas gift. (*Australian *18 and 30 December 1841)*

Herald wrote of the book:

COLONIAL LITERATURE — A very useful little publication entitled 'A Mother's Offering to her Children', issued from the Colonial Press last week. The work is written in a very unpretending style, similar to Aitken's Evenings at Home, and some of Mrs. Barbould's works, and, to use the words of the authoress, 'it may claim some trifling mercy from being the first work written in the Colony expressly for children'. It is written in the form of a dialogue between a Mrs. Savelle and her children, in which the former relates the particulars of the wreck of the *Charles Eaton*, the loss of the *Stirling Castle*, the history of Joseph Forbes, the formation of the settlement at Port Essington, together with chapters on various natural phenomena in the Colony. — As a Christmas present, more especially for new-comers, the work is well adapted, and the community are under no small obligation to the authoress for having provided such a fund of amusement and instruction for the rising generation.[18]

The *Sydney Gazette* said:

'The Mother's Offering' ... should be in the hands of every young person. ... we can confidently recommend it to the notice of parents, guardians and teachers, who will all find it a powerful auxiliary in inculcating true morality and profitable information in the minds of those intrusted to their care and supervision, and for whose mental improvement they are responsible . . .

We trust that the 'Mother's Offering' will obtain a cordial welcome in the house of every colonist in New South Wales, as, independent of its intrinsic merits — the successful attempt by Mrs. Barton to elevate the character of the rising generation of her adopted land, by her excellent work, gives her a claim upon the public that entitle her to their best wishes and patronage.[19]

Charlotte Barton died in 1867 at the age of seventy. By then her youngest daughter, Louisa Atkinson, had become an established novelist and writer on nature.

Mary Theresa Vidal

> Satan soon will gain the rule,
> Where he once hath enter'd in.

Mary Theresa Vidal was twenty-four years old when she arrived in Sydney on the *Earl Grey* on 25 February 1840 with a sick husband and three sons aged four, two and six months. The family had made the long voyage by sailing ship in the hope that a few years' residence in the healthy climate of New South Wales would restore Rev. Francis Vidal's health, which had been undermined during a period he had spent as chaplain in the damp cells at Exeter gaol.

A fellow passenger on the *Earl Grey*, Arthur Wilcox Manning, a member of the well-known New South Wales legal, commercial and squatting family, making his third trip to Australia, kept a diary of the voyage. He described Mary Vidal as 'genteel' in appearance, an 'excellent sailor' but 'so inanimate that one cannot take much interest in her'.[20] Beneath her quiet exterior, Mary Vidal was a deeply religious woman with a talent for writing and a great urge to impart to others, particularly those she regarded as her inferiors, her views on correct, moral behaviour.

Mary Theresa Vidal, née Johnson, was born on 25 July 1815 at Torrington, Devon, the eldest child and only daughter of William Charles Johnson, of a well-to-do family connected to the landed gentry, and his wife Mary Theresa (née Furse), a Devon heiress. In 1835, at nineteen, Mary Theresa married Rev. Francis Vidal, the curate at North Torrington.

After their arrival in Sydney the Vidals lived for some time at Balmain where two more children were born, their only daughter, Elizabeth Theresa, in 1841, and a fourth son, Robert Wellington, in 1843.[21] When Francis

Vidal's health recovered sufficiently for him to take a position as a clergyman, he was appointed to Penrith and there Mary Vidal observed the Australian settings used in some of her writing.

Her first book, *Tales for the bush*, published in Sydney in 1845, proved so popular that only one year later it was published in its third edition in England and it ran to at least five editions.[22] It consists of a series of moral tales in the form of short novels divided into brief chapters. The themes emphasise the virtues of observance of the Sabbath, truthfulness, proper manners and subservience to 'betters'—the sort of virtues the upper classes preferred to find in their servants and among the lower classes generally. Mrs Vidal, like many other observers fresh from class-stratified English society, was astonished at the lack of these 'virtues' among native-born Australians. Most of her stories concern newly arrived, generally poor, English migrants who are distinguished from their native-born counterparts by their honesty, politeness and cleanliness and their propensity for religious observance, or who fall by the wayside under the influence of the lax life around them. Her grand-daughter, Faith Compton Mackenzie, wrote many years later that initially Mary Vidal wrote the stories for the instruction of her servants.[23]

One of her stories 'Marion Martin; or, the Month's Trial' was preceded by a homily in verse form typical of the author's simple moral attitude:

Petty Thefts once learnt at school,
Will proceed to greater sin;
Satan soon will gain the rule,
Where he once hath enter'd in.[24]

The book provides many insights into distinctive Australian attitudes in the 1840s. A story about a recent emigrant, Ruth Walsh, provokes a comment about the lack of class distinction in Australia. As the drayman nears the property where Ruth is to be employed, he says 'Now we're coming to Manley's run.' Ruth asks '. . . is he not a gentleman . . . Are not gentlemen called "Mr." here?' The drayman replies:

Why, darling, in this country we're all gentlemen; we don't think of Misters and titles, d'ye see? we all get good pay, and there's no need for bowing and courtesying, sir-ing and ma'am-ing; we servants are great folk out here, and I advise you, my dear, to speak up more and forget your English manners, unless you want to be the laugh of the whole settlement . . .[25]

The cleanliness of recently-arrived English migrants is contrasted with the slovenly and dirty Australians—a striking reversal of more recent perceptions. Mary Vidal has her character, Ruth Walsh, put on her Sunday gown, bonnet and shawl to call on the Australian Brown family in the next cottage. There she finds a squalid scene with tubs and pans lying about, the floor unswept, Brown unshaven sitting in a corner smoking and a daughter Sally dressed in

Mary Theresa Vidal wrote her moral tales Tales for the bush *to instruct her servants. They were published first in Sydney in eight parts enclosed in coloured wrappers selling for sixpence a part. Within a year her tales had become so popular they were published in England in a third edition.* (Australasian Book News and Library Journal March 1947)

dirty clothes making damper. Ruth by contrast was 'always neat', not only on Sundays. Mary Vidal told her readers:

> To be habitually clean and neat, — neat without show nor display, neat whether people are by to see it or not — is a sort of proof that that person is also careful of her ways — careful to be modest, humble, and regular in her temper.[26]

The moralising attitudes of *Tales for the bush* found a wide and receptive audience in the 1840s. In their limited way the stories are well written and constructed and Mary Vidal's uncomplicated faith in her views shines through.

After their return to England from Australia in 1845, Rev. Francis Vidal succeeded Mary's brother, William Johnson, as tutor at Eton and master of one of the boarding houses. There Mary Vidal, by then the mother of six sons and one daughter, continued to write novels. She was referred to by A. E. Shipley, Master of Christ's College, Cambridge, as 'a lady of some distinction as a writer'.[27] Only two of the remaining ten books she wrote had connections with Australia. *Cabramatta and Woodleigh Farm*, published in 1849, consisted of two long stories, the first set in the Penrith and Nepean district west of Sydney where the Vidals had lived, the second in provincial England. Mary Vidal offered the profits from the sales of this book to the Bishop of Sydney for the cathedral building fund.[28] A more elaborate book with an Australian setting, *Bengala: or, some time ago*, was published in two volumes in London in 1860, after the gold-rushes had transformed the colony Mary Vidal had known. She wrote in the preface:

> It may possibly be deemed strange, if not presumptuous, that after the more recent and highly-coloured pictures of the same subject, this homelier and greyer tinted sketch should be brought forward. But though life is the same in one hemisphere as in another, the accidental and surrounding circumstances vary, and there is a more rapid and continual change in a new colony. To seize one of these shifting scenes — a transient period with its own peculiar characteristics, its hopes, fears, evils, and enjoyments — has been my endeavour . . .[29]

Like her other Australian stories, *Bengala* is set in the country to the west of Sydney. It concerns pastoral life among station owners and their families, their financial difficulties and their convict servants in the 1830s and 1840s.

Mary Vidal's other books were all set in England. In later life she suffered from *tic douloureux*, a severe form of neuralgia of the face and she died in England in 1869 aged fifty-four. The sincere, moralistic style of writing which she introduced to Australia continued to have a following for many years.

3

A Degree of Professionalism

> '. . . the woman question . . . the difficulty of a woman earning a
> livelihood even when she had as much ability, industry, and
> perseverance as a man.'
>
> Catherine Helen Spence

By the time Mary Vidal returned to England to some moderate acclaim as a novelist, a talented woman writer had arrived in Australia from England intending to stay only a few years. She was Louisa Meredith who, while still a girl, had achieved great success as a poet and illustrator in her home city of Birmingham. Together with two other writers, Scottish-born Catherine Spence, who was to become a prominent pioneer feminist in Australia, and Australian-born Louisa Atkinson, she was to introduce a more professional element to women's writing in Australia. With the Victorian era's emphasis on conservative domestic values, the social climate was if anything less favourable to the emergence of women writers than in previous years, and all three struggled against considerable odds.

Louisa Meredith was the first of the three to be published. She arrived as a visitor but spent the rest of her long life in Australia where, although she made a mark as a writer and illustrator, particularly of nature subjects, circumstances were against her building on the fame she had enjoyed as a young woman in England. Her life contained other disappointments. Though interested in radical politics in Birmingham, any interest she had in Australian politics was expressed only through her husband's career as a conservative member of parliament. Married life in the Australian bush did not dull Louisa Meredith's enthusiasm for writing but it probably denied her the success she could have achieved had she stayed in England.

It is interesting to compare Louisa Meredith's career with that of another woman writer/naturalist, Australian-born Louisa Atkinson. Louisa Atkinson, although she became a botanical expert respected internationally, concentrated on writing for the Sydney press, becoming the first woman in Australia to contribute a regular column to a capital city newspaper. Louisa Meredith, perhaps because she lived in Tasmania with its small population and limited range of newspapers and periodicals, concentrated on writing beautifully illustrated books for the overseas market.

Catherine Helen Spence

Contemporaneously with the achievements of Louisa Atkinson and Louisa Meredith, a remarkable woman of strong character began writing novels and newspaper articles and serials in Adelaide. Catherine Helen Spence, described towards the end of her life as 'the grand old woman' of Australia[1] preferred to describe herself as a 'new woman . . . an awakened woman . . . awakened to a sense of capacity and responsibility, not merely to the family and the household, but to the State'[2]. A pioneer feminist, journalist, novelist, preacher, electoral and social reformer, she was in the forefront among women in nineteenth century Australia.

During her lifetime and at her death Spence was lauded chiefly for her achievements as a political and social reformer. In recent years most of her novels have been either reprinted after being out of print for over a hundred years or, if previously only printed as serials in newspapers, have become available in book form for the first time. In this account her considerable achievements as a pioneer journalist are emphasised. Her struggles and limited success in this field indicate just how difficult it was for women to break into journalism. Although on her eightieth birthday she was described as 'the oldest and one of the most distinguished journalists in the Commonwealth'[3] she never achieved a permanent staff position as a journalist. Her autobiography, which she began writing in the last few months of her life, describes her struggles and the stratagems she had to employ to be accepted as a journalist and is the only record of its kind available on women's earnings from writing in the nineteenth century. At the time of her death on 3 April 1910 she had corrected the proofs of the first three chapters. Her friend, fellow electoral reformer Jeanne F. Young, revised the rest of the manuscript and then completed Catherine Spence's life story. Publication in serial form began in the Adelaide *Observer* on the same day and the same page as the long and laudatory obituary about her, and concluded the following November.[4]

Catherine Helen Spence, born in 1825 at Melrose on the Tweed River, a daughter of David Spence and his wife formerly Helen Brodie, arrived in Adelaide at the age of fourteen in 1839 only three years after the establishment of the South Australian colony. A year after the family's arrival, David Spence was appointed Town Clerk of Adelaide but he later lost the job when the municipal corporation failed from lack of money. After the loss of his job her father's health failed, her brothers who had gone up-country as farmers returned to Adelaide defeated, and her sister's husband, Andrew Murray, floundered in his mercantile business. Catherine Spence probably did not need the spectre of failing family finances to spur her into looking for employment and ways of earning money. She was well educated, had a strong character and was not the sort of person to be content in a purely domestic sphere. Her response was unusual however. Although she was to spend some years as a governess and running a school, she turned also to writing. Not only did she write novels, but she also wrote for newspapers, which was considered barely respectable for a woman. Her brother-in-law, Andrew Murray became editor of the *South Australian* early in 1843 and was proprietor from 1844 to 1851. Through the family association with this paper Catherine Spence by the age of seventeen had had the occasional letter and some verses published.

When gold was discovered in Victoria, Andrew Murray, deserted by both subscribers and printers of the *South Australian*, went to Melbourne where he obtained employment on the *Argus*, leaving Catherine Spence and her brother, John Brodie Spence, to carry on his paper as best they could. This gave Catherine an opportunity to contribute, but the arrangement was shortlived as funds ran out. Such writing (she was also by this time writing for the Adelaide *Register*) gained her some notoriety in Adelaide and the attitude to women liberated enough to undertake such work is apparent in this anecdote recorded in her autobiography.

> At a subscription ball to which my brother John took me and my younger
> sister Mary, she found she had been pointed out and talked of as the
> lady who wrote for newspapers. I did not like it even to be supposed of
> myself, but Mary was indignant, and I wrote an injured letter to my
> friend. [John Taylor, owner of the *Register* soon to sell it for £1000] He
> apologised and said he thought I would be proud of doing disinterested
> work, and he was sorry the mistake had been made regarding the sister
> who did it.[5]

At the same time as she began writing for newspapers Catherine Spence also began writing novels. Her experience of life in a colony depopulated by the rush of gold seekers to the Victorian goldfields provided the background for her first novel *Clara Morison—A tale of South Australia during the gold fever*. She entrusted the manuscript to John Taylor to take to London publishers Smith, Elder and Co. hoping that it might realise £100 because of the great interest in the gold discoveries in Australia. The reader for Smith, Elder, Mr Williams, who had discovered indications of Charlotte Bronte's genius in her first manuscript (he advised her she could do better and she produced *Jane Eyre*), gave similar advice to Catherine Spence. However another publisher, J. W. Parker and Sons, took *Clara Morison* and published it anonymously in

Catherine Helen Spence, described when she died as the 'grand old woman' of Australia, was a towering figure as a feminist and political and social reformer in nineteenth century Australia. She was also a pioneer journalist, who, when she first began writing for newspapers, had to use her brother's name because contributions from a woman would not have been accepted. (National Library of Australia)

two volumes in 1854. Catherine Spence was to receive £40 but the publisher deducted £10 for abridging it. Commenting on this poor return for the work of writing a novel she wrote:

> Novel writing had not been to me a lucrative occupation, I had given up teaching altogether at the age of 25, and I felt that, though Australia was to be a great country, there was no market for literary work, and the handicap of distance from the reading world was great.[6]

The literary critic Frederick Sinnett thought *Clara Morison* was the best Australian novel published to that time:

> It stands ... quite alone among all Australian stories yet published, in that it is free from the defect of being a book of travels in disguise. It is not written exclusively for distant readers ... The story is thoroughly Australian, but at the same time is not a deliberate attempt to describe the peculiar 'manners and customs' of the Australians.[7]

Catherine Spence's second novel *Tender and true: a colonial tale* was published anonymously by Smith, Elder in London in two volumes in 1856 but she received only £20 for the copyright. The only one of her books to go into more than one edition, it was issued in two or three large editions, but she received no further payment. She was told that 'nothing could be made out of shilling editions'.[8]

Even with information from her *Autobiography* it is difficult to pinpoint Catherine Spence's newspaper writing to exact dates but it seems that by the 1850s she was, in a surreptitious way, Adelaide correspondent for the

Melbourne *Argus*. Her brother was officially the correspondent, but she wrote the reports from news he supplied. Although a few years later the *Sydney Morning Herald* began publishing Louisa Atkinson's 'Voice from the Country' series, editors and readers were at this time far from ready to accept a 'hard news' column from a woman.

It was also during the 1850s that Catherine Spence became absorbed in the proportional representation voting system, (which she referred to as 'effective voting') advocated by Thomas Hare. It was to become one of the great causes of her life and her enthusiasm for it spilled over into her journalism. After reading John Stuart Mill's advocacy of Thomas Hare's system she wrote a leader and sent it to the *Argus* which, holding other views, did not even offer to print her contribution as a letter. Soon after, her employment with the *Argus* ceased although not because of her advocacy of proportional representation: the introduction of the telegraph between Melbourne and Adelaide in 1858 meant papers did not need to wait for weekly columns of news to arrive by post. Her loss of income of £50 a year was made up for by a regular gift of the same amount from her maiden aunts.

Catherine Spence continued writing for the Adelaide *Register* and in 1861 she published a pamphlet on proportional representation entitled, 'A Plea for Pure Democracy'. Although not one copy was sold in Adelaide, Frederick Sinnett, by then editor and proprietor of the *Daily Telegraph*, set up in August 1862 as Adelaide's first evening newspaper, was very impressed and English experts including Thomas Hare thought her arguments were the best put forward. She wrote her third novel, under its original title of *Uphill Work*, at the same time as the pamphlet and when Sinnett wanted to bring it out as a serial in the weekly edition of the *Telegraph* she decided to work in Thomas Hare as a character in an effort to publicise his proportional representation scheme. The novel, she wrote, dealt with 'the woman question, as it appeared to me at the time, the difficulty of a woman earning a livelihood, even when she had as much ability, industry, and perseverance as a man'.[9] She received £50 for the serial rights and when she visited England some years later she persuaded publisher George Bentley to publish it in book form. He agreed on condition its name was changed 'as the first critic would say it was uphill work to read it'.[10] When it was published in 1865 in three volumes under its new title, *Mr Hogarth's Will*, she received £35 as a half share of the profits.

During a trip to England she wrote articles for periodicals including 'An Australian's Impressions of England' published in the *Cornhill Magazine* in January 1866 for which she received £12, a large sum. She described it as the best paid work she had had to that time. After her return to Australia she wrote another novel which was serialised in 1867 in the *Observer* as *Hugh Lindsay's Ghost*. (The London edition was called *The Author's Daughter*.)

Gradually, as she became more of a public figure through her advocacy of proportional representation, her work in the placing of destitute children with families rather than in institutional care, and her preaching in Unitarian churches (all unusual occupations and causes for a woman at the time) Catherine Spence found more openings for writing for the press. 'My life now became more interesting and varied. A wider field for my journalistic capabilities was open to me', she wrote.[11] She became a contributor to the *Melbourne Review*, a literary periodical run by banker and historian, H. G. Turner, author Alexander Sutherland, and litterateur A. Patchett Martin. Although unpaid, the work brought her views to public notice and she continued to contribute literary and political articles until the *Melbourne Review* ceased in 1885.

Catherine Spence became a regular contributor to the Adelaide *Register* and the *Observer* in 1877. By then she had been writing for the press for over twenty years in a casual capacity, but clearly this appointment was a considerable achievement for her, as evidenced by her elation:

> Leading articles were to be written at my own risk. If they suited the policy of the paper they would be accepted, otherwise not. What a glorious opening for my ambition and for my literary proclivities came to me in July 1878, when I was in my fifty-third year! Many leading articles were rejected but not one literary or social article. Generally these last appeared in both daily and weekly papers. . . .
>
> I felt as if the round woman had got at last into the round hole which fitted her . . .[12]

A columnist in the Adelaide *Advertiser* on 13 November 1931, more than twenty years after her death, wrote that when a boy he often saw Miss Spence climbing the *Register* stairs, and after

> . . . taking a breather on the landing going along to the then editor John Harvey Finlayson with one of her articles on Effective Voting. Later in the evening I heard the comps. calling the dear old lady everything when they could not read her awful scrawl.[13]

From 1878 to 1893 when she left to visit America and Europe, she held the position of 'Outside Contributor' on 'the oldest newspaper in the State', she wrote, 'and for those 14 years I had great latitude'.[14] Apart from this major writing activity she also contributed to other publications and in 1878 published a pamphlet containing four papers entitled 'Some Social Aspects of Early Colonial Life' under the pseudonym 'A colonist of 1839', which she also used for some newspaper writing. Her friend Dr Andrew Garran, editor of the *Sydney Morning Herald*, took reviews and articles, and the *Australasian* published a short story 'Afloat and Ashore' plus a social article on 'Wealth, Waste, and Want'. Apart from the *Melbourne Review* she also contributed to the *Victorian Review*, which began by paying well, but these payments gradually ceased. She wrote:

I found journalism a better paying business for me than novel writing, and I delighted in the breadth of the canvas on which I could draw my sketches of books and of life. I believe that my work on newspapers and reviews is more characteristic of me, and intrinsically better work than what I have done in fiction; but when I began to wield the pen, the novel was the line of least resistance. When I was introduced in 1894 to Mrs. Croly, the oldest woman journalist in the United States, as an Australian journalist, I found that her work, though good enough, was essentially women's work, dress, fashion, functions, with educational and social outlooks from the feminine point of view. My work might show the bias of sex, but it dealt with the larger questions which were common to humanity; and when I recall the causes which I furthered, and which in some instances I started, I feel inclined to magnify the office of the anonymous contributor to the daily press. And I acknowledge . . . the large-minded tolerance of the Editors of The Register, who gave me such a free hand in the treatment of books, of men, and of public questions.[15]

Catherine Spence wrote on a great number of public issues including women's rights, law reform, child welfare, electoral reform and proportional representation. Although, she wrote, she was 'so engrossed with work on The Register and The Observer that my time was quite well enough accounted for', she still continued to write novels. She entered a competition for a prize of £100 offered by the *Sydney Mail* in 1879 with a manuscript called 'Handfasted' but was not successful, '. . . for the judge feared that it was calculated to loosen the marriage tie — it was too socialistic and consequently dangerous'.[16] This novel, *Handfasted: A romance*, written under the pseudonym Hugh Victor Keith, which remained unpublished until 1984, dealt with the old Scottish custom of trial marriages (handfasting) for a period of a year and a day. It was set in a Utopian society called Columba, giving Spence scope to challenge some of the prevailing social standards regarding illegitimate children, inheritance laws and chastity. Another novel, *Gathered in*, was serialised in the Adelaide *Advertiser* in 1881–82 and simultaneously in the *Queenslander*, but not published in book form until nearly a century later — in 1977. She wrote of it:

I believe it to be my best novel — the novel into which I put the most of myself, the only novel I wrote with tears of emotion . . . in [this novel] — still unpublished I felt quite satisfied that I had at last achieved my ambition to create characters that stood out distinctly and real.[17]

A friend took the manuscript to England but it was rejected by Smith, Elder, Bentley and Macmillan. Years later Spence tried a Sydney publisher but she was told the only novels that would appeal to an Australian public at that time were sporting or political novels. Another work, 'A Week in the Future' was serialised in the *Centennial Magazine* beginning in January 1889 and the manuscript of another story, 'A Last Word', was lost when the *Centennial Magazine* ceased.

Following the death in December 1887 of her mother, whom she had cared for, Catherine Spence was freer to take up a public life involving lecturing and travel and from that time her literary work became a secondary interest. In 1893–94 she visited the United States, Canada, Britain and Europe where she lectured in many cities on proportional representation and the de-institutionalisation of child care. After she returned she found, 'My journalistic work... was neither so regular nor so profitable as before I left Adelaide'.[18] In 1897 she became the first woman in Australia to seek election in a political contest when she was a South Australian candidate for election to the Federal Convention. She received 7501 votes, placing her twenty-second out of thirty-three candidates.

When she died on 3 April 1910 at the age of eighty-four, in addition to all the praise for her work for social and political reform, she was described as 'the doyenne of Australasian women-writers'.[19] The fact that she did not marry — in her autobiography she said she had refused several offers of marriage — left her with more freedom to pursue her aims as a reformer and writer. Despite this, the meagre returns she received for her writing and the uncertainty of her position as a newspaper contributor indicate the difficulty of achieving writing success even for a woman with time to devote to a career.

Louisa Anne Meredith

> '. . . *colonial ladies seldom speak of aught besides dress,*
> *and domestic events and troubles . . .*'

As a young woman of great talent, Louisa Meredith gave promise of a working life as distinctive and pioneering as that of Catherine Spence, but being tied by marriage to life away from the centres of population meant her opportunities were to some extent limited.

Louisa Meredith was born Louisa Anne Twamley on 20 July 1812 in Birmingham to elderly parents, Thomas Twamley, a corn dealer and miller, and Louisa Anne Twamley, a member of the influential and well-to-do Meredith family of lawyers and businessmen. Taught by her accomplished mother, she was by the age of ten writing poetry and stories, painting, drawing and sketching. Through a friendship with the editor W. G. Lewis, she had poems and literary critiques published in the radical *Birmingham Journal* under a nom de plume. Her interests also extended to politics, becoming involved in the Birmingham Political Union which developed into the Chartist movement. She wrote newspaper articles in support of Chartism and years later found that one of her readers was the young Henry Parkes (their correspondence is held in the Mitchell Library). After her father's death when she was twenty, she took over his position as Corn Inspector at Birmingham, an unusual job for a woman which involved providing a weekly account to the London office of quantity, kind and price of grain.

By the age of twenty-six Louisa Twamley was the author of five books of poetry (all self-illustrated) many articles, poems and critiques and had made many flower paintings and sketches. She was famous in Birmingham as an author and painter, and was well enough known in a wider sphere to gain William Wordsworth's permission to dedicate her book *The romance of nature, or, The flower seasons illustrated* to him. She had also come to the attention of Leigh Hunt, who had made a light-hearted reference to her in a poem, 'Blue stocking revels, or the feast of violets'.[20]

At this time she agreed to marry Charles Meredith, a cousin on her mother's side, who was visiting England from Tasmania where his family were landowners. On 18 April 1839 they were married in Birmingham and sailed soon after for Australia where they intended to settle for a few years. Ironically Louisa had earlier rejected the offer of becoming governess to her uncle's younger children in Tasmania. Her reply then had been, 'Where would my literature be in Van Dieman's Land? Writing sonnets to whales and porpoises, canzonets to kangaroos, madrigals to "prime merinos" and dirges to black swans...'[21]

Louisa and Charles Meredith's destination was New South Wales where Charles Meredith had a station on the Murrumbidgee River. They stayed for a short time in Sydney then Charles Meredith visited his sheep station, Louisa travelling over the Blue Mountains as far as Bathurst with him. He found that all vegetation on his land had died in the drought which had blanketed New South Wales. At the beginning of 1840 the Merediths moved to Homebush, a dilapidated, depressing house outside Sydney, previously owned by D'Arcy Wentworth. Here Louisa took up colonial housekeeping in a lonely environment where there were few visitors, certainly none of the cultivated society she had been used to in Birmingham, and where a gang of bushrangers regularly held up passers-by on the road outside her home. Her first child was born on 1 July 1840. Soon after, Charles Meredith lost his land in the general collapse of property values and with no financial resources he found himself obliged to take his wife and baby son to live with his parents near Swansea on the east coast of Tasmania.[22]

After such experiences it is not surprising that Louisa Meredith liked little in New South Wales. Nevertheless she was able to turn her views to advantage by reporting them in a book *Notes and sketches of New South Wales during a residence in that Colony from 1839 to 1845.* When it was published in London in Murray's Home and Colonial Library it became one of the most popular books in the series. Her views on colonial society have continued to be valued by social historians:

> I soon found that Colonial ladies seldom speak of aught besides dress, and domestic events and troubles, 'bad servants' being the staple topic. And most gentlemen have their whole souls so felted up in wools, fleeces, flocks, and stock, that I have often sat through a weary dinner and evening of incessant talking, without hearing a single syllable on any other subject . . . However fascinating may be the company of his 'fine-wool sheep' and peerless breed of Merinos, he should not insist on taking them out to dinner . . . the eternity of wool, wool, wool — wearied my very soul. Perhaps some excuse is admissable for this unsocial style of conversation in Colonial gentlemen, from the rarity of Colonial ladies who are disposed to take a part in any topic under discussion, and many, though not disposed or qualified to express an opinion on general subjects, would feel insulted if you asked their advice how to make butter or cure a ham; thus rendering it difficult to know what they would like to talk about when the servant-stories are exhausted, which usually prove lengthy and very circumstantial.[23]

Her comments were resented in Sydney. The *Sydney Morning Herald* said 'we cannot see what there is in it that could have induced Mr. Murray to publish it'[24] but the Melbourne *Argus* described the author as a 'shrewd and cultivated observer'.[25]

Louisa Meredith is said to have gained little income from her writing but the success of this book must have provided some financial relief, being released in the same year as another financial failure overwhelmed her husband. Close to bankruptcy he was fortunate to obtain the position of Assistant Police Magistrate at Port Sorell on the north coast of Tasmania. There at first they lived in a cottage Louisa derisively called 'Lath Hall' (it was built of upright slabs, lathed and plastered inside and lathed outside) then later in a more pleasant home they built themselves. After four years they returned to Swansea where Charles managed his father's property, but family quarrels resulted in Charles and Louisa moving out of the family home. With great strength of character Louisa maintained her own interests in writing and sketching while she observed bitterly the loss of the inheritance she thought should have been her husband's. During this time she wrote another very successful descriptive book *My home in Tasmania, during a residence of nine years*, published in 1852 in London. The following year it was published in New York by Bunce and Brothers, the preface stating that the work had met with an 'unmixed meed of approval' by 'the whole body of British critics, from the lengthy review in the mighty "Quarterly", to the passing notice or brief compliment in the provincial paper'.[26] It was the first such description of life

Before she left her home city of Birmingham at the age of twenty-six, Louisa Anne Meredith was famous as the author and illustrator of five books of poetry. During more than fifty years in Australia she continued to write books of social commentary, verse and beautifully illustrated descriptive books on Tasmanian animals, birds and insects. (Allport Library and Museum of Fine Arts, State Library of Tasmania)

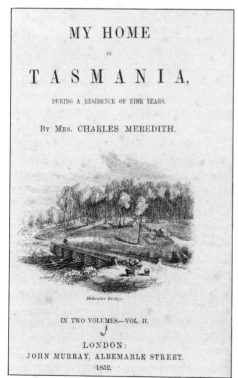

MY HOME

IN

TASMANIA,

DURING A RESIDENCE OF NINE YEARS.

BY MRS. CHARLES MEREDITH.

Deloraine Bridge.

IN TWO VOLUMES.—VOL. II.

LONDON:
JOHN MURRAY, ALBEMARLE STREET.
1852.

Louisa Meredith wrote several books of social commentary. The first, Notes and sketches of New South Wales, like My home in Tasmania was published in Murray's Home and Colonial Library and was one of the most popular in the series. Her criticism of social life in Sydney was not appreciated at the time but has been a rich source for social historians ever since. Her two-volume work on Tasmania was the first such description of life in Tasmania written by a woman. It was illustrated by the author and by the Bishop of Tasmania, Dr Francis R. Nixon and was printed in an American as well as an English edition. (Title page of My home in Tasmania) in Tasmania written by a woman.

Again this must have brought some badly-needed income, for the family was once more in financial difficulties. Contemplating her husband's disastrous financial dealings Louisa Meredith suggested that he become a politician. In 1856 he was elected to the Tasmanian Legislative Council where, ironically, he soon became Colonial Treasurer, remaining a politician until his death in 1880.

In 1861, following a visit to Victoria, Louisa Meredith wrote the third of her social reportage/travel books, *Over the Straits, a visit to Victoria*, which again met with success. At the same time she was working on the nature books for both adults and children which gained her great renown. In 1860 *Some of my bush friends in Tasmania*, a large and elaborate work on the flowers and animals of Tasmania containing numerous drawings and poems, was published, followed by books of verse and sketches. In 1880 her book *Tasmanian friends and foes, feathered, furred and finned* was released, described by the publisher, J. Walch of Hobart, as, 'A family chronicle of country life, natural history and veritable adventure with coloured plates, from drawings by the author'.[27] When *Bush friends in Tasmania Last Series* was published in 1891 by Macmillan in London, Louisa Meredith was described on the title page as '. . . recipient of prize medals for botanical drawings in exhibitions in London, Sydney, Melbourne and Calcutta; Honorary Member of the Royal Society, Tasmania'.[28] The book itself was a magnificent large-format work with gilt edging and gilt lettering on the cover, the poems (some of which had appeared previously in periodicals) and articles illustrated by beautiful colour plates including the Tasmanian laurel, the kangaroo apple, the pepper tree and the native holly. Unfortunately this book was published at her own expense in an edition of 700 copies at two guineas a copy and in the depression of the 1890s this price was beyond the means of many potential buyers.

Like many other colonial writers, Louisa Meredith also tapped the extensive Australian market for serial publication of novels, in 1866 her first novel *Ebba* being published in serial form in the *Australasian*.

Louisa Meredith published nineteen major books in her lifetime, fourteen of them after she moved to Australia. Nearly all her works reached a large Australian and international audience through numerous editions. Despite her success, however, she was left in poor circumstances in later life. In 1884 the Tasmanian Parliament authorised the payment of a pension of £100 a year for her services to science, literature and art, a forerunner of the Commonwealth Literary Fund pensions given to writers in later years.

Following Louisa Meredith's death on 21 October 1895 at the age of eighty-three while on a visit to Melbourne, the London *Times* said:

> Mrs. Meredith's facile and clever pencil has enriched the world with
> many valuable and life-like reproductions of the curious fauna and flora

Louisa Meredith wrote eleven books describing the animals, birds and insects she observed and drew around her homes on the east coast and in the north of Tasmania. Many went into several editions. The 1891 edition of Bush friends in Tasmania was an elaborate large format book with many coloured plates. (Title page of Bush friends in Tasmania)

of the island colony ... In 1891, at the age of nearly 80, Mrs. Meredith undertook the voyage to England, her first visit to her old home, after an absence of more than half a century. She remained in London for nearly two years, during which time she succeeded, after many disappointments, in seeing through the press her latest important work, called 'Last Series of Bush-Friends in Tasmania'.[29]

Louisa Atkinson

> 'This excellent lady ... cut down like a flower.'
> Sydney Morning Herald

Like Louisa Meredith, Louisa Atkinson had a great interest in nature and a talent for writing and drawing. She was the first native-born woman writer to achieve success and the first woman writer to exploit the newspaper and periodical market, having a long-running series of articles published in the Sydney Morning Herald and the Sydney Mail in the 1860s. Her mother Charlotte Barton was well educated and had herself inherited a love of nature from her father. Louisa's father, James Atkinson, was a successful public servant, farmer and author of a book on agriculture, although he had no direct influence on her upbringing as he died when she was two months old.

Caroline Louisa Waring Atkinson was born at Oldbury, near Berrima, New South Wales on 25 February 1834. After the failure of her mother's second marriage, to George Barton, the family lived for some time at an isolated outstation near the Shoalhaven River, then in Sydney. Later they moved to the Blue Mountains because of Louisa's delicate health, her mother deciding that the higher altitude and pure air might suit her. She built a house named Fernhurst on Kurrajong Heights and Louisa soon became immersed in the plant life around her. Walking or riding through the bush she observed and noted birds, insects, flowers and ferns, collecting plants for pressing and mounting and making sketches. A deeply religious woman, she began Sunday school classes at Kurrajong, but she also had an unorthodox streak. She and her friend, Mrs Selkirk, wife of a local doctor, scandalised the locals by wearing practical, unfeminine clothes in the bush instead of conventional long skirts. It was said that they caused 'some twitterings in the ranks of the colonial Mrs. Grundy'.[30]

At the age of twenty-six she had acquired sufficient skill in writing about nature to approach the editor of the Sydney Morning Herald with a proposal to supply a regular series of articles. Beginning on 1 March 1860 she contributed a series entitled 'A Voice from the Country' which were republished in the weekly Sydney Mail. Written in a clear, factual, journalistic style they

Louisa Atkinson was the first native-born Australian woman to achieve success at writing. She was the author of several novels, and was the first woman in Australia to have a long-running series of articles published in a major newspaper. Her popular series, 'A voice from the country' based on her observation of plants and natural phenomena in the Blue Mountains and Berrima districts of New South Wales, began in the Sydney Morning Herald *and the* Sydney Mail *in March 1860. She achieved such fame as a naturalist that Baron von Mueller named several plants after her. (National Library of Australia. RAHS Journal 1929)*

became, judging from the length of time they continued, a very popular series. Between 1864 and 1870 she was also a regular contributor to the *Horticultural Magazine.* Her articles attracted the attention of Dr William Woolls, a famous teacher and prominent amateur botantist and through this friendship her botanical specimens reached the naturalist Baron von Mueller. He sent them to England where they were described in volumes of *Flora Australiensis.* Baron von Mueller thought so highly of her work he named several plants, including *Atkinsonia ligustrina,* in her honour.

In 1857, a few years before the start of her 'A Voice from the Country' series, Louisa Atkinson's first novel, *Getrude the emigrant,* was published by J. R. Clarke in Sydney, ascribed to 'an Australian lady'. A highly moral love story of a young emigrant, Gertrude Gonthier, who on arrival in Sydney is engaged as housekeeper by station-owner Mrs Doherty, *Gertrude* was early in featuring what were to become staples of nineteenth century Australian fiction. The titles of some of the twenty-three engravings (by William Mason) with which the book is illustrated indicate the themes of the story: 'The stampede', 'The new chum', 'The bush fire', 'The kangaroo at bay', 'Burning off', 'The miner rescued', 'The Aboriginals'. *Gertrude the emigrant*'s great virtue was that it was written for an Australian audience. Contemporary critic, G. B. Barton wrote:

> The scene is laid wholly in the Colony, principally in the bush; and nowhere are the peculiar features of bush life more accurately or graphically pourtrayed [sic]. The tale abounds in incident, the characters

41

THE BUSH FIRE.

In her books Louisa Atkinson included many events such as bushfires that were to become common ingredients of nineteenth century Australian fiction. (Illustration from Gertrude, the emigrant)

THE NEW CHUM.

The best character in Louisa Atkinson's first novel, Gertrude, the emigrant is a newly arrived emigrant, a 'new chum' who goes up bush intending to ridicule native-born land owners and workers but instead finds himself a figure of fun. (Illustration from Gertrude, the emigrant) are skilfully drawn, and the literary execution is quite equal to that of ordinary novels.[31]

In 1859 her second novel, *Cowanda, the veteran's grant, an Australian story* appeared, also published by J. R. Clarke, with a woodcut cover from a design by colonial artist S. T. Gill. While not now a very readable story, it includes interesting descriptions of station life in the 1840s and 1850s and of office life in Sydney. The *Empire* wrote:

> Altogether, we have been very much pleased with Cowanda, It strikes us as having the great and unusual merit of being a sincere book — by one who looks at things with his [sic] own eyes, and describes them as he sees them.[32]

No more of Louisa Atkinson's novels were published in book form but she became a favourite author of serials published in the *Sydney Mail*. They included *Debatable ground; or, the Carlillawarra claimants* which began on 30 March 1861 and *Myra* on 7 February 1864.

After some years living in the Blue Mountains Louisa and her mother had returned to Oldbury near Berrima where her mother died in 1868. In March the following year at the age of thirty-five Louisa married James Snowden Calvert, a man with a background as an explorer who shared her interest in botany. He was then manager of Cavan station near Wee Jasper south of Yass.

James Calvert as a young man had travelled to Australia in 1841 on the same ship as Ludwig Leichhardt. When Leichhardt set out in August 1844 from the Darling Downs to attempt to reach the north coast at Port Essington, Calvert, then only nineteen, was one of his party. During the journey of nearly eighteen months the party suffered greatly from hunger and thirst and Calvert was severely wounded when the party was attacked by Aborigines. Leichhardt named Calvert's Plains on the Dawson River, Calvert's Peak and the Calvert River on the western shore of the Gulf of Carpentaria after him.

After her marriage Louisa Atkinson continued to have serials published in the *Sydney Mail*. The first instalment of *Tom Hellicar's children* appeared on 4 March 1871. When he sent her the cheque for the story John Fairfax wrote that the story had been 'much admired'.[34] Louisa Atkinson's marriage to James Calvert ended after only about three years with her death at the age of thirty-eight in April 1872, eighteen days after the birth of her only child, Louisa. An obituary in the *Sydney Morning Herald* said:

> This excellent lady, who has been cut down like a flower in the midst of her days, was highly distinguished for her literary and artistic attainments, as well as for the Christian principles and expansive charity which marked her career. As an authoress she distinguished herself by the publication of "Gertrude," "Kiandra," [sic] and other simple and

interesting tales, exhibiting many of the most striking features of colonial
life, and inculcating in the most attractive manner the claims of virtue
and morality. Her drawings — which were, for the most part, illustrations
of Australian animals and flowers — displayed great natural talent,
unaffected elegance, and extreme accuracy, and some of her latest efforts
are now in course of publication under the auspices of the University
of Kiel.[35] . . . But Mrs. Calvert was remarkable for higher excellences
than those of a literary and scientific character; for when residing
at Kurrajong, she . . . endeared herself to the inhabitants by visiting
the sick, comforting the afflicted . . . whilst for the uneducated she was in
the habit of composing letters, drawing up petitions, and sometimes
even preparing the last will and testament . . .[36]

Louisa Atkinson's last story, *Tressa's resolve*, was published after her death.
The first instalment appeared in the *Sydney Mail* on 31 August 1872 as 'A
Tale by the late Mrs. Calvert' with an editorial note:

The writings of this lamented authoress are well known to Australian
readers, having appeared periodically under the signature of 'L. A.' and
'L. C.' The most prominent of her writings are to be found in the early
numbers of this journal . . . the series of papers entitled 'A Voice from
the Country', appearing both in the *Herald* and *Mail*, are looked upon
somewhat as authorities in matters relating to Australian natural history
and botany . . . The present tale, 'Tressa's Resolve,' we hope will be
kindly criticised as a last production of an Australian authoress.[37]

Louisa Atkinson was a distinguished forerunner of many women writers during
the next decades who were to find an outlet for their writings both factual and
fictional in the daily and periodical press. With her delicate concern and
interest in the natural phenomena about her she was also a forerunner of
today's writers on the environment.

4

Visitors and Lady Travellers

'The age of Victoria was the age of the lady travellers . . .'
Alexandra Allen, 1980[1]

This chapter is something of an interregnum in the development of the theme that there was a considerable interdependence between women writers in Australia and newspapers. The works of visitors and travellers being in general published overseas, their authors had little connection with the Australian press, but it would be a mistake to overlook entirely women visitors who wrote about Australia. Lady travellers were to be a striking feature of the emerging independence of a certain class of women in Victorian England, and there were those who came to Australia with the specific intention of writing. Some, like Caroline Chisholm, came with great social purpose, and their writing was a by-product of their main concerns. Many came because of family commitments, while others were caught up in the influx of humanity from around the world to gold-rush Melbourne. Some, like Thérèse Huber, were armchair travellers who wrote about Australia and its oddities without ever making a visit.

A distinguishing feature of visiting writers when compared with resident women authors was their greater awareness of the features of Australian life which overseas readers would want to read about. Louisa Meredith, though a resident for most of her life, saw Australia in this way. She had the desire and ability to describe Australia's natural phenomena to overseas readers and her books were always published overseas.

In the 1850s and 1860s convicts remained a subject of great interest in England. Towards the end of 1859, Caroline Leakey's remarkably acute observation of the convict system in Tasmania and her sympathy for its victims were expressed in her novel *The broad arrow*, which enjoyed a very successful publishing history. Even in the 1860s Mrs Elizabeth P. Ramsay-Laye, wife of a clergyman, still found an eager public for a book, set in Sydney, whose story was based on the 'convict stain'. Published under the name of 'Isabel Massary' in Edinburgh in 1866, her novel *Social life in Sydney; or colonial experience: an Australian tale*, continued to be reprinted for many years, appearing as late as 1914 under the author's own name.

The gold-rush was also good value as a topic for a book. The crowded streets and tent towns of Melbourne, the sensational changes of fortune brought about through a lucky strike on the goldfields, and the extreme liveliness and lawlessness were portrayed most effectively by Celeste de Chabrillan, a Paris courtesan who had married into the French aristocracy, and Ellen Clacy, apparently a refined young Englishwoman.

When interest in the convict past and the gold rushes began to decline, social comment on Australian life became popular. Clara Aspinall, an English clergyman's daughter, visited her barrister and journalist brother, Butler Cole Aspinall, in Melbourne in the late 1850s. When she returned to London she published in 1862 a charming book, *Three years in Melbourne* expressing conventional views on progress in Melbourne. Elizabeth Murray in her novel about the life of a governess, *Ella Norman; or, A woman's perils*, published in 1864 was a more critical observer. For some time, however, the best social comment on Australia remained that of Louisa Meredith who, when she wrote *Notes and Sketches of New South Wales*, thought she was a visitor soon to return to England.

Isabella Bird was in the great tradition of the English lady travellers who, defying hardship and danger, spent their lives travelling to out-of-the-way places and recording their adventures and observations for a fascinated public. She visited Australia at the beginning of what was to become a lifetime of travelling to exotic places.

Caroline Woolmer Leakey

> '. . . such an atmosphere of sin, suffering, and sorrow.'
>
> *Australasian*

Caroline Woolmer Leakey, a retiring, extremely religious English lady was an unlikely author of a work about a woman convict sentenced to transportation for life. Her novel *The broad arrow: being passages from the history of Maida Gwynnham, a lifer*, published in 1859 under the pseudonym Oline Keese, predated by eleven years the serial publication of Marcus Clarke's convict novel *For the term of his natural life*.

The book was so successful it appeared in three English and three Australian editions. It would appear to have become one of the most widely read Australian works by women writers prior to the last decade of the nineteenth century, reaching, for instance, a much wider readership than Catherine Spence's novels.

In an adulatory book written about her by her sister, Emily, after her death, Caroline Leakey appears as a person of saintly qualities and marked spirituality who lived a holy and guileless life, while suffering constant ill health. Her family was steeped in evangelical religion and good works. When Emily's book *Clear shining light* was published it was dedicated to Caroline's three surviving brothers, all clergymen, and to her brother-in-law, Rev. J. G. Medland. Caroline herself was the author of many penny tracts and she worked for such causes as the Church Missionary Society, the Seaman's Society and saving the Jews.[3]

Caroline Woolmer Leakey was born at Exeter on 8 March 1827, the fourth daughter and sixth child of James Leakey, an eminent artist. One of eleven children, she was always frail. She was kept away from school because of her ill health but developed an intense love of books, particularly poetry, and sat for many hours as a model for her artist father. (None of these portraits seems to have survived and no photograph of Caroline Leakey has been located.)

In 1847 at the age of twenty she sailed for Van Dieman's Land at the request of her sister, Eliza, who wanted her to help care for her children otherwise dependent on convict nurses. Caroline arrived in Hobart in January 1848 and joined the household of Eliza and her husband Rev. James Gould Medland. Her letters to her family during her stay with her sister are taken up, to a great extent, with cloying accounts of the cute sayings and actions of her sister's young children. There is little in them to indicate that Caroline Leakey was absorbing the atmosphere and knowledge of the convict system that was to emerge in her novel.[4]

The year after her arrival she contracted colonial fever and then hip disease followed by other complications which kept her a semi-invalid for the rest of the five years she spent in Tasmania. In 1850 she stayed with Bishop Francis Russell Nixon, the first Anglican Bishop of Tasmania, and Mrs Anna Maria Nixon, both of whom were interested in the fine arts and encouraged her in writing poetry. (She used their home, Boa Vista, as a setting in her novel.) While with them she wrote some poetry and, encouraged by Bishop Nixon, submitted a book of poems for publication. This was published in 1854 as *Lyra Australis, or attempts to sing in a strange land* under her own name in both London and Hobart. All the poems are strongly religious and deal with household and family matters, sickness, death, infancy and motherhood. Two are addressed to her doctor, J. W. Agnew, and his wife, who were family friends. A section of the book containing poems written by Caroline Leakey while she was staying at Boa Vista is dedicated to Lady Denison, wife of the Governor.

In 1851–52 she stayed for a year with the Rev. T. B. Garlick and his family at the parsonage at the infamous prison settlement at Port Arthur, where only officials connected with convict administration were permitted to

THE

BROAD ARROW:

BEING PASSAGES FROM THE HISTORY

OF

MAIDA GWYNNHAM,

A LIFER.

BY OLINE KEESE.

IN ONE VOLUME.

TASMANIA:
J. WALCH AND SONS,
HOBART TOWN AND LAUNCESTON.
1860.

[*The right of Translation is reserved.*]

Caroline Leakey, like many other women writers of the nineteenth century, disguised her identity under a pseudonym. Her powerful novel, The broad arrow, *about a woman sentenced to transportation for life to Tasmania was first published in 1859 under the name of Oline Keese. It was so successful it was published in three editions in England and three in Australia. Caroline Leakey based her novel on her observation of the convict system during a visit of five years to Tasmania from 1848 to 1853. (Title page from* The broad arrow)

live. It is clear that it was here, in a community of convicts sentenced for the second or third time for offences committed after transportation, that Caroline Leakey gained much of the knowledge she used in *The broad arrow*. She wrote to her sister that the parsonage was 'built in sight of that sadly-solemn sea-girt graveyard, "the isle of the dead" '.[5] Caroline Leakey suffered further ill-health after the visit to Port Arthur and Dr Agnew advised her to return to England. She sailed from Tasmania in March 1853 at the age of twenty-six and, after a trip confined to her cabin, arrived in London in June. Plagued by illness, she was nevertheless able, following the death of a sister, to take charge of the school the sister had run in London. The following year, after the death of her mother, she returned to Exeter to care for her father.

She spent a year from March 1857 to March 1858 writing *The broad arrow*, a long work in two volumes. In a preface she said she had been told 'the subject is unbecoming to a woman's pen'. She had replied that she intended it as a warning to any 'sister, now trembling on the brink of ruin'.

She added 'loss of virtue is (in most cases) the first and fatal impulse towards those depths of sin whose end it has been my painful lot to witness in Tasmania'.[6] In England the *Athenaeum* wrote:

> We are hardened novel readers and stony-hearted critics, but we have read some parts of the *Broad Arrow* more than once. It contains as much as half a dozen ordinary novels put together. The book is written with great force and earnestness. The *Broad Arrow* may take its place beside De Foe's stories for its lifelike interest and graphic reality.[7]

The broad arrow was reviewed in the *Australasian* following publication of an Australian edition by George Robertson in Melbourne in 1887. The reviewer said the story was 'not very artistically constructed' and the incidents 'of such a uniformly painful character that the reader experiences a sense of relief on reaching the end of the last chapter, and escaping from such an atmosphere of sin, suffering, and sorrow'. The review ended:

> The story is rather crude in conception and execution, but where the writer deals with the convict population of the island in the former days, and with the abuses of the penal system, he (or she?) is forcible and effective.[8]

The story is melodramatic and permeated with religious comments. Maida Gwynnham, the heroine, an unusual convict being the daughter of a country gentleman, is the victim of a heartless lover, Captain Henry Norwell, who seduces her and induces her to commit forgery on his behalf. She has a child who dies and whom she buries secretly. Arrested for child murder she is tried, convicted and sentenced to death, but the sentence is commuted to life imprisonment. She is transported to Hobart and assigned as a servant to Mr and Mrs Evelyn. The humiliations she undergoes, the people she has to mix with, and the iniquities of the convict system take up many chapters. After a life of great trials and humiliations Maida Gwynnham dies from a lung haemorrhage, Captain Norwell arriving in Hobart just in time to see her corpse in the morgue. Shocked, he loses his reason and becomes an inmate of a lunatic asylum.

The book is lengthy and poorly organised but it contains some scenes of startling drama. An example is an incident concerning two convicts, Bradley and Pragg, who hate each other but who are chained together for a long period:

> But just out of spite the overseer *would* release them: he had barely done so, than, with the roar of an uncaged lion, upstarted Bradley, knocked him down, caught up a handcuff and struck Pragg a blow that felled him to the deck, and made the blood flow from his head. Bradley then flung himself on his hands and knees and lapped up the blood.
>
> 'I swore to hell I'd never rest till I'd spit your own blackguard blood in your face; now, here it is!'[9]

After this one novel Caroline Leakey reverted to writing on religious topics. In 1861 she wrote *God's tenth*, a penny tract, the first of a series issued each year until her death. She also wrote moral poems for the *Girls' Own Paper* and worked for the Exeter Home for Fallen Women. For many years she did not buy clothes for herself so that she could give £14 a year to an old servant. She suffered great pain from corns on the soles of her feet which she treated by bathing them with laudanum but towards the end of her life she decided to give up this treatment 'for Christ's sake'. She died on 12 July 1881 at the age of fifty-four.[10]

Celeste de Chabrillan (Mogador)

> *'During two nights I sat up until dawn reading* Voleurs d'Or'
> Alexandre Dumas

Of the many thousands of people from around the world who flocked to Melbourne in the early 1850s, few could rival the extraordinary background and achievement of Celeste de Chabrillan. After a girlhood spent in Paris brothels she had, in the face of his family's violent opposition, become the wife of Count Lionel de Chabrillan, a member of one of the oldest French noble families, and travelled to Melbourne with him in 1854. Celeste, snubbed by Melbourne society because of her past, spent her time writing a lively novel of the gold rushes *Les voleurs d'or* (The gold robbers) into which she packed all her experiences of the feverish, boom-town atmosphere of Melbourne and of the Victorian gold diggings.[11]

Celeste Venard was born in Paris on 27 December 1824, the illegitimate daughter of Anne-Victoire Venard and a man who joined the army and disappeared before her birth. In her childhood her mother had several lovers and Celeste witnessed many violent quarrels. With this upbringing it is difficult to know how she gained the education and mental stimulus that enabled her to become a well-known writer and playwright. She had unusual descriptive powers, was an acute observer and wrote lively dialogue. She also had the ability, to an amazing degree, to attract the interest of famous men, not only as lovers but as admirers of her literary ability. When fourteen, her mother's lover attempted to rape her while her mother was absent. She ran away and, found on the streets, was sent to Saint-Lazare women's prison. At sixteen she became a registered prostitute indebted to a brothel-keeper, then a dancer at Bal Mabille, one of the most popular dance halls in Paris. Her male partner, Brididi, when Celeste became popular and everyone wanted to dance the new dance sensation, the polka, with her, said 'I should have less trouble to defend Mogador than my partner'. (Mogador was a name

CÉLESTE MOGADOR

When Celeste Mogador, formerly a Paris courtesan, actress and circus performer, arrived in Melbourne in 1854 with her husband Count Lionel de Chabrillan who had been appointed French consul, she was ostracised by Melbourne society because of her background. She spent her time writing a lively novel about the gold-rush, Les voleurs d'or, which became a great success after being praised highly by the famous French novelist Alexandre Dumas. (Phot. Bibl. Nat. Paris) of the moment, being a fortress in Morocco bombarded by the French in 1844. The name of Mogador stayed with her for the rest of her life.) When the dance hall closed down she moved on to a circus where she became a famous rider.

By 1845 at the age of twenty-two she was the star of the Hippodrome, the toast of Paris and mistress of the Italian Duke of Ossuna, but had to give up circus performances when she was badly hurt in a chariot race. She then fell in love with Count Lionel de Chabrillan, heir to a large fortune and an inveterate gambler. They had a stormy relationship, separated several times and Celeste had other lovers, one of whom she arranged to marry but left at the church door.

Count de Chabrillan, besieged by creditors and disowned by his family because of his association with Celeste, left Paris in 1852 for Victoria, one of thousands of young men lured there by the newly discovered goldfields. He returned the following year without having made his fortune but determined to marry Mogador. In an effort to stop this marriage his family obtained for him the position of French Consular Agent in Melbourne. He accepted the position but he also married Mogador — in London on 4 January 1854 — and together with Solange, Mogador's adopted daughter, they sailed for Melbourne. Their ship the Croesus was so late reaching Melbourne that it was assumed to have sunk and the papers carried obituaries of the prominent people aboard, among them the new French consul, Count Lionel de Chabrillan. He was described as the husband of 'the notorious Celeste Mogador, the first two volumes of whose curious Memoirs have been published by the Librairie Nouvelle in Paris (they can also be purchased in Melbourne)'.[12] Mogador's memoirs Adieux au Monde, released in Paris in five volumes, gave a frank account of her life as a prostitute, dancer, circus performer and courtesan. This was too much for Melbourne society and she found herself left out when her husband was invited to Government House. In Melbourne they found rents high and at first, like many others, lived very uncomfortably. However, with great foresight Celeste had bought a prefabricated house in Bordeaux and, when it arrived, they had it erected at St Kilda.

Late in 1856, Chabrillan's finances deteriorated after a venture in flour speculation failed. In an effort to raise money, Celeste, who had been ill, returned to France taking with her the manuscript she had written in Melbourne gaol — all appear. Alexandre Dumas in his review described 'absolutely extraordinary'[13] by Alexandre Dumas and became famous overnight. It is a fast-moving tale of Melida, the daughter of an English physician, Dr Iwans, who migrates to Australia with his family. The heroine's wealthy suitor, known to the family as Mr Fulton, proves to be Max, an escaped convict and the leader of a ferocious coach-robbing gang. He seduces and leaves Melida but after many twists and turns of the plot, Melida sees him hanged, watching from the window of the Iwans' home overlooking Melbourne gaol. The book is written with great vitality which tends to carry the story over improbable patches. The life of Melbourne and the goldfields—the violent duststorms of summer, shipboard tragedies, fights and the hangings at Melbourne gaol—all appear. Alexandre Dumas in his review described Celeste de Chabrillan as a 'valiant heart' and said of the book 'During two nights I sat up until dawn reading *Les Voleurs d'Or*'.[14]

While a sensation in Paris, with its wild story and exciting exotic setting, *Les voleurs d'or* was not universally admired. Hubert de Castella, landowner and wine grower who had arrived in Melbourne from Switzerland in 1854, wrote a book *Les squatters Australiens*, published in Paris in 1861, about his first years in Australia as a cattle farmer, as a rejoinder to *Les voleurs d'or*. He said Celeste de Chabrillan's book was 'full of guile and of disparagement of a land and people she had not known'.[15]

Lionel de Chabrillan died in Melbourne in December 1858. A notice in the *Argus* of 30 December 1858 invited the friends of the late 'Comte Lionel de Moreton de Chabrillan' to follow his remains to the Melbourne General Cemetery the next day.[16] By then Celeste, who had remained in Paris, had written two more novels with Australian settings. She later wrote a large number of plays, many of which were performed successfully. Altogether she wrote twelve novels and twenty-six plays, as well as poems, songs and operettas. In 1870 when the Prussian siege of Paris was imminent she formed the sisters of France which organised ambulance stations in empty houses on the outskirts of the city where she helped to nurse the wounded. She died at an old people's home at Montmartre on 18 February 1909 at the age of eighty-five, more than half a century after her brief residence in Melbourne.

Ellen Clacy

Ellen Clacy is something of a mystery reporter on the Victorian goldfields. She arrived in Melbourne in 1852 and set out almost immediately for the gold diggings with her brother and several other young Englishmen. Goodnaturedly enduring considerable discomfort she managed not only to find some gold but to write an appealing book about her short stay in Victoria, entitled *A lady's visit to the gold diggings of Australia in 1852–53*.

If her account is to be taken as factual there was a conventional happy ending to her stay with her marriage to one of her brother's friends, Charles Clacy, although there does not appear to be any evidence of such a marriage in the records of the time, nor of their supposed departure from Melbourne by ship to England soon after.[17] Within a short time of her arrival back in London in February 1853, her book was published. It proved very popular and after selling out quickly was reprinted. The *Daily News* said it was 'the most graphic account of the diggings and the gold country in general that is to be had'.

Despite some doubts about Mrs Clacy's identity, the author must be credited with the writing of an engaging account of a young woman's trip to the goldfields at a time when interest in Victoria was intense. It included vivid descriptions of the excitement and lawlessness that gripped Melbourne, the hardship and destitution among many of the new arrivals who crowded into temporary tent towns and the chaos of overburdened public services such as the scenes at the Post Office when a ship arrived with mail.

Ellen Clacy also wrote *Lights and shadows of Australian life*, published in London in 1854, which included many of the usual themes of nineteenth century Australian fiction including bushrangers, floods, an Aboriginal attack and convicts.

Elizabeth Murray

Elizabeth A. Murray, author of a novel containing very critical comments on Australian society at the time of the gold-rushes, was born in 1820 in Jamaica, where her father Lieutenant-Colonel Charles Poitier was serving with the British Army. Her mother, formerly Sara Hunter, came from a family established in the Bahamas and after leaving the Army, her father stayed on in Nassau as Collector of Customs.

After the death of her parents Elizabeth went to live in Ireland where, at the age of eighteen, she married Captain Virginius Murray. Following service in Canada and Britain, Murray left the Army and, attracted by the opportunities in Victoria following the discovery of gold, decided to emigrate. He soon gained appointment as a Goldfields Commissioner, first at Beechworth and later in the Dunolly area. A colourful character with a reputation as a ladies' man, Murray became a friend of explorer Robert O'Hara Burke while stationed at Beechworth where they were regarded as two eccentrics.

When his stay became protracted his wife in 1855 followed him out to Melbourne with their five sons. She found life in Melbourne uncongenial and was disappointed with the educational opportunities for her children. At the end of 1859 she left to return to England leaving behind her husband and her eldest son, Reginald. A year later Virginius Murray became ill and he died on Christmas Day 1861, aged forty-four.

Elizabeth did not know for some time that she was a widow. Thrown on her own resources (she received only £325 from the Victorian Government as compensation for the death of her husband, not the £2000 she had expected) she settled in Harrow and having previously written novels with some success, decided to write *Ella Norman; or, A woman's perils*, a novel set in the colony

In 1855 Elizabeth Murray arrived in Victoria with her five sons to join her husband Captain Virginius Murray who had been appointed a gold commissioner at Beechworth. She was critical of what she saw as the gross vulgarity and personal and commercial immorality of life in Victoria. After her return to England and the death of her husband she wrote a novel Ella Norman; or, a woman's perils *about a governess, containing acute observations on Australian society. (Lady Murray, Murrumbateman, NSW)*

of Victoria.

She was described by a descendant, Sir Brian Murray, in the preface to the recent Australian edition of this book, as 'intelligent, artistic (she painted in oils and water colour), fastidious, extremely feminine, and although gentle in manner, possessed of considerable character and strong convictions'.

Ella Norman is the story of a young woman whose family's sudden impoverishment leads them to seek opportunities in gold-rush Australia. To earn money Ella Norman takes a position as a governess in Victoria, at a time when young Englishwomen were being led to believe that their services as governesses were in great demand in Australia and that rich husbands were waiting on the wharf for genteel and refined English females. Similarly, well-bred young Englishmen believed fortunes were ready to be plucked from trees. Elizabeth Murray's book had some value in helping to expose these myths.

In her preface she wrote:

> My own personal sympathies are, and have long been, strongly excited by the sufferings of members of my own sex, exposed too often to a heartrending fate, by the mistaken kindness of 'friends at home'.
>
> The noble and true-hearted who have the real interests of their *protegees* at heart, will appreciate my motives in offering them a sketch suggestive of the probable future of some of their helpless victims — victims to a philanthropy not the less cruel in effect because mistaken, and *meant for the best*. It may at least stimulate further inquiry into these regions, comparatively unknown to writers of fiction, and seldom approached by writers of fact, at least in their *inner* life.

A character in the book remarks on the fate of governesses:

> Who can doubt the amiable intentions of the good people who
> inundated the country with those hapless girls, who came out only to
> meet their ruin? . . . It drives me mad sometimes to think of the
> benevolent feelings and the money expended by injudicious great people
> in working out unmitigated evil for their fellow-creatures, when
> possessed by some ridiculous crochet or whim; as it often happens they
> are worked upon by some scheming adventurer.

The book also contains attacks on many aspects of life in Victoria including
corruption in high places and the manners and mores of what Elizabeth
Murray saw as a 'mob-ascendant' society. A reviewer in the London *Athenaeum*
was rather suspicious of Mrs Murray's objectivity: 'Whether she is actuated by
personal pique, we cannot, of course, decide; but her bitter invectives might
almost lead us to form that conclusion.'

The London *Saturday Review* wrote: 'Yet, even though it is an exaggerated
and ill-looking likeness of the whole colony, Mrs Murray's book may do
good . . . (if, this book will induce its readers only to think, and to use
common sense, before taking a plunge to the Antipodes — it is a comparatively
small demerit that the book is in itself obviously onesided.)'

From a different perspective, the Melbourne *Age* said:

> It is not a bad thing for social health at times to see ourselves as others
> see us, even though the reflection should involve some exaggeration of
> the proportions of our noble selves. The fair author of the Victorian
> novel and sketch book before us is a plain speaker and no mistake; and,
> if the absence of malice prepense cannot certainly be predicated in the
> revelations of what she has at some time or other of our history seen with
> her own eyes, she extenuates nothing.[18]

Perhaps without intending to do so, Elizabeth Murray presents native-born
Australian women as attractively assertive and independent, some of those
with means already running farms and businesses, others throwing off class
attitudes brought from 'home' and moving across social barriers. There is a
delightful scene at a registry office where a girl looking for work as a servant
questions a would-be employer about the work and conditions and when these
do not please her turning down the offer of a situation.

Although it subsequently became a forgotten work until republished in
1985, Elizabeth Murray's novel must have been a financial success at the time
of its first publication in England in 1864, as the author was enabled to send
her sons to the famous Harrow school for their education.

Mrs R. E. (Sarah) Lee

*'. . . without a chart, and with an erring compass, I can but guess at
what I saw . . .'*

Adventures in Australia

Armchair travellers who wrote about Australia without ever visiting the country, satisfied a demand for adventure stories set in strange places. To English readers, particularly children, Australia, while perhaps not as interesting as Africa or the East, was still a fascinating locale. As a setting it presented unusual animals, birds and plants, the opportunity for exploration and adventure in a huge land, frequent natural disasters, such as bushfires and floods, and the opportunity, after the discovery of gold, for exciting and rapid changes in fortune.

Sarah Bowdich, later Mrs R. E. (Sarah) Lee was a very successful exponent of this type of writing. Although she did not visit Australia she wrote *Adventures in Australia: or, the wanderings of Captain Spencer in the bush and the wilds,* (in other editions called *The Australian Wanderers; or, the Adventures of Captain Spencer, his horse and dog*) which was published in 1851. The first edition contained illustrations by J. S. Prout, the colonial artist who worked from 1840 to 1848 in Australia. The hero of Sarah Lee's book, Captain Spencer, after being shipwrecked on the north-west coast of Australia, sets out for the Swan River (Perth) but ends in crossing the continent to the east coast, accompanied by his dog, his horse and his talking parrot plus a faithful Aborigine, Kinchela. Explorers had only a few years before crossed Australia for the first time and Sarah Lee acknowledged her debt to their accounts in a preface:

> . . . as the natural products of the newer world are even more extraordinary than those longer discovered, it is the object of the present work rather to dwell upon them, than in the fast increasing riches of the settlements. . . .
>
> The author is desirous to express her gratitude for the assistance she has received from private sources, and from the adventurous travels which have been written on the same subject. The names of Stokes, Gray, Sturt, Eyre, and several others, give authority to her assertions . . .[19]

After missing the Swan River settlement (it has been suggested that Mrs Lee did not have a good description of the settlement at Perth on which to base

Englishwoman Sarah Lee, an 'armchair traveller' who did not ever visit Australia, wrote a very successful adventure book for young readers about a shipwrecked sea captain who found his way from the north-west to the east coast. The book, which was published in 1851 not long after Australia had been crossed by explorers for the first time, contains many improbable adventures. The title page is a good example of the long, explanatory titles which were very common in the nineteenth century. In other editions the book was called The Australian wanderers; or, the adventures of Captain Spencer, his horse and his dog. *(Title page of Adventures in Australia)*

ADVENTURES IN AUSTRALIA;

OR, THE

WANDERINGS OF CAPTAIN SPENCER

IN THE BUSH AND THE WILDS.

CONTAINING ACCURATE
DESCRIPTIONS OF THE HABITS OF THE NATIVES,

AND THE

NATURAL PRODUCTIONS AND FEATURES OF
THE COUNTRY.

BY

MRS. R. LEE,

(Formerly Mrs. T. E. Bowdich,)

AUTHOR OF "THE AFRICAN WANDERERS," "MEMOIRS OF
CUVIER," &c.

WITH ILLUSTRATIONS BY J. S. PROUT,

Member of the New Water-Colour Society.

LONDON:
GRANT AND GRIFFITH,

SUCCESSORS TO

J. HARRIS, CORNER OF ST. PAUL'S CHURCHYARD.

M.DCCC.LI.

her writing) Captain Spencer arrives after many adventures at the Murray River where he meets miners from Adelaide and an overlander, and by the last chapter he manages to reach Sydney. On his journey he sees frigate birds and crocodiles, flying foxes, green ants, hawks, pelicans, cranes, porpoises, kangaroos, frilled lizards, bowerbirds, venomous snakes and possums. In addition he is speared by an Aborigine, bitten by a snake, nearly dies of thirst, and saves an Aborigine by dressing his wounds. Of his extraordinary crossing of Australia, Captain Spencer is made to remark:

> . . . without a chart, and with an erring compass, I can but guess at what I saw, further than that I was in the Bight of Australia, to the east of King George's Sound, and that I believe I skirted Lake Torrens. You tell me we are now on the Darling.[20]

The story ends with Captain Spencer back in Bombay where he receives a letter from friends he had made on a station in New South Wales, telling him of the discovery of gold, but he decides against joining the gold diggers.

The fictitious nature of the book did not prevent it becoming immensely

PAGE 260.

Sarah Lee's book Adventures in Australia; or, the wanderings of Captain Spencer in the bush and the wilds *was illustrated by artist John Skinner Prout, who had returned to London in 1848 after eight years in Australia during which he executed many highly regarded watercolours and pencil sketches. Sarah Lee's descriptions of the Aborigines and the strange birds and animals Captain Spencer came across during his adventurous trip across Australia added to the popularity of her book. ('The kangaroo hunt' by John Skinner Prout from* Adventures in Australia)

---

popular. The sixth edition was published in London in 1879 and another appeared in 1891. There were American editions in 1872, 1873 and in 1898, and probably many others in between. Mrs Lee was a prolific writer of children's travel stories and books on nature subjects. Some of her other books published in many editions included The African wanderers; or, the adventures of Carlos and Antonio.

Born about 1791, the daughter of John Eglington Wallis of Colchester, she married in 1813 Thomas Edward Bowdich who became famous for his travels in and writings on Africa. Sarah accompanied him on many of his adventurous trips in Africa and after his death, at the age of thirty-three completed and published the last part of the story of his adventures. Left a widow with three children, she later remarried and as Mrs R. Lee became a popular writer and illustrator of books on scientific subjects for young readers. She died in 1865.[21]

Anne Bowman

Anne Bowman was another prolific children's author who wrote popular adventure stories set in exotic places including Mesopotamia, the Rocky Mountains and the wilds of Africa. Her work set in an Australian locale was *The kangaroo hunters; or, adventures in the bush* published in London in 1859. She wrote in the preface:

> The rapid spread of education creates a continual demand for new books, of a character to gratify the taste of the young, and at the same time to satisfy the scruples of their instructors . . .
> In this belief, we are encouraged to continue to supply the young with books which do not profess to be true, though they are composed of truths. They are doubtless romantic, but cannot mislead the judgment or corrupt the taste; their aim is to describe the marvellous works of creation . . .[22]

In the thirty-four chapters of adventure the protagonists, the Maybury family, have to abandon ship among coral reefs, meet alligators, kangaroos, snakes, frilled lizards, laughing jackasses, emus and wombats, and traverse mountains, mangrove swamps and deserts. They encounter friendly and unfriendly Aborigines and bushrangers:

> . . . the privations of the barren and dry desert, the perils of the rude mountain-passes, and the fording deep and foaming rivers, besides the subtle and vindictive pursuit of various unfriendly tribes of natives. At length they attained in safety the fertile banks of a broad and rapid river . . .[23]

While there are extensive descriptions of rugged country containing deserts, rivers, ravines, wild country and strange animals, there is no sense of the enormous extent of the interior of Australia. The story ends when the Mayburys reach the estate of a friend, their supposed path through Australia remaining obscure to the end.

Adventures written from afar would be judged harshly today but this type of story written by competent authors satisfied an apparently insatiable demand for exotic adventures in little known lands, particularly among young readers.

Isabella Lucy Bird

Isabella Bird was one of a number of eccentric British women who made a career of travelling and writing about foreign places in the nineteenth century. High minded and intrepid, for thirty years she spent her life seeking the odd places in the world, producing many books of travel and adventure. She travelled on horses, yaks, mules and elephants over mountain passes and through river rapids and lived in places never before reached by Europeans. She visited Australia early in her travels but it rated only some articles, apparently not being sufficiently exotic to warrant a book. She was handicapped, in any case, by having visited only Victoria.

Isabella Lucy Bird was born in 1831 at Boroughbridge, Yorkshire where her father was the curate. She and her sister Henrietta were brought up in an evangelical household and they took up causes such as Sunday observance and temperance. When the family moved to Edinburgh Isabella visited the slums to care for the poor and when her sister moved to the Isle of Mull Isabella during frequent visits busied herself bettering the lot of the islanders and encouraging them to emigrate to Canada. Following an operation for a tumour on her spine she suffered constant ill health and in 1872, being prescribed a change of air, she sailed for Australia. She landed at Melbourne and spent some time in the Victorian Western District, then left for New Zealand and at the beginning of 1873 sailed from Auckland for the Sandwich (Hawaiian) Islands. Despite hurricanes, cockroaches and mutinous stewards she enjoyed the trip so much she began her travelling/writing career with *Six months in the Sandwich Islands.*[24]

During this trip she wrote a series of seven articles entitled 'Australia Felix. Impressions of Victoria' which appeared in a periodical of which no records remain, ascribed to the author of *Six months in the Sandwich Islands.* From her temperance standpoint she looked behind the burgeoning buildings of Melbourne and the obvious signs of affluence to write:

> Nowhere, except in the young frontier towns of America, have I seen such a redundancy of billiard-saloons and 'rowdy'-looking restaurants and bar rooms. Facilities for intoxication abound in Melbourne, and though the use of alcohol in that dry and over-stimulating climate is a fruitful cause of lunacy and death, drinking increases, and hundreds of men, and some women, go to hopeless wreck on brandy every year in a month after landing . . .
>
> The 'larrikin' is an embryo ruffian, a boy in years, a man in vices. He gambles, cheats, drinks, chews, smokes, sets outhouses on fire, rifles drunken citizens' pockets, insults respectable women, rings bells, wrenches off knockers, and has a fatal precision in the use of obnoxious missiles . . .[25]

Isabella Bird spent the rest of her life visiting remote places. In 1878 she was the first European to visit some parts of Japan and she lived for a time among the hairy Ainu in a remote part of Hokkaido. In 1880 she married Dr John Bishop, the Birds' family doctor, ten years her junior. When asked how such a frail lady could accomplish such arduous journeys he said she had 'the appetite

Isabella Bird Bishop was one of a number of intrepid British women who gained fame in the nineteenth century as lady travellers — women who spent most of their lives travelling to exotic, little known parts of the world and writing about their travels. Isabella Bird made some forthright comments on Melbourne when she visited Australia in 1872, but she is more famous for her series of books describing her travels in remote parts of Asia and America. She is dressed in Manchu dress in this photograph illustrating her adventures on a journey up the Yangtse River in China. (The author — Manchu dress. The Yangtze Valley and beyond)

of a tiger and the digestion of an ostrich'. After his death in 1886 she resumed travelling. She rode through Persia into seldom visited provinces, travelled up the Yangtse River in China in a small boat, and rode around Korea on half-tamed ponies. As a result of her travels and writing she was the first woman elected to the Royal Geographical Society. When she died in 1904 she was planning another journey to China.

Lady Broome

Lady Broome (Barker) was more than a lady traveller, becoming famous in the late nineteenth century for her books on colonial countries, some of which she had lived in as a governor's wife. She was born Mary Anne Stewart in Spanish Town, Jamaica, educated in England and at the age of twenty-one married Captain George Barker of the Royal Artillery, who was knighted in 1859 for distinguished service during the Indian Mutiny. He died in England in

1861 and four years later, at the age of thirty-four, she married a sheep farmer from New Zealand, Frederick Broome. They sailed to his large sheep run, Steventon on the Selwyn River, North Canterbury where writing as Lady Barker, Mary Anne Broome described their life vividly in *Station Life in New Zealand*. The book proved very popular and was reprinted several times.

After a disastrous season, Frederick Broome sold Steventon and he and Mary returned to England where they both took up journalism to make a living. Mary wrote *Station amusements in New Zealand* in 1873 and for the next ten years wrote for magazines, edited travel books and published eight of her own books, including an autobiography and a cookery book. During all this time she preferred to use the more aristocratic name of Lady Barker. In 1875 Frederick Broome was appointed colonial secretary in Natal and there Lady Barker wrote *A year's housekeeping in South Africa*. Her husband's next position was Governor of Western Australia, a post he held from 1882 to 1889.

After their arrival in Western Australia with their younger son Louis, Mary Anne Broome wrote to her son Guy at school in England about Perth and about the places she visited when she accompanied her husband on official tours in the state. Later she edited these letters into *Letters to Guy*, one of her most successful books.[26] Mary Anne Broome's husband was knighted in 1884. Left badly off when he died in 1896, she took up journalistic work again and in 1904 her autobiographical collection of stories, *Colonial memories*, was published in London under the name of Lady Broome.

5

Eccentric Entrepreneurs

'*We desired to show that WOMAN is capable of something higher and nobler than the trivial and circumscribed duties which are generally considered as belonging exclusively to our sex.*'

Spectator

The publishing of women's magazines had a long history in England, dating back to the *Ladies' Mercury* which appeared in the last decade of the seventeenth century. This magazine consisted mainly of questions and answers, whereas a successor, the *Female Tatler*, begun in 1709, was described as 'a vehicle for the violently Tory invective of "Mrs Crackenthorpe, a Lady that knows Everything" '.[1] Apart from political and society scandal the *Tatler* contained lively descriptions of contemporary life and events, but the editor (not the fictitious Mrs Crackenthorpe but Mrs Mary de la Riviere Manley, author of several scandalous books of gossip disguised as fiction) had to hand over editorship to a 'Society of Modest Ladies' after encountering libel problems. Other women's magazines followed through the eighteenth century, most of them far more earnest and instructional than the *Tatler*. By the early part of the nineteenth century there was a well established tradition of women's periodicals, some aimed at educating readers, others aimed at entertainment and amusement.

This was a tradition that was slow to come to Australia, despite the fact that a large number of periodicals of other types, mostly literary, were begun in Australia in the nineteenth century. The most successful general magazines were weeklies brought out by the major newspaper publishers. Most of the others were short-lived, failing, as similar publications (not supported by grants) have done in the twentieth century, because of a small and scattered market.

Until the 1880s there were but two small and curious women's magazines published in Australia. The women who ventured into the field of magazine publishing needed unusual talents and a good deal of perseverance. They required not only writing, literary and editing skills, but also some business and finance ability and some knowledge of printing and layout. Such skills were not easy for women to acquire.

Not surprisingly the first women in this field were unusual characters. One, with her husband in the background, set up a periodical in Sydney with the aim, according to her detractors, of collecting subscriptions and decamping with the proceeds. Her publication, the *Spectator*, begun in Sydney in 1858, was surprisingly professional. In Melbourne in 1861 two women of very different character began a periodical, the *Interpreter*, that lasted a mere two issues. Caroline Dexter was a pioneer of the 'bloomer' revolution in England, an unconventional woman who became a patron of the arts. Her partner, Harriet Clisby, became one of the first women doctors in the world and a leader in international women's organisations.

Cora Anna Weekes of the *Spectator*

> 'A Jeremy Diddler in Petticoats'
> Sydney Morning Herald

The *Spectator*, begun in 1858, was ostensibly a literary rather than a women's magazine, but the editor made her target clear when she wrote that she wanted to make the paper acceptable to ladies and did not 'care a fig for the gentlemen'.[2] Mrs Weekes started her magazine at a time when it was unusual for a woman to undertake any sort of business enterprise. Not only did she initiate, edit and publish the fortnightly periodical but she personally solicited subscriptions among the business houses of Sydney and Melbourne. In the first few issues however her identity was hidden behind an anonymous 'association of ladies'.

On Saturday 3 July 1858 this 'association' began what appeared to be a brave venture into periodical journalism with the release in Sydney of the first issue of sixteen pages of *The Spectator—Journal of Literature and Art*, subtitled 'For the cultivation of the memorable and the beautiful'. In this issue it was stated that the *Spectator* would be published semi-monthly simultaneously in Sydney and Melbourne. Agents were named in London and New York. The first three pages were taken up by an editorial on 'The Colonial Literature', setting 'the course we have marked out for ourselves'. This contained a strange combination of adherence to 'the landmarks of Christian conservatism and virtue' and a challenge to the traditional role of women:

> It has been intimated by some who have expressed a desire to see a high-class Literary Journal established in our midst, that such an enterprise is

65

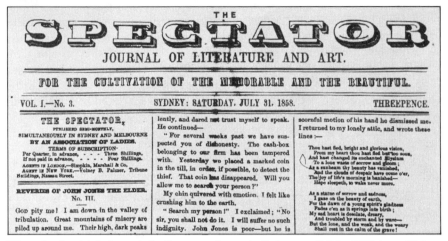

When the fortnightly journal the Spectator began in Sydney on 3 July 1858 its publishers claimed to be 'an association of ladies'. It soon became clear that the paper was owned and edited by Cora Anna Weekes who also, very unusually for a woman, solicited for subscriptions among the business houses of Sydney and Melbourne. Cora Weekes expressed very high ideals for her periodical but the contents hardly lived up to her claim that the Spectator would be a 'high-class Literary Journal'. (Spectator 31 July 1858)

> not altogether suited to the tastes and capacities of our sex. Particularly have some of our best friends seemed to doubt the propriety of a lady entering personally into the field of competition, and calling on gentlemen to solicit their subscriptions.[3]

The writer claimed that subscribers had been found among leading bankers, merchants and, in many instances, a dozen subscribers had been found in a single business house. The articles in the first issue hardly lived up to the publication's stated high ideals. Apart from the three-page article on colonial literature there was a laboured two-page essay on 'The Philosophy of Kissing' by 'An Elizabeth Street Barrister'; a critique of Robert Browning's 'Aurora Leigh'; an article on roads and railways; a piece entitled 'An Elder Brother's Misfortunes' by 'An Elder Brother' from Melbourne; an essay on 'Temper' taken from 'A Woman's Preaching for Woman's Practice' by Augusta Johnstone; and a few other filler articles. Approximately one of the sixteen pages was taken up with advertisements mainly for schools or for supplies, such as coffee.

The second issue, published on 17 July 1858, announced that the principal editor of the Spectator was leaving that day by steamer for Melbourne where she would open offices of the publication and hoped to obtain more than a thousand subscriptions as she had done by canvassing Sydney. An addition to the contents in the second issue was a column of replies to correspondents. One read 'Your communication is excellent, but not exactly suited to our columns. We would avoid everything of a political or sectarian nature.' Another whose contribution was accepted was told, 'We *aim* to make this paper acceptable to Ladies — our sympathies are with our own sex — if we only please *them*, we don't care a fig for the gentlemen!'

To this date the proprietor or 'association of ladies' had remained anonymous but this changed following publication of a sensational story in the *Empire*, the *Sydney Morning Herald* and the Melbourne *Age*. Henry Parkes's *Empire* was the first with the news which it gleaned from the San Francisco papers as soon as they arrived in Sydney. Without linking Mrs Weekes to the Australian periodical she had started in Sydney, the *Empire*, quoting from the San Francisco *Evening Bulletin* of 19 April, claimed that Mrs Cora Anna Weekes and her husband had disappeared from San Francisco soon after starting a weekly literary journal, the *Athenaeum*. After the first issue she had solicited subscriptions in advance in San Francisco, Sacremento, and other places, collecting many thousands of dollars. 'It was then discovered,' the *Evening Bulletin* stated, 'that her editorials were mere plagiarisms'. Soon after, Mrs Weekes and her husband had left 'surreptitiously' for Australia on the barque *Glimpse* under assumed names. Quoting from another paper, the *Alta California* of 20 April, the *Empire* said Mrs Weekes and her husband had used the assumed names of 'Mr. and Mrs. Percival' when they left for Australia, taking 'some 1500 dollars which she had precollected from subscribers, and leaving several hundred dollars of debts. The affair has created no small flutter in literary circles.'[4] These quotes, published without comment under the heading 'Literary Intelligence', were replied to in a letter to the editor from Mrs Weekes' husband George W. Weekes published on the following day:

> In your issue of yesterday, a paragraph appears by which the present proprietors of the *Spectator* may be seriously injured. Although this paragraph has not in any way identified the persons spoken of by the Californian press, in connection with the *Athenaeum*, with those at present conducting the *Spectator* in this city, I desire to state at once, that Mrs. Cora Anna Weekes who presides over the editorial department of the *Spectator* is the same person who established the *Athenaeum* in San Francisco. From the first appearance of this Journal in San Francisco, the most determined efforts were made by the press of that city for the purpose of destroying it, and with an amount of virulence happily in the newspaper world confined almost exclusively to Californian journalists. This very bitter antagonism arose simply from these reasons. In San Francisco at this period there were four papers of a purely literary character, whose interest it was to put down any publication of a precisely similar nature. There were in all 35 established papers in the city, and their proprietors very naturally considered that any increase to the number would impair the circulation and prospects of their own journals . . . The most outrageous libels were constantly

published upon Mrs. Weekes, and those associated with her in her enterprise, and I am not surprised that the *Alta California* and the *Evening Bulletin* should have continued their malicious attacks after our departure . . .

From the *Alta California*, it would appear that Mrs. Weekes had only issued one number of the *Athenaeum*, when she clandestinely left America. You will perceive by the papers sent herewith, that the fourth number of the *Athenaeum* had appeared in San Francisco under the immediate superintendence of Mrs. Weekes. She then openly and fairly disposed of her interest in the journal to Mr. Galacar, of San Francisco, for the sum of five hundred dollars, and left that city in her own name — having discharged, to the last farthing, every debt she had contracted in California.

As to the charge of her articles having been plagiarisms, some copies of the *Athenaeum* forwarded to you contain a sufficient refutation of this accusation . . .[5]

The *Sydney Morning Herald*, scooped on 19 July by the *Empire* caught up on 20 July with new revelations from American papers under the heading A JEREMY DIDDLER IN PETTICOATS.[6] Quoting from the *San Francisco Herald* of 20 April Mrs Weekes was described as a 'neat, pretty, well-dressed little woman', so anxious to gather as many subscribers as possible for her literary weekly that 'laying aside the native delicacy of her sex', she had visited saloons and even 'common "grogshops" ' seeking subscriptions of five dollars each 'from every unlucky wight exposed to the blandishment of her charms, or within hearing of her soft, silvery voice'. The paper continued:

> After literally sacking the warm-hearted citizens of 'Frisco', she proceeded to the capital, and besieged the members of the Legislature with a *vim* that elicited their warmest sympathies. Her bright, expressive eyes, *petite* yet graceful form and air, soft, sympathetic voice, and look of trusting, confiding dependence, took the gentlemen, especially those from distant districts, by storm, and with one accord they furnished forth the needful, regretting that it was not more, to the bewitching little mendicant.[7]

The *Sydney Morning Herald* claimed that this was not the first time Mrs Cora Anna Weekes had used this tactic. Previously in Galveston, Texas, where she had started the *Southern Age* she had visited the House of Representatives where according to the Baton Rouge correspondent of the New Orleans *Picayune*, 'With her handsome face, killing smile and graceful manners, Mrs. W. did tremendous execution among the honourable representatives for the space of about half an hour — obtaining subscribers right and left.' In further quotes from American papers, Mrs Weekes was accused of 'shamefaced literary piracy' and 'unblushing fraud'. The *Sydney Morning Herald* also reprinted George Weekes' letter in defence of his wife, including his claim

THE SPECTATOR

JOURNAL OF LITERATURE AND ART.

FOR THE CULTIVATION OF THE MEMORABLE AND THE BEAUTIFUL.

VOL. I.—No. 4.　　　　SYDNEY: WEDNESDAY, SEPTEMBER 1, 1858.　　　　PRICE SIXPENCE.

PERSONAL.

We owe both an explanation and apology to our subscribers, and we proceed to give both in as brief a manner as possible. Immediately after the issue of our second number we left this city for Melbourne, purposing to remain in that city several weeks. Our back was scarcely turned, however, before the Sydney press, with one or two honourable exceptions, commenced a furious onslaught upon us, our motives, and our character; giving copious extracts reflecting upon us from the California press, applying to us the most abusive and shameful epithets, in language of too coarse and indelicate a nature to quote in these columns;—and even intimating that we had taken "French leave," and that we should never more be seen in Sydney. These attacks were copied in detail by the Melbourne papers, within a day or two after our arrival. We were alone, in a strange community, without a friend or adviser. We could have believed that our unprotected situation in Melbourne would have shielded us from attack; or at least that the press would have been generous enough to delay the expression of their opinions until such times as we could correspond with our friends in Sydney, and receive advice as to the proper course to pursue in the emergency. But no! the newspaper magnates of Melbourne, with the single exception of the *Argus*, lent their columns to the vilest abuse of the SPECTATOR and its editor, naming us as a swindler, and our publication a fraud.

To add to our distress, we heard not one word from Sydney for nearly three weeks— (on account of some irregularity in the mails, as letters were regularly posted to our address.) Finally, after undergoing such suffering as we would not wish our most vindictive enemy, were she the vilest of her sex, to endure, we returned to Sydney. On our arrival home, we found our business nearly ruined, and a general impression among our subscribers that they were victimized, and that our paper was defunct.

In our dire extremity, traduced and slandered by the press of Sydney and the surrounding districts, sick at heart and almost fainting,—we looked around in the desperate hope that we might find at least one word of sympathy and encouragement. To our sur-

prise, almost, we found that the "MONTH" literary journal had defended us in our absence, had spoken in vindication of our conduct, and had expressed its confidence in our honesty. This was peculiarly gratifying, coming as it did from a publication which might have regarded us, humble as we were, in some sense as a business rival; and coming, too, from literary gentlemen with whom we had no personal acquaintance. Subsequently, some of the friends of both periodicals induced the proprietors of the "MONTH" and ourselves to unite the two publications, sincerely believing as they did that such an union would be beneficial to all parties, would prove satisfactory to our own subscribers, and would give a new impetus to Literature in New South Wales. We at once fell in with their views, and joyfully assented to the proposed amalgamation. Accordingly, the necessary steps for the consummation of the arrangement were taken, and due notice was given to the public through the advertising columns of the Sydney *Herald*.

But now appeared a difficulty which we had not anticipated. On comparing the subscription books of the MONTH and the SPECTATOR, we found that *the subscribers, in a large majority of instances, were identical*; that the subscribers to the SPECTATOR were also patrons of the MONTH. Of course, under such circumstances, the amalgamation was impracticable. Our own subscribers had very generally paid in advance; they were entitled to the paper for three months; and we therefore felt obliged to cancel our agreement with the MONTH, or stand convicted and guilty of having broken faith with the public. To end a long story, the MONTH proprietors very generously released us from our engagements with them; and—here is No. 4 of the SPECTATOR.

We have issued this number in the midst of great difficulties. Our expenses are heavy. Every penny received for subscriptions has been expended in this publication. We have embarked in this undertaking, and have staked all we possess in the world on the issue. Whether we succeed in a pecuniary point of view, the future only will tell. But with us the loss of money is a minor consideration. Our reputation and our good fame are at stake. Besides, it was in recognition of a great and important *principle*, that we

undertook the editorial management of this journal. We desired to show that Woman is capable of something higher and nobler than the trivial and circumscribed duties which are generally considered as belonging exclusively to our sex. Why, is there nothing for us, higher than kitchen drudgery and needlework? Shall all our high aspirations, our love of art and letters, our yearnings for the poet's wreath, our strivings for a position and a place among the world's noble ones, be regarded as unworthy of respect or reward? Shall not Woman be permitted to work with brain as well as with fingers? Look around you, citizens of Sydney, at the hundreds of poor unfortunates who throng the streets and crowd the "labour offices" in search of employment. Think of the large numbers of respectable and delicately-nurtured females, thrown by some ruthless stroke upon the mercies of the world, and struggling in menial occupations, with enervated frames and despairing hearts, to earn for themselves a shelter and a crust! Is it not plain, then, to every reflecting mind, *that new avenues of employment must be opened up to our sex?* Is it not a too glaring truth, that the market for female labour is largely overstocked, and that unless some remedy be speedily applied, thousands of poor girls must sink into destitution and infamy?

For our own part, our path is plain before us. We are but a woman, and we are weak; yet we feel that we owe a duty not only to ourselves, but to our sex and to the public. It may be that it is our lot to bear a large measure of censure and abuse; we at least shall strive not to deserve it. Patience will blunt the edge of persecution. Confident in our own good purposes, in the justice of the community, and in Providential aid and direction, we feel that like some of old we too may walk unscorched through the furnace of fire, and that this affliction may bring at last a blessing and a recompense.

In conclusion, we have only a few words to say. The press of New South Wales took a most unfair advantage of us, by attacking us when we were not here to defend ourselves. They have acted cowardly—we now ask them simply to do us the justice to state to the public, who have been misled by their former statements, that the SPECTATOR has not been discontinued.

Following the third issue of the Spectator, *Sydney and Melbourne newspapers published sensational stories of Cora Weekes' activities in America where she had apparently begun several similar papers and after soliciting subscriptions in advance had decamped with the proceeds. She was referred to as a 'Jeremy Diddler in Petticoats' and accused of plagiarism. Cora Weekes replied to her critics in the next issue of the* Spectator (above) *and her husband, George, defended her in letters to the press. She continued her journal for over six months but a question mark remains. Was she a charlatan? (*Spectator *1 September 1858)* that they had left San Francisco openly.[8]

All the material printed in the *Sydney Morning Herald* was reprinted in the Melbourne *Age* after Mrs Weekes had appeared there in her efforts to gain more subscribers in Melbourne and start a Melbourne edition. The *Age* began its story under the heading FEMALE ENTERPRISE:

> We were favoured a day or two ago with a call from the fair Editress of the *Spectator*, a new periodical, which has recently appeared in Sydney. This lady introduced herself as Mrs. Weekes, and submitted to us the first two numbers of her periodical, stating that it was owned by a proprietory of ladies, and edited and managed by ladies, with a special view to lady readers. The project commended itself as novel, not to say a graceful one, and from the address of its fair representative, who had just arrived from Sydney for the purpose of prosecuting an active canvass for subscribers in Melbourne, we should have augured certain success for it. But, unfortunately for the prospects of the *Spectator* and its fair proprietors, 'later' from San Francisco has furnished the Sydney papers with several paragraphs, conveying very equivocal compliments to their character.[9]

The *Age* then reprinted the 'Jeremy Diddler' story from the *Sydney Morning Herald*.

Readers of the *Spectator* were informed for the first time in the third issue on 31 July that the name of the principal editor was Mrs Weekes. It also referred to press stories:

> ... a rumour is abroad to the effect that this paper is to be given up. We would simply state here, that it is the intention of Mrs. Weekes to publish this journal regularly, without regard to the sneers or attacks of the contemporary press; also, that she intends to pursue her duties as canvasser for subscribers.[10]

A letter published in this issue gave a description of Mrs Weekes canvassing for subscriptions, with an indication of how unusual it was for a woman to do this. The writer described his business as one where ladies seldom went as he was a wholesale dealer in articles not used by ladies and operated from a warehouse packed with heavy boxes. Nevertheless Mrs Weekes entered his warehouse to canvass a subscription to her periodical at three shillings for three months paid in advance. Later he heard much of the 'lady canvasser' who apparently created a ripple of interest as she canvassed the business houses of Sydney:

> She swept our whole street (Macquarie Place), I learned, taking subscribers right and left, and sparing nobody. In fact, she obtained more subscribers in this street, and now distributes more than double the number of papers than any other Sydney newspaper, not excluding even the *Morning Herald*.

The letter writer advised Mrs Weekes to ignore her attackers and maintain the standard of her paper:

> If the Sydney press continue to evince a disposition to disparage you — if they even attack you day after day, as was done in California — *do not answer one word.* Trust to the justice of this community, to your own pure purpose, and to God's grace and mercy, and all will be well.[11]

While the letter might be genuine, it is possible that Mrs Weekes wrote it herself!

In later issues more about the history of Cora Ann Weekes appeared. She claimed to have left England with her husband on 4 March 1857 on the *Baden* for New Orleans. They had proceeded to Texas where she had started a literary paper, the *Southern Age*, under the patronage of Governor Pease of Texas and Rt Rev. Dr Odin, Bishop of Texas. The paper had continued for some time but had to be abandoned because of the sparse population and she had left Texas penniless. She had then started the *Athenaeum* in San Francisco but had been attacked in rival papers as 'a base literary imposter' 'a foreigner and stranger to our institutions', 'a detestable Englishwoman', 'an outrageous plagiarist', and 'a literary thief'.[12]

The fourth issue of the Sydney *Spectator* was delayed until 1 September 1858 and then was issued in the midst of great difficulties. 'Our expenses are heavy. Every penny received for subscriptions has been expended in this publication', she wrote. During her absence, Mrs Weekes said, the Sydney press had begun a 'furious onslaught' on her character, quoting 'copious abusive and shameful epithets from the California press and intimating that she had taken "French leave" '. These attacks had been taken up in the Melbourne papers (apart from the *Argus*), and she had been named a swindler and the publication a fraud. On her return to Sydney there had been a proposal that the *Month*, which had been the only publication to defend her, would amalgamate with the *Spectator* but it was found that the lists of subscribers were almost identical and as the *Spectator* subscribers had paid in advance they were entitled to continued production. The fourth issue contained an interesting defence of the right of women to move into journalism:

> ... it was in recognition of a great and important *principle* that we undertook the editorial management of this journal. We desired to show that WOMAN is capable of something higher and nobler than the trivial and circumscribed duties which are generally considered as belonging exclusively to our sex. Why, is there nothing for us, higher than kitchen drudgery and needlework? ... Shall not Woman be permitted to work with brain as well as with fingers? Look around you, citizens of Sydney, at the hundreds of poor unfortunates who throng the streets and crowd the 'labour offices' in search of employment. Think of the large numbers of respectable and delicately nurtured females, thrown by some ruthless stroke upon the mercies of the world, and struggling in menial

occupations, with enervated frames and despairing hearts, to earn for themselves a shelter and a crust! Is it not plain, then, to every reflecting mind, *that new avenues of employment MUST be opened up to our sex*? Is it not a too glaring truth, that the market for female labour is largely overstocked, and that unless some remedy be speedily applied, thousands of poor girls must sink into destitution and infamy?[13]

The issue included a small sympathetic item on the death of Henry Parkes's *Empire* newspaper. It had been the first to attack the *Spectator*, calling Mrs Weekes a swindler, but she commented on its demise: 'We sincerely sympathise with him in his misfortunes'.[14]

Issue five contained a very long poem by Mrs Cora A. Weekes, taking up all of page one and continuing on further pages. She claimed to have written it in one day while oppressed by onerous business duties and frequent interruptions, maintaining it to be original although she may have 'unconsciously' fallen into imitation.[15] In the sixth issue on 2 October there was an editorial TO OUR SUBSCRIBERS to mark the first quarter of the *Spectator's* existence. It stated that the magazine would continue to be published, that there were upwards of one thousand subscribers, and that receipts had been sufficient to cover all expenses of publication leaving a small balance. Nevertheless, Mrs Weekes wrote, this was small recompense for working fifteen hours a day — canvassing all day for subscriptions and frequently spending half the night 'with pen in hand'. In addition she had had to bear such abuse from the press 'as perhaps never before fell to the lot of woman'. She ended optimistically:

> ... this journal has met with a greater measure of success ... than has
> ever before been extended to any similar publication in New South
> Wales in the same length of time; indeed, we have reason to believe that
> the circulation it has already attained is second to none in the colony,
> with the single exception of 'the leading journal'.[16]

She urged subscribers to pay their subscriptions for the second quarter. Though individually small, they amounted in total to £150, a sum which would enable the purchase of a printing-press, greatly improve the paper and allow economies on business expenses so that the journal would be built up 'beyond the fear of disaster'. Already Mrs Weekes' Sydney effort had survived for longer than all her American papers put together. Her appeal for subscriptions must have been successful as in the 16 October issue she announced that she had purchased a good assortment of new type and printing materials and could take orders for all types of letterpress printing, including book work, billheads, labels and cards at her Hunter Street premises.

Issue nine contained a long editorial on the press in New South Wales. It deplored the fact that following the cessation of the *Empire* and the short-lived Sydney *Dispatch*, the *Sydney Morning Herald* was the only newspaper remaining.

> We have one solitary daily, overgrown and unsightly, old-fashioned and ugly, with just talent enough to make it tolerable, and just honesty enough to make it respectable; but surely, (and we speak with all due respect) unworthy of the place it occupies, as the *only* exponent of the principles and the sentiments of the citizens of New South Wales.[17]

The demise of the *Empire* was blamed on 'the apathy, the indifference, the "penny wise and pound foolish" conduct' of the public. Issue eleven contained an impassioned appeal for printers thrown out of work with the closure of the *Empire*, some of them Indians brought to Sydney by Henry Parkes to work on his paper. Even before his paper ceased, the printers had been paid only a fraction of the wages due to them, the editorial alleged.

> We know of unemployed printers in this city whose sufferings, if made known, would scarcely be credited. One a large creditor of Mr. PARKES, has sold his furniture to get food for his family, till he has nothing left. In conversation with him the other day, he facetiously remarked: —
> 'Last week we lived on the headboard of our last bedstead — this week we are living on the footboard.'[18]

With issue twelve the *Spectator* completed a half-year's existence. There was a self-congratulatory editorial claiming 'decided SUCCESS' commercially although not yet 'in a purely literary sense'. Plans were announced to make the paper 'more purely AUSTRALIAN' with liberal payments for articles. Forthcoming features would include 'an original Nouvellette, by the Editor ... laid mostly in New South Wales'; the continuation of the 'POEM by the Editor, commenced in a former number'; articles by a newly engaged 'POLITICAL writer of talent and experience'; a 'Fine Arts' department; the latest 'Paris Fashions'; a fortnightly summary of leading events; and extracts from the 'choicest' English magazines and reviews. The editorial ended with a plea for the payment of the next quarter's subscriptions — 'only three shillings' — and an appeal for the payment of overdue subscriptions by 300 subscribers.[19]

The main feature of the next issue, Vol. II No. 13, was a four-page report of a lecture on 'Female Heroism in the Nineteenth Century' given at the School of Arts, Sydney on 30 December by Mrs Weekes. A note on the editorial page stated that Mrs Weekes would visit Windsor shortly to canvass for subscribers in that district and would give a lecture during her stay.[20]

There were no further issues of the *Spectator*. Either the subscriptions failed to arrive in sufficient volume for the paper to be continued or enough money was raised for Mrs Weekes and her husband to leave with the proceeds. Cora and George Weekes seem to have disappeared from Sydney. There is no trace of them in the street directories of the time and there is also no record of the death of Cora Anna Weekes in New South Wales. It seems

Caroline Dexter, a most unusual woman, published Australia's first 'Ladies Almanack' in time for sale as a gift at New Year 1858. She also practised in Melbourne as a herbal physician, mesmerist and clairvoyant, and with Harriet Clisby began a very earnest, 'blue stocking' style monthly magazine, the Interpreter *in 1861. (Art in Australia National Library of Australia)*

likely that she and her husband moved on to another colony or another country—perhaps again to start some obscure, short-lived paper.

Although probably a charlatan, Cora Weekes was a competent editor who produced a professional looking paper. With so little time to write or solicit articles, it is not surprising that the *Spectator* contained some very mediocre articles, no doubt culled from other obscure papers, but when Mrs Weekes wrote on subjects on which she held strong views, she expressed herself forcibly and well.

Caroline Dexter and Harriet Clisby of the *Interpreter*

*'the present period of time seems to sanction and require an
Interpreter . . .'*

Interpreter January 1861

Harriet Clisby and Caroline Dexter, joint editors and proprietors of Australia's other early women's periodical, the *Interpreter*, begun in Melbourne in 1861, were extremely unconventional women.

Caroline Dexter was born Caroline Harper in Nottingham on 6 January 1819, a daughter of a watchmaker and jeweller, apparently well enough off to send her to Paris to be educated. As a young woman she is believed to have given lectures in London in favour of the 'bloomer' costume.[21] The bloomer revolution was begun by Amelia Bloomer, an American temperance reformer and advocate of women's rights who, in 1851, became famous for wearing 'Turkish pantaloons' called bloomers which she advocated in her journal, the *Lily* as sensible, unrestricting dress for women. When it reached London, the 'bloomer revolution' campaign created a sensation.

At the age of twenty-four in Nottingham Caroline Harper married an artist, William Dexter, born in Melbourne, Derbyshire, who had exhibited paintings at the Royal Academy. They had probably met in Paris where Dexter had lived for some time after serving an apprenticeship painting china at the Derby China Factory. In 1852 Caroline and William Dexter decided to emigrate to Australia, Dexter arriving in October 1852 and Caroline some time later. At first Dexter taught painting at Lyndhurst College, Glebe, then he went to the Bendigo goldfields where he took part in the agitation against the licensing of miners. William Howitt, who heard him speak to a meeting of 10 000 diggers, said Dexter claimed to represent the French nation. He spoke in favour of a republican Australia and had painted the digger's flag.[22]

In 1855 back in Sydney he opened a Gallery of Arts and School of Design in Bathurst Street, Sydney, where Caroline, according to a contem-

BLOOMERISM!

Strong-Minded Female. "Now, DO, PRAY, ALFRED, PUT DOWN THAT FOOLISH NOVEL, AND DO SOMETHING RATIONAL. GO AND PLAY SOMETHING ON THE PIANO ; YOU NEVER PRACTISE, NOW YOU 'RE MARRIED."

The 'bloomer' revolution, begun by Amelia Bloomer in America who advocated 'Turkish pantaloons' as sensible dress for women, created a sensation when it reached London. The subject fascinated London Punch which ran many satirical, sexist cartoons, articles and poems, most on the theme of role reversal, lampooning women wearing trousers. As a young woman Caroline Dexter is believed to have been a campaigner for the bloomer movement in London. (Punch 1851) porary advertisement, taught 'elocution, composition and literature, grammar, writing and conversation'.[23] The next year — the reason is unknown — the Dexters moved to Gippsland, in eastern Victoria, where their home was a primitive hut near Stratford on the banks of the Avon River.

In this unlikely setting, Caroline Dexter planned the 'First Australian Ladies' Almanack published in the Colonies'. Its full title was *Ladies Almanack 1858. The Southern Cross or Australian Album and New Years Gift* and it was 'respectfully inscribed to the Ladies of Victoria by the Authoress'. Partly written in an extremely hyperbolic style, it is remarkable more for the fact that it was produced than for what it contains. In the first article Caroline Dexter hailed an 'auspicious year': 'All Hail! — "New Year" we welcome thee', ending with the hope that the memory of the year will be honoured 'by the prosperous and happy children of our highly favoured land and BLESSED AUSTRALIA. GOD SPEED HER GREATNESS'. Underneath is an illustration of an eagle with spreading wings holding a five-starred cross over a kangaroo and an emu standing on the top of the world. The inscription is 'The home of the world. Australia'. Such refreshing and unabashed patriotism seems to have been unusual at the time but tied in with William Dexter's involvement in the goldfields agitation.

William Dexter illustrated the magazine with several other sketches including Gippsland scenes, an opossum by moonlight and McArdell's steam flour mill erected in Gippsland in 1854. For the frontispiece he drew Hothpathapatha, 'the favourite lubra of the Dargo Chief' and the drawing on the last page is of a woman in a sunbonnet sitting outside a rough slab hut — probably Caroline herself.[24] *The Southern Cross* contained some original axioms such as 'To ensure your husband's affections, look after his shirt-buttons' (one feels Caroline did not spend her time in such trivial pursuits), 'Before you marry study domestic economy' and 'Play with hoops do not wear them'. She also advised on the growing of native plants. The most interesting article in the magazine was her account of Angus McMillan and his famous grey horse Clifton in which she defended his claims to be the discoverer of 'Caledonia Australis' (Gippsland) against Count Strzelecki. The Dexters moved to Melbourne in 1857 in time for *The Southern Cross* to be printed and published by W. Calvert of East Melbourne for the beginning of 1858. In a leaflet she described it:

> This entirely Colonial Production comprises: — An Almanac, an Album, and Original Letterpress of Poetry and Prose, beautifully Illustrated with Artistic Talent . . .
>   The greatest claim which this little offering lays to the support of Victorian Patronage is, its being strictly National; even every effusion of thought concerning its production has emanated under our own sunny sky. It makes its trembling advent as the 'First-born among Women' in the world of Australasia, and if that be its only merit, surely our noble

Caroline Dexter prepared the material for her 'ladies' almanack' while living near Stratford in Gippsland. Illustrated by her husband, artist William Dexter, it included a calendar, signs of the zodiac and poems, articles and stories. Its most remarkable feature was its unabashed nationalism. Although Caroline Dexter had emigrated from England only a few years before its publication she adopted Australia enthusiastically, ending her introductory article with 'Blessed Australia. God speed her greatness. The home of the world. Australia'. (Title of Ladies' Almanack 1858.)

brethren will tender it infant appeal for fosterage, 'The Right Hand of Fellowship.' Its hopeful Mamma promises that it shall grow in grace and beauty as its years increase, and trusts that its novel features may be lighted with a welcome smile, that the bud of its childhood be not withered.

The first Ladies' Almanac published in the Colonies, must be looked upon as a tribute of respect paid to the Sex; and Gentlemen cannot pay a higher compliment to Woman than by presenting a LADIES' ALMANAC, 'by a Lady,' to a Lady.

The price was £1 1s. Potential subscribers were asked to register their names 'at an early date' with the publisher. An addition in Caroline Dexter's handwriting stated that subscriptions would also be received by Mrs Dexter, Domain Road, South Yarra, Melbourne, Victoria.[25]

By the time the *Almanack* was published William Dexter had returned to Sydney after having an exhibition of his paintings in 1857 but selling none. At first the separation was to enable William to earn money working in the signpainting firm of a relative, William Smedley, after which he would send for Caroline. The letters passing between the two were at first very loving but in time the relationship deteriorated. In May 1859, after they had been separated two years, during which time Caroline had supported herself,

William demanded her presence in Sydney on 13 June, a month from the date of his letter. She replied on 29 May:

> Do you look on me as a piece of furniture or as a purchased slave?
> . . . When I leave Melbourne I shall leave it of my own free and
> independent *will*, without persuasion, without force, and as I have left all
> other places behind me creditably and honourably . . .
> I have read the last of any letters you may send me; and this ends
> the beautiful and peaceful happy home you promised me.[26]

William Dexter started divorce proceedings and there were more acrimonious letters between the two until his death at Redfern in February 1860, aged forty-two.

Caroline Dexter was a strikingly handsome woman with an unconventional mind and a love of nature and of art. Thrown upon her own resources in Melbourne, in addition to producing the *Southern Cross*, she prepared a publication 'Lives of the Victorian Legislators' (it is not clear whether this was published) and opened a Mesmeric Institution at the corner of Collins and Russell Streets as Madame Carole, 'Medical Mesmerist and Clairvoyante'. In a handbill advertising the practice she listed testimonials from people in London as well as Sydney and Melbourne, suggesting that she had practised as a medical adviser before emigrating to Australia. One testimonial came from a homoepathic practitioner in London who stated:

> Madame Carole has been to my knowledge a curative operator as a
> Medical Mesmerist, in many of those dangerous and debilitating diseases
> which are peculiarly incident to females.[27]

Among the herbal remedies Caroline Dexter made and sold were 'Female Corrective Pills', a description for supposed abortifacients. The emphasis on women's health made her venture ahead of its time, well before the advent of trained women nurses and doctors. It was probably through this practice that Caroline Dexter came in contact with Harriet Clisby, and together they decided to bring out a periodical to be called the *Interpreter*.

Harriet Clisby was born in London on 31 August 1830 and with her parents and other family members arrived in Adelaide in 1838 on the *Rajasthan*, just two years after the first European settlers. On her hundredth birthday she recalled the adventures of the five months' voyage and her impressions of arriving in the tent-town of Adelaide as a child of eight. Her father, Charles Clisby, purchased an acre of land on what was later King William Street. While he cleared it and built a mud hut with a thatched roof the family slept in hammocks slung between trees. Later the Clisbys moved to the Inman Valley, south of Adelaide, where 'Old Colonist' writing of 1850–51 described Charles Clisby's farm as having 'good-looking crops of potatoes'.[28]

After five years in the Inman Valley, the family returned to Adelaide where Harriet, showing extraordinary independence for a young woman at the time, decided on a career in journalism and as a first step began to learn shorthand. At the age of twenty and semi-independent after being left £100 a year, Harriet Clisby after rejecting offers of marriage, sailed for Melbourne and an independent life. She became involved in several social enterprises, many of them far in advance of thinking at the time. She started a community farm at Glenferrie, now a suburb but then a rural area, on the lines of the rural communes of recent years; she started a community laundry; she worked as an apprentice with a doctor, caring for poor patients and learning physiology and anatomy; she started a scheme for assisting women migrants (her registry office conducted from a dray became well-known at Port Melbourne) and when she returned to Adelaide for a time she conducted a community home for women ex-prisoners.[29]

Her first venture into journalism and magazine production was to start an eccentric monthly magazine named the *Southern Phonographic Harmonica*, said to be 'edited by a lady'. It contained articles on phonographic and general topics, short stories and pars, all written in Pitman's shorthand or, as was stated in a sub-title, 'written in the initiatory corresponding and reporting style'. While Harriet Clisby was editor from January to June 1857 the magazine ran a great deal of English news and this led to her receiving in her mail a pamphlet from England written by Elizabeth Blackwell on the medical training of women. This began her interest in undertaking medical training overseas.

Before leaving Australia she began the *Interpreter* with Caroline Dexter, an extraordinary journal containing a hotch-potch of articles with a blue-stocking approach. Described as 'an Australian monthly magazine of Science, Literature, Art etc.' it was published in Melbourne by Gordon and Gotch and sold for one shilling. The only advertisement was a full page one advertising 'Madame Carole, Herbal Physician, Mesmerist and Clairvoyante'. The magazine's contents were listed in a very contrived fashion:

SUBJECTS	*No.*	CONTENTS	*Page*
Interpreter	1	Interpreter	1
Invocator	2	Spirit of the New Year	1
Recreator	3	My Acquaintance	2
Vindicator	4	Woman's Capabilities	6
Delineator	5	Life and Love	8
Elevator	6	Our Volunteers	17
Explanator	7	Beauty	18
Detector	8	Photographs	20
Translator	9	A Thought	30
Instructor	10	Language	31
Biographer	11	Empress Eugenie	35
Reformator	12	Lord Brougham	40
Medicator	13	Our Medical Page	43
Extractor	14	Quartz Crushings	44

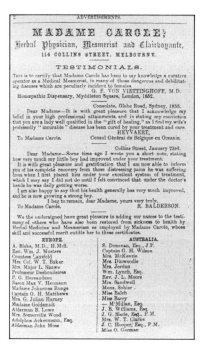
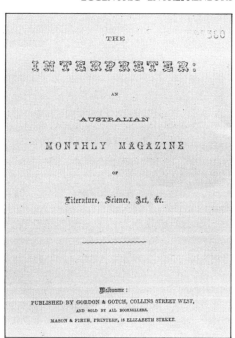

Caroline Dexter and Harriet Clisby began the Interpreter *magazine in Melbourne in 1861 but it lasted only two issues. It was a brave venture for two women to undertake but its contents were disappointing, a critic describing it as having 'the smirking gush of esthetic twaddle'. The only advertisement was for 'Madame Carole', the professional name used by Caroline Dexter for her unusual venture into alternative medicine. (Title page and page 2 of the* Interpreter)

The first item was an apologia for the *Interpreter*:

It is a name fraught with sweet promises of Hope; pregnate with the Faith that 'Hopes *even* against Hope,' though evidence be obscured. The present period of time seems to sanction and require an Interpreter, and though high the ground we take, still it is with the lowliest humility — the humility which seeks in its aspiration to be of *use* to others, for the human mind in its progress seeks unvaryingly new modes and mediums of communication suited to the several stages of its development.

However perilous the position, still we feel *no* hesitation in taking it, meaning to interpret 'aright' the thoughts, sentiments, and feelings of all those whose interest *is* the advancement of humanity. We are not insensible to the significance of the title, still we trust that the name does not imply more than an earnest endeavour of being truthful in all things, that we may expect to reap a harvest of satisfaction from the field our own tillage will open up to us.

> Our subjects will be given under certain heads, and the contents of
> the subjects will be the interpreter thereof.[30]

The first issue contained several poems, including one by J. Sheridan Moore,
who had been briefly editor of the *Month*, a short-lived journal started in
Sydney in 1857, and formerly a teacher at Lyndhurst where Caroline Dexter's
husband had taught; several essays, including a fulsome piece on Lord
Brougham ('this gifted man of genius') and an article headed 'Woman's
Capabilities' taken from 'Mrs Ellet's "Women Artists"' on Anna Maria
Schurmann, a seventeenth century linguist, artist and musician, called by her
contemporaries 'the wonder of creation'. There were two long articles apparently written by the editors. 'My "Acquaintance" of the South Australian
Range' referred probably to an experience of Harriet Clisby's while living in
the Inman Valley concerning a young Aboriginal girl betrothed at birth to a
man whom she did not love, who was that day coming to claim her. The
other, the first part of a serial set in the lace-making factories of Nottingham,
was apparently written by Caroline Dexter and drew on her knowledge of her
childhood home.

The most interesting feature of the magazine was the medical page,
which contained advice on how to avoid 'Inflammatory disease, and Consumption':

> We must try and prevent this, by attention to our dress, our exercise,
> and our diet. We should never be clad too lightly, or too heavily —
> never going out (if ladies) in damp weather with thin shoes, and never
> keeping them on in the house. Always to wear flannel in winter, *next* the
> skin; in the summer, the second garment *from* the skin. To have
> moderate exercise in all weather. Rising early, and never sitting up very
> late. To partake of light food in summer, with a more solid diet in
> winter. This is very simple treatment as a preventative, but it will be
> found the most effectual.

A collection of miscellaneous items and snippets concluded the forty-eight
page issue. They included Lord Jeffrey's 'Description of an Englishwoman of
Fashion', Sir Walter Raleigh's 'Last Words', and a quote on fashion: 'Fashion
is a chain on the soul. It is a yoke laid by superiors on inferiors through
opinion'.

The second and last issue, which came out in February 1861, contained a
similar collection of articles and gave no indication that the periodical would
cease. Henry Gyles Turner described the *Interpreter* as 'the most distinctive
in character' of periodicals begun in Victoria. He also captured the strange
atmosphere of much of the contents:

> It is pitched throughout in the superlative, and the English language has
> no words that can properly describe the lofty conceit, the smug, self-

*Before becoming joint proprietor of the Inter-
preter Harriet Clisby had been involved in
several social enterprises far in advance of the
time. She began a rural commune near Melbourne, conducted an employment registry
from a dray at Port Melbourne to assist newly
arrived women migrants and in Adelaide conducted a community home for women ex-
prisoners. After she left Australia she became
one of the first women doctors in the world
and later founded L'Union des Femmes in
Geneva. She lived to the age of 101. (Adelaide
Chronicle 24 October 1940)*

satisfied gentility, and the smirking gush of esthetic twaddle which
distinguishes many of the articles.[31]

The *Interpreter* was a brave venture but even allowing for the reading tastes of
the period it was somewhat boring and esoteric. Its creators' lives were of
much greater interest than the magazine they produced.

After the failure of the magazine Harriet Clisby decided to go to England
and take up medicine as a career. She worked at first at Guy's hospital as a
nurse, since women were not admitted to medical studies. She eventually
saved enough money, from the proceeds of public lectures she gave, to be able
to go to New York where she entered the Medical College and Hospital for
Women, the only college in the world that would then admit women as
medical students. The mayor of New York provided the women students with
a guard as there was strong opposition from male students to their admission.
She graduated in 1865 and some years later moved to Boston where she stayed
for twenty years and where she organised the first free religious movement for
women. She also founded and became first president of the Women's Educational and Industrial Union which later spread over the United States. One
of her friends in Boston was Louisa M. Alcott.

In 1885 Harriet Clisby went to Europe and settled in Geneva where she
founded L'Union des Femmes and kept up an interest in women's work. She

returned to England in 1911 and lived at Kensington until her death at the age of 101 in 1931. Although never an active worker for women's suffrage she worked all her life for women's freedom and advancement. The reporter from the London *Observer* who called to interview her on a hot afternoon on her hundredth birthday found her doing physical exercises. He described her as 'still essentially energetic, both mentally and physically'. Up to a few years before her hundredth birthday she had continued to give drawing-room lectures.[32]

Caroline Dexter remained in Melbourne after the demise of the *Interpreter* and in the same year as the magazine failed married William Lynch, a former pupil of her late husband's. He was aged twenty-one, more than twenty years her junior and financially secure. It was a happy marriage. He said later 'It was my wife's mind that attracted me, and from her I learned all I know of art'. At their home in Brighton they cultivated the friendship of artists such as Louis Buvelot, offering them encouragement, and were among the first private citizens to collect Australian paintings.[33] Caroline died at the age of sixty-five in Brighton while her husband was travelling overseas.

6

Mostly Moral and Earnest

'. . . if one sinking spirit has been revived and strengthened in the Christian path . . . [my] highest ambition is more than satisfied.'
Maud Jean Franc (Matilda Evans)

The absence of humour in the writing by women in nineteenth century Australia is marked. Perhaps it was because the writers were determined to be taken seriously, or perhaps they were a particularly humourless group. A noticeable number certainly shared a narrowly moralistic and religious view of life. Over the decades many women followed Mary Vidal's moral tales with their own contributions to the cause of virtuous living, pointing their readers towards the paths of righteousness. Far from the 'lady novelists', these were women writing with a purpose.

Although present throughout the century, there were probably more women writers of this type in the 1860s and 1870s, a period when conservative thought predominated, although there were several evangelical writers in the 1880s and 1890s. A prominent example in the earlier period was Matilda Evans, a clergyman's widow, who found an appreciative market for her series of novels spreading the gospel of Christian living. Another was Maria Scott who founded a training school for Protestant domestic servants and preached acceptance of the will of divine providence. Henrietta Foott wrote of her family's stirring experiences in the outback, including homilies on the need to live a good life. Others mentioned in this chapter held similar, if less blatantly expressed views. The first Australian women poets also tended to be extremely serious and frequently moralistic.

Fortunately there was also a little light relief. Elizabeth Selby, under the pseudonym of 'Bess of the Forest, the Lincolnshire Lass' wrote *Long Bay*[1], a small book of naive verse and stories written in a rollicking, humorous style. She was one of the few women writing at this time in whose material there were echoes of the irrepressible vitality in many anecdotal stories of women convicts and migrants. Eliza Winstanley also was not entirely in the moral mould. Her stories were humdrum but as one of Australia's earliest actresses she had more than a hint of the unconventional in her background.

In the 1860s and 1870s there were also some women writers of regional stories, a genre that continued in later years. H. G. Turner probably summed up the standard of most of them when he said of Cecilia Hill's *Checkmated*, that it would be 'a matter for deep regret' if the book 'should ever be read outside the colony'.[2] His remarks referred not only to the standard of the writing but also to the book's crudity. While the works of most of the other writers were more sensitive, they were of limited literary merit and most are now obscure. Ellen Liston is a good example. She is noted here not because of the quality of her writing but because of her efforts to make money as a correspondent for a country newspaper, and a contributor of articles and serials to newspapers.

Matilda Jane Evans ('Maud Jean Franc')

Matilda Jane Evans wrote her moral, Sunday-school stories under the rather exotic name of Maud (sometimes spelt Maude) Jean (sometimes spelt Jeanne) Franc. As far as is known she gave no explanation for the choice of this quasi-French pseudonym. She was a straitlaced woman who, when widowed in South Australia with children and stepchildren to support, turned — after a few efforts at running schools — to writing novels. Judging by the number of books she wrote and the buoyant demand for them, she was very successful.

Matilda Jane was born on 7 August 1827 at Peckham Park, Surrey, England, the eldest daughter of Henry Congreve, a doctor who won a reputation for a medicine he developed as a cure for coughs and colds, which was also said to be a cure for consumption. Given the enormous sum of £10 000 by his wealthy father, he invested the money and lost it, and in 1852 sailed with his family for South Australia. It was a disastrous move as Matilda's mother died on the voyage and Dr Congreve died at North Adelaide only a few months after their arrival, leaving Matilda to support the younger children. One of her first engagements was as governess to the Walter Paterson family at Kunyanga where she taught in a slab room especially erected for the purpose. She was to use her experiences there in her first novel *Marian; Or, The light of some one's home*. Later she moved into town and started a school which she kept for some years. In 1858 she moved to Mount Barker to run a school, spending her spare time sitting under an old chestnut tree where she wrote *Marian*. It was first printed by a Mr Waddy of Mount Barker in monthly instalments. Later Matilda sent it to a firm of publishers, Messrs Binns and Goodman of Bath, England, who issued it in book form. When this firm failed the London firm of Sampson, Low became her publishers and nearly all her subsequent fourteen books were published by them.[3]

Readers must have identified with the true-to-life depiction of simple bush and country town life and the moral tone of *Marian*. It was a great success, eventually reaching at least eleven editions. The end of *Marian* is typical of much of her writing. Following the death of one of the characters, a saintly young girl, the author comments:

> Our tale is told. If but one heart through its quiet teachings has learnt to discern a beauty in holiness; if one sinking spirit has been revived and strengthened in the Christian path; if one young friend has found that the paths of obedience are those of happiness, through the humble medium of the author's pen, — her highest ambition is more than satisfied.[4]

In 1860, before the publication of *Marian*, Matilda Congreve had married a widower, Rev. Ephraim Evans, Baptist Minister of Nuriootpa, at the Zion Chapel, Adelaide. Only three years later he died at South Rhine aged thirty-eight of hemiplegia[5] leaving Matilda with two baby sons and several step-children to support. A public subscription helped her to start a school at Nuriootpa and soon after she moved to nearby Angaston where she began a ladies' college. In 1868 she moved to North Adelaide where she started a school called 'Angaston House' but later she gave up teaching and devoted herself to the work of the North Adelaide Baptist Church as a deaconess and to writing. During her writing life in addition to novels, she contributed many short stories and articles to Adelaide journals.

She was South Australia's second woman novelist, after Catherine Spence. Her field was more restricted and her talent limited but she was successful in finding a prolific market for her simple stories of life ruled by the Gospel. All her novels reached at least two editions, some many more, and were popular as Sunday school prizes. Her inspiration came from her own life and the lives of the people around her. In *Beatrice Melton's Discipline*, published in London in 1880, she describes the main character's loss of her father, based on her own grief at the death of her husband:

> The past year! can I bear to review it? It has been such a hard, hard year to us all. We have truly been 'shorn to the wind!' yet 'God tempers the wind to the shorn lamb'. So they tell me, and my gentle mother, in all her heavy trouble, by her very gentleness proclaims it true; yet I cannot see it, cannot feel it.
>
> We were so happy, and had been so prosperous. Dear father seemed so well, so useful; how ill could he be spared by any of us. Still more did the Church seem to need him; for the earnest, self-devoted labourers are so few, and the harvests very great; and yet, in the midst of all our happiness, he was stricken, taken from us in a few short hours. 'God took him, and he was not.'

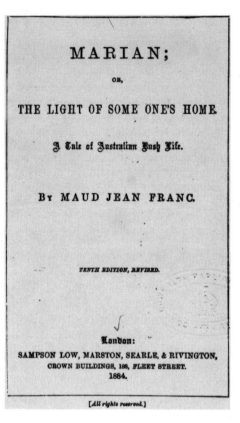

MARIAN;

OR,

THE LIGHT OF SOME ONE'S HOME

A Tale of Australian Bush Life.

BY MAUD JEAN FRANC.

TENTH EDITION, REVISED.

London:
SAMPSON LOW, MARSTON, SEARLE, & RIVINGTON,
CROWN BUILDINGS, 188, FLEET STREET.
1884.

[All rights reserved.]

Matilda Jean Evans, widow of a South Australian Baptist clergyman, wrote a succession of highly successful novels between 1860, when Marian was first published, and her death in 1886. Most of her novels went into several editions — Marian was reprinted at least eleven times — indicating the popularity of their simple moral message. Matilda Evans wrote under the name of Maud Jean Franc. (Title page of tenth edition of Marian)

'God took him.' Ah! they tell me that should be my consolation.[6]

Some of her other fourteen novels were Minnie's Mission, an Australian Temperance Tale which was set in Mount Barker; Vermont Vale; or, Home Pictures in Australia, set in the Angaston district and Hall's Vineyard which she wrote by special request in an effort to combat wine-drinking. It won a prize offered by the Scottish Temperance Society for the best story dealing with the liquor question and subsequently had a large circulation.[7] The fact that despite their colonial and provincial settings all her novels were published in London indicates their wide appeal.

One at least of her stories was serialised in a country paper. In 1867 the Kapunda Herald ran Golden Gifts, described as 'by the author of Marian, Vermont Vale etc. etc.'.[8] In 1881 she contributed stories to the South Australian Christmas Annual and in 1888 a collected edition of her tales was produced by her London publishers, but by then Matilda Evans was dead. She died at her home at Prospect on 22 October 1886 of peritonitis, aged fifty-nine.[9] The Adelaide Observer described her as 'a pleasant writer of homely stories':

Her works are full of the highest aspirations, and the gentle disposition of the deceased lady made itself manifest in the characters which are so gracefully depicted. Mrs Evans was of a very retiring nature, but her conversation was full of vivacity.[10]

Not a great deal is known of Matilda Evans' life, nothing of her appearance and only what can be deduced from her novels of her character. Within the framework of her intensely moralistic approach to life, it is possible that there was a little more humour and sophistication in her makeup than appears on the surface. She was very close to her two sons, both of whom were part of the artistic, literary and newspaper world of Adelaide.

The elder, Henry Congreve Evans, at 24, was chief of staff of the Adelaide *Advertiser* and in 1889 with Alfred C. Chandler founded *Quiz*, a satirical, social and sporting weekly which carried social and political comment, short stories, verse, social notes (written in a satirical way) theatrical and literary notes and cartoons.[11] Henry Evans was also author of the libretto *Immomeena: An Australian Comic Opera* written in 1893. He died in 1899, aged 38.

The second son, William James Evans, also a journalist and at one time employed in the commercial department of the Adelaide *Advertiser*, collaborated with his mother in a book, *Christmas Bells* published in 1882, which she edited and which contained short stories by both mother and son. In 1898 William James Evans published a book of light-hearted rhyming verse entitled *Rhymes without Reason*, published in Adelaide by J. L. Bonython. He died in 1904 aged 41.[12]

Maria Scott ('Mist')

Maria Scott, who wrote under the name of 'Mist', sometimes 'M.I.S.T.' and once as 'Spray', was another female writer who wrote semi-religious moral novels including *Annine: A Novel* published in London in 1871 and *A Brother or Lover? a Sister or Bride? and The Lights and Shadows of Hazelglen* published in 1872. Her stories were based on Christian ideals and her saintly characters were often people doomed to die young.

Maria J. Scott was the daughter of Colonel George Barney, colonial engineer, superintendent of the failed convict settlement Gladstone Colony at Port Curtis, Surveyor-General and member of the Legislative Council. He had arrived in Sydney in 1836 with the Royal Engineers, accompanied by his wife formerly Portia Peale and family. Maria probably accompanied her parents when they returned to England for some years in the mid-1840s. Back in Australia she married David Charles Scott, a retired captain of the East India Co., Police Magistrate and pastoralist, a cousin of Rose Scott, the noted feminist and social reformer and of David Mitchell, founder of the Mitchell Library.

An indication of Maria Scott's interests is that, with her husband (who died in 1881) she founded the Female Protestant Training School for Domestic Servants which later came to be housed in their home and was called 'Lisgar' after it. After her death in 1899 it became the Deaconess Institute.[13] Like several other women authors she was also an artist. She was a pupil of Conrad Martens and two books of her pencil drawings are in the Mitchell Library.

Ellen Liston

> 'Alas, poor girl! she only brought £2, because she was not colonial!'

Ellen Liston was another writer whose works were imbued with seriousness. She was born in London in 1838 to deeply religious parents, David and Mary Liston, who both wrote essays, reminiscences and verse on political and religious subjects. She arrived with her parents in Adelaide in 1850 at the age of twelve. A delicate child, she was educated at home.

In Adelaide the family and a few friends formed a society to improve the minds of members, producing many essays and papers on religious subjects. Together with the Harwood family, a member of which, Joseph Harwood, later married Ellen's sister Mary, they formed a church of 'Free-thinking Christians'. The church had no ministers, services being conducted by members, and the congregation was made up of men and women who believed in church reform.

In 1867 with her parents dead and her brothers and sisters married, Ellen became a governess at Nilkerloo Station on Eyre's Peninsula. Here she began writing stories and verses, some of which were published in the Adelaide *Observer*. Of one serial, *Montie* (the heroine's name) she said, 'Alas, poor girl, she only brought £2, because she was not colonial!',[14] an indication of the interest of colonial readers in reading about their own heroes and heroines.

Ellen Liston became extremely popular among the people of the west coast not only for her character and her writing but also for her abilities as a horserider and bushwoman. Her fame must have been widespread, for when the name of a new township between Port Lincoln and Ceduna was being considered the settlers decided unanimously to name it after her, combining her name into Elliston.

After five years at Nilkerloo, Ellen Liston joined the Education Department and took charge of a school near East Wellington. With no accommodation available near the school she lived on the opposite side of the river and

Ellen Liston had many short stories published in Adelaide papers and the provincial press but she had to hold full-time jobs to earn a living because the rewards from writing were so small. She wrote while working as a governess on remote Eyre's Peninsula, (where she was such a popular figure the town of Elliston was named after her,) and later as a school teacher and a telegraphist. In 1836, nearly half a century after her death, a collection of her short stories was published with the title Pioneers. (Pioneers by Ellen Liston, comp. E. A. Harwood)

during floods had to wade through water on her way to and from school. This caused an illness from which she never recovered. When she became too ill to continue teaching she joined the Postal Department as a telegraphist at Watervale Post Office. While there she wrote a long serial, *Auckland Marston* which in 1879 won a £20 prize offered by the Melbourne *Leader*. Shortly after she was transferred to the Marrabel Post Office where she remained until her death on 19 August 1885 at the age of forty-seven.[15]

Ellen Liston was successful in exploiting the market for serials and stories in newspapers. She was on the corresponding staff of the *Kapunda Herald* and had many stories published in the Adelaide *Observer*, particularly at Christmas time. Yet despite this relative success as a writer she had to hold full-time jobs to keep herself, any money she earned from writing being an uncertain extra. In 1936, nearly half a century after her death, her niece Ellen A. Harwood published a collection of her short stories, *Pioneers*, and one of her stories, 'Doctor', appeared in *A book of South Australia* published for the centenary in 1936.

Henrietta Foott

'. . . *a lesson of thankfulness to the Giver of all goodness, and contentment with the lot he has chosen for them* . . .'[16]

In 1872 Henrietta Foott published a book about her family's journey to the

outback and their life there which is an epic of cheerful endurance interspersed with moral strictures. *Sketches of life in the bush: or, Ten years in the
Interior*, published in Sydney, told the story of her family's long journey in
1860 from Melbourne to newly-settled country in north-western New South
Wales known as Fort Bourke.

Mrs Foott was born Henrietta Anne Lumsden, daughter of Henry
Lumsden, a member of a distinguished Scottish family of Clova, Aberdeenshire, many of the male members of which were courageous soldiers. In 1842
she married James Foott, of an Anglo-Irish family of Carrigacunna and
Springfort, County Cork, a dashing man who squandered his inheritance on
extravagant living. According to a descendant, his claret was marked with his
name etched into a glass seal above the cork and his dinner service, painted
to his own design with his initials stamped in raised gold on a shield, was sent
to him from China in a tea clipper. His best Queen Anne silver was heavily
chased and even his everyday silver was engraved with his crest.[17]

As a result of his extravagance, he found it necessary to emigrate to
Australia and with his wife, Henrietta, and six children, he arrived in gold-
rush Melbourne in 1853 on the *Ivanhoe*. After some years in Victoria the
family left Melbourne in May 1860 for life in the outback. They travelled
from Kilmore to Deniliquin then down the Murrumbidgee to the Murray
where they camped for some weeks, being afraid to continue on to the
Darling River until rain had fallen to bring grass for their horses. Here James
Foott and his sons spent exciting hours pig-hunting and shooting game for
food and Henrietta, who had never cooked a meal before, turned out meals of
roast duck, cockatoo soup and galah stew. Mrs Foott's narrative of this
journey is broken by homilies on the number of public houses which caused
the ruin of families and observations such as that contentment and sweetness
of temper can make the discomfort of roughing it slight. 'How many families
are plunged in distress and ruin by workmen yielding to the temptation of the
public-house!' she wrote.[18]

After nearly six months' travelling over 1100 miles, they reached Jandra
holding near Fort Bourke. Here they started to build a homestead on a high
bank on a bend of the river, in the meantime living under tarpaulins. Often
in summer the temperature soared to 115 °F in the shade, hot winds searing
through the tent by night and the scorching sun making the sand underfoot
like red hot ashes. There were a surprising number of visitors, some of them
men tramping between stations fifty or sixty miles apart looking for work. One
was the explorer, William Landsborough, sent out in 1861 to search for Burke
and Wills. When a man came along accompanied by two small children,
having been deserted by his wife, Mrs Foott was judgmental: '. . . women too
often forget God's holy commandments, forget the love and obedience they
owe their husbands, and throw away for ever the sacred name of mother . . .'[19]

In 1864 after heavy rain the Darling River rose rapidly and their house

Henrietta Foott wrote a book, Sketches of life in the bush: or, Ten years in the Interior, *about her family's life in the outback at Jandra station, near Fort Bourke. When they arrived from Melbourne after a journey of six months in 1860 they set up home in tents on the banks of the Darling River (above). At first their station prospered, but following disastrous floods in 1864 the family had to abandon their home and spent seven weeks marooned on a sandhill. Henrietta Foott illustrated her story of the family's life at Bourke with sketches of their surroundings. (Sketch of the Darling River by Henrietta Foott in* Sketches of life in the bush*)*

had to be abandoned. The family moved to a sandhill a quarter of a mile away where they were terrorised by large numbers of snakes and tormented by mosquitoes. Marooned here for seven weeks, the family lived in makeshift tents, and when they returned to their home mud was everywhere. James Foott, who in a few years had succeeded in clearing Jandra, building a homestead and stocking the run with sheep, never recovered from the effects of the flood. Some years later the family moved into the small settlement at Bourke where Mrs Foott ran a school. In 1871 they left Bourke for Sydney where James Foott died some years later.

In 1872 Henrietta Foott's *Sketches of life in the bush* illustrated by some of her drawings, was published in Sydney and it went into a second edition in 1878. She was a competent artist and when a widow earned money giving painting lessons. She made a gift of one of her paintings, of a buttercup, to Dame Mary Gilmore who later gave it to writer and artist, Ethel Anderson. Dame Mary Gilmore wrote on the painting:

After ten years Henrietta Foott and her family abandoned life in the bush and went to live in Sydney where her book, Sketches of life in the bush went into a second edition in 1878. She was a competent artist and as a widow earned money giving painting lessons. She gave a painting of a buttercup to Dame Mary Gilmore who said she was one of the first artists in Australia to paint Australian flowers for decorative purposes. (Gladys Cooney, Broadbeach Waters, Queensland)

Dear Mrs Anderson: This is a small picture painted for my birthday by Mrs. Ffoott [sic] whose (great) grandson married your daughter. It is not great painting, but she was one of the very first here, apart from botanists, to make a study, for decorative purposes, of Australian flowers. It was she, if I am not mistaken, who started Mrs. Ellis Rowan — in fact, I am certain. I remember some paintings of heath, boronia and flannelflowers which she did to interest Lady Jersey (for me) and that was YEARS, after she began. History COUNTS, and so I make this note for you.[20]

Henrietta Foott lived in a small wooden cottage in Woollahra until her death in 1916 at the age of ninety-four. Her daughter-in-law, Mary Hannay Foott, was a poet and journalist (see Chapter 11).

Eliza (Winstanley) O'Flaherty

'The editor of "Bow Bells" . . . pronounces Mrs. Winstanley's new tale to be a most remarkable and powerful production.'
Bow Bells

Eliza Winstanley, one of Australia's earliest actresses, was a remarkably able and versatile woman who, after her stage career in Australia, England and America, became a most prolific author. She was born in Blackburn,

Lancashire in 1818, a daughter of William and Eliza Winstanley and in 1833 migrated with her family to Sydney where her mother became a straw-bonnet maker and her father a signwriter and theatre scene painter. Eliza made her first stage appearance in the leading role in the melodrama, 'Clari, or the Maid of Milan', at the Theatre Royal on 31 October 1834 at a benefit for her father. The critics praised her natural talent, remarkable speaking voice and power of expression and soon she was the leading actress in Sydney. In the next few years she played many Shakespearean parts, including Desdemona in 'Othello' at the first performance at the Royal Victoria Theatre on 26 March 1838.

In 1841 at the age of twenty-three, Eliza Winstanley married Henry Charles O'Flaherty, a musician in the theatre orchestra, actor and playwright. Later that year she played Portia, Lady Macbeth and other leading parts but, after an argument with the management she and her husband left Sydney to perform in Hobart, Launceston and later Melbourne. By the time she left Australia in 1846 it was said that 'she had acquired here a position that had not been reached by any other actress up to that time'.[21] In England Eliza played leading Shakespearean roles in Manchester, Newcastle-on-Tyne and at the Princess Theatre in London and she appeared in several command performances before Queen Victoria at Windsor Castle, one as Mrs Malaprop. During a visit to New York in 1848 she appeared as Mistress Quickly in the Merry Wives of Windsor and in 1851 she was included among the distinguished actors and actresses in Tallis's Shakespeare Gallery in this role.

In England Eliza had reverted to her maiden name, apparently believing it was more acceptable than her married, Irish name. Her husband died about 1854 and some time after this, becoming too stout and old for many of the parts she had played previously, she took up her second career as an author. Her first book Shifting Scenes of Theatrical Life was published in London in 1859. The following year her novel, Bitter Sweet — So is the World, was serialised in the Sydney Mail under the pseudonym Ariel, beginning on 25 August 1860. (She may also have been the author of Lucy Cooper, a short novel published anonymously in the Illustrated Sydney News in 1854.) Gradually she abandoned acting and novels flowed from her pen, many of them being serialised in the London Bow Bells magazine, and in 1865 she became editor of the weekly Fiction for Family Reading, a subsidiary of Bow Bells. The themes of her books were based on her theatrical experiences and on the memories of her young life in Australia. Among the novels set in Australia were Margaret Falconer (1860), The Mistress of Hawk's Crag (1864), Twenty Straws (1864), What is To Be Will Be (1867) and For the Term of Her Natural Life: A Tale of 1830 (1876). In a preview Bow Bells magazine claimed that Twenty Straws, a story of life in Sydney in the 1830s, was founded on fact:

... the hero and many of the characters did exist, and the principal scenes and events therein depicted really did occur to the personal

Eliza Winstanley was one of Australia's earliest actresses who later gained renown on the English and American stage in Shakespearean parts. When she became too old and stout for the theatre she turned to writing and is credited with being the author of at least thirty books, many issued as paperbacks in a popular English series selling at sixpence each. In 1865 she became editor of Fiction for family reading, *a subsidiary of* Bow Bells *in which many of her stories wree serialised. (Eliza Winstanley as 'Mistress Quickly' in Tallis' Shakespeare Gallery, 1851)*

knowledge and observation of the writer who had been engaged for upwards of two years writing the work. The Editor of 'Bow Bells' having read the MSS., pronounces Mrs. Winstanley's new tale to be a most remarkable and powerful production.[22]

Correspondence in Old Chum's column in *Truth* in 1919 and 1920 canvassed the idea that Sir Richard Nolkinghame in the novel was Governor Sir Richard Bourke and that the 'villain' Colonel Stackhouse was Colonel Kenneth Snodgrass, at one time acting Governor of New South Wales. The claims of the 'truth' of the story are exaggerated as it attributes a fictitious second marriage to Sir Richard Bourke (alias Nolkinghame). Altogether Eliza Winstanley wrote probably more than thirty books, by one estimate between forty and fifty. Many of them were issued in London publisher, John Dicks' English Novels series, in paper covers selling at sixpence a copy, in editions of several thousand.

Many legends grew up about Eliza Winstanley, one being that she was governess to Governor Bourke's daughters, but this seems unlikely as she began her theatrical career soon after her arrival in Australia, leaving little time for governessing. Although absent from Australia for more than thirty years, she returned about 1880 and died in Sydney on 2 December 1882 at the age of sixty-four.[23]

Sarah Susannah Perry

> '*To utter oaths and swear and lie,*
> *This is* colonial *styled.*'
>
> Sarah Perry

As with many of the prose writers, the poets in the third part of the nineteenth century exuded morality and earnestness. Of the poets of this period Caroline Carleton is remembered best, mainly because her 'Song of Australia' was put forward for consideration as Australia's national song. She was the author of the first book of verse by a woman to be published in South Australia. Three years earlier, in 1857, Sarah Perry and Susan Talbot both had written books of poetry in Victoria. In Queensland Eva O'Doherty, who had achieved fame as a revolutionary poet in Ireland, in her new home wrote sad, nostalgic verse and in New South Wales Emily Manning, (see Chapter 7), who was a pioneer journalist, wrote some fine poems published in book form in London in 1877.

Sarah Susannah Perry epitomised the moral approach. Her '*Durable Riches*', *or A Voice from the Golden Land* was published in London in 1857 to honour her memory. A 'sweetly unobtrusive and genuine character' Sarah

97

Perry, an intensely religious woman, had died the previous year at the age of twenty-eight.[24] Born Sarah Hollett in London in 1827, she was brought up in a very religious atmosphere and at fifteen started a diary of her spiritual progress which she continued until close to her death. Well educated, a fine pianist and a student of German, she worked in London as a governess and a teacher. From an early age she wrote poetry, at first secretly but she later had several poems accepted for publication by magazines in England.

After the death of her mother she emigrated to Melbourne with other family members, sailing on 1 August 1853 on the *Blackwall*. On board she met Charles Stuart Perry whom she married in Melbourne on 21 January 1854, on her marriage changing from the non-conformist faith in which she had been brought up to her husband's Anglican religion. Her 'whole expression spoke of intelligence, meekness, and heavenward aspirations', her memorialist, Emma Falkner, wrote. Not surprisingly the robust colonial life of post-gold-rush Melbourne horrified her. In her poem 'Colonial' she wrote:

> For little urchins pipes to smoke,
>   Scarce in their teens installed,
> To quaff their glass and 'crack a joke,'
>   This is *colonial* called.
>
> For rude and gentle, low and high,
>   For aged man and child,
> To utter oaths and swear and lie,
>   This is *colonial* styled.

After further verses condemning the evils of drink and desecration of the Sabbath, she appealed to newly arrived migrants,

> 'Beware, lest this *colonial* brand
>   Deface and injure you.'[25]

Sarah Perry died on 17 May 1856 and was buried in Melbourne in the grave in which her child had been buried previously.

Caroline Carleton

Caroline Carleton, whose 'Song of Australia' was proposed, along with 'Waltzing Matilda' and 'Advance Australia Fair', as a contender in a referendum held in 1974 to choose an Australian national song, was the author of *South Australian Lyrics*, a small book of verse, published in 1860.

Caroline Carleton was born at Bonnan Hall near London on 1 July 1820, a daughter of William Baynes and granddaughter of Count and Countess de la Mere who had fled France during the Revolution. As a child she learnt French, Italian and Latin. In 1836, at the age of sixteen, she married Charles

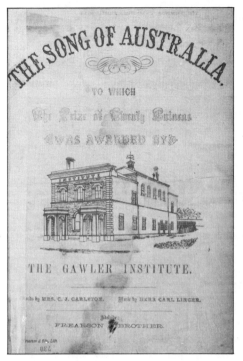

Caroline Carleton was the winner of a prize of twenty guineas offered by the Gawler Institute, in 1859, for the best 'Song of Australia'. Set to music by Herr Carl Linger her song was a contender, together with 'Waltzing Matilda' and 'Advance Australia Fair', in a referendum held in 1974 to choose an Australian national song. Caroline Carleton's South Australian Lyrics, published in 1860, was the first book of verse by a woman to be published in South Australia. (Title page of 'The song of Australia')

James Carleton, a medical student at Guy's Hospital. In 1839 she sailed on the *Prince Regent* for Adelaide with two infants and her husband who, although he had not completed his medical degree, acted as ship's surgeon. In the course of a dreadful voyage both of their children died and were buried at sea.

Arriving on 26 September 1839 they settled in Adelaide where Charles Carleton worked as a dispenser at Adelaide Hospital. In 1847 they moved to Kapunda where he became medical officer and assayer at the mines and when gold was discovered in Victoria he followed the rush to the goldfields but was unsuccessful. Back in Adelaide he was appointed Curator of West Terrace Cemetery where, after a long illness, he died on 20 July 1861 at the age of forty-seven, leaving his wife with five young children to support. Caroline Carleton had, in effect, carried on his job for the last two years of his life, but when after his death she applied for his job she was rejected because, she was told, no woman had ever held the position before.[26]

Caroline Carleton had been writing poetry for some years before her husband's death. In 1859 when the Gawler Institute offered a special prize of twenty guineas for the best 'Song of Australia' she submitted an entry under the nom de plume 'Nil desperandum', indicating that she was not hopeful of success and also to conceal her sex. Her entry won the competition.[27] The song, beginning 'There is a land where summer skies', was set to music by Herr Carl Linger, a German migrant who had arrived in Adelaide in 1849 and who died in 1862 at the age of fifty-two. Many years later, in June 1936, a memorial to Linger was unveiled in the West Terrace cemetery by the South Australian Premier, Mr R. L. Butler. In his speech he referred to Caroline Carleton's poetry, saying 'Her verses were a means of creating a stronger national sentiment among Australians.'[28]

After her brief fame as winner of the Gawler Institute prize and publication of her book of poetry, Caroline Carleton turned to running primary schools in Adelaide to support her children. She later established a school at Wallaroo during a boom period after mines opened in the region. She died aged fifty-four at Matta Flat near Kadina on 10 July 1874.

Mary Eva O'Doherty

Poet Eva O'Doherty lived in Queensland for most of the last fifty years of her life until her death in 1910. Although her poetry remained closely linked to her native Ireland she was the earliest woman poet of any note in Queensland. Born Mary Eva Kelly at Headford, County Galway, Ireland in 1829 she began to write verse when a child and in her early teens sent her first contribution to the *Nation*, the famous Irish paper started by Charles Gavan Duffy in 1842. During the exciting days of the revolutionary 'Young Ireland' movement she wrote ballads imbued with stirring patriotism, becoming known as 'Eva of the *Nation*'. It was at this time she became engaged to one of the movement's leaders, Kevin Izod O'Doherty, a doctor.

After the suppression of the 'Young Ireland' uprising in 1848, Kevin O'Doherty was arrested, tried for high treason and after the jury had disagreed twice was tried a third time and sentenced to ten years' transportation to Van Dieman's Land. In 1854 O'Doherty was freed on condition he did not live in Ireland and after their marriage in 1855 he and Eva lived for some time in Paris. About 1860 the O'Dohertys migrated to Australia, first to Victoria then Sydney and in 1865 they settled in Queensland where they entered the social, political and literary life of Brisbane. O'Doherty became renowned as a surgeon, was appointed Surgeon-Major of the Queensland defence force, elected to the Legislative Assembly and was later a member of the Legislative Council.[29]

In 1877 a book of Eva O'Doherty's poems containing many written in Australia was published in San Francisco and another edition of *Poems* appeared in 1880. Her best poetry was written in the 'Young Ireland' period when she was stirred by patriotic emotion. Her Queensland verse became progressively sadder. In 'Remembrance' she wrote:

Eva O'Doherty was the earliest woman poet of any note in Queensland but her poetry remained closely linked to her native Ireland. During the stirring days of the 'Young Ireland' movement she wrote patriotic ballads published under the name of 'Eva of the Nation'. She married one of the leaders of the 'Young Ireland' rebellion, Kevin O'Doherty, who had served a sentence of transportation to Australia. Eva O'Doherty lived in Queensland from about 1860 to her death in 1910. (John Oxley Library, State Library of Queensland)

Down the black river of life as I go —
    Drifting all wearily,
    Onward so drearily,
While the rain falls and the wild tempests blow.[30]

A tall, distinguished looking woman, she was unassuming and candid. At a time when her poetry was highly esteemed, she said 'The best that we can do must have in it some inspiration from outside things — patriotism, affection, and events; but of my best I do not think there is much that counts.'[31]

After her husband's death she lived at Auchenflower, occasionally contributing to Queensland journals and one of her poems was included in *A book of Queensland verse* published in 1924. She died on 22 May 1910 survived by only one of her eight children and was buried in Toowong Cemetry where admirers erected a monument to Kevin O'Doherty 'the Irish patriot' and his 'gifted wife' 'Eva of the *Nation*'.

Francis Hopkins, editor of the *Australian Ladies' Annual*

> '. . . men and women talk and act as they never do outside the walls of a lunatic asylum.'
>
> *Melbourne Review*

The first venture into an anthology of women's writing appeared in 1878 when Francis Rawdon Chesney Hopkins, a grazier and writer, edited *The Australian Ladies' Annual*. Apart from a few well known contributors it consisted of very mediocre contributions by authors now unknown. It may have been an idiosyncratic selection but in its ordinariness it probably reflected much of women's writing of the period.

The production of a *Ladies' Annual* appears a strange venture for a squatter but it is important in recording at least one man's views on the women writers he considered worthy of inclusion. Intended as an annual it was not followed by any further collections. Francis Hopkins, born in Bombay, migrated to Victoria at sixteen and spent his life managing or owning stations. He worked first in the Wimmera for an uncle, then on the Murray and later in New South Wales. In 1885 with partners he bought and managed a station near Carcoar and later took over stations in the Gwydir district. During this time he wrote plays which although undistinguished were produced on the stage and he published several collections of stories. For years he did book reviews for the *Australasian Pastoralists' Review*.[32]

In his preface to *The Australian Ladies' Annual* Hopkins claimed the book was a novelty. 'So far as I can learn,' he wrote, 'no book written exclusively by ladies, has been yet published in this, or any other country.' When he had first suggested the idea to his friends they had laughed saying, 'There are no lady-writers here; and, granting a sufficiency of numbers, you would not get people to believe that the contributions *were* written by them'.[33] Why he decided to produce a ladies' annual is unknown. He dedicated it to Miss Evelin Carmichael and noted in the preface, written from Perricoote, New South Wales in November 1878, that he regretted she had been unable to contribute to the book. Like a number of other contributors Evelin Carmichael is an obscure figure. They included some who used pseudonyms — 'Sylvia', 'Little Rosebud', 'Constance Craig', and 'Eene Rolf' — and other unknown or little-known writers who used their own names, including Mrs Kate Dampier, Annie C. Donnelly (a New Zealander, who wrote 'Heroines of Fiction'), Clara E. Cheeseman (also a New Zealander), Margaret Chesholt and Mary Card.

Three well-known writers were included — 'Tasma', (see Chapter 9), Mrs Cross (Ada Cambridge) (see Chapter 9), who contributed 'By the camp fire' a poem taken from her latest book of verse, and Louisa Meredith who contributed two poems, 'To my husband' and 'The cockatoo'. The latter was taken from *Grandmama's Australian verse-book*, published in Hobart in 1878. 'Tasma' contributed 'The Rubria ghost' and an essay 'Concerning the forthcoming Melbourne Cup'. The *Annual* was released to coincide with the Melbourne Cup in November rather than at Christmas which Hopkins thought was not kept up properly in Australia.

When the *Annual* was reviewed in the *Melbourne Review* it was hailed as not a bad idea. If carried out yearly it 'may enable us to see what kind and

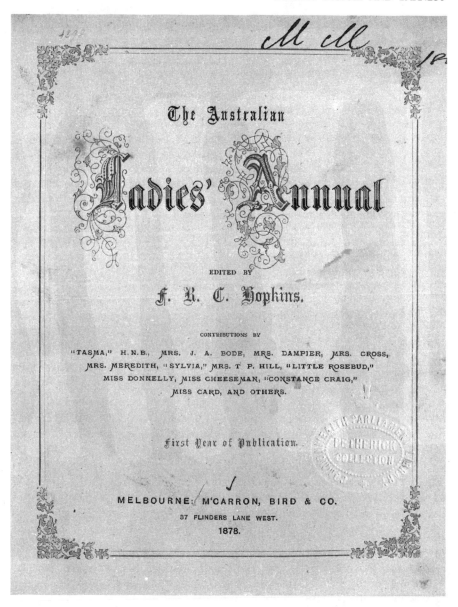

The first collection of women's writing to be published in Australia was published in Melbourne in 1878 in time for Melbourne Cup Day. The editor, grazier and writer Francis R. C. Hopkins, believed this was more appropriate than release at Christmas, which he believed was not kept up properly in Australia. The publication was intended to be an annual but only one issue appeared. Apart from a few well-known writers, most of the contributors were obscure. (Title page of Ladies' Annual 1878)

103

degree of literary talent there is in these colonies among the fairer half'. The reviewer found the volume interesting as 'showing some of the tendencies we may expect to find in the poetry and fiction contributed to our scanty colonial literature by the women of Australia'. He continued:

> Chief among their faults is one which is mainly attributable to their want of experience and knowledge of human nature — namely, the unreality and extravagance which pervade most of the tales in this volume. Instead of describing faithfully the incidents and characters of real life, the writers invent wild and absurd stories, and make men and women talk and act as they never do outside the walls of a lunatic asylum. We have been tempted to notice this fault, as the writer of a critical article, the last in the book, entitled 'Heroines of Fiction', remarks that women, though less practical, are more imaginative than men. This is a great mistake. Women have far less imagination than men, and nothing shows it more strongly than their tendency to depart from truth and nature in their delineation of life and character. True imagination is based upon experience, and is shown far more in a faithful and life-like description than in the wildest and most fantastic departure from reality. Without this basis of knowledge and experience the imagination can produce little better than the visions of a dreamer, or the crude outpourings of children and savages.[34]

Apart from some praise for 'Tasma' most of the stories in the volume were described as 'wild and improbable', notably 'The three troopers' by Cecilia H. W. Hill and 'The empty house' by 'Little Rosebud'. A 'slight sketch', 'A romance of Coma' by 'Mura Leigh', (Letty H. Martin) was described as 'better and more promising, as the writer keeps on the plain pathway of every day life, instead of wandering into the hopeless mazes of sensational incident and melodramatic character.'

Cecilia H. W. Hill, author of 'The three troopers', was the wife of Thomas Padmore Hill, a teacher of elocution in Melbourne. In the same year as her story appeared in the *Annual* she published a novel, *Checkmated*, set in suburban Melbourne, Bendigo, South Australia, England and France. It was scathingly reviewed by H. G. Turner in the *Melbourne Review*:

> The characters are flashed on the pages with the effect of phantasmagoria, strike violent attitudes, snarl ferocious defiance, purr the most transparent flatteries, swear the roundest oaths, and vanish suddenly into outer darkness for the next tableau.
> There is scarcely an actor in the whole story who is not either revoltingly detestable or disgustingly contemptible. Such a gathering of the representatives of loathsome wickedness and inherent imbecility was never grouped in one book before . . .[35]

Another contributor, Mrs J. A. (Ettie E.) Bode of Sunningdale Park, South Australia, was probably a sister of Cecilia Hill (both had the maiden name

Ayliffe). Ettie E. Bode had a poem 'Lubra' included in Douglas Sladen's *Australian Poets 1788–1888* and in 1885 at Strathalbyn, South Australia published *Original Poems*. Another contributor 'H. N. B.', author of 'Some of Australia's claims on her women', was Mrs Hannah Newton Baker, who published a collection of bush and mining stories, *Sketches of Australian Life and Scenery* in 1876; *Frank Carey: A Story of Victorian life*, a story of an English settler who became a member of the Victorian Parliament; and *Wytha Wytha: A Tale of Australian Life*, a novel of station life and mining set in central Victoria and Melbourne, published in 1903.[36]

7

Early Journalists and Country Editors

*'The train by which your correspondent quitted the capital was
delayed three hours . . .'*
Sydney Morning Herald 31 October 1870

The anonymous nature of much early journalism in Australia makes the task
of tracing women writers on newspapers and periodicals difficult. It is usually
only when clues have been left in autobiographical or biographical writing, or
by friends of the writers, that women writers can be traced in mid-nineteenth
century newspaper writing. In the 1850s and 1860s, Catherine Spence's
writing of editorials under her brother's name is known because she wrote
about it in her autobiography; Louisa Atkinson's 'A Voice from the Country'
articles are identified easily because they are signed L.A. or L.C. and were
attributed to her in a newspaper obituary. Adelaide Ironside was better known
as a painter, yet there is an indication that she too wrote for the Sydney press.

Adelaide Eliza Ironside

Adelaide Eliza Ironside impressed many people with her gifts. When she died
the London *Athenaeum* wrote, 'Full of nervous sensibility, she was the
impersonation of Genius. Her mind was too active for the delicate frame in
which it dwelt...'[1] The *Town and Country Journal* began a full page article
with, 'In the records of Australian genius, the memorials of this lady's short
but brilliant career, will always be looked upon with great interest'.[2] Adelaide
Ironside was born in Sydney on 17 November 1831, the only surviving child
of Scottish-born James Ironside, commission agent and accountant, and his
wife Martha. Her parents were members of the congregation of Presbyterian

Adelaide Ironside was regarded as a genius during her short life. From an early age she showed great talent in art and literature and she became the first Australian to study art overseas when she left for Italy in 1855. Before that she was a leader-writer and contributor of poetry to radical papers in Sydney. (Town and Country Journal 14 January 1871)

Minister and politician, Dr John Dunmore Lang. During her childhood spent living with her mother in a small cottage on the North Shore she showed signs of great talent in languages, art and literature and developed an interest in the supernatural, later becoming a medium.

She began early to write poetry, some being published under her initials in Sydney periodicals. Her views were stirringly republican and national-istic — she even designed a banner for the First Volunteer Artillery Company of New South Wales. Some of her poems and articles attacking enemies of democratic ideals, published in the *People's Advocate and the New South Wales Vindicator* and other periodicals, were described by the *Town and Country Journal* as of 'considerable merit' but of 'erratic construction'.[3]

In her early twenties she is said to have been a leader-writer for the Sydney press. Leader-writers are always anonymous so it is not possible to check the extent of her writing. This information is contained in the memoir of Daniel Henry Deniehy written by Miss E. A. Martin. Described by E. A. Martin as a woman of 'commanding intellect and rare literary genius', Adelaide Ironside was, she said, 'one of the very few of her sex who have ever aspired to and reached the position of leader-writer on the press'.[4] Adelaide Ironside was a close friend of Daniel Deniehy, the son of convicts who became a brilliant orator, lawyer and politician before his early death. E. A. Martin suggests that Adelaide Ironside remained in love with Deniehy until his death in 1865 but that he did not return her love. They remained correspondents after Deniehy's marriage in 1852 and Adelaide Ironside is said to have refused many 'brilliant' offers of marriage. Deniehy, along with Dr Lang, urged her to study painting in Europe. According to Martin he saw 'at a glance the splendid and untried capabilities of her budding genius, and

107

earnestly advised her to pursue her studies in Rome'.[5]

Adelaide Ironside left Sydney with her mother with introductions to important people in London and she was later to become friendly with John Ruskin. By the beginning of 1856 she had begun studying painting in Rome. Her fame as a painter spread; the Prince of Wales and W. C. Wentworth visited her and both bought paintings for £500 each. Pope Pius IX received her at a private audience and gave her permission to study the paintings of Bento Angelico at St Mark's Convent, Florence and to copy works in the papal collection.

In 1860, while she was in Rome, Dr Lang proposed to the New South Wales Parliament that the Government pay her an allowance of £200 a year, but this was rejected. She showed two pictures, 'Marriage at Cana of Galilee' and 'The Pilgrim of Art' in the New South Wales court of the London Exhibition of 1862. A proposal put forward to purchase the former for £1000 for New South Wales failed through lack of funds. She died in Rome in 1867 of tuberculosis at the age of thirty-five, her brilliant talent at painting not fully realised and her efforts as a pioneer woman leader-writer buried in obscure radical papers.

Anna Blackwell

By 1860 only a handful of women in Australia had any journalistic association with newspapers. It is surprising, therefore, to find a woman appointed in that year to the coveted position of foreign correspondent with the *Sydney Morning Herald*, a job that was to remain a male province for the following century and more. The appointment went to Anna Blackwell in Paris. She was not an Australian and never visited the country but the high regard in which she was held by the Fairfax family, owners of the *Sydney Morning Herald*, ensured her keeping the appointment for an extraordinary period of well over thirty years.

Anna Blackwell was born in Bristol, England, on 21 June 1816, the eldest of nine surviving children of Samuel and Hannah Blackwell. (Another daughter, Elizabeth Blackwell, became famous as the world's first qualified woman doctor.) In 1832 when Anna was sixteen the family emigrated to New York and in 1838 moved to Cincinnati where Samuel Blackwell died. Anna, as one of the supporting members of the family, took various teaching jobs but by the early 1840s had begun writing articles for papers and magazines. She later moved to Paris and by the end of the 1840s was supporting herself by sending regular despatches to newspapers in the United States and some British colonies. Her columns, signed 'Fidelitas', consisted of lively news items combining the reporting of political and international events with gossipy accounts of life in Paris. She was a successful poet also, and in 1853 a collection of her poems was published in England.[6]

One of her first columns for the *Sydney Morning Herald*, signed 'Stella', the pseudonym she used for this paper, was datelined 24 October 1860, Paris. Consisting of six full length columns of closely packed type, it contained news covering practically every European country. It was despatched, as all overseas news was, by ship mail and appeared in the paper on 18 December 1860. The column included reports on Garibaldi's progress in the liberation of Italy and the intricate manoeuvres between Garibaldi and Cavour; Queen Victoria's recent visit to Hesse; the abnormally cold weather; a theory about the correlation between weather conditions and moral health; the acceptance of potatoes as a food by the French; the French Emperor and Empress's tour of Algiers, Lyons and the south of France; free-trader Richard Cobden's negotiations for a trade treaty with the French Government; and several examples of the harsh rule of the prince who governed Serbia. The beginning of this item is a good example of her chatty style as she shared confidences from the capitals of Europe with her readers in far-off Sydney:

> A highly intelligent Frenchman, who has for several years occupied an important public post at Bucharest, and who is intimately acquainted with all the region which Austria would so much like to add to her dominions at the expense of Turkey, has given me some curious particulars of the late Prince Milosch, and the way in which he governed.

Among the incidents that followed was one in which the Prince ordered a bishop to be buried alive for allegedly fleecing his flock. The despatch concluded with a postscript of details of 'telegraphic despatches' from Naples of another attack on the Garibaldians by the Royalists.[7]

When the proprietor of the *Sydney Morning Herald*, John Fairfax, was overseas early in 1865, his son James R. Fairfax wrote telling him he could pick up a copy of the *Sydney Morning Herald* from 'Miss Blackwell in Paris'. In another letter he wrote concerning her style, which had been discussed, apparently, in previous letters. James Fairfax defended her, commenting that the articles of another writer on social affairs were very good 'but the gossiping style of Miss Blackwell I think is appreciated'.[8]

In September 1870 when Paris was besieged by the Prussians, Anna, then fifty-four, escaped from France to England. Her despatch began in Paris on 18 August but was added to on several occasions. On 31 August from Boulogne she gave a graphic account of her departure from Paris just ahead of the invading forces. Her enormously long despatch made up nearly two pages of very small print in the *Herald* of 31 October 1870. It began with a report that the Prussians were expected in a few days and a placard had been placed on walls in the city warning 'all foreigners and useless mouths' that they would be ejected summarily from the city when the Prussians arrived. This, she wrote, 'determined your correspondent to follow the example so generally set by the foreign residents and to seek residence in the "English colony" [Boulogne]'.[9]

When she left the usually gay city of Paris she described the 'grave and anxious' faces and the 'vague and dubious bits of intelligence given out by the authorities'. Huge numbers of people were moving to the centre of the city preparing to withstand a siege. She continued:

> The train by which your correspondent quitted the capital was delayed three hours on the road by the enormous crowding of the line, train after train, of interminable length, bringing stores of grain, flour, provisions, cattle, sheep, forage, coal, &c, to the city so soon to be beleagured [sic] by the foe. It really seemed, as the long lines of laden waggons went by, as though all France were being drained for the last scene of the sad drama in progress. All night, before I left Paris, the bleating of sheep and lowing of cattle filled the streets; reserves for living food being created in all the vacant lots within the fortifications. Immediately around the city were huge piles of trunks of trees, hastily cut down to deprive the advancing host of cover; the boughs, thriftily prepared for the baker's ovens, being neatly packed in goods waggons for transportation to the capital. In places the air was filled with the smell of sap. At every station, even the smallest, was a group of people eagerly waiting for news, and a squad of country bumpkins being drafted off to war. It was heartrending to see all the young faces, all the figures, generally small, going off thus to form "flesh for cannon," according to the saying of the first of the now extinct 'Napoleons'; for whatever else may, or may not, be the results of this war, the downfall of the Empire is sure to be one of them.[10]

After this crisis was over Anna Blackwell returned to Paris and continued to support herself by sending despatches of European news. In the 1870s her columns went to newspapers in many countries including Australia, India, South Africa and Canada. By this time, however, she was rather eccentric, devoting her spare time to translating books about spiritualism and reincarnation. A relative described her as 'odder than before but still handsome'.[11]

More than twenty years after they first began appearing in the *Sydney Morning Herald*, Anna Blackwell's long columns were still being printed. Their emphasis had changed, another correspondent apparently having been appointed to cover political events. Her columns appearing under the heading 'Continental Gossip' remained as popular as ever. Apparently there had been some talk about changing their emphasis but on 4 June 1881 James R. Fairfax wrote to Anna:

> ... we have been reconsidering the matter and think it better that you should continue the monthly budget as formerly and not trouble to write upon politics more than you used to do. We think it better for our readers here to have a special letter from Paris from a correspondent

At a time when it was very unusual for women to be employed on newspapers, American Anna Blackwell became Paris correspondent for the Sydney Morning Herald. She held the position from 1860 for well over thirty years. In September 1870 when Paris was besieged by the Prussians, Anna Blackwell sent graphic descriptions to the Herald as she prepared to leave the city ahead of the invading forces. (U.S. Library of Congress. Blackwell Family Papers)

devoted more especially to the political aspect of affairs. So please consider the arrangement for your continental gossip undisturbed. There appears to be some probability of my being in Europe towards the end of the present or the beginning of next year when I shall do myself the pleasure of seeing you.[12]

In her later years Anna Blackwell became involved in some implausible money-making schemes, including one aimed at digging up treasure supposedly buried in France by the fleeing James II in the seventeenth century. She was ruined financially by her involvement in this project. At the same time changes in world conditions and the advent of the cable, providing a rapid means of communication, drastically reduced her newspaper outlets until, of an original eleven, only two remained. One of these, a Montreal paper, dispensed with her column in 1885 leaving her with the *Sydney Morning Herald* alone. Apart from £100 a year she received from the *Sydney Morning Herald*, her only other source of income was £100 a year which her brother Henry provided. In 1890 the *Sydney Morning Herald* raised her fee from £100 to £125 a year. This, she recorded, gave her no pleasure as she believed they should have raised her payment twenty-five years before. During the 1890s, when nearly eighty, she decided to give up writing and move to England instead of, she said, working herself to death to pay for what she described as her 'coming cremation'.[13] She died on 4 January 1900, aged eighty-four, after an attack of influenza and bronchitis.

The *Sydney Morning Herald* did not note Anna Blackwell's death at the time it occurred, apparently because of some coolness at their parting. But when her more famous sister, Dr Elizabeth Blackwell, died in 1910 the paper used the occasion to write about Anna:

Dr Elizabeth Blackwell . . . was a sister of Miss Anna Blackwell, for very many years the Paris correspondent of the 'Sydney Morning Herald'. Miss Anna Blackwell, who adopted the nom de plume 'Stella' was a lady of brilliant attainments, and was almost as distinguished in the world of literature as her sister was in the world of medicine. She was a contributor to the columns of the 'Herald' at the time of the Franco-Prussian war, and was compelled to leave Paris during the siege. Upon the termination of hostilities, however, she returned to her duties, and continued to act as the Paris correspondent of this journal until 15 or 20 years ago, when she retired with her sister from active work. Miss Anna Blackwell took a deep interest in a wide range of subjects, and published a number of poems.[14]

Emily Manning ('Australie')

*'The journalistic veil of anonymity has concealed so much of her press
work . . .'*
Centennial Magazine September 1890

Emily Manning was in her lifetime accorded much praise as a poet. It was not
until after her death that her great contribution as one of the first women in
journalism in Australia was recognised.

Emily Matilda Manning was born into a well-to-do upper class family in
Sydney on 12 May 1845, a daughter of Sir William Manning, the famous
lawyer and politician, and his first wife formerly Emily Wise who died the year
after Emily's birth. She was educated at a private school and later Professor
John Woolley, first professor of classics at Sydney University, encouraged her
to take an interest in literature. From 1860 she lived at Wallaroy, the
mansion her father, at the time a very wealthy man, had built at Edgecliff.

When Emily was about nineteen she is believed to have been romanti-
cally involved with David Scott Mitchell, later the benefactor whose book
collection formed the basis of the Mitchell Library. The two were part of the
same social circle and exchanged some light-hearted poems in October and
November 1864.[15] Emily Manning left soon after for London. On the voyage
a fellow passenger, a Catholic priest, impressed by her mental ability, offered
to teach her logic and she spent a portion of each day of the voyage in study.
In England she had connections and introductions which allowed her to move
into the literary world, meeting Tennyson, Browning, Huxley and George
Eliot. She began her journalistic career writing for periodicals including C. F.
Yonge's *Monthly Packet of Evening Readings*, which specialised in refined
reading for teenage girls, and *Golden Hours*. Both publications had many
distinguished literary contributors. With this experience she was able, after
her return to Sydney at the beginning of the 1870s, to become one of the first
regular women contributors to newspapers and periodicals. From the early
1870s her articles began appearing in the *Town and Country Journal*, *Sydney
Morning Herald* and *Sydney Mail*, either anonymously or under the pen-name
'Australie'.

On 22 December 1873 at the age of twenty-eight she married Henry
Heron, a Sydney solicitor, in due course having six children. William L.
Curnow, a clergyman and a journalist on the *Sydney Morning Herald*, knew
her well and said that she was a 'womanly woman . . . She had the old ideas

Australian-born Emily Manning was praised highly as a poet during her lifetime. It was only after her death that her great achievements as one of the first women to be involved in journalism in Australia were revealed. For twenty years to her death in 1890 she wrote editorials and articles on a great range of subjects for the Sydney Morning Herald *and other papers.* (Centennial Magazine *September 1890*)

touching what is due from a wife and a mother'.[16] Yet from her early years to the time of her death she combined the roles of wife and mother with the writing of a constant stream of contributed articles to magazines and newspapers, her constancy being remarked on as much as her versatility. Apart from general articles she was also a literary critic, one example being a long review of John Le Gay Brereton's *Genesis and the Beatitudes* which appeared in the *Sydney Quarterly Magazine* in 1887 under the name E. Heron.

Much of Emily Manning's press work remained behind the 'journalistic veil of anonymity'[17] so that to the public she was known chiefly as the author of a book of poems *The Balance of Pain and other Poems*, published under the name of 'Australie', in London in 1877. The *Illustrated Sydney News*, in an enthusiastic review, said the author was 'well-known as a contributor of both prose and verse to the public journals':

> 'Australie' undoubtedly possesses the true poetic instinct combined with more intellectual power than is oftentimes associated with the writing of poetry. Her poems are characterised by great purity of tone and loftiness of purpose, while many of the pieces breathe a touching sentiment and earnest sympathy for the sufferings and trials that frequently beset the path of humanity.[18]

During the last months of her life it was said that she was 'more systematically engaged in journalism' than ever before and a few days before her death she reported on the opening of the Anglo-Australian Art Exhibition.[19] At her death an obituary stated that she loved journalism and had hoped to spend many more years in such work. She died at the age of forty-five on 25 August 1890 at Blandville. Her husband had been in financial difficulties from the early 1880s and at her death there were references to her withdrawal from society. It was probably the need to contribute to the family finances that led to her greater involvement in journalism.

Evidence from obituaries and other sources indicate that for twenty years from 1870 she was a contributor to the *Sydney Morning Herald* and for part of that time one of its leader-writers. In 1888 and 1889 she appears to have been the principal female journalist on the *Herald's* Women's Column begun at that time and for the year before her death she was associate editor of the *Illustrated Sydney News* where, it was said she was 'distinguished for her critical and painstaking work'.[20]

William Curnow who was appointed editor of the *Sydney Morning Herald* in 1886, said of her death:

> She may truly be said to have died in harness, and her death means a loss not only to those associated with her in her labors, but to the colony generally. Australia has many women who write, not a few who have given us books and pamphlets, but the number of trained women writers and authors is not large, and among the foremost of these stood Mrs. Heron. Our scanty literature was made richer by her labors, and will be poorer for her death.[21]

The *Sydney Morning Herald* commented that her journalistic work had continued 'almost to the last' until 'the busy pen of the journalist is done' and praised her professional approach:

> The strong and easy style of which she was mistress singled her out among women writers as much as her man-like grasp for her subject, indeed, within her own lines, few men had an equal command of the qualities that go to make up the character of an effective writer. She had incisiveness and earnestness, an intense interest in those public questions that appealed to her, and much sterling honesty of purpose. This journal has frequently published contributions from her pen, sometimes under the usual journalistic veil of anonymity, and sometimes under an initial or *nom de plume*. Not more than a few weeks ago we printed a thoughtful and well-considered paper on a stirring subject of discussion at the time, which we have reason to believe made an impression in many quarters where the name of the writer was not so much as suspected. Her practical skill as a literary worker was not more marked than her comprehensive taste, which was singularly broad. To social subjects she gave much of her mind, and some of her contributions to the discussion of questions of sanitation, prison discipline, forestry, as well as those domestic matters of interest that might seem to come more directly within the province of a woman's treatment have all been dealt with at

different periods by her versatile pen. This choice of subject was characteristic of her intensely earnest mind and her restless passion for inquiry, which led her to seek the best and latest information on all subjects, as well as to keep abreast of current questions of the day.[22]

The paper added 'in larger European centres of intellectual activity Mrs. Heron might have moved among the noticeable women of the time'.

Mrs Carl (Jane) Fischer

'In those days women journalists were almost unknown . . .'
Bulletin

In addition to employing the first woman foreign correspondent and printing leaders and articles on a wide range of subjects from Emily Manning, the *Sydney Morning Herald* was the employer of the first woman music and drama reviewer. She was Mrs Carl Fischer, described in a history of the paper as 'a vigorous writer of strong and sometimes prejudiced views, influenced by personal likes and dislikes'.[23]

Jane (or Jenny) Fischer was by the time she became associated with the *Sydney Morning Herald* a mature woman with a wealth of experience. Born Jane Sara Edwards in 1834 in Gloucestershire, the daughter of a teacher, she was apparently well trained in music. She arrived in Melbourne in 1856 and that year married William Gilpin Dredge, a well-known Melbourne musician. In the following eight years she had five children, of whom only one girl and one boy survived. In 1864 her husband died and two years later she was married at St Kilda to Wilhelm Carl Fischer, a merchant. There was one child of this marriage. From 1870 to 1877 Mrs Fischer was principal/proprietor of Geelong Ladies' College, a large girls' school. During this time she began contributing musical critiques to several Melbourne papers, being probably the first woman apart from Catherine Spence to write for newspapers in Melbourne.[24]

In 1879 the Fischer family moved to Sydney and almost immediately Mrs Fischer began contributing music and drama critiques and social notes to the *Sydney Morning Herald* and its sister paper the weekly *Sydney Mail*, her position later being formalised. Until her death in 1896 she was music and drama critic for the *Sydney Mail*, also conducting the social columns and what was referred to as the 'ladies department'. During this time she continued to do music and drama criticism for the *Sydney Morning Herald*.[25] Of her work the *Mail* said:

It was as a musical critic that she won the highest reputation, and did so

Mrs Carl Fischer wrote music and drama criticisms for Melbourne papers in the 1870s and in 1879 joined the Sydney Morning Herald *as music and drama critic. Later she was among the first journalists to edit a women's page when she began 'Hausfrau's Lucky Bag' in which she replied to readers' queries in the* Sydney Mail. *(Sydney Mail 17 October 1896)*

much to promote the art in this city and colony, and to raise it to a higher plane. Those who can recollect the class of music that satisfied the public some years ago, and can compare it with the high standard that now prevails, will be ready to concede to Mrs. Fischer the commendation which is her due for having fulfilled so completely a task that was congenial, though sometimes in its fulfilment distasteful . . . She was just and generous to a degree, and her judgment was rarely at fault . . .

For many years she had charge of the social columns of this journal, and also of the ladies' department. Her contributions to our pages were as interesting as they were valuable, and formed a leading feature in the *Mail.* "Hausfrau's Lucky Bag" was one in which very many dipped for information, and never in vain.[26]

Jenny Fischer died at the age of sixty-two at her home in Upper William Street, Sydney on 6 October 1896 from the effects of catching a chill. The extraordinary position she had achieved in Sydney was apparent during her illness when many prominent people including Lady Hampden, the Governor's wife, inquired about her. On the day of her death Cardinal Moran called to pay his respects to her husband and many people well known in journalistic, musical, dramatic and charitable circles attended her funeral at Waverley Cemetery. They included many members of the Fairfax family and *Sydney Morning Herald* editor William Curnow. After her death admirers subscribed to a memorial fund which reached £125. It was used to educate and support her grandson.[27]

Writing nearly fifty years later of the days when Jane Fischer began working for the *Sydney Morning Herald* a correspondent in the *Bulletin* said:

In those days women journalists were almost unknown . . . The only prominent woman worker on the Sydney newspapers was old Mrs. Carl Fischer.[28]

Elizabeth Macfaull, Mercy Shenton, Sarah Gill

The involvement of women in the running of newspapers in colonial Australia is, like the existence of women writers on metropolitan papers, a little-known story. Like Mrs Ann Howe who gained control of the *Sydney Gazette* when widowed, most women proprietors acquired their newspapers following the deaths of their husbands. The extent of their involvement is sometimes obscure but in several cases it is clear that the women proprietors were editors as well.

In a few cases women were involved in capital city newspapers. Two women have a place in the early history of the paper that later became the *West Australian*. Begun as the *Perth Gazette and Western Australian Journal* in 1833 by Charles Macfaull in association with W. K. Shenton, the paper was conducted by Macfaull for some years. Following his death his widow, Elizabeth Macfaull, became proprietor and, although there is no direct evidence, she is believed to have been involved in editorial work on the paper. She later disposed of her interest and at the beginning of 1848, Arthur Shenton, a printer and journalist, became editor. In 1870 he was involved in a highly contentious libel case which, although he had much public support, resulted in his being fined and sentenced to two months' imprisonment. This was said to have caused his death in March 1871. His wife, formerly Mercy Heal, of York, England, took over the management of the paper and, like Elizabeth Macfaull, is believed to have done some editorial work.[29]

In Hobart the daily *Tasmanian News* was owned and managed for many years by Mrs Sarah Gill. She was regarded as a good manager but according to the *Bulletin* she chose reporters partly 'for their "respectable and quiet appearance"; and a respectable and quiet appearance isn't much real value as journalistic equipment'.[30] Sarah Gill, née Sarah Inez Jacobs, was the wife of Henry Horatio Gill (1840–1914) explorer, farmer, prospector and newspaper proprietor, a native-born Tasmanian whose grandfather had been Lord Mayor of London. In 1881 Gill bought the Hobart *Southern Star* and in November 1883 launched the *Tasmanian News*, an evening paper. The paper continued for about twenty-eight years but by 1896 Gill had retired from journalism. From about 1890 to its demise in 1911, the paper was run by Sarah Gill.[31]

Margaret Falls, Mrs D. G. Jones

Several women became proprietors of newspapers in New South Wales country towns, among them Mrs Margaret Falls at Maitland and Mrs Jones at Deniliquin. Margaret Falls was born in Mallow, County Cork, Ireland, a daughter of John Flynn. In 1849 at the age of nineteen she married Alexander Falls, manager and later owner of the *Maitland Mercury*. After he died in 1870 Margaret Falls ran the paper until her own death in 1873. The extent of her involvement in editorial work is not known but Mrs Jones, widow of Welsh-born David Griffiths Jones, a medical practitioner as well as a journalist, is known to have edited the *Pastoral Times* in Deniliquin following her husband's death in 1876. For some years after his arrival in Sydney in 1848 David Jones was correspondent for the *Sydney Morning Herald*. Later he settled in Deniliquin to practise as a doctor but soon began the *Pastoral Times*, being regarded as the pioneer of journalism in the area.[32]

Mrs Jones edited the paper for four years until her death in 1880 when the *Bulletin* reported:

> By the death of Mrs. D. G. Jones of the Pastoral Times, Deniliquin, New South Wales has lost its only female editor. Victoria has an editress, who conducts a Kyneton paper. She writes vigorous leaders and once cowhided a man.[33]

No further details have been found about the Kyneton 'editress'.[34]

Marion Leathem

> '. . . she had a high conception of her duty . . . as the proprietress of a public journal.'
>
> *Molong Express*

The *Bulletin* may have been correct when it stated that New South Wales had lost its only female editor, but a few months before Mrs Jones' death Mrs Marion Leathem had taken over the management, if not the editorship, of the *Molong Express* after the death of her husband in 1879. She continued to run this paper for the next thirty-nine years. Marion Leathem was born in Belfast, Ireland, on 15 June 1842, the third daughter of Dr William Large,

Mrs Marion Leathem took over the Molong Express following her husband's death in 1879 and ran the paper for nearly forty years. Although she employed editors she retained editorial control and was known as a woman of strong character and opinions, her views being reflected in the paper's policies. She was one of several women who took control of newspapers following the deaths of their husbands. (Molong Express 9 August 1919, reprinted in Molong Express Centenary Special November 1976. Reproduced by permission of Norm Bloomfield, editor, Molong Express)

and was brought to Melbourne by her family when six months old. Later the family lived at Tumut and Marion attended the Ladies Seminary at Wagga. In 1866 she married Henry Vale Leathem and on 1 October 1876 her husband and his brother established the *Molong Express*. When Henry Leathem died on 9 July 1879 Marion Leathem was left a widow with six young children. With the help of her eldest son, who started work at the age of ten, she managed the paper until her death in 1919.

Although she employed editors she retained editorial control. Known as a woman of strong character and opinions, her views were reflected in the paper's policies. A political opponent, Dr Andrew Ross MP, started a rival paper, the *Molong Argus*, in August 1895 because he held different views from Mrs Leathem on the free trade/protection debate, the raging issue of the time.[35] After Marion Leathem's death the *Molong Express* said:

> ... she adhered undeviatingly to the path which she believed to be the right one, notwithstanding that she lost considerable pecuniary profit in consequence. Efforts were made on several occasions to induce her to haul down her colors, more especially in connection with political questions, but, irrespective of the consequences, she could not be turned aside from her convictions, and the greater the pressure that was brought to bear the more she smiled and the more resolutely she pursued the policy which she believed in. But, fair and honest to a degree she recognised that there were two sides in every question, and her paper was ever ready to publish the views of her opponents, even when those views contained strong castigations of her opinions ...
>
> Principle was to her a jewel of great value, and she had a high conception of her duty to the public as the proprietress of a public journal.[36]

Her sons, Charles and John Leathem, ran the paper until the 1930s. After the paper reached the half-century mark it was remarked that it was a record for a western New South Wales paper to have been in the hands of one family for such a time.[37]

Mary (Boyle) Garland

> 'We sing but the heroic deeds
> Of lovely Mary of Carcoar.'
>
> Bulletin

By far the most colourful character among the women editors in New South Wales in the nineteenth century was Mrs Mary Boyle (née Newland), later Mrs Mary Garland, who ran the Carcoar Chronicle and the Mount McDonald Miner.

Mrs Mary Boyle took over the Carcoar Chronicle after the death of her first husband, Edward Hugh Boyle, in 1880 and in July the following year the Bulletin made the first of its comments about her:

> If there is a paper published in New South Wales that we have lately read with breathless interest, it is the CARCOAR CHRONICLE. In the first place, every issue of the journal is filled up with the very kind of matter that interests — nay, absorbs us. Those leaders, sharply criticising the fiscal policy of the Uruguay Opposition, have entranced us, and the pars which liken Andy Lynch to a modern Coriolanus will live in our memories a life-time. And, in the second place, the paper being edited by a lady, the matter all through has a footstool and work-box flavour, which makes the CHRONICLE stand out pre-eminently as the domestic paper of the hour.[38]

Four months later the Bulletin reported that Mary Boyle:

> ... with meretorious energy and hardihood, rode through the pouring rain on Monday alone (but not uncared for), from Carcoar to Mount M'Donald and back, something like fifty-two miles, upon business in connection with the MOUNT M'DONALD MINER, which she establishes this week. May fortune reward the brave, and bedeck her with a Garland. — COWRA SOMETHING.

The Bulletin continued its mockery of Mrs Boyle with a poem:

> Let hist'ry's heroines hide their heads,
> Their names will thrill our souls no more;

We sing but the heroic deeds
    Of lovely Mary of Carcoar.
We've read of Joan, of Isabella,
    And female fightists, full a score;
But we, the fame will only beller,
    Of lovely Mary of Carcoar.[39]

A later verse implied that Mrs Boyle was about to remarry and in February 1882 the *Bulletin* reported:

> The bolt has fallen. We are undone. Here is the key to our sorrow. The only lady editor NSW possesses is married:-
>
> 'GARLAND-BOYLE — February 8th; at St. Andrew's Cathedral, by the Rev. Dr. Ellis, Charles Launcelot, youngest son of Captain W. R. Garland, to Mary relict of the late E. H. Boyle, of Carcoar.' . . .
>
> The bride, who looked lovely, but slightly nervous, was supported by the joint staffs of her papers, the CARCOAR CHRONICLE, and MOUNT M'DONALD MINER. He (that's to say, the staff) was a man of venerable aspect, and he appeared conscious of the honour of escorting one for whom he had turned so long. The bridegroom was a heavenly vision of blue frock coat and lavender pants, and appeared deeply interested in the lining of his hat and the ceremony. Dr. Ellis read the service with his customary eloquence, and not a hitch occurred until the staff broke down when signing his name in the vestry.[40]

To the *Bulletin* writers Mary (Boyle) Garland was a figure of fun but while they were at the most employees, more probably 'penny-a-liners', 'Carcoar Mary' managed and edited her own paper. When her husband stood for election to the New South Wales Parliament the *Bulletin* commented:

> Our esteemed friend, Mrs. GARLAND, the beautiful and accomplished editress of the CARCOAR (N.S.W.) CHRONICLE, runs her paper in purely feminine principles at election time. Mr. FREEHILL, the protectionist candidate, made a good speech, and the lady polished him off with 13 lines. Mr. GARLAND, who is a Freetrader, and also the husband of the paper, likewise made a speech, and he got 3½ columns.[41]

Hector Lamond, later editor of the *Worker* and then a Nationalist politician, served his apprenticeship as a compositor under 'Carcoar Mary' on the *Carcoar Chronicle* and for a time was editor. Carcoar proved too limited for his ambition and he moved to Sydney.[42]

Mary Garland's husband, Charles Launcelot Garland, a well known identity in Australia's early mining history, was involved in many great mining ventures, including the Palmer rush in north Queensland, and he pioneered the gold bucket dredging system. He was a member of the New

South Wales Legislative Assembly for Carcoar for three terms. Mary Garland died at the end of 1929 and her husband a month later in January 1930.[43]

Annie Christie Massy

'. . . this Labor organ shall either uphold political principles in keeping with the People's Party or close.'
Port Denison Times and Bowen Advocate

Annie Christie Massy was born in the Bowen district on 15 April 1864 to squatter James Hall Scott and his wife. Both her parents were Scottish and Annie was sent to Scotland and the Continent to be educated and trained as a teacher. After she returned to Bowen she began a boarding school where she taught languages and music. Some time later she married a grazier, John Eyre Massy, and went to live on his property Sanoma on the Bowen River, but he failed financially and in an effort to get work had to travel as far as the Gulf of Carpentaria where he was employed at the Burketown Meatworks. Annie Massy tried to make money running a school in Bowen but this was not a success and in 1899 she grasped an opportunity to buy the plant of a defunct paper, the Bowen Mirror, cheaply and used it to launch the Bowen Advocate. Surprisingly for a woman from the squattocracy she proclaimed her policies as democratic and Labor. After the death in June 1900 of the proprietor of another Bowen paper, the twice-weekly conservative Port Denison Times and Kennedy District Advertiser, she also bought that paper, with financial help from her brother.[44]

On 1 September 1900 she combined her two papers under the new name of Port Denison Times and Bowen Advocate. In her introductory article Annie Massy wrote 'a Progressive party is indispensable to the future prosperity of this district' and indicated that the progressive policies of the Bowen Advocate would not be submerged under the Tory policies of the Port Denison Times in the amalgamation.[45]

Unfortunately she did not live long enough to achieve her aims for the paper. One of her last editorials advocated a Labor vote at the coming Federal election.[46] She was admitted to Townsville Hospital early in 1901, originally for a specialist opinion, but subsequently she caught dengue fever. She became increasingly furious with the conservative views expressed by the acting editor, J. A. Thuman, in her absence and from her hospital bed issued a statement to be printed in the paper:

The Ministerial stand lately taken by the P. D. Times and Bowen Advocate, owing to the unexpected illness of the Editor,

Annie Christie Massy was a most unusual newspaper proprietor. The daughter of a squatter and wife of a grazier she was a strong supporter of the recently emergent Labor Party. When she gained control of a conservative newspaper in Bowen, North Queensland, in 1900 she attempted to change its political policies and from her bed in Townsville Hospital sacked an editor who tried to thwart her. (Rod Kirkpatrick, author of Sworn to no master)

necessitating a sojourn in the Townsville Hospital, and compelling hurried steps to be taken to fill up the vacancy, has made the proprietor decide this Labor organ shall either uphold political *principles in keeping with the People's Party or close.*[47]

She dismissed the editor and issued a statement of the paper's policy. The *Worker* reported, however, that, 'before the printers' ink had wet the type that embodied the expression of her brave and indomitable soul, "God's finger touched her and she slept" '.[48]

Annie Massy's statement on the federal election indicates that Labor's White Australia policy was one of the major reasons for her support of the party:

> ... Labor must sweep victoriously to the front if workers decide to fight for the welfare of the masses on the principle of 'No surrender'. The hour has arrived for all in sympathy with the mighty socialistic approval of the world to stand together. If we value the purity of the nation above capitalistic interest, human souls above the sugar industry *as it is carried on by the companies*, let Australians vote solidly against the Asiatic Coloured Curse and the Kanaka, with their vile contaminating influences, and their unmentionable vices. Let us as men and women, for our own safety and the protection of our children, realise if a White Australia is to be a reality, not a dream, Labor must first organise, then fight. Remember, we must finally win the day if the cry goes ringing down the ranks of Democracy: 'Australia for Australians, and Australians for Australia.'

A note in brackets stated that it was published 'under special orders from the proprietor' from Townsville Hospital.[49]

Annie Massy died in Townsville Hospital on 15 February 1901 at the age of thirty-six leaving two children. After her death her husband, John Eyre Massy, assumed control of the paper and ran it for eight and a half years. In August 1909 he leased the *Port Denison Times* to E. S. Emerson, a writer for the *Lone Hand* and the *Bulletin*, and Messrs Walker and Greenhalgh. The lessees took over the paper for a term of years with high hopes but left after only three months. For five months from November 1909, Francis Kenna, Labor Member of Parliament for Bowen 1902–09, and a former editor of the *Worker*, the *Charters Towers Telegraph* and the Brisbane *Sun*, edited the paper but it ceased publication in 1910.[50]

8

Voices from the Bush

'A wind-blown, shimmering, shifting, awful waste ...'
Barbara Baynton[1]

The initiation of many women into Australian life in the first century of European colonisation was a story of the bush, of adapting to an immense, strange and wild land and a life they found harsh and lonely. It was not until the 1890s, when Barbara Baynton wrote her stories of country women living on the edge of destitution that the poor and deprived were depicted in writing by a woman. Before that, country stories were written by, and largely about, middle-class women. Some wrote of great privations and loneliness but usually shining through was the women's courage and spirit, often bolstered by religious faith, as they made long journeys through unknown country and spent months or years on isolated stations. In their writing there was usually some sense of a settled life, of a servant in the offing or the possibility of a visit (even though the journey might take weeks) to a relative or to town.

Many of the women included in previous chapters wrote about the bush. Mary Vidal's *Tales for the bush* are illuminating on some aspects of bush life but she wrote of the closely settled districts near Sydney. Louisa Atkinson and Louisa Meredith wrote perceptively of the plants and animals of Australia but neither experienced the extreme isolation that women on outback stations endured. Henrietta Foott was a true pioneer of the outback and her story, illuminated by her stirring faith, was typical of many women previously unaccustomed to hardship who found themselves weeks or months from civilisation.

Katherine Kirkland, Annie (Baxter) Dawbin, Harriet Daly, Mrs Edward Millett

One of the first published descriptions of bush life written by a woman was 'Life in the Bush by a Lady' published anonymously in *Chambers's Miscellany* in Edinburgh in 1847[2]. The author, Katherine Kirkland, wrote of her experiences as a pioneer in the first wave of settlers in Victoria's Western District. Living herself in a primitive hut with doors made of rushes, she reported her disgust at the 'dirty and uncomfortable' way the settlers lived with nothing to eat but mutton, tea and damper; she wrote of a dangerous journey through flooded rivers while on her way to give birth in Melbourne and later of living in a tent at Darebin near Melbourne while the temperature soared to over 100 °F day after day. With her husband away, she barely saved the lives of her children and herself when bushfires singed the tent. Katherine Kirkland became ill under the strain of pioneering life and after three years in Australia returned to Glasgow in 1841.

Annie Baxter who arrived at Hobart in 1837 with her husband Lieutenant Andrew Baxter wrote of station life in *Memories of the past by a Lady in Australia* published in 1873.[3] Her experiences of life at Yessaba, near Port Macquarie, where her husband farmed in the early 1840s and then at Yambuck, in the Victorian Western District, and the two months' journey between the two, are briskly told. From later knowledge of what she was confiding to her diaries of her unhappy married life it is obvious her published account is a superficial version. It did, however, add to the picture of the hardships and isolation of life in the bush and of the courage of the women who lived there.

Annie Baxter's book covers the period of her early married life to Andrew Baxter. She left her husband in 1849 and returned to England. Eight years later she returned to Melbourne to wind up the affairs of her husband who had committed suicide in 1855. On the voyage she met Robert Dawbin. They were married soon after their arrival in Melbourne and took up stations in the Western District where Annie Dawbin resumed her friendship with many of the pioneer families she had known while living at Yambuck. A few years later Dawbin became insolvent. After an unsuccessful attempt at making a living in New Zealand, the Dawbins left the country and Annie Dawbin returned to Victoria. She died in 1905 at her small farm at South Yan Yean outside Melbourne. The volumes of the diary she kept between 1834 and 1865 provide an invaluable insight into social life in colonial Australia.

Harriet W. Daly, in *Digging, Squatting and Pioneering Life in the Northern Territory of South Australia*,[4] wrote of her experiences living at the recently established settlement at Darwin where her father, Captain Bloomfield Douglas, was Government Resident in 1870. The family lived at first in rough huts in a country 'destitute not only of any road, but absolutely devoid of any cleared track'. But as a member of the leading family in the Territory, Harriet lived better than most. In 1871 she returned to Adelaide to marry Dominic Daly, the nephew of a former Governor, Sir Dominick Daly.

Mrs Edward Millett, wife of a clergyman sent from England to a parsonage east of Perth in the 1860s, wrote cheerfully in *An Australian parsonage*[5] of her experiences living in a rough bush-built home at a place which she left unnamed because of the 'limited character of the population of the colony'. She wrote of convicts — she saw fettered road gangs long after the convict system had ceased in New South Wales — and of Aborigines, but most of all she wrote to dispel the ignorance in England of the huge extent of Australia. She described with cheerful acceptance the difficulties of everyday life, the extreme climate and the limitations of diet and wrote with enthusiasm about the peculiar animal life.

The women described in detail later in this chapter were different in degree. They were women who went to the outback far beyond the distance Mrs Millett travelled, further and into wilder more extreme country than Annie Baxter experienced. Australians by the late 1870s, 1880s and 1890s wanted to read of these adventures. They had become accustomed to the stories of Rolf Boldrewood and others in the *Town and Country Journal*, the *Sydney Mail*, the *Illustrated Sydney News*, the *Australasian* and the *Queenslander* and, in 1880, with the start of the *Bulletin* factual and fictional stories of the hardships and the romance of the bush became more popular than ever. The writings of Jessie Lloyd, K. Langloh Parker and Laura Palmer-Archer, in different ways catered to the demand for such outback stories.

Jessie Lloyd

> '. . . it is the women . . . who have to endure the worst part of this
> species of poverty.'
> Illustrated Sydney News 13 May 1882

The topics that are almost cliches of country life — searing droughts and hazardous floods, financial insecurity and crushing mortgages, the dangers of isolation, the conservative, homely virtues of the country housewife — were the subjects of Jessie Lloyd's writing. Some of her best writing was of droughts:

> All improvements come to an end, no more money is to spare for fencing, dam-making, building, or other ways of improving the run. Money laid by is absorbed, and additional sums are borrowed, as the sinews of war are needed in abundance when a contest has to be waged against this most dreaded of all enemies in the interior of Australia — drought . . . Many men send away their wives and families to the metropolis or country towns, where they will not be witnesses of the daily fever and frets and wearing anxiety of hope deferred. But some women elect to share the anxiety, divide the trouble, and endure the discomfort, in the hope of being able, if only by one feather's weight, to lighten the burden that is bowing the head and crushing the heart.[6]

Mrs Jessie Lloyd, under the name of 'Silverleaf', contributed a very successful long running series of articles on life in the bush to the Illustrated Sydney News *beginning in January 1881 and continuing until May 1883. Her articles reflected her own life as the wife of a squatter weighed down by debt at Terembone station, near Coonamble. She used money earned from writing to send her elder sons to boarding school in Sydney.* (Illustrated Sydney News *29 August 1885*)

When she wrote an article on 'Poor People' her sympathy was for the genteel poor, those brought down by circumstances but compelled by convention to keep up with their neighbours:

> The painfully poor are those well-born and well-educated, of refined tastes and sensitive natures, whom circumstances have put in such a position that they have to take their place and creep step by step with those whose incomes are perhaps double their own . . .
>   But it is the women . . . who have to endure the worst part of this species of poverty, to whom fall the petty economies . . . Those who have to struggle like this, whether men or women, seldom live long, circumstances are too strong . . .[7]

To a great extent this applied to her own life. She and her husband arrived at Terembone as youthful pioneers full of hope and with the expectation of leading successful lives as squatters. Gradually these hopes were eroded, the optimism of the good seasons giving way to the harrowing uncertainty of seasons of drought and the weight of mortgages. She also experienced the dangers of outback life — a long and difficult birth without medical help that resulted in the birth of a sickly child who suffered from epilepsy all his life; a confrontation with a threatening tramp fended off with a revolver when she was alone with her children.

Jessie Georgina Bell was born at Longford Farm, near Launceston on 4 June 1843, the third child of Joseph William Bell and his second wife, Georgina. As a child of two she was taken by her parents to live in

Melbourne where she witnessed the extraordinary excesses and vitality of life during the gold-rush. Her father's furniture emporium failed after the gold-rush period and her mother's efforts to support the family through school-teaching had to be abandoned when she again became pregnant. When Jessie was sixteen they returned to Tasmania to live on a small farm at Glenorchy, near Hobart. With her mother in ill health she undertook the teaching and care of the younger children and for the next six years had charge of the large family.

Through her mother's relatives, the Lasseters, she met her future husband George Alfred Lloyd Jnr, son of George Alfred Lloyd, New South Wales merchant and politician. After their marriage at the Wesleyan Chapel, Glenorchy, on 6 September 1866 George Lloyd gained experience on the land on runs held by the Lasseter family in the Liverpool Plains area near Gunnedah. He then took over a managing partnership in the heavily mortgaged 65 000-acre Terembone run about thirty miles north-west of Coonamble in north-western New South Wales.[8]

After a journey of some weeks over the Blue Mountains and up through Mudgee to Coonamble Jessie arrived at a bare, primitive dwelling set in the midst of vast plains stretching to the horizon. Supplies came in only once a year and when they ran out their diet consisted of birds, emu eggs, kangaroo meat and wild duck. Her journey to this isolated homestead on Teridgerie Creek and her life there were to provide the ingredients for her stories and articles.

During the drought years Jessie Lloyd wrote partly as an outlet for her creative talents and perhaps to blot out her dispiriting surroundings, but also to earn some desperately needed money. In the custom of the day (very few women writers used their own names) she chose the pseudonym 'Silverleaf', inspired by the leaves of the myall trees which take on a silver appearance when seen against the rays of the sun. When she had finished her first novel *The Wheel of Life. A domestic story of bush experience in Australia*, she took it to Sydney to a representative of publisher George Robertson, and a few weeks later heard the manuscript had been accepted for publication. A reviewer in the *Echo* wrote:

> The tale is not in any way tedious, for no attempt at fine writing is made; and, although the moral is a good one, the book is not of the goody-goody character too often found among colonial authors. The heroine is introduced to the reader in the first chapter, and her fortunes are followed with interest through girlhood until she meets her fate in the person of a handsome, sunburnt young squatter; while the record of her married life, the troubles that beset the young couple in their early years of matrimony, and their successful outcome in the end, form a very interesting chapter of Australian life.[9]

The story was close to the story of her own life. By the time this review appeared another of her stories, 'All aboard. A tale for Christmas', had been published in the Sydney evening paper, the *Echo*. Written in the form of a series of travellers' tales, the first episode appeared on 13 December 1879 and

FATHER CHRISTMAS IN AUSTRALIA.

One of Jessie Lloyd's articles in her 'Silverleaf Papers' series, entitled 'Christmas in the bush' appeared in the Illustrated Sydney News *on 23 December 1882. The issue contained many Christmas stories and had an extraordinary cover depicting Father Christmas mounted on a kangaroo with handmaidens riding sidesaddle on emus. (Illustrated Sydney News 23 December 1882. National Library of Australia)*

the last on 27 December, the series concluding with 'Jack's Revenge' and 'The Young Mother's Story'.

In January 1881 Jessie Lloyd's series of articles on bush life called 'The Silverleaf Papers' began appearing regularly in the *Illustrated Sydney News*. In her essay-style articles she sometimes wrote on domestic subjects, such as 'Town and Country Housekeeping' but more usually on wider aspects of country life such as 'New Chums', 'Squatters versus selectors', 'Black sheep', 'Aborigines of New South Wales' and 'Thoughts on Land Legislation'.

About mid-1883 Jessie Lloyd turned from the writing of articles to

"*RETRIBUTION,*" By *SILVERLEAF.*
Author of "*The Wheel of Life,*" "*All Aboard,*" &c., &c.
Author's rights Reserved.

"*RETRIBUTION,*" By *SILVERLEAF.*
Author of "*The Wheel of Life,*" "*All Aboard,*" &c., &c.
Author's rights Reserved.

Serials were very popular with readers of Australian newspapers and periodicals in the second half of the nineteenth century. At the height of their popularity some periodicals ran three or four serial stories simultaneously, each instalment appearing with an illustration to increase interest. These drawings illustrated Jessie Lloyd's Retribution, *which ran for fifty-seven chapters for a year beginning in June 1884 in the* Illustrated Sydney News. *The illustration on the left for Chapter 15 is captioned 'Norah had grown into a charming young woman' and the illustration on the right for Chapter 41 is captioned 'But I see I am shocking you with my worldly sentiments; you have been brought up with different notions'. (*Illustrated Sydney News *26 August 1884 and 14 February 1885)*

another novel. Called *Retribution*, it was never published in book form but ran for fifty-seven chapters for a year from 7 June 1884 in the *Illustrated Sydney News*. In it she used Melbourne during and after the gold-rush and Tasmania as settings for a rather melodramatic story. The paper described it as 'a powerfully conceived and vigorously worked out story of Australian life and character'.[10] She died at the age of forty-two at her home at Terembone on 30 July 1885 after what was described as 'a long and painful illness'. At the time of her death she had completed four chapters of a new book, 'On Turbulent Waters'. The *Illustrated Sydney News* wrote in an obituary:

> Mrs Lloyd was a graphic and graceful writer, possessing the faculty of presenting her characters in a clear and unmistakable light, and capable of commanding the love, the respect, or the detestation, she intended the reader to feel, at the touch of her pen, which in this respect appeared

to partake of the mysterious quality of the fabled wand of the magician. The tone of her novels is always high and moral, and the aspiration of her heroes and heroines always lofty. There can be no doubt that in a few years Mrs Lloyd would have taken the highest rank among writers of fiction in the guild of literature, as she already occupied a good position in the first flight of Australian writers.[11]

Jessie Lloyd was buried on Terembone station where her grave remains, surrounded by a simple fence. At a memorial service Rev. G. T. Geer of Coonamble said she had '. . . a view that throws a halo of romance and beauty about life in the bush . . . such a philosophy has not been without influence in bringing refinement and comfort and home life into the back-blocks of the bush'.[12]

Following his wife's death George Lloyd left Terembone with their children and soon after lost the station following foreclosure of the mortgage. Much of what was then Terembone station is now included in the Pilliga State Forest. Jessie's eldest son, Walter, worked as a journalist in Western Australia where he was editor and co-owner of several newspapers including the Perth *Daily News*.

K. Langloh Parker

'With endless patience she set herself to win the confidence and affection of the tribes about her.'
Lone Hand 2 December 1912

K. Langloh Parker (later Catherine Stow) wrote the first sympathetic and substantial account of Aboriginal legends and culture available to white Australians. At the time other writers were portraying Aborigines as barely human or as humorous characters of low intelligence. Where others observed without understanding, K. Langloh Parker listened to and recorded the legends of the Noongahburrah tribe whose language she learned while living in the far north of New South Wales.

Catherine (Katie) Eliza Somerville Field was born in May 1856 to parents who were members of early pioneering families in South Australia. When she was a young child the family moved to a huge station, Marra, on the west side of the Darling River beyond Wilcannia. While there two of the Fields' three young daughters drowned while swimming in the Darling, Catherine, the only survivor, being saved by an Aboriginal nursemaid. She was educated by her mother, an unusually well educated woman who had been brought up in a family where she learned to read the New Testament in Hebrew and the Old Testament in Greek.[13]

At Marra Catherine Field grew up accustomed to life on an outback station and this was to be her way of life after her marriage. From a photograph of her, taken in later life, she appears a determined and proud woman of strong character, perhaps indicating that at eighteen she was sufficiently mature to handle the entry into her life of Langloh Parker, a man nearly twice her age, a larger than life character, well known among Melbourne and Sydney society as a dashing, charming and extravagant squatter. His ride of 320 miles in twenty-four hours with seven changes of horses through outback New South Wales had become a legend. Born in Tasmania, the son of a British Army officer, he had as a young man worked on his uncle's huge outback stations.[14] So great was his reputation that he appeared as a character under the name of 'Lal Parklands' in Rolf Boldrewood's A Colonial Reformer, serialised in the Town and Country Journal.[15] The serial, a satirical outback story about Ernest Neuchamp (New-chum) (another character was Geoffrey Hasbene) began on 1 July 1876, the character of Parklands appearing in Chapter XIV:

> He was well known to have explored a very large proportion of the Australian continent, to have formed, managed, bought, or sold, at least a score of cattle and sheep stations. His transactions comprised incidentally thousands of cattle and tens of thousands of sheep. He had recently returned from another colony where he had acquired an immense area of newly discovered country . . .
>
> Lal Parklands was popular. A good-looking, pleasant fellow, went in for everything — billiards, loo, racquets, dinners, theatres and balls, with the same zest, energy and enjoyment which he threw into all his business operations.

Another character commented that if Mr Neuchamp 'takes Mr. Parklands as his model in speculation, management, and conversation, he must succeed in everything he undertakes'.[16]

Catherine Field and Langloh Parker were married in 1875 and spent the first few years of their marriage visiting squatter friends and enjoying society events in Melbourne and Sydney. Four years after their marriage Langloh Parker took over Bangate, a station of over 200 000 acres in the Goodooga, Angledool district near the Queensland border. Although the purchase was financed by enormous loans from the cattle king, James Tyson, and Dalgetys, in good years the Parkers made money and enjoyed the life of the squattocracy. Catherine Parker, however, was not a typical squatter's wife. With her experiences with Aborigines as a child at Marra she rose above the prejudices of the time to develop a rapport with the Aborigines employed on Bangate station. She wrote in The Euahlayi Tribe:

> . . . if they [the Aboriginals] know you well, and know you are really interested, then they tell you the stories as they would tell them to one

At a time when Aborigines were being portrayed with little understanding, if not with hostility, K. Langloh Parker recorded and published the legends of the tribes living near her station home, Bangate near Lightning Ridge in the far north of New South Wales. Her books of Aboriginal legends were the first substantial account of Aboriginal legends and culture available to white Australians. (Lone Hand 2 December 1912)

another, giving them a new life and adding considerably to their poetical expression.[17]

Her appreciation of Aborigines was unusual at the time, although she adopted the offensive terms then standard, referring to them as 'blacks', 'darkies' and 'gins'. One story she wrote for the *Sydney Mail* was called 'My darkie friends'.[18] Nevertheless over the years she earned their trust and gathered and recorded their legends. In a series on 'Representative Women of Australia' in the *Lone Hand* 'Ann Cornstalk' said:

> She brought to her task affection and comprehension, and she found in the people who have been crudely dismissed as 'the lowest on earth', poetic feeling, religious conception and a definite social ethic. With endless patience she set herself to win the confidence and affection of the tribes about her . . .[19]

In 1896 the first edition of *Australian Legendary Tales. Folk-lore of the Noongahburrahs as told to the Piccaninnies* was published in London under the name of Mrs K. Langloh Parker. She apparently chose to use her husband's Christian name Langloh as well as Parker, because it was highly recognisable. The book was dedicated to Peter Hippi, King of the Noongahburrahs. In the preface dated 24 June 1895 she wrote:

> A neighbour of mine exclaimed, when I mentioned that I proposed

making a small collection of the folk-lore legends of the tribe of blacks I knew so well living on this station, 'But have the blacks any legends?' — thus showing that people may live in a country and yet know little of the aboriginal inhabitants; and though there are probably many who do know these particular legends, yet I think that this is the first attempt that has been made to collect the tales of any particular tribe, and publish them alone.[20]

The introduction was written by Andrew Lang, writer on myths and a pioneer in anthropology, whose brother Dr W. H. Lang of Corowa, New South Wales obtained the illustrations by an Aboriginal artist, known as Tommy Macrae. In 1897 a second edition was issued and in 1898 *More Legendary Tales* was published.

It is not known whether Catherine Parker received much return for the books but by this time some income from writing may have been welcome. Following the disastrous drought and the depression of the early 1890s, James Tyson foreclosed on their mortgage and although Langloh Parker stayed on for some time as manager, they were forced by weight of debts to leave Bangate in 1901. In Sydney Catherine Parker continued writing. In addition to her books of Aboriginal legends, she wrote tales and sketches for the *Lone Hand*, the *Bulletin* and other weeklies. She also wrote a delightful story for the *Emu*, the periodical of the Ornithologists Union, entitled 'My tame wild birds'.[21]

With his life as a squatter over, Langloh Parker died in Sydney in 1903, a broken man.[22] His wife, then forty-seven, travelled abroad, sending articles on her impressions of England back to the *Pastoralists Review*. During her travels she met Percy Randolph Stow, a lawyer from a well-known Adelaide family. They were married in London on 7 November 1905,[23] and returning to Australia settled at Glenelg. Catherine Stow, still using the name of K. Langloh Parker, published a factual book, *The Euahlayi Tribe*, in 1905 and two more books of Aboriginal legends, *The Walkabouts of Wur-run-ah* in Adelaide in 1918 and *Woggheeguy* in Adelaide in 1930, both based on material collected at Bangate.

When *A Book of South Australia — women in the first hundred years* was published in the South Australian centenary year (1936) two of K. Langloh Parker's Aboriginal legends were included. In later life Catherine Stow was prominent in Adelaide society but did little writing.[24] She died in Adelaide on 26 March 1940 at the age of eighty-three. In 1953 some of her Aboriginal stories were selected and edited by H. Drake Brockman and illustrated by Elizabeth Durack. In the next twenty years there were many reprints, an indication of the enduring attraction of the tales and legends.

Laura Palmer-Archer, who wrote under the name of 'Bushwoman', was born in Melbourne but spent her life after her marriage in outback Queensland. There she wrote stories of bush life for the Town and Country Journal *and the* Australasian. *Her first volume of stories,* Racing in the Never-Never, *was published in 1899 and a second,* A bush honeymoon, *in 1904. (National Library of Australia)*

Laura Maude Palmer-Archer

Laura Maude Palmer-Archer was born in Melbourne in 1864, a daughter of Hugh O'Ferrall and his wife formerly Mary Brophy, both from County Limerick, Ireland. Her maternal grandfather was one of Melbourne's pioneer pressmen. In 1888 in Melbourne she married Tasmanian Tom Palmer-Archer and they moved to Queensland where her husband took over a station which, from the setting of some of her stories, appears to have been near the Warrego River in the south-west of the state. Later, perhaps after failing financially during the depression of the 1890s, her husband became stock and station agent for New Zealand Loan and Mercantile Agency at Hughenden, 236 miles south-west of Townsville. The property on which Laura Palmer-Archer lived and outback life in general were the settings for her stories written under the pseudonym of 'Bushwoman' and published in the *Town and Country Journal* and the *Australasian*. Based on the dramas and conventions of bush life, her stories were entertaining, sentimental tales similar to many written by male writers for the *Bulletin*.

In 1899 a collection of her stories, *Racing in the Never-Never* was published and in 1904 another collection entitled *A bush honeymoon and other stories* appeared. In the foreword Rolf Boldrewood (T. A. Browne) said '. . . work of such genuine merit should find a permanent place in literature'.[25] He vouched for the accuracy of the 'dialect'—the portrayal of the speech of Aboriginals, children's talk and the slang of the woolshed and the stockyard. Literary critic Catherine Hay Thomson in an article in *Cassell's Magazine* commented that 'The "accuracy" has sometimes been termed photographic; rather from the artistic selection of essentials, the result is the living effect presented by an outline picture on a Greek vase'.[26] Of particular interest is the glossary she added at the end of the book to explain Australian bush terms to English readers.

Laura Palmer-Archer died in 1929. Her younger sister Nancy O'Ferrall, who wrote under the name of 'Bohemienne', had stories published in the *Australasian, Lone Hand* and other periodicals. Her brother Ernest O'Ferrall wrote humorous stories of city life for the *Bulletin* under the pseudonym 'Kodak' and had several volumes of stories published.

Barbara Baynton

'[Bush Studies] *ranks with the masterpieces of literary realism in any language.*'
Bulletin 4 February 1903

Barbara Baynton wrote at the time when the 'bush legend' was enjoying popularity through the *Bulletin* school of writing, but when she escaped, at the age of thirty, from the bush in which she had been born, she revealed it as grim and hostile, a cruel place peopled by warped men and pathetic women. She wrote little but her stories once read are not easily forgotten. They have a power absent from the writing of other Australian women writers of the century.

Barbara Baynton was born in 1857 at Scone, New South Wales, youngest daughter of John Lawrence, a carpenter and his wife formerly Elizabeth Ewart, who had arrived in Australia in 1840 from Londonderry, Ireland. By 1866 the Lawrences had moved to the district around Murrurundi where Barbara was educated either at home or at small local schools. Despite her family's comparatively poor background she read Dickens and the Russian authors as a child and was sufficiently well educated to get a position as a governess with the Frater family at Merrylong Park, south of Quirindi. In 1880 she married a son of the family, Alexander Frater jnr, a selector. The following year they moved to the Coonamble district (in the district where

Barbara Baynton, a woman of strong character and commanding presence, was born in the bush. Although she left her life in the country behind for ever at the age of thirty, it provided the grim and hostile setting for her short stories. Her writing has a forcefulness not found in other Australian women writers of the century. (H. B. Gullett, Griffith, ACT)

Barbara Baynton, who married three times, did most of her writing during her marriage to her second husband, Dr Thomas Baynton, a Sydney surgeon. In later life she was a successful investor on the stock exchange and increased her wealth buying and selling antiques. She was also a collector of jewellery and when she died in Melbourne in 1929 had an unrivalled collection of black opals. Her third marriage to Lord Headley lasted only a short time. (H. B. Gullet, Griffith, ACT)

139

Jessie Lloyd was writing her 'Silverleaf' articles) where they had two sons and a daughter. Seven years after their marriage Frater left Barbara for their servant, Sarah Glover, his cousin, and Barbara took her children to Sydney.[27]

Little is known of how she survived and kept her children during the next three years. One of her money-making ventures was to run a hat shop[28] and she is also believed to have sold Bibles door-to-door. Somehow she met a seventy-year-old widower, Thomas Baynton, a well-to-do retired surgeon with literary and cultural interests. In March 1890, on the day after she gained a divorce, she married Thomas Baynton and moved into social and cultural circles quite different from those she had previously experienced. She had already had some poems published under a pseudonym in the *Bulletin* and, financially secure after her marriage, she began writing short stories, verse and articles, most of them based on her experiences and observations of life in the bush. Her first story written under her own name (later added to and published in her collected book of stories as 'The chosen vessel') was published in the *Bulletin* in December 1896. Short poems followed: 'A noon, an eve, a night' in 1897 and a few others at intervals to 1902. A. G. Stephens, editor of the *Bulletin* became a close friend who advised her on writing and revised her manuscripts.

After failing to find a publisher for her collection of six short stories, Barbara Baynton visited London in 1902 where after many rejections, *Bush studies* was accepted by Duckworth and Co. A review in the *Bulletin's* Red Page said:

> The book contains only half-a-dozen sketches; and four of them are in all essentials perfect as far as they go. This is uncompromising commendation; but *Bush Studies* deserves uncompromising commendation. So precise, so complete, with such insight into detail and such force of statement, it ranks with the masterpieces of literary realism in any language.[29]

In 1903 Barbara Baynton returned to Sydney where her husband died the following year. Unconventionally for a woman at the time, she began investing on the stock exchange, particularly in the Law Book Co. of Australasia Ltd, of which she later became chairman of directors. She became friendly with many of the leading figures of Sydney society and gained a secure social position. She wrote a few articles for the *Sydney Morning Herald* on women's issues, one, for example, on the 'Indignity of domestic service', but she was far from a feminist. Of the popularity of factory work over domestic service she wrote:

> No hated caps, or other 'I serve' insignia, and, above all, that paramount privilege, men as masters.
> This may sound disloyal to my sex, yet, it is a common truth; show me a woman in power and I will show you a despot. Indeed, in my anti-

suffrage canvass in London, my surest and most successful weapon for anti-votes was to just ask shopgirls, "Would you rather have a woman over you than a man?".[30]

An astute businesswoman, she bought and sold antiques and collected jewellery, her collection when she died included an unrivalled collection of black opals.[31] She lived alternately in Sydney and London where she became a literary celebrity. In 1907 her only novel, *Human Toll* was published. Like her short stories it is based on her experiences in her early life in the bush and appears to contain some autobiographical material. It has been criticised for faults in construction and in the development of plot and character and is not regarded as being nearly so successful as her short stories. A. G. Stephens wrote:

> Nebulous and unfocussed, the characters drift in and out of the scenes; they come, they pass, leaving us vainly guessing, striving to picture them, to clothe them with actuality. Yet the disjointed scenes are vivid and rememberable . . .
> The book is really a collection of detached scenes, the life of a bush-orphan in a sinister setting. *Human Toll* bears the impress of an autobiography, loosely held together by a plot of hidden treasure that is lost sight of long before the end of the book.[32]

The book ends with the heroine fleeing with a child she has taken from a mother about to murder it. She becomes lost in the bush, the child dies in her arms and, still carrying the child's body she gradually goes mad with thirst. At the end she imagines she sees in the shape of the bark hanging from a gumtree the figure of Christ crucified.

Barbara Baynton was in England during World War I, in which her sons were severely wounded serving with the British Army, and kept open house for both Australian and British soldiers. It was at that time that *Bush studies* was reissued with the inclusion of two new stories under the title *Cobbers*. In Australia in 1920 she said in an interview that she was writing a novel to be called 'Wet Paint' in which 'the bush, Sydney society and London scenes' would appear.[33] This was never published and unfortunately much of her manuscript material has been lost, including a collection of stories she wrote for her grandchildren.[34] She returned to Sydney in 1920 to sell her property there, intending to settle in Australia the following year, but in London in 1921 she married Lord Headley, president of the Society of Engineers and of the Muslim Society. The marriage lasted only a short time and she returned to Australia to live, dying at her home at Toorak in 1929 without publishing any further work.

9

Renown, Mostly Abroad

'. . . [she] takes with her a substantial part of the slight literary
achievement accredited to Australia.'
Bookfellow 1 May 1912

The three women writers regarded as the best to emerge in Australia in the
period almost to the end of the nineteenth century were Ada Cambridge,
Jessie Couvreur and Rosa Praed. Ada Cambridge, born in England, arrived in
Australia as a young married woman and although she ended in accepting
Australia as her home wrote from an Anglo-Australian viewpoint. Jessie
Couvreur, born in England of Dutch and Anglo-French parents, spent her
childhood and young married life in Australia but, although she set her novels
in Australia, achieved fame after she had returned to Europe to live. Rosa
Praed was born in Australia but left as a young woman and although she used
her Australian experiences in her writing, she achieved her success as a writer
in the literary world of London.

Other creative women writers were prominent in the latter part of the
nineteenth century. The reputations of most of those who shone at the time
have become dimmed through their limited talent and changes in reading
taste, although one, Catherine Martin, is more highly regarded now than
when her work was first published. The works of some of these women writers
were included in two anthologies which give an interesting glimpse of the
standard of writing at the time, even if allowance is made for the fact that
they were compiled in England and drew heavily on expatriate writers.

Ada Cambridge

'Hers was a passionate spirit thwarted, a strong voice silenced . . .'
Bookfellow 1 May 1912

Towards the end of the 1870s Ada Cambridge was becoming known as a
writer of quality serials. She was a much more polished and competent writer

Ada Cambridge arrived in Melbourne with her husband, Rev. George Cross, in 1870 and spent over forty years as a parson's wife in the parishes to which he was posted, first in Victorian country towns and then at Williamstown, a suburb on the west of Port Phillip Bay. In need of extra money 'to buy nice things' for her babies she began writing novels, the first, Up the Murray, *being serialised in the* Australasian *in 1875. She was the author of over twenty novels, three volumes of poetry and two autobiographical works. (National Library of Australia)*

with a greater range of ability to portray character and situation than her predecessors. She was also a good poet; there is nothing in her novels to equal the haunting rhythm or the unconventional thoughts of the best of her poetry. With her twenty novels, three volumes of poetry and two autobiographical works, she was the first woman writer of fiction in Australia to reach a status of renown.

Ada Cambridge was born in Norfolk in 1844, daughter of a gentleman farmer, Henry Cambridge, and his wife Thomasina, a doctor's daughter. She grew up in a cultured, comfortable and devoutly religious home and at the age of twenty-one published two religious works — *Hymns on the Litany* and *Two Surplices. A Tale.* At twenty-five she married George Frederick Cross, an Anglican curate who had decided to serve in the colonies, and they left almost immediately for Australia, arriving in Melbourne in August 1870. Over the next forty years they lived in the Victorian country towns to which Rev. Cross was posted — first as curate to Wangaratta, then to his own parishes at Yackandandah, Ballan, Coleraine, Bendigo, Beechworth and finally in 1893 to Williamstown, a Melbourne suburb on the west side of Port Phillip Bay. Ada Cambridge's life was very much that of the country parson's wife. She was involved in the affairs of the parish from bazaars and church teas to conducting Sunday school, playing the organ and training the choir, and also in dealing with the arguments and social pretensions of small town life. She had the usual chores of a home where there was little money to pay for help — cooking, sewing and looking after her children, even helping her husband make their own furniture in their first parish. The Anglican Bishop of Melbourne, Bishop Perry, agreed with her that the strain on parsons' wives was 'literally killing'.[1] The demands on her stamina were great, particularly as

143

her health was not good and there was 'always a new baby in every house'. Two, at least, of her children died in early childhood.[2]

In 1873 she began writing, she wrote, 'to add something to the family resources when they threatened to give out'[3]; 'I think I wrote most of my books to buy nice things for my babies'.[4] In December 1874, with her first Australian novel partly written, she wrote from the parsonage at Ballan to the editor of the *Australasian* offering two chapters of a serial 'to be one of Australian life' with a promise to complete the work as required. She said that magazine editors in England had accepted her stories without seeing them and she asked for an agreement that she was to be paid 'at a fixed rate per number, with regard to the merit of my story' before any of the material had been printed[5] — an indication both of her need for money and her confidence in her writing. The reply was favourable and she promised to finish the work in the stipulated time. Her first novel, *Up the Murray*, was published in the *Australasian* in 1875, the first of many to be published in that periodical in the next fifteen years. It had qualities above the usual run of serials and it excited curiosity about its unknown author. When she became known as the author, Ada Cambridge found her writing gained her acceptance into the congenial and exclusive social circle of pre-gold-rush wealth — 'a small inter-related, highly exclusive circle of about half a dozen families, who had had time and the means to read, travel, and generally sustain the traditions of refinement to which they were born'.[6] She was probably the first woman in Australia to attain upward social mobility through writing. Her writing also, combined with ill health, enabled her to escape to some extent from the pervasive demands of parish work.

Although the financial rewards were small, she persevered, turning out nine serials for the *Australasian* in the next twelve years, and had another, *A Little minx*, serialised in the *Sydney Mail*. Six of her serials, including *Up the Murray*, were never published in book form. The rest were published in London where her fourth novel, *A Marked Man* (1890), was her first financial success. When it was first published under its original title of 'A black sheep' Ada Cambridge received the considerable sum of £197 for the serial rights but, as she remarked, that was in the boom of the 1880s. She was to receive much less for subsequent serials.

Parts at least of all her novels were set in Australia but the characters were usually English and the world she wrote about was that of Anglo-Australians. At the time it was remarked that her novels contained little more than superficial descriptions of Australian life. A contemporary critic Desmond Byrne said of *A Marriage Ceremony* (1894), after its main female character had arrived in Melbourne in 1893 with its bank crashes and depression:

> Here, it might be supposed, was an opportunity for one or two vivid and instructive sketches of the sensational period that witnessed the proof of

so much folly and its punishment, and wrought so many more effects on all classes of Australian society than could be noted on the common records of the time. But the great crisis is almost ignored in the novel.[7]

Even the very successful *The Three Miss Kings* (serialised in 1882 and published in 1891) and *A Mere Chance* (serialised in 1880 and published in 1882) although set partly in Melbourne, tell little of city life in Australia. Strangely Ada Cambridge wrote effectively of the 'Marvellous Melbourne' of the boom years of the 1880s and of the city during the collapse in the 1890s in her autobiographical *Thirty Years in Australia*.

Another contemporary critic writing in the *Melbourne Review* about *A Mere Chance* commented on what are recognised as the strengths of Ada Cambridge's writing:

> There are not many novels of the season which can be considered its equal. It contains a reasonable yet interesting plot. The people are all natural, and such as we meet every day; yet they are·neither conventional nor commonplace. The leading characteristic of the authoress is quiet good sense, but there is also a keen insight into character, a considerable power of literary expression, and the power of making a very ordinary, and by no means improbable, story highly interesting.[8]

Apart from her novels, Ada Cambridge's poetry was highly regarded. In her later poetry she expressed unconventional views, and *Unspoken Thoughts* published in London in 1887 was withdrawn from sale, although most of the poems were published in a later volume. It contained some explicitly sexual references to an unhappy marriage. In 'A Wife's Protest' she wrote:

> I lay me down upon my bed,
>   A prisoner on the rack . . .
>
> What creeping terrors chill my blood
>   As each black night draws on.

She prays that 'he may die' and 'O Nature give no child to me'.[9] There is no indication that she was referring to her own marriage, which appears to have been reasonably happy, but the expression of such sentiments by a clergyman's wife must have appeared surprising and shocking in the 1890s.

After she had retired to England at the age of sixty-seven the *Bookfellow* said she took a 'substantial part of the slight literary achievement accredited to Australia':

> Ada Cambridge had the writer's instinct; she had ideas to express and the faculty to express them. In the field of family fiction her original talent did not develop: all her life she was limited by environment, her true mind never found a full utterance. Hers was a passionate spirit thwarted, a strong voice silenced — with her consent, yet unwillingly.

She remained a rebel behind the bars her own hands had fixed in place. That poignant autobiography *Thirty Years in Australia*, gives some clue to the striving and sorrow of a life that, with many acknowledged blessings, never was adjusted to her ideal. And now a gentle, frail, white-haired lady goes sadly from the land that has been her home for forty years, to bury her dreams in the land of her birth.[10]

Ada Cambridge and her husband lived in England for five years until his death in 1917, after which she returned to Melbourne where her two surviving children lived. In her later years she contributed articles to Australian papers and up to a year or two before her death was a regular contributor to the American *Atlantic Monthly*. She was president of the Women Writers' Club and second life member of the Melbourne Lyceum Club for women. Her autobiographical work, *Thirty years in Australia* remains an affecting account of the life of an interesting woman. Just before her death her reminiscences were published in *Women's World*.

Towards the end of her life, crippled and partly paralysed by a stroke, she found herself 'by a series of accidents and misfortunes... destitute in the money sense', a humiliating situation for a woman who had earned money for herself and her children nearly all her adult life. She had been corresponding with George Robertson of Angus and Robertson since 1920, when she had tried unsuccessfully to interest him in publishing a book of short stories (he paid her £10 for the manuscript without rights of publication), and, reluctant to accept help from her son, a Collins Street medical specialist, she offered to sell Robertson the rights to all her books. He sent her £100 for the rights, although he does not seem to have had any intention of republishing any.[11] The gesture gave her spirits a wonderful lift and enabled her to pay for assistance and continue living in a boarding house for semi-invalids rather than enter a hospital. She died a few years later, in 1926. By the time she died her works had faded, to a great extent, from popular memory but were recalled in an obituary in the *Argus*:

She was one of the few Australian novelists who have made a permanent name in literature, and apart from her literary gifts, her personality had endeared her to a wide circle of friends.[12]

The London *Times* commented first on her poetry:

... [her poems] showed an intense sensitiveness and sympathy with suffering, added to the sturdy courage that comes to many who have lost their hold on revealed religion ... But it is as a novelist that she will be chiefly remembered, and here her achievement was curiously unequal. Her best stories were 'A Marked Man' and 'Not All in Vain'.[13]

Her fame as a novelist did not outlive her. Ironically with the renewed interest in what women were writing in nineteenth century Australia, Ada

Cambridge's 1880 novel A Marked Man has been issued in a new edition as part of a series in which Rosa Praed and Catherine Martin have also been republished. It is intended that other 'forgotten' women writers will be included in the series in due course.[14]

Jessie Catherine Couvreur ('Tasma')

'. . . the Australian novelist par excellence . . . has found a congenial
resting-place in Brussels.'
Illustrated Sydney News 25 April 1891

Jessie Catherine Couvreur was an unlikely person to spend her youth in the very uncosmopolitan Hobart of the nineteenth century, yet she perpetuated her association with Tasmania by adopting the pseudonym 'Tasma' in honour of the place where she had spent her childhood and youth. She was born in Highgate, London, on 28 October 1848, the second child and eldest daughter of James Alfred Huybers, one of a long line of merchants and mariners from Antwerp. His wife, formerly Charlotte Ogleby, was of English and French descent.

In 1852 the Huybers migrated to Hobart where James Huybers estab-lished a warehousing and merchant's business that was at one time the largest in Tasmania. The family lived comfortably in a large residence in Hobart and at a suburban summer house on a spur of Mt Knocklofty at the foot of Mount Wellington. The children were educated by their mother who had been brought up on strict pre-Victorian lines to be an austere person, and was regarded as eccentric. She gave her children a cultural, literary and artistic education.[15] According to her brother Edward Huybers, the chronicler of the family, Jessie grew up a person of consummate charm. From the best-known illustration of her, dressed in clothes vaguely reminiscent of a fortune teller or gypsy, she seems to have had a theatrical streak. She began to write early and as a girl of sixteen had a verse accepted by the *Australian Journal* entitled *Lines Addressed by a Mother to Her Idiot Son*.

At the age of eighteen Jessie Huybers married into a distinguished family. Her husband was Charles Forbes Fraser, son of Major James Fraser, who was a family friend and Usher of the Black Rod in the Tasmanian Parliament. His uncle was Sir James Agnew, later Premier of Tasmania. They went to live at the Victorian country town of Kyneton where Charles was employed in the flourmilling business of his brother-in-law, William Degraves. Later he took up a property near Malmsbury and became the first stipendiary steward and a judge of the Victorian Racing Club. These were not activities of interest to his wife and she was to depict characters having her husband's supposed anti-

147

Author and journalist Jessie Couvreur used the pseudonym of 'Tasma', a name which commemorated her childhood and youth spent in Tasmania. After the failure of an unhappy marriage to a Victorian farmer she became a freelance journalist and lecturer in Europe. Later she married Belgian journalist and former politician M. Auguste Couvreur and lived in Brussels where she wrote some very popular novels, beginning with Uncle Piper of Piper's Hill. After her husband's death she took over his prestigious position as Brussels correspondent for the London Times. (National Library of Australia)

intellectual, gambling, horseracing style of life, as well as his affairs with other women, in some partly autobiographical novels. The breakdown of their marriage began in these years. The faults were probably not all on Fraser's side; Jessie wrote in her journal 'I am not born with a wife's instincts, I fancy'.[16]

From time to time she returned to her parents in Hobart and in 1873, leaving her husband in Victoria, she went with her mother and several of her brothers and sisters to England and Europe, where she spent nearly three years visiting art galleries, and attending concerts and theatres. Following the collapse of her father's business, the family returned to Australia in 1875 and Jessie resumed her marriage with Charles Fraser, but their relationship deteriorated further. With her interest in a wide range of issues stimulated by her visit to Europe, Jessie began contributing stories and articles to Australian publications, including the *Vagabond Annual* 1877, *Australian Ladies' Annual* 1878 and the *Australasian*. She had an article published in the *Melbourne Review* advocating cremation, an 'advanced' social topic of the time.

Following a complete break with her husband, she returned to Europe in 1879. Receiving little of the financial support he had promised, she supported herself by writing and lecturing. An article she wrote for the *Nouvelle Revue* advocating European migration to the Tasmanian fruit-growing areas attracted the attention of the French Geographical Society and she was invited to speak to the Society. This address was a great success and she became an acclaimed public speaker, lecturing on Australia in the chief cities and towns of France, Belgium and Italy. Halls were crowded wherever she spoke. The French Government conferred on her the decoration of *Officier de l'Academie*, the Bordeaux Geographical Society presented her with a specially struck silver medal and the King of the Belgians received her in private audience to discuss schemes for improving communication between Belgium and Australia. On a personal level while visiting Venice she met M. Auguste Couvreur, a well-known Belgian statesman, who was later to become her second husband.[17]

In 1883 she returned briefly to Australia to begin divorce proceedings from Charles Fraser, and the marriage, which was childless, was dissolved on 13 December 1883 on the grounds of his adultery and desertion.[18] While in Australia she wrote for the *Australasian*. The following year on returning to England as a journalist to report on the international Health Exhibition being held in London, she again met M. Couvreur, who was president of the Belgian section of the Exhibition. They were married in London in August 1885. Couvreur had been a Liberal Member of the Belgian Parliament from 1864–84, was a prominent freetrader and friend of John Bright and Richard Cobden, and was for many years political editor of the *L'Indépendence Belge*.

The marriage relieved Jessie Couvreur of the pressing need to make money to keep herself and gave her the opportunity to expand her writing beyond articles, literary criticism and short stories into novel-writing. Settled in Brussels where her husband was correspondent for the London *Times* she made their home a centre of intellectual and political life. Her first novel *Uncle Piper of Piper's Hill*, was a story of middle-class society in colonial Melbourne. It appeared at first as a serial in the *Australian Journal* as *The Pipers of Piper's Hill* from 7 January to 12 May 1888. When it was published in London in 1889 under the pseudonym 'Tasma' it was an immediate success and went through three editions before January 1890. The London *Times* said:

> The human interest and reality of the characters were extraordinary, and presented for the first time to English readers the social side of Australian life . . . Mme Couvreur possessed remarkable insight into character and, like many persons who enjoy that gift, she delighted in studying children. They played a great part in her stories . . . [*Uncle Piper of Piper's Hill* was] the best novel she ever wrote.[19]

Her brother thought her work should have left 'a more lasting record'. The *Spectator* described it as 'only the third work of fiction possessing remarkable merit that has come to us from the Antipodes'. (The others were Marcus Clarke's *For the Term of His Natural Life* and Rolf Boldrewood's *Robbery Under Arms*.) In the *World* it was praised as 'a valuable example of that excellent gift of humour so rare in women'.[20] A stream of novels followed this success, most partly autobiographical, depicting aspects of her first marriage. They included a story of girlhood *In her Earliest Youth* (1890), the largely autobiographical *The Penance of Portia James* (1891), which appeared as a serial in the *World*, *Not Counting the Cost* (1895), and *A Fiery Ordeal* (1897).

In Brussels Jessie Couvreur through her husband's position entered diplomatic circles and with him travelled the continent. She kept up-to-date with all the intellectual preoccupations of the time such as agnosticism, physiognomy and phrenology, mentioning them in her novels. The Couvreurs lived in a beautiful house in the Chaussée de Vleurgat where their way of life was described in an article published in the *Illustrated Sydney News* in 1891. They worked at their writing at each end of a table in a long, narrow room which traversed the house from the road in front to the garden at the back. Panels of rare medieval glass decorated the centre of the windows which were darkened by leaded panes and the broad leaves of the birthwort growing outside. A black bookcase lined half of one wall. Jessie Couvreur was described as:

> . . . a beautiful woman, still 'in her earliest youth,' with dark hair and eyes, a clear Spanish complexion, and a singularly intelligent forehead. This is 'Tasma,' the Australian novelist *par excellence*, who, like Charles Lever and Charlotte Bronte before her, has found a congenial resting-place in Brussels.[21]

After her husband died in 1894 she took over his position as Brussels correspondent for the London *Times*, an unusual post for a woman at the time. Her journalistic work was praised by the *Times*:

> ... most conscientious and painstaking, and at the same time keenly alive to all political, intellectual, and social movements likely to interest her readers. Though she had, like her husband, strong liberal convictions of the Belgian type, she showed judgment and moderation in her comments on the conduct of other parties — virtues which are not common in a country where political passions run exceptionally high.[22]

Two of her despatches to the London *Times* published on 20 May 1895 give an example of the scope of her work. One, dated Brussels 18 May, headed 'Belgium and the Congo State' described a meeting of the special commission of the Belgian parliament set up to examine the treaty between Belgium and the Congo. The second, dated Brussels 19 May, explained a complicated clash between rival political groups, the Clerical and Liberal Societies, which had organised demonstrations on the same day. Both were signed 'Our Correspondent'. Similar despatches continued until her death.[23]

Jessie Couvreur died in Brussels in 1897 from heart disease, just before her forty-ninth birthday, after an illness of only two days.

Rosa Caroline Campbell Praed

> *'Write that again and you will be famous.'*
> George Meredith 1884

Rosa Praed was the first native-born Australian woman writer to gain international recognition. Although born in Australia she spent only the first twenty-five years of her life in her homeland. Rosa Caroline Murray-Prior was born on 27 March 1851 at a property near Maroon, on the Logan River in south-east Queensland, daughter of Thomas Lodge Murray-Prior, a well-known station owner, member of Parliament and Minister in the Queensland Government. Until the age of seven she was brought up on stations in the Burnett River district, from which the family moved following the massacre by Aborigines of the Fraser family at Hornet Bank station and the retaliatory massacre of Aborigines by whites. She lived then at Maroon and was sent to school in Brisbane where she associated with squatting families and observed politics through her father's involvement. She returned home to a life of ease and amused herself by editing the *Maroon Magazine*, a handwritten production to which she tried unsuccessfully to get Brunton Stephens, then a tutor on a nearby station, to contribute a manuscript later published as *Convict Once*.[24]

In 1872, at the age of twenty-one, she married Arthur Campbell Mackworth Praed, son of a London banker and nephew of the poet Winthrop

Mackworth Praed. Their ᴇarly married life was spent in very isolated circumstances on a cattle station on Curtis Island, off Gladstone on the Queensland coast. Rosa was to use the solitude and monotony of this life in her first book *An Australian Heroine* (1880), and also in *The Romance of a Station* (1889) and *Sister Sorrow* (1916). After four years on Curtis Island the Praeds left Australia in 1876 to live in England. Rosa was then twenty-five and had written nothing that had been published, but she arrived in London with an adventurous life in the bush behind her and this was to provide her with settings and action for her books which were new and fresh to English readers. She was unlike almost all other Australian writers in not using periodicals and newspapers as publication outlets. When her writing career began there were publishers on hand, London being the centre of publishing in the English language, and she did not need to use this form of publication. Being well-to-do she also did not need to maximise her earnings.

After she had written her first manuscript Rosa Praed was fortunate to meet the novelist George Meredith, then reader for Chapman and Hall, who advised and encouraged her. When he saw the draft of her first novel *An Australian Heroine* he said 'Write that again and you will be famous'. She rewrote the draft not once but three times. The book went into one edition after another and, as he had prophesied, made her famous.[25]

Young, talented and well known after the success of her first book she was welcomed into the literary society of the day. In 1884, after she had published several novels, she met the Irish politician and writer Justin McCarthy, the leader of the anti-Parnellites in the House of Commons, and the following year began a literary collaboration with him. The books they wrote together, including *The Right Honourable* and *The Ladies' Gallery*, were set in England and Europe, but after McCarthy's death she reverted to Australian settings with *My Australian Girlhood*, *Lady Bridget of the Never-Never Land* and *Sister Sorrow*.[26] In all she wrote about forty novels, about half with Australian themes and nearly all of them bestsellers in England and America. An account of her work published in 1938 drew attention to one aspect of her writing:

> She wrote exclusively, too, from the feminine viewpoint; male characters almost invariably seem to be introduced only for the sake of, and entirely as affecting, the heroine. And these heroines are mostly women of the 'seventies and their stories are chronicles of sentiment.[27]

After separating from her husband (who died in 1901), Rosa Praed lived with her friend Nancy Harward for 28 years from 1899. By this time she had a great interest in the occult and believed Nancy Harward to be the reincarnation of a Roman slave girl, a theory she explained in *Nyria*, which caused a sensation when published in 1904.

In her life she experienced deep personal tragedies. Her three sons died

For the first four years of her married life, Queensland-born Rosa Campbell Praed lived in harsh conditions on an isolated cattle station on Curtis Island off the coast from Gladstone, Queensland. She used this and her earlier experiences as the daughter of a Queensland government minister and station owner in many of the books she wrote after she left Australia at the age of twenty-five to live in London. There she was encouraged to write by English novelist George Meredith. (National Library of Australia)

violently — one in a car accident, another gored by a rhinoceros and the third committed suicide. Her daughter, the only child to survive her, had been born deaf and died in a mental asylum. After Rosa Praed's death on 10 April 1935 at Torquay at the age of eighty-four the *Sydney Morning Herald* said in an obituary:

> It is difficult at present to assess the value of Mrs. Campbell Praed's English work. She wrote of her time and she wrote well, and a future generation may re-read her books. Her Australian books come into another category. They give vivid pictures of phases of Australian life which are over and done with. The value of well-written truthful pictures of a life which is past and gone is historical, as well as literary . . .[28]

Catherine Martin

Catherine Martin's work was first published in the 1870s and while she did not achieve the fame of Ada Cambridge, Jessie Couvreur and Rosa Praed there is now more interest in her work than when it was first published.

Catherine Martin was born on the Isle of Skye, Hebrides, in Scotland about 1845, the seventh child of Samuel Mackay, a poor Highlands crofter and his wife Janet. The family migrated to South Australia in 1855 and with other Scottish Highland families settled at Robe and later Naracoorte in the south-east. She seems to have gained her education from her father who taught children on the voyage out to Australia but somehow she also acquired a love of German language and literature. In her early twenties she contributed poems and translations of German poetry to the *Border Watch* and while living at Mount Gambier in 1874 published *The explorers and other poems* under the initials 'M.C.'. About half the book comprised a 132 page poem on the Burke and Wills expedition and the rest comprised a miscellany of poems, including 'By the Blue Lake of Mount Gambier' and a group of poems translated from German and other European languages. *The Explorers* opens with the departure of the Burke and Wills expedition from Melbourne in 1860 for the first staging point where, gathered around the camp fire, the members of the party tell a series of tales. The main story of the expedition is then recounted in parts.[29]

Catherine Martin moved to Adelaide about 1875 and tried to make a living in journalism. Catherine Spence, who in her *Autobiography* gives some of the little information available about Catherine Martin, describes meeting her at the inauguration of Adelaide University:

> ... I at first thought her the daughter of a wealthy squatter of the south-east, but when I found she was a litterateur trying to make a living by her pen, bringing out a serial tale, 'Bohemian Born,' and writing occasional articles, I drew to her at once. So long as the serial tale lasted she could hold her own; but no one can make a living at occasional articles in Australia, and she became a clerk in the Education Office, but still cultivated literature in her leisure hours. She has published two novels 'An Australian Girl' and 'The Silent Sea' — which so good a judge as F. W. H. Myers pronounced to be on the highest level ever reached in Australian fiction, and in that opinion I heartily concur. I take a very humble second place beside her ...[30]

As Catherine Spence knew from her own experience, it was impossible for a woman to earn a living by casual journalism. In 1877 Catherine Mackay joined the Education Department as a clerk but, because she was a woman, did not gain a permanent appointment, and was dismissed in 1885. On 4 March 1882 she had married Frederick Martin, an accountant who shared her interest in literature, and they lived for a time near Waukaringa where her husband worked.

The serial mentioned by Catherine Spence, 'Bohemian Born', was never published in book form. Catherine Martin's first published novel was *An Australian Girl* which appeared anonymously in London in 1890. It attracted attention at the time but was later criticised as a bluestocking romance and largely ignored. Catherine Spence wrote 'Except for my friend, Mrs. Mackay

(Mrs. F. Martin) I know no Australian novelist of genius'[31] but Miles Franklin described *An Australian Girl* as a:

> . . . trying rigmarole about a girl who does not know what to do with herself or her lovers — Ted Ritchie, the rich, crude, squatter with £15,000 a year, and a doctor, one of those cultured, idle creatures who filled the role of hero in the era of practising gentlemen. There is literary conversation and worrying about religion, but praise be! the girl, Stella Courtland, never had a day's illness. This was a great advance when the frown of a lover could reduce a thoroughbred maiden to lying on a couch with the megrims, while her social inferiors had to produce and rear half a dozen children on a pound a week plus odds and ends of provisions and any old clothes handed to them.[32]

Considering Catherine Martin's poor family background it is ironic that her heroine should be derided for being so upper class and that on first meeting her Catherine Spence mistakenly thought her to be a rich squatter's daughter. It suggests that Catherine Martin had acquired not only a cosmopolitan education but an insight into the lives of people of other classes and was of an appearance that belied her origins.

An Australian Girl, in which the action moves from the Mallee to Berlin, fell into obscurity and was out of print for many years. It is now regarded highly for its treatment of wider themes than the conventional novels of the time, dealing as it does with religion, scepticism about marriage, the quest for happiness, social issues and philosophy.[33] Catherine Martin published another novel *The silent sea. A novel* under the pseudonym 'Mrs. Alick Macleod' in London and New York in 1892. In the early 1890s she and her husband travelled in Europe. As a result of the trip she wrote *The Old Roof Tree. Letters of Ishbel to her half-brother Mark Latimer*, a book written in the form of letters mainly from London and a provincial English city, describing from a socialist point of view the writer's horror at the social inequalities and suffering of English life. In a dedication to her mother she wrote of 'the strange chaos of misery that underlies Britain's social system'.[34] The final part of the book includes similar letters from Amsterdam and Zwolle in Holland, the Lower Rhine, Bonn and Venice.

Catherine Martin and her husband returned several times to England and Europe in the early 1900s. The couple had no children and Frederick Martin died in Adelaide in 1907. Some years later, in 1923, Catherine Martin published, under her own name, *The Incredible Journey*, a book written from an Aboriginal woman's point of view about a desert journey to recover her son taken by a white man. She died on 15 March 1937 at Unley Park at the age of eighty-eight, being described on her death certificate as a journalist,[35] a reminder of the efforts she had made to earn a living as a journalist sixty years before.

Coo-ee, Harriette Anne Martin, Kathleen Caffyn, Margaret Thomas

'A rather curious feature of the volume is the amusing way in which it evidences many of the peculiar characteristics of the "woman writer" . . .'

Sydney Morning Herald 23 May 1891

Anthologies of the works of women writers are of interest in indicating the popularity of writers at a particular time. Two Australian anthologies were published in London in the 1890s, the contributions being selected by editors living there, so expatriate writers figure largely. Probably also the circle of friends of the editors may have been over-represented. One of the anthologies, *Coo-ee* was entirely an anthology of women's writing, the other, *By creek and gully*, included male and female authors.

Coo-ee: Tales of Australian Life by Australian Ladies, published in London in 1891, was edited by Harriette Anne Martin. Born in Queensland, the daughter of Dr John Moore Cookesley, she became Harriette Bullen on her first marriage. After being widowed she married Australian writer Arthur Patchett Martin in London in 1886. Patchett, with Henry Gyles Turner, had started the *Melbourne Review* in 1876 and was prominent in Bohemian circles in Melbourne as a wit, writer, poet and theatregoer. In 1883 he left Australia after being involved as co-respondent in a divorce case and became a journalist in London writing for the *Pall Mall Gazette*.

Harriette Anne Martin edited three anthologies: *Under the Gum Tree* in 1890, which included contributions from men and women including Rosa Praed; *Volcanic Gold and Other Tales* to which Victor Daley was one of the contributors, and *Coo-ee*. The title *Coo-ee* gave the collection an obviously Australian expatriate flavour. The contributors included some well-known women writers, but there were also some who have disappeared without trace. Those well known included 'Tasma' who wrote 'An Old-Time Episode in Tasmania', a melodramatic but very readable tale of convict times; Mrs Mannington Caffyn ('Iota') who contributed 'Victims of Circe', an involved love story set on a Victorian station; and Rosa Praed who wrote 'The Bunyip'. Other writers included Mrs Henry Day, Mrs Lance Rawson, Margaret Thomas and the editor, who contributed a two-part story. The *Sydney Morning Herald* described it as an 'agreeable little book':

> . . . by far the two best [stories] in style and matter are 'Victims of Circe' and 'An Old-time Episode in Tasmania'. The others are more or less amateurish and conventional. A rather curious feature of the volume is

the amusing way in which it evidences many of the peculiar
characteristics of the 'woman writer,' especially of stories. Thus we read
here of 'a person out on the prowl,' 'a large fat man in a greasy coat, with
big, dazed leather eyes,' and a church 'looking rather proud and high-
stomachy' . . .

In some of the stories the men talk like girls in tearful drawing-room
comedies . . .

There is, as a rule, a good deal of sameness and poverty of invention
about Australian stories, and this volume is not an exception. 'Tasma's'
story, however, is a little gem of its kind, and it can hardly be said that
the volume as a whole is dull — any more so, that is, than this kind of
set volume usually is.[36]

One of the two writers singled out in this review, Kathleen Caffyn, was the
author of the novel *The Yellow Aster*, a great success in its day but now
forgotten. She was born Kathleen Hunt in Co. Tipperary, Ireland in 1853,
the daughter of William de Vere Hunt. After being educated by English and
German governesses she moved to London where she trained as a nurse and
in 1879 married Dr Stephen Mannington Caffyn. They arrived in New South
Wales in 1880 where Dr Caffyn worked as a government medical officer in
Sydney and Wollongong, before moving to Melbourne in 1883 where they
became public figures in the literary and medical worlds. They returned to
London to live in 1892 and Dr Caffyn died four years later.[37]

Kathleen Caffyn wrote *The Yellow Aster* while living in Australia.
Published in London in 1894 under the pseudonym 'Iota', it went into four
editions and was feted as the 'book of the day'.[38] The *Australasian* said it was
written in the style 'affected by the advanced literary women of the time', and
Australian journalist, Mrs Hirst Alexander said it was 'classed among the
"New Woman" books of the day'.[39] Following the success of her first book in
the next twenty years she wrote sixteen others on romantic and sexual
themes, several of which achieved great popularity. When one of her novels,
The Fire-Seeker, the story of a girl's first encounter with the world, appeared,
the *Bookfellow* said 'The interest is sustained page by page and sentence by
sentence'.[40]

Another contributor to *Coo-ee*, Margaret Thomas, was better known as
an artist and sculptor than as an author. Born in Croydon, Surrey, England in
1843 she was brought by her parents to Melbourne at the age of nine. She
became the first woman to study sculpture in Victoria and when she returned
to England had several of her portraits exhibited at famous galleries. At the
same time she wrote poetry which was published in English, American and
Australian periodicals, including the *Australasian*. Seven of her poems
appeared in Douglas Sladen's *Australian Poets, 1788–1888* published in
London in 1888.

157

By creek and gully, Mary Lucy (Lala) Fisher

The second anthology, *By creek and gully,* sub-titled 'Stories and sketches mostly of bush life told in prose and rhyme by Australian writers in England', published in London in 1899, was edited by Lala Fisher. She dedicated it to her uncle, W. Knox D'Arcy, one of the founders and a director of the rich Mount Morgan gold mine, south of Rockhampton. A millionaire, he was then living at Stanmore Hall, a mansion in Middlesex. Mary Lucy (Lala) Fisher, born in Rockhampton, Queensland in 1872, daughter of a surveyor, Archibald Richardson and his wife formerly Lucy Knox D'Arcy, was by the age of fifteen contributing to the local press. In 1893 she married at Rockhampton English-born Francis Fisher, her father's assistant. In the middle of 1897 the family left with their two sons for England where Lala, an attractive, independent woman, gained some fame as a writer, poet, lecturer and long-distance swimmer. They remained in England for four years during which she published, in 1898, a book of verse *A twilight teaching and other poems* and, in 1899, *By creek and gully.* She became a member of the writers' club and was president for Queensland in the International Congress of Women.[41]

Her poetry was highly regarded. When *A twilight teaching* was published the English *Observer* said:

> Mrs Fisher bids fair to become the poet of Australia. There are passages in her volume which far surpass anything written by Gordon . . .

The *Morning Bulletin* in her home town of Rockhampton said:

> Mrs Fisher is not a great poet, but that she possesses the faculty divine, few who have read her effusions, and know what real poetry means, will deny.[42]

Many of the contributors to *By creek and gully* had been represented a few years before in *Coo-ee.* The most distinguished of the women writers included in the anthology were Mrs Campbell Praed who wrote a sketch 'The old scenes'; Mrs Caffyn ('Iota') who contributed 'Lenchen'; Margaret Thomas who wrote a sketch, 'Struck gold', and a poem of four verses, 'To my cigarette'; and Mrs Patchett Martin who wrote a story and a poem. Lala Fisher included two of her own stories, 'His luck' and 'The sleeping sickness of Lui the Kanaka', and two poems, 'To the story-makers' and 'Heimweh'. The other contributors were male. They included Hon. Pember Reeves, H. B. Marriott Watson, E. W. Hornung, A. Patchett Martin, Hume Nisbet, Oliphant Smeaton, Douglas Sladen, E. S. Rawson, John Elkin, Louis Becke and Frank Richardson.

When she returned to Australia Lala Fisher became involved in radical

While living in London in the 1890s Lala Fisher, an impulsive, talented young woman born and brought up in Rockhampton, published an anthology of Australian writing called By creek and gully *in 1899. Like a previous Australian anthology of Australian women's writing,* Coo-ee, *collected in London in 1891 by Harriette Anne Martin, its contents were of mediocre quality. The best contributions were from Rosa Campbell Praed and Kathleen Caffyn ('Iota'). (National Library of Australia)*

journalism. Separated from her husband, she lived in Queensland, first at Charters Towers, where she wrote for the radical New Eagle, edited by Frank Hill, then at Rockhampton and Brisbane where she wrote for various papers, including the Australian Worker, the Queensland Worker and Steele Rudd's Magazine. Later reunited with her family she moved to Sydney and in 1909 bought the Theatre Magazine, in which Frank Hill became a partner, and she edited the magazine for some years. She published two further books of poetry, Grass Flowering in 1915 and Earth Spiritual in 1918. In her late forties she became mentally ill and she died in 1929.

10

New Women in Print

'. . . there are paths out of most labyrinths, and we will set up
finger posts.'

Dawn 15 May 1888

Louisa Lawson and *Dawn*

When Louisa Lawson's monthly publication *The Dawn. A Journal for Australian Women* began on 15 May 1888 the time was right for a paper that
espoused the views of women who wanted to free themselves from a purely
domestic role. There were those who had begun to work for the vote for
women, others wanted the freedom to work at jobs previously restricted to
men, some believed that before any other reform better education opportunities were needed, some wanted release from unhappy marriages, others
wanted more freedom in dress and in recreation. The *Dawn* took up all these
causes, surviving the great depression of the 1890s to appear for seventeen
years. Written, edited, produced and printed by women it was tangible proof
of what women (mostly one woman) could achieve.

Women's columns and pages of social news published in the daily and
weekly papers were already providing news to women satisfied with the status
quo. Louisa Lawson saw there was a need to present the views of women
working for women's suffrage and for other feminist ideas. Self-reliant,
resourceful and practical, her background had provided her with the experiences that moulded her ideas on the freedom women needed. Half Australia's
women's lives were unhappy, she wrote, but the *Dawn* would set the 'finger
posts' out of 'the labyrinths'.

Louisa Lawson was born in 1848 at Guntawang, a station near Mudgee,
New South Wales, where her father, Henry Albury, was employed as a
stationhand and teamster. Her mother, Harriet, a clergyman's daughter, was a

Louisa Lawson was separated from her husband and had supported herself and her children in Sydney for some years before she started Dawn. A Journal for Australian Women *on 15 May 1888. She was a woman of strong and independent character quite prepared to battle the Typographical Association and overcome any obstacles that stood in the way of the success of her paper.* Dawn *was remarkably effective in fighting for women's rights for seventeen years. (RAHS Journal 1933. National Library of Australia)*

cultured and well educated woman. Louisa was educated at the Mudgee National School and wanted to become a student teacher, but was kept at home to help care for ten younger brothers and sisters. Her mother, no doubt desperate to retain her services in the home, is supposed by one account to have burnt her books.[1]

At eighteen, in 1886 Louisa married Norwegian-born Niels Larsen, known as Peter Lawson, a sailor turned gold-digger. They joined the gold-rush to the Weddin Mountains and later selected forty acres at Eurunderee where their first child, Henry, later famous as the poet and short story writer, was born in 1867. In the next ten years Louisa had four more children. With her husband often away, either at the goldfields or contract building with his father-in-law, she took in sewing, sold dairy produce and fattened cattle to make money. Her life provided a model for the hard-working, resourceful and long-suffering bushwomen who appeared in some of her son's stories.

After seventeen years of marriage Louisa Lawson separated from her husband, moving with her children to Sydney where for a time she conducted a boarding house in Phillip Street and took in sewing and washing. She had begun writing while still living in the bush. A poem she wrote commemorating the loss of an infant daughter, Annette, entitled 'My Nettie' had been published in the *Mudgee Independent* in February 1878 and this led to more writing. In 1887, with her son Henry becoming well known as a poet, she bought a small news-sheet, the *Republican*, which she and Henry edited. However this was only a tryout for a much bigger venture, the publication of *Dawn*.

In the first issue of the *Dawn* she outlined the aims of the paper. Initially, bowing to convention, she used a pseudonym — 'Dora Falconer' — discarding it some years later for her own name. She wrote:

Every eccentricity of belief, and every variety of bias in mankind allies itself with a printing-machine, and gets its singularities bruited about in type, but where is the printing-ink champion of mankind's better half? There has hitherto been no trumpet through which the concerted voice of womankind could publish their grievances and their opinions. Men legislate on divorce, on hours of labor, and many another question intimately affecting women, but neither ask nor know the wishes of those whose lives and happiness are most concerned. Many a tale might be told by women, and many a useful hint given, even to the omniscient male, which would materially strengthen and guide the hands of law-makers and benefactors aspiring to be just and generous to weak and unrepresented womankind.

Here then is DAWN, the Australian Woman's Journal and mouthpiece — phonograph to wind out audibly the whispers, pleadings and demands of the sisterhood.

Here we will give publicity to women's wrongs, will fight their battles, assist to repair what evils we can, and give advice to the best of

THE DAWN.

A Journal for Australian Women.

EDITED BY DORA FALCONER

VOL I. No. 1.   SYDNEY, MAY 15, 188¿.   PRICE, 3D.

About Ourselves.

"WOMAN is not uncompleted man, but diverse." says Tennyson, and being diverse why should she not have her journal in which her divergent hopes, aims, and opinions may have representation. Every eccentricity of belief, and every variety of bias in mankind allies itself with a printing-machine, and gets its singularities bruited about in type, but where is the printing-ink champion of mankind's better half? There has hitherto been no trumpet through which the concentrated voice of womankind could publish their grievances and their opinions. Men legislate on divorce, on hours of labor, and many another question intimately affecting women, but neither ask nor know the wishes of those whose lives and happiness are most concerned. Many a tale might be told by women, and many a useful hint given, even to the omniscient male, which would materially strengthen and guide the hands of law-makers and benefactors aspiring to be just and generous to weak and unrepresented womankind.

Here then is DAWN, the Australian Woman's Journal and mouthpiece—

In the first issue of Dawn *Louisa Lawson stridently proclaimed the aims of the paper as the mouthpiece for Australian women. The fact that a woman of such independent character still felt it necessary to use a pseudonym ('Dora Falconer') indicates how widespread this practice was in nineteenth century newspapers and magazines.* (Dawn 15 May 1888) our ability.

Half of Australia's women lives are unhappy, but there are paths out
of most labyrinths, and we will set up finger-posts. . . . This most potent
constituency we seek to represent, and for their suffrages we sue.[2]

A second editorial, prompted by the defeat of the Divorce Extension Bill,
argued for divorce reform. 'There are few questions so important', she wrote,
'since full half the sorrows of women arise from marriages, foolishly made, or
from nuptual ties which being made cry out for severence'.

Louisa Lawson was a pragmatic woman out to make the *Dawn* a success,
so in addition to polemics there were also general articles in later issues, on
more practical topics than in the first, which included where to buy good
original works of art and the use of artificial flowers for decoration. There was
also a useful offer to secure accommodation in Sydney for new arrivals and
country families, a short story and poetry and many stories of women's
successes, including one about a girl reporter employed on the *Denver
Republican* in America. Four pages of advertisements, some of them full page,
gave the publication a healthy appearance. Throughout the *Dawn's* existence
Louisa Lawson was to be very successful in soliciting support from advertisers.

The production of the paper was a saga in itself. Years later Louisa
Lawson described how she got a printing machine and some type and with her
female employees started to print a paper:

> How did we learn to set type and lock up formes? Goodness knows! Just
> worked at it till we puzzled it out! And how the men used to come and
> patronise us, and try to get something out of us! I remember one day a
> man from the CHRISTIAN WORLD came round to borrow a block — a
> picture. I wouldn't lend it to him; I said we had paid a pound for it, and
> couldn't afford to go and buy blocks for other papers. Then he stood by
> the stone and sneered at the girls locking up the formes. We were just
> going to press, and you know how locking up isn't always an easy matter
> — particularly for new chums like we were.
>
>   Well, he stood there and said nasty things, and poor Miss Greig —
> she's my forewoman — and the girls, they got as white as chalk; the tears
> were in their eyes. I asked him three times to go, and he wouldn't, so I
> took a watering pot full of water that we had for sweeping the floor, and I
> let him have it.[3]

Two weeks after founding the *Dawn* she decided that there was nothing
peculiarly masculine about the skill involved in typesetting so she sacked her
two male employees and employed girls for this work also.

By the first anniversary issue Louisa Lawson was able to report its great
success:

> . . . THE DAWN is the pioneer paper of its kind in Australia, being
> edited, printed, and published by women, in the interest of women. It

has been looked upon, by many, as an uncertain venture, and we have frequently been asked, by subscribers and advertisers, the question, 'Will it live?' to all such we have but one reply. THE DAWN has been a success from its first issue, while a glance at our subscriber's [sic] list convinces the most skeptical.[4]

She expressed the hope that during the next year of the *Dawn's* existence Australian women would join in working for the 'elevation of women'.

By the second year the *Dawn* was employing ten women, full- and part-time, either producing the journal or in the job printing side of the business. This was a challenge to an entrenched field of male employment and provoked a boycott by the New South Wales Typographical Association. This was not, as Louisa Lawson pointed out, because her staff were undercutting male rates but because the typographers objected to competition from women in a previously all-male field. The Typographical Association, which refused membership to women, tried to force her to dismiss her printers. It appealed to advertisers to boycott the *Dawn*, attempted to get the Post Office to prevent the paper being sent through the mails and harassed the women at work. Louisa Lawson countered with a proclamation of her support for trade unionism and called on her readers to combat the boycott by supporting the *Dawn's* advertisers.[5] All this provided the *Dawn* with great copy. There were full reports when a *Dawn* reporter was excluded forcibly from a meeting held to organise a Tailoresses' Union and when Louisa and her staff were heckled in the streets near their George Street office.[6]

The typographers put their case in the daily press, contending that the printing trade was unhealthy, caused tuberculosis and was unfit work for women. Louisa replied by interviewing the General Manager of the *Sydney Morning Herald*, Mr Cook, the Superintendent of the Government Printing Office, Mr Chapman, and the Manager of the *Town and Country Journal* and the *Evening News*. She reported that Mr Cook considered typesetting 'when confined to reasonable hours and carried out under proper sanitary conditions "as healthy as agriculture", and he could not understand on what grounds the contrary was asserted'. After inspecting 200 men at work at the Government Printing Office she wrote that she did not 'notice any signs of emaciation or slow decay on the men, nor was there apparent the universal coughing and blood-spitting which the romanticists of the Typographical Association would lead the outsider to anticipate'.[7] The boycott was not withdrawn until about nine years later but it does not appear to have impeded *Dawn*.

The July 1889 issue reported the inauguration of the 'Dawn Club' described as a social reform club for women, at a meeting called by Louisa Lawson at which she read a paper on women's suffrage. The club's aims included working for women's suffrage but also:

To gather together a nucleus of those women who, having themselves

A JOURNAL FOR AUSTRALIAN WOMEN.

Edited by DORA FALCONER.

[REGISTERED AS A NEWSPAPER.

FOR TRANSMISSION ·····]

VOL. 2: No. 6.   SYDNEY, OCTOBER 5, 1889   PRICE 3D.

BOYCOTTING THE DAWN.

ASSOCIATED labour seems to be in its own small way just as selfish and dictatorial as associated capital. The strength which comes of union has made labour strong enough, not only to demand its rights but strong enough also to bully what seems weak enough to quietly suffer under petty tyranny.

We have a notable example of this in the boycott which the Typographical Society has proclaimed against *The Dawn*. The compositors have abandoned the old just grounds on which their Union is established, viz: the linking together of workers for the protection of labour, they have confessed themselves by this act an association merely for the protection of the interests of its own members.

The Dawn office gives whole or partial employment to about ten women, working either on this journal or in the printing business, and the fact that women are earning an honest living in a business hitherto monopolised by men, is the reason why the Typographical Association, and all the affiliated societies it can influence, have resolved to boycott *The Dawn.*

They have not said to the women "we object to your working because women usually accept low wages and so injure the cause of labour everywhere," they simply object on selfish grounds to the competition of women at all.

Now we distinctly assert that we do not employ women because they work more cheaply ; we have no sympathy whatever with those who employ a woman in preference to a man, merely because they think she will do as much work for a lower wage. We will be the first to aid the formation of trades' unions among working women, whether they be compositors, tailors, or any others, so that women who try to earn a living honestly may win as good an income in proportion to the quantity and

quality of their work as men can do. In this object we know we have the sympathy of our readers, and as to the boycott we only need their co-operation to entirely neutralise its effect.

A great many women have written to us at various times wishing to be able to help us and begging to know how. There is now an opportunity to help us, and the woman's cause generally, with pronounced effect, and we can give a comprehensive reply to all our kind well-wishers. The aid can be given by those who have no time to write for us, no time to attend women's meetings, no time for anything but the duties of their own household.

It can be given us in the most powerful form, merely in the course of the necessary expenditure of your weekly income, whether that be large or small.

If it is made clear to your tradesmen that you deal with them because they advertise with us, the boycott is immediately defeated

Subscribers alone never entirely support a newspaper : the expense could not be borne without the profit of advertisements, therefore, of course, the most effective way to injure any publication is to prevent the possibility of advertisement support.

We are told that a Sydney journal on which two women were engaged, was recently interfered with and effectually extinguished in this way. Union men personally visited those who advertised in that journal, and threatened them with a Union boycott if they continued their support. As a consequence the tradesmen withdrew their advertisements, and some news agents who had also been visited, refused to sell the paper, producing of necessity the stoppage of the journal and the bankruptcy of the proprietor.

When Louisa Lawson decided to employ women typographers the all-male Typographical Association placed a boycott on her paper. She fought the ban successfully and her battles provided front page stories for Dawn. (Dawn 5 October 1889) faced the realities of life, in its work, its poverty, its trials, have or hope they have, gained through these things, useful experience which might help others in the same battlefield.[8]

In the same issue she reprinted an article by Frances Gillam Holden entitled 'Women's Work' which had won the Silver Medal at the 1888 Exhibition of Women's Industries.

Articles on the work available to women and new spheres into which they could move were a feature of the *Dawn* throughout its existence. In one editorial entitled 'Wanted; — Women' she argued for women physicians, lawyers, factory inspectors, women prison warders and magistrates.[9] Other articles urged women to be efficient and good housekeepers and mothers. Most issues included advice on the health and care of children, diet and exercise. The fashion pages included practical patterns and urged women to dress sensibly and attractively. Probably the first illustration carried by the *Dawn* (apart from those in advertisements) was a 'ladies' costume' on the fashion page in the 1 May 1893 issue. Almost every issue had news on women's suffrage, including despatches from other states.

The journalists known to have worked on the *Dawn* included Mrs Cooper, who was Queensland correspondent[10], Mrs E. (R. H.) Todd, who contributed to the paper for some years around 1900 when she wrote an article about Louisa Lawson's illness following a fall from a tram,[11] and Louisa's daughter Gertrude Lawson. When the paper was ten years old Louisa Lawson looked back on the enemies that 'cannot hurt us now, we are strong enough to smile at them'. She printed testimonials from her readers, referred to as 'DAWN sisters':

'I would not like to be without THE DAWN, I should fancy I missed someone to come and see me.'
'I hardly know where to find the rent, but I must have THE DAWN.'
'I cannot imagine how anyone once seeing THE DAWN, could refuse to subscribe to it.'[12]

Several wrote that their husbands read the paper from cover to cover. The anniversary was also marked by the adoption of a new cover incorporating an unfortunate combination of typefaces.

In an interview with the *Bulletin's* A. G. Stephens, ironically printed under the heading 'A Poet's Mother', Louisa Lawson expressed her advanced feminist views. Accused of being unkind to weak and helpless women when she spoke stridently to them Mrs Lawson said:

And why shouldn't a woman be tall and strong? I feel sorry for some of the women that come to see me sometimes; they look so weak and helpless — as if they expected me to pick 'em up and pull 'em to pieces

Throughout Dawn's *existence Louisa Lawson was very successful in attracting advertisements. Even the first issue had four pages of advertisements and for the next seventeen years* Dawn *continued to attract good advertising revenue.* (Dawn, 1 July 1890)

and put 'em together again. I try to speak softly to them; but somehow I can't help letting out, and then they go away and say, 'Mrs. Lawson was so unkind to us'.

And whose fault is it but men's? Women are what men make them. Why, a woman can't bear a child without it being received into the hands of a male doctor; it is baptised by a fat old male parson; a girl goes straight through life obeying laws made by men; and if she breaks them, a male magistrate sends her to gaol where a male warder handles her and locks her in her cell at night to see she's all right. If she gets so far as to be hanged, a male hangman puts the rope around her neck; she is buried by a male grave digger; and she goes to Heaven ruled over by a male God or a hell managed by a male devil. Isn't it a wonder men didn't make the devil a woman? . . .

I declare it's the most pitiful thing in the world. When I come sometimes to a meeting of these poor working women — little, dowdy, shabby things all worn down with care and babies — doing their best to bring up a family on the pittance they get from their husband and keep those husbands at home and away from the public-house — when I see their poor lined faces I feel inclined to cry. They suffer so much.

And listen to their talk! so quiet and sensible. If you want real practical wisdom, go to an old washerwoman patching clothes on the Rocks with a black eye, and you'll hear more true philosophy than a Parliament of men will talk in a twelve-month.

No, I don't run down men, but I run down their vanity —

⨯ Fashions. ⨯

THE stylish bodice shown on this page is suitable to be made in any firm material, and may be worn either for home or walking-dress , the lining of the bodice is cut to fasten down the front; the smaller front in pattern is for the material ; the vest is cut without join in front, it is sewn in under the strap of trimming on the right side, and is hooked over with invisible hooks and eyes under the trimming on the left side. Any sleeve may be worn with this bodice, tight to the elbow, with balloon-top, gigot, or the Bedouin sleeves are all suitable. The paper patterns of this stylish bodice and skirt sent for 6d. each.

THE materials appropriate for blouse bodices are various. First in favour are the crêpes, shot silk, surah, trilby and striped velveteens.

Trimmings of ribbon are much affected, and may be disposed in many ways. One exceedingly stylish mode is that of placing two straps of ribbon over the puff of the sleeve, these meeting at the shoulder and elbow, and ending in bows or rosettes. With this may be simply a belt and collar of ribbon or bretelle straps over the shoulders falling loose like the waist. and ending in the band, back, and front.

Another fashion is that of trimming only the lower sleeve with bands encircling the arm, with two bands to match, which may be of ribbon, lace, or other trimming across the bust, set about two inches apart.

Twisted folds of velvet are used to festoon, being finished at the top with rosettes. In making rosettes of material, cut a circular piece and gather the edge, and draw up close and fasten in the centre.

THE zouave jacket effect so popular is often of jet, yellow or heavy lace. Others are of a contrasting material, whilst some are of the dress material, with a fancy trimming.

Some bodices show a trimming at the neck and waist line of two bands of ribbon, either silk, satin, or moiré, finished with rosettes of the same, a little to the left of the front, or directly in front for the belt, and in the centre front or back for the collar. A narrower width is of course necessary for the neck where two are used.

BUCKLES of gold, silver pearl or jet. are used on collars and belts, the ribbon or material forming a little frill on each side of it. These little frills appear also when no buckles are used, about four to six inches apart, turning from the centre, either in the front or in the back. On collars they are somewhat nearer together.

SOME of the new bonnets are scarcely larger than one's hand. The trimming is the main portion.

A NOVELTY in neckwear is a narrow velvet collar with small bows and very long ends of velvet ribbon from the back of the neck.

ROSETTE bows of silk with very long ribbon ends, finish the belts of many of the new dresses.

A FAVOURITE style of bonnet has the brim made of bias velvet, set on in full plaits large enough to form a background to the face.

Louisa Lawson was pragmatic in including in Dawn *features of wide appeal such as fashion pages. She offered patterns at a moderate price and urged women to dress sensibly and attractively.* (Dawn, 1 June 1896)

The sub-title of Dawn *changed in 1891 from 'A Journal for Australian Women' to 'A Journal for the Household'. Although women's suffrage and women's rights remained the major issues, in later years* Dawn *included more articles on subjects such as gardening and poultrykeeping. Some women readers told Louisa Lawson that their husbands enjoyed reading the paper. (Cover of* Dawn *March 1891)*

especially when they're talking and writing about women. A man editing a ladies' paper! or talking about women's questions in Parliament! I don't know whether to laugh or cry; they know so little about us . . .

Did you ever think what it was to be a woman and have to try to make a living by yourself, with so many men's hands against her. It's all right if she puts herself under the thumb of a man — she's respectable then; but woe betide her if she strikes out for herself and tries to compete with men on what they call 'their own ground'. Who made it their ground?[13]

Louisa Lawson never abandoned her strongly held views but with some battles won and women's suffrage nearly achieved the *Dawn* became less crusading. Its subtitle had changed much earlier to 'A Journal for the Household' and in its later years there were more articles on subjects such as gardening and poultry keeping, along with medical notes, fashions, recipes and a children's page.

On 1 April 1905, in an advertisement which wrongly claimed that the *Dawn* had reached its nineteenth year, the paper appealed for new subscribers, claiming to be 'the only paper . . . printed and published by women, and the only one that has lived and paid its way without outside subsidy',

Dawn ceased in July 1905 soon after its seventeenth anniversary. Although still apparently a viable business, Louisa Lawson, who had had a long illness following a tram accident, and was involved in a complicated legal wrangle with the government, decided she had had enough. The paper had been such an expression of her own individuality that she could find no woman journalist she felt worthy to succeed her (Dawn, May 1905)

Louisa Lawson even on occasion earning money in other ways to 'tide through the bad times'.[14] By then Louisa Lawson had nearly had enough. The end came for the *Dawn* in July 1905 when, weighed down by a lengthy legal case with the government over a device she had invented for closing and securing mail bags, she decided to give up the paper. She wrote:

> Death, madness, and financial ruin have overtaken many connected in this smothered-up case, and Mrs. Lawson's existence has been made almost unendurable, overshadowed as she is by detectives, slanderers, and persecutors of the vilest type. Suffering from a keen sense of injustice, her health is again failing . . . And as she knows none whom she could trust to continue this Journal on the unbiassed and independent lines which has characterised it in the past — the independent woman journalist being almost as scarce as the good man politician — she contemplates ending her paper as she started it, quite upon her own responsibility.[15]

Louisa Lawson lived for another fifteen years, dying in Sydney on 12 August 1920 aged seventy-two. Her success in keeping a radical paper in print for seventeen years had been remarkable. By the time of her death an entirely different era had begun for women's papers.

171

The Australian Woman's Magazine and Domestic Journal and Woman's World: Australian Magazine of Literature and Art

'The Proprietors of this Journal are desirous of presenting to the Women
of Australia a truly representative paper.'
Woman's World May 1886

The *Dawn* was not Australia's first women's magazine. Several others had
been started in the 1880s but their aim was entertainment rather than the
achievement of women's rights. One was the *Australian Woman's Magazine
and Domestic Journal*, published in Melbourne from April 1882 to September
1884. Mainly a vehicle for serials, often having three or four running
simultaneously, it also included a series of colonial sketches, poetry, knitting,
crochet, fancy work patterns, fashion notes, a section on books and music
(including on some occasions the reproduction of a piece of music), recipes
and answers to correspondents. It seems likely its editor was a woman but her
identity is unknown. Most of the writers used pseudonyms, including 'Indi',
'Vera', 'Alfra', 'Alcyone', 'Castalia', 'Chloe' and 'Ruby'. Other frequent
contributors included F. S. Hunter, A. Chesney (author of a novel titled
Mona; or an Australian waif published in 1879), Frances Gillam Holden, one
of the first trained nurses in Sydney, who contributed health articles sometimes under her pen-name 'Australienne', 'E.A.C.' (Mrs Ellen Chads) and
'Icneoral' (Mrs A. E. Clarke). Ellen Augusta Chads appears, from some semi-
autobiographical stories, to have been the wife of an English Army officer
who spent some time stationed in India and other British colonies. After his
retirement they settled in Melbourne where Mrs Chads wrote many stories
based on her experiences as a young person in England and later in overseas
posts. She published several collections of stories — *Tried as Pure Gold, and
other Tales* (1882), *The Snowdrop's Message, and other Tales* (1888) which was
dedicated to the Anglican Bishop of Melbourne, and *Tracked by Bushrangers*
(1891), dedicated to her husband who had died the previous year. At the end
of *Tracked by Bushrangers* there was a section entitled 'Work for the Master', a
series of sermon-type articles expounding ways in which women could lead
morally upright lives. Her novel *Dora's Repentance* was praised in a review for
its 'purity of thought' and the 'cleanliness' of the author's imagination.[16]

The *Australian Woman's Magazine and Domestic Journal* ceased in September 1884 after being sold, although it was stated that it would be produced
in a larger form. A similar magazine, the *Woman's World: Australian Magazine
of Literature and Art*, begun first as a monthly in Melbourne in May 1886 and
continued from July as a weekly, survived until October 1887. The prospectus
claimed that its main aim was to foster 'a literature of our own' and that it

This very genteel version of a ladies' bicycle appeared in an advertisement for John Payne's clothing shop in the Eastern Arcade, Melbourne, in the October 1883 issue of the Australian Woman's Magazine and Domestic Journal. *The caption read 'Ladies can procure Costumes, as above, Ready-made or to order, at Moderate Prices (Making, from 12/6)'. (*Australian Woman's Magazine and Domestic Journal *October 1883)*

would be 'entirely conducted by Women'. It had many of the same contributors as the *Australian Woman's Magazine*, including F. G. Holden whose article, later reproduced as a best-selling pamphlet, 'Woman's Ignorance and the World's Need' appeared in the May 1886 issue (see Chapter 11). It contained many serials aimed at entertainment but included a few more significant items about work being undertaken by women, including a report of the success of a woman journalist in New York[17] and an article on 'Ladies as Reporters' by W. B. Yaldwyn.[18]

Maybanke Susannah Wolstenholme and the *Woman's Voice*

'... *womanly, but not weak; democratic, but not revolutionary* ... '
Woman's Voice *9 August 1894*

In the mid-1890s, at a time when the *Dawn* had lost a little of its crusading spirit and was taking on some aspects of a family magazine, another women's paper, the *Woman's Voice*, dealing with serious feminist issues, was begun in Sydney by Maybanke Susannah Wolstenholme. It was successful for some time but without the widespread support Louisa Lawson gained for the *Dawn* both in numbers of satisfied subscribers and in advertising revenue, the paper

173

*After divorcing her first husband, May-
banke Susannah Wolstenholme, a prominent supporter of women's suffrage and
other women's rights issues, began a feminist periodical in Sydney in 1894. For
some years she had run a very successful
school, Maybanke College, and later in her
life she was a leading worker for free
kindergartens and the provision of playgrounds. In 1899 she married Professor
(Sir) Francis Anderson, professor of philosophy at the University of Sydney. (Lone
Hand 2 February 1914. National Library
of Australia)*

folded after about eighteen months.

Maybanke Susannah was the only daughter of Henry Selfe, a plumber.
She was born at Kingston-on-Thames, near London in 1846 and arrived in
Sydney at the age of nine with her parents and brothers. Her mother was a
woman of strong personality who thought that every girl should be brought up
to earn her own living. Maybanke was educated to become a teacher but
married before she had begun her career. On 3 September 1867 at the age of
twenty-two she married Edmund Kay Wolstenholme, a timber merchant from
West Maitland who later became a successful accountant in Balmain. Late in
the 1870s the Wolstenholmes moved to Dulwich Hill and by 1882 had built a
large home, called Maybanke, set in spacious grounds.[19] The marriage
produced six children but in December 1884 Maybanke was deserted by her
husband who ceased supporting her soon after, and they were divorced in
1892.[20] In 1885 she began a school in her home. Over the next decade
Maybanke College gained a reputation through its modern teaching methods,
the success of its pupils, especially in university examinations, and through
Maybanke Wolstenholme's public activities. Her first public work was as a
founder and later president of the Women's Literary Society. The meetings
were generally devoted to books but on one 'free' evening Mrs Wolstenholme
raised the issue of women's suffrage by drawing members' attention to the
move by women's groups in England for the vote. An indignant member
insisted that such a subject should not be raised and she was supported by a

NEW WOMEN IN PRINT

The
Woman's Voice

EDITOR:
M. S. WOLSTENHOLME,
" *Maybanke*," *Dulwich Hill*.

DEMOCRATIC BUT NOT REVOLUTIONARY.——'
WOMANLY BUT NOT WEAK.——'
'——FEARLESS WITHOUT EFFRONTERY. · · ·
'——LIBERAL WITHOUT LICENSE.

SYDNEY AGENT:
E. B. ROBSON
Woman's Guild, Sydney Arcade.

VOL. I.—No. 1.   THURSDAY, AUGUST 9, 1894.   Two PENCE.

BUSINESS NOTICE.

ANY Person desirous of becoming a subscriber to the WOMAN'S VOICE is requested to send name and address to Miss E. B. Robson Sydney Agent, No. 3 Sydney Arcade. Subscription, 4s. per annum, in advance; postage to neighbouring colonies, 2s. 2d. extra. Subscriptions may be sent in postage stamps, postal note, or P.O. order.

E. B. ROBSON,
Sydney Agent.

EDITOR'S NOTE.

THE COLUMNS of the WOMAN'S VOICE will be open to the free expression of opinion. These opinions will be welcomed, however widely they may differ from our own, because our object is to encourage thought, the great lever of humanity. The paper is published especially in the interests of Women, but it will exclude the opinion of no individual and no class, so long as the subject is treated with moderation and in a spirit of calm inquiry.

INTRODUCTORY.

Another paper! Yes, truly, another paper! But a paper that competes with no other: a paper to express the opinion of the home by the voice of a woman—to deal especially with the subjects that interest thinking women, and to form, so we hope, a slight bond of union among all the women who work for the common good in New South Wales, and perhaps in Australasia. Such a paper is needed. Though our large dailies and weeklies do each in their own way devote some space to women's work, they do not give us all the news we need, or discuss all the questions we think important. Besides the eternal fret and worry, recrimination and deceit of politics, from which many women turn with infinite disgust; besides the reiterated spiral of cabled news and accidents, meetings of companies and creditors, money-making and fraud, which crowds the columns of the news-paper, there are many thoughts, many facts, small, it may be, to tradesman, shopkeeper, or merchant on his daily round of work, but large to the quiet eye that watches in the home. These facts, these thoughts we desire to chronicle and comment on.

Some day, when the women of a future generation shall stand, thanks to the climbing of their foremothers, upon the same level as their brothers, there will be no need for a paper devoted to the woman's cause, for the welfare of the woman

will be one with the welfare of the race, one with the welfare of humanity; and the journals of that bright day will meet the united demands of a higher and purer life. But that time is not yet. Before the dawn of the harvest home there must be the ploughing of the fallow field of mind, there many a seed of love and truth. Women must wake up to wider knowledge of themselves, their work, and their responsibilities; and the women who can see the need of such knowledge must learn to do the work of pioneers, and must endeavor to lead their sisters to a larger life. Some of this work—our little share—we hope in all humility to do.

So long as women are allowed to give to the nation their money in taxes, their help in charity, their energy in citizen-ship, their patriotism, their devotion, and are not allowed to do the simple duty of casting a vote, which every free country offers to its men; so long as women are permitted to do the same work as men for lower wages, and so make the rich man richer and the poor man poorer, and thus benefit neither; so long as it is counted shame for a woman to sell herself—rather than starve—to the man who has grown rich on the profit of her labor, and not shame for the man who buys her, when by his neglect of duty she (heaven help her!) can do no other; so long as women must bear children to die in hundreds in their infancy, or to crowd our gaols and lunatic asylums—larrikins and outcasts—in their riper years; so long as there is need for prisons and reformatories, for maternity wards and foundling hospitals, so long there will be teaching work for thinking women and need for a woman's paper.

But these matters, and the great need for reform in them, though they will be of vital interest to us, will not be per-mitted to monopolize our space. We hope to give our readers some literary news, to keep them informed of new books and papers, and to tell them of what women are doing in education, in art, and in literature, in other countries as well as in our own.

The WOMAN'S VOICE will be womanly, but not weak; democratic, but not revolutionary; fearless without effrontery, liberal without license. It will try to keep pace with the leaders of thought in older countries, and at the same time will open its columns to all those who work for home and humanity near at hand. It will be entirely free from sectarian bias, and will recognise without distinction of class or creed the good work of every organization. It will record the work of women in all the centres of population, and thus encourage sympathy and stimulate energy; and it will, so long as it lives, endeavor to keep its motive pure, its method simple, and its aim the common good.

The front page of the first issue of Maybanke Wolstenholme's Woman's Voice *set out the aims of the periodical. Although not nearly as successful as* Dawn, Woman's Voice *continued for about eighteen months to the end of 1895. The paper dealt with many important feminist issues, including divorce, prostitution and sex education.* (Woman's Voice) large majority. Following this Maybanke Wolstenholme joined with Rose Scott and Margaret Windeyer in forming the Womanhood Suffrage League of New South Wales. She and Rose Scott addressed the first public meeting, 'an ordeal' as she wrote:

> I had never spoken in public before. But I foresaw many years of struggle and much public speaking, and I determined to do without notes, or break down and retire. After that, we spoke at drawing rooms and public meetings wherever we were invited. I did so sometimes two or three times a week.[21]

Maybanke Wolstenholme began her fortnightly women's paper, the *Woman's Voice*, of which she was proprietor and editor, in 1894, to further the cause of women's suffrage. Following Louisa Lawson's example, women were employed to set the type. The Sydney agent was Miss E. B. Robson of the Women's Industrial Guild, and organisation set up to promote and sell women's work to relieve the distress and poverty among women of all classes during the 1890s depression.

Maybanke Wolstenholme set out the aims of the new paper in the first issue, and in an advertisement for the paper indicated that she intended it to be a paper covering the nation — 'Most of the women who take a leading part in Women's Work in all the colonies will contribute to its columns'.[22] The first issue, dated Thursday 9 August 1894, included articles on some of the major concerns of the paper: women's suffrage, women's work and education for women. Mary Sanger Evans of the Women's Cooperative Silk Association wrote on 'Industrial Independence for Women'; Ellen Julia Gould, Matron and superintendent of the training school at Sydney Hospital, on 'Trained Nursing'; and Rose Scott, General Secretary of the Womanhood Suffrage League on 'Thoughts on Woman Suffrage'. There was a report of speeches made at a meeting held in London on 'Women and the Franchise' by Sir John Hall, ex-Premier of New Zealand, where women had won the right to vote, and by Mrs Sheppard, who had been prominent in its achievement. Other items were of the type that would appeal to women interested in feminist issues.

A column entitled 'Chit Chat', which was to continue as a regular feature, contained many items recording successes of women in many fields, for example, in obtaining degrees, taking up bicycling and starting businesses. A small scathing item entitled 'The Woman's Craze for War' criticised the Ladies Volunteer Movement, an organisation recently started in England to train women for war. 'Surely no more foolish work was ever begun by women', *Woman's Voice* said:

> ... every true-hearted woman must turn away in disgust from the spectacle of women drilling, practising the loading of rifles and wielding of swords, in order that they may make children orphans and wives widows.

In a move predating similar techniques in more recent women's struggles, a list of members of the new Legislative Assembly was published, indicating with an asterisk those who had replied affirmatively to questions from the Womanhood Suffrage League.

The first issue also contained a plea for the appointment of police matrons: 'the most glaring example of the absence of women when other women require their presence — viz., in the police stations'. There was a report of a factory to be run on cooperative lines in Christchurch, New Zealand — 'Our sisters there are leading in more ways than one'; an announcement of the imminent arrival of Annie Besant; and an interview with American-born Mrs Anne Lane, wife of William Lane, who had led a group of Australians to the Utopian settlement 'New Australia' in Paraguay in 1893.

The second issue contained an article by Frances G. Holden on cremation which emerged as one of the issues of continuing interest to readers. Frances Holden contributed several health articles to later issues including 'Commonsense about Cancer' and 'Diphtheria Simplified'. There was also the first illustration to be published in Woman's Voice — a photograph of English writer, Sarah Grand, accompanying an article about her in which she was described as 'one of the most valuable recruits which the women's cause has gained in recent years'. This issue also contained a despatch on 'Women in Hobart' by a 'Special Correspondent' and in following issues there were intermittent columns from Hobart, New Zealand, Victoria and South Australia. A regular feature added later was an 'Open Column of Letters to the Editor' which became an important part of the paper.[23]

In issue four, readers were asked to send in names of possible new subscribers and there was an appeal for every woman in a trade or profession to advertise. Well-off buyers were asked to make it known that they spent their money at establishments advertised in Woman's Voice:

> When women stand by women we shall be able to move the world. We do not want to abate one jot, one tittle of our happy confidence in money, so we speak plainly, and ask for the help which in helping us will help the mass.[24]

In issue eight, prostitution was tackled in an article entitled 'Problem of the Streets' by 'Orare' which emphasised the unfairness of punishing of women prostitutes rather than their clients. Further articles on this subject were published at intervals.[25] The following issue also contained a pathetic story written in the first person by a woman forced to drown her illegitimate baby, at first unwanted but then dearly loved, because of attitudes in the place where she lived.[26] In all issues there were editorial comments in a column entitled 'From the Casement'.

At the end of a year's existence, Mrs Wolstenholme reported that financial difficulties were to a great extent conquered but the paper needed to expand:

> There is not, so far as we know, beside ourselves, and our sisters (the DAWN in Sydney, and DAYBREAK, in New Zealand) another woman's reform paper on this side of the equator, and in England the number is very limited.[27]

Despite this sanguine comment about finances the paper must have been in difficulties, although at about this time the number and size of advertisements increased. There were regular advertisements for Butterick's patterns; for an employment agency for governesses and superior servants; for a 'hand' camera for ladies; a hair dye; boots; a woman dentist; Dr Waugh's baking powder; French millinery; Granuma 'the most valuable food on earth'; and lawn tennis racquets. In August regular full page advertisements began for Dr Steinmeyer's Celebrated Elegant Pills—'A boon to stout people'; for Madame Eugene's toilet preparations; and for 'high class' wines, teas and whisky. The 10 August 1895 issue contained approximately seven pages of advertisements, one of which displaced the editorial item from the first to the third page, but the financial difficulties which emerged later suggest that some of these advertisements may have been free or paid for at minimal rates.

Some renowned women authors contributed stories. The 20 April 1895 issue contained a story, 'Mother', written 'expressly' for the *Woman's Voice* by M. Louise Mack and on 7 December 1895 there was a note entitled 'A new book by one of our own women', about *Family at Misrule* by Ethel Turner.

A series on sex education for children begun on 5 October 1895 with 'Shall we tell the children?' was a daring inclusion for the time. The series, which continued with 'Shall we confide in the girls?'[28] and 'Shall we talk to the boys?'[29] later was published in pamphlet form and brought several appreciative letters.

But time was running out for the paper. In the last issue of eight pages published on 21 December 1895, Maybanke Wolstenholme wrote:

> ... the VOICE may have to cease. The reason is simple, and very few words will suffice to tell it. The subscription list is not large enough to pay for its publication, I cannot get advertisements which would help to support it, and I can no longer largely supplement its income. To edit a little paper like this is easy, and the money needed to maintain it is not a large sum, but to work at the first with the writing and correspondence it involves, after one has finished a day's work to earn some of the second, is just now more than I can manage ... For my own labour I never expected to be paid. But eighteen months have passed, and the VOICE income is not yet sufficient to pay for the manual labour involved in its production, and the necessary postage, materials, &c, so I have to choose between lessening expenses somehow, or letting the whole business drop. I am very loath to completely destroy the beginning I have

The promotion of cycling was a women's issue in the 1890s. It was seen as a liberating influence allowing women to travel independently. On 8 April 1895 Woman's Voice had a full page article on 'Cycling for Women', illustrated with a photograph (above) of Mrs Maddock, captain of the Sydney Ladies Bicycle Club, who had ridden a bicycle from Sydney to Melbourne. The Club planned a cycling tour to Wollongong for the Easter holidays. (Woman's Voice 8 April 1895)

made. Australasia surely holds two-thousand women who are in sympathy with the reforms the VOICE demands and who can at the same time afford a penny a week to make their advocacy known. I can not believe that the paper does not fill a vacant niche, and, naturally, I shall be sorry to disappoint the hundreds of subscribers who now write their warm approval. But, at the same time, I can not contract liabilities. If the VOICE must cease, I shall not regret it, but shall conclude that it was born ten years in advance of the times, and I shall lay down my pen with the certain knowledge that the thoughts I have sent out, feeble and imperfect though they be, as they are the expression of living Truth, will do the work Truth always does. They may be shunned as disagreeable, or flouted as vulgar, but they will live when fashion and foolishness are forgotten. And though my feeble woman's voice may cease, I shall know that I have done a little of the rough work of the pioneer, and have made the path a trifle clearer for the women, a crowd of which no man can humble, who, in a few years will follow.

Maybanke Wolstenholme remained a writer and contributor to newspapers and magazines and continued to be active in the suffrage movement. She also became general secretary of the Australian Home Reading Union started by Professor Edward Ellis Morris, Professor of Modern Languages and Literatures at the University of Melbourne. At her school, Maybanke College, she had established a kindergarten section and in 1895, while still editing *Woman's Voice*, the establishment of free kindergartens became another interest. She helped set up the first free kindergarten at Woolloomooloo and continued to work for the establishment of free kindergartens for many years. Through this work she met her future husband, Professor Francis Anderson, Professor of Philosophy at Sydney University, educational reformer and a supporter of the free kindergarten movement. Her later interests included the Playgrounds Association, which she founded; the Citizens Association, which worked to obtain the right for women to be elected to municipal councils; the University Women's Society and the Women's Evening Students Association.[30]

Mrs Maybanke Anderson died in 1927 at the age of eighty-two at St Germaine-en-Laye near Paris while on a holiday visit abroad with her husband.

The Sun: an Australian Illustrated Newspaper for the Home and Society and Happy Homes: A Journal of Pure Literature for the Household

Many other periodicals, most of them short-lived, were published either by and for women, or by men for women in the latter part of the nineteenth century. Some aimed at entertainment, others to promote women's causes.[31]

180

One which went through both phases was the *Sun: An Australian Illustrated Newspaper for the Home and Society*, a weekly published in Melbourne. It began in December 1888 as a society paper run by male owners. From August 1897 to January 1899 it was owned by Henry Hyde Champion, a controversial socialist married to Elsie Goldstein, sister of prominent feminist Vida Goldstein, and he introduced some material on social subjects in which he was interested.

In January 1899 two women writers, prominent in women's organisations in Melbourne, Catherine Hay Thomson and Evelyn Gough, took over the *Sun* from Champion. Catherine Hay Thomson, born in Glasgow, had been educated in Melbourne, matriculating from Melbourne University before women were accepted as university students. She was principal of Queen's College, Ballarat for some time and in 1881 opened a boarding and day school for girls in Spring Street, Melbourne.[32] Later she began writing investigative articles, being referred to in the *Bulletin* in 1886 as 'the female "Vagabond"[33] of Melbourne'. Referring to an article she had written after entering Kew Asylum pretending to be a 'mad woman', the *Bulletin* said it disappointed 'sensation-hunters' as 'She did not find the eyes gouged out of a single lunatic, nor one hip joint "broken into smithereens" '.[34] After disposing of the *Sun* she became a literary agent.[35] In 1909 she was the author of an interesting article on 'Women Writers of Australasia' for *Cassell's Magazine*.[36]

Mrs Evelyn Gough, born in Canada, spent part of her childhood in New Zealand before marrying an Army officer. As a widow in Melbourne in the 1890s she taught elocution, wrote articles and plays (she played the leading part in her own play 'Her Majesty's Yacht Squadron' performed at the Austral Salon in 1896),[37] was prominent in several suffrage organisations and interested in the labour movement. She was a great friend of Alice Henry's. After 1903 she devoted most of her time to the National Council of Women.[38]

Under the ownership of Catherine Hay Thomson and Evelyn Gough the *Sun* continued regular columns on music and art, ran book reviews and a children's page and an occasional health column, but there were more features on social matters. The 12 January 1900 issue contained a feature on the Central Methodist Mission home, expressing sympathy for the 'fallen and friendless women' cared for at the home and in the 3 August 1900 issue there was an article on the work of district nurses. An editorial on 'Housing the Poor' stated: 'The poor ought to be as certain of decent shelter as the rich of the luxurious home'. At the height of the anti-suffrage agitation in 1900 the paper carried hard-hitting editorials attacking anti-suffrage proponents, particularly the *Argus* newspaper and women opposed to women's suffrage. In 1903 the *Sun* was incorporated into *Arena* and the involvement of Catherine Hay Thomson and Evelyn Gough in its publication ceased.

Several other magazines for women were published but were mainly domestic. *Happy Homes: A Journal of Pure Literature for the Household*, a monthly published in Sydney, ran from July 1891 to January 1892, and then continued as *Good Health* for a short time. The first editor and proprietor was Florence Hope, followed by Mrs W. Keep. *Dawn* summed up its aims with a comment on the first issue:

> On its cover it portrays the contented family group whose domestic serenity is to be cultivated and enhanced by the contents of the journal.[39]

Florence Hope, under her married name of Mrs E. P. Wright, was referred to by Louisa Lawson as one of the six women editors in Sydney in 1895. The others were Louisa Lawson, Miss Levvy (sic), Miss [?Mrs] Fotheringhame, Mrs C. Bright and Mrs Wolstenholme.[40] Although referred to by Louisa Lawson as Miss Fotheringhame, this was probably Mrs Fotheringhame, who started her career as the first woman journalist employed by the *Bulletin* and was the founder and editor of *Young Australia*, a magazine for children.[41] Annie (Mrs Charles) Bright was editor of the prestigious monthly magazine *Cosmos* from 1894 to 1896.

Cosmos was aimed at a serious audience, men and women, and included contributions from well-known writers including 'Price Warung', G. B. Barton, Alexander Sutherland, Charles Bright and Frank Mahoney. Its main features were illustrated interviews of political and other prominent figures and articles on a wide range of social topics. These included 'Modern Journalism' in September 1895 and 'The Sydney Hospital and its matron' in December 1895, written by Annie Bright herself. Annie Bright encouraged other women writers to contribute, including Louise Mack, Ethel Turner and 'Iota' (Kathleen Caffyn). Louise Mack's *In an Australian city* ran as a serial and there was also an interview with her by Annie Bright. *Cosmos* continued until 1899 when it was incorporated in *Southern Cross*.

Two other short-lived women's magazines were *Lady's Newsletter: A Journal for Women Only*, published in Melbourne in 1892 and then incorporated in *Table Talk*; and *Woman: A Journal devoted to Women in Art, Fashion, Politics and Literature* published in Sydney in 1892, which began with grandiose ideas of distributing 30 000 copies free per issue as an advertisement but ceased after only six months.[42]

In the early years of the twentieth century *Woman's Sphere*, begun by feminist Vida Goldstein, carried on the cause of women's suffrage until it ceased publication in 1905, the year in which *Dawn* ceased in Sydney.

11

Women's Voices, Very Diverse

'A spokeswoman for millions of her sex.'

US Evening World

Women made their views known in a variety of ways during the ferment of developing feminist ideas in the 1880s and 1890s. Through articles in newspapers and periodicals, through books and public speaking they brought to public notice their divergent views on many issues. Women's suffrage was an issue that brought many together but there were other women who maintained a very conservative view of women's role. Some demonstrated through their lives that a wider non-traditional role in the workforce was available to women with the strength and independence to grasp opportunities. Feminist Alice Henry was not to realise her full potential until she was well over fifty and a leader of women in the United States, but in Australia she was an important pioneer woman journalist. Writer Mary Gaunt, lonely and desolate in London, persevered to become probably the first Australian woman to make a reasonable living from writing books. Other women devoted their lives to spreading messages. Frances Holden, a trained nurse, worked for education, particularly health education, for women; Bessie Lee preached temperance and celibacy; Jennings Carmichael spread the message of compassion for the sick.

Alice Henry

Alice Henry's feminist outlook came from her upbringing. She was born in the inner Melbourne suburb of Richmond in 1857 to Scottish emigrant parents, Charles Henry, an accountant, and his wife Margaret, a seamstress. While Alice was a small child her father lost his job with a cotton importing firm when the American Civil War ruined the cotton trade. He decided to go on the land, taking a block on what is now the site of the Beaconsfield railway station east of Melbourne, but which was then bush on the edge of the Gippsland forests. Alice and her brother were taught by their mother who had a Scottish regard for education. They were well grounded in Hans Christian Andersen's tales and Lamb's *Tales from Shakespeare* but Alice also read boys' adventure books and expected her life to be filled with adventure and travel. Later she wrote in her autobiographical notes:

> ... no sex division, still less sex inferiority, obtruded itself on my mental picture ... the distinctions between qualities and standing between boys and girls were literally unknown to me, though it was in my hearing that my mother remarked upon it, when a visitor offered a ride upon his pony to my little brother and took no notice of me. That was perhaps my first lesson in feminism.[1]

When the family returned to Melbourne after about three years Alice Henry attended a private school run by Mrs John R. Wood in Richmond, but when it was taken over by a temperance advocate who wanted her pupils to sign a total abstinence pledge, she was withdrawn. She later attended public schools and on Saturdays went to literature and French classes run by Florence Williams who was a daughter of the then popular novelist G.P.R. James and who had been a drama critic while living in Europe. Florence Williams was ahead of her time in also giving lessons in sex education. To finish her schooling Alice Henry went to Richard Hale Budd's 'Educational Institute for Girls', one of the first schools for girls to follow the traditional classical teaching of the English public schools for boys. Melbourne University had only recently agreed to females sitting for matriculation, although they were still not accepted as university students, so Alice Henry finished her education with matriculation. She became a pupil teacher at Budd's College and later worked as a private tutor preparing students for matriculation and for civil service examinations.

At about this time she came under the influence of Harriet Elphinstone Dick, an English cross-Channel swimmer who after emigrating to Melbourne taught swimming and gymnastics to women and girls and promoted the cause of physical education for women. Alice Henry wrote: 'She was also a good, though unobtrusive, feminist, and instilled ambition and increased self-respect into the heart of many a girl'.[2]

Alice Henry's first success in journalism did not come until 1884 when, at the age of twenty-seven, she had an article published in the *Australasian* advocating the use of coke as a fuel. As a journalist she did not see herself as a woman writer but as a writer on all topics. However her start was conventional enough, for when she secured a position on the *Australasian*, the

184

Alice Henry (left) and Evelyn Gough (right) at Russell Falls on the slopes of Mt Wellington in 1902. Alice Henry after her work as a pioneer journalist in Melbourne was soon to leave for America where she achieved fame for her work for women and trade unionism. Mrs Evelyn Gough was joint editor and proprietor with Catherine Hay Thomson of a Melbourne periodical, the Sun, from 1899 to 1903. The widow of an Army officer she was prominent in women's suffrage organisations and interested in the labour movement. (National Library of Australia)

weekly country paper associated with the daily *Argus*, she began in what she described as a 'humble' position 'at the bottom of the ladder', reporting society functions and supplying cookery recipes. Using the initiative that was to be a feature of her career, she gave the cookery column a fresh look by submitting American recipes obtained from the wife of an American dentist settled in Melbourne. All her work at this stage was written under the nom de plume, 'Pomona', taken from the name given to stone jars.[3]

At this time few women had succeeded in breaking into journalism, and then usually only as contributors. Alice Henry was almost certainly the first woman journalist in Australia to be taken on to a newspaper staff and trained on the job. She trained under editor David Watterston, a Scotsman who had begun work as a journalist in Queensland and who had reported the Philadelphia Centennial Exposition of 1876 for the *Argus*. A conservative man and a strict disciplinarian, Watterston succeeded Henry Gullett as editor of the *Australasian* in 1885 and remained in the position until 1903. Alice Henry's account of the training she received from him is one of the few records of this aspect of journalism before the advent of the cadet training system:

> My editor's standards of accuracy and of good English were high as well as his sense of balance in arranging news. On little points of journalistic etiquette he expected his staff to be well informed and I owe him much for the training he gave me. But progressive in his opinions he was not. He felt that both the labor movement and the feminist movement should either be ignored or actively opposed.[4]

Alice Henry was an enterprising reporter always on the lookout for unusual stories, but was at times thwarted by Watterston's conservative views. She got around this to some extent by submitting some stories on labour and feminist subjects under the nom de plume of A.L.F. (her brother Alfred's initials). She found 'gentler and more encouraging influences' than Watterston among other staff members — (Sir) Edward Cunningham, *Argus* chief-of-staff, later editor, and Edward Fricker, later editor of the *Australasian*. For the next twenty years she wrote on a wide range of subjects from the sawmill industry to children's courts (her article describing the Juvenile Court set up in Adelaide in 1892 was reprinted in the London *Times*); from an obituary for Mrs Annette Bear-Crawford (a worker for the protection of girls and women's suffrage), to an interview with a visiting German socialist.

The *Argus* was a bitter opponent of women's suffrage so most of Alice Henry's articles on this subject were published in the *Champion* or other outlets, but even after she had severed her full-time connection with the *Argus* it continued to publish her articles on social issues. She wrote several articles on the training of intellectually disabled people, among them 'Brightening the dull', which described the teaching of backward children by Laeta Fishbourne, and 'Teaching the unteachable'. She also wrote about the care of people with epilepsy and was one of the founders of the Talbot Epileptic Colony at Clayton. In March 1898 her eyewitness accounts of the extensive bushfires which raged through Gippsland were published in the *British Australasian*. She made a point of interviewing interesting visitors. When Sidney Webb and his wife toured Australia in 1898 she obtained an interview with Mrs Webb who told her she was going to attend the Melbourne Cup. Alice Henry advised her 'don't be content with sitting in the grandstand. Go down on the flat where all the people are'. Mrs Webb took her advice and later sent a postcard of thanks for the interview and the interesting time she had had on the flat.[5]

Catherine Spence's biographer states that at one stage David Watterston proposed to restrict Alice Henry 'to the women's columns of fashions, frills, and frivolities'. At this 'she revolted and gave up the work'.[6] This was probably in the mid-1890s when apparently finding little stimulation in journalism and probably wanting to earn more money (she was later to complain about the poor pay for women journalists)[7] she started an enterprising business in Queen's Walk, an arcade off Swanston Street, offering services which included a town shopper for country women, an employment agency for governesses and domestic servants, a travel agent who would meet visitors and conduct them on tours of the city and an arranger of home and amateur theatricals and entertainments. Her new venture was described by Florence Blair, writing as 'Cleo' in the *Bulletin*: 'Miss Alice Henry, a penwoman whose level head is associated with prematurely gray hair, has started operations in Melbourne as a 'town shopper' and general undertaker of female commissions'.[8] For some years until she sold the business in July 1899 Alice Henry was a part-time journalist only, but she continued to contribute many articles to newspapers and periodicals and was also the social correspondent for the *Queenslander* and secretary of the women's Warrawee Club.

Alice Henry had met Catherine Spence in 1893 when she passed through Melbourne on her way to represent Australia at the International Conference of Charities at the World's Columbian Exposition held in Chicago to celebrate the 400th anniversary of Christopher Columbus' arrival in America. They shared similar views on women's rights and women's suffrage and an enthusiasm for proportional representation, and a great friendship began. Influenced by Catherine Spence about the wider opportunities available overseas for a woman of reforming views, Alice Henry in 1905 left Australia as a delegate from the Melbourne Charity Organisation Society, travelling first to Europe and England, and then to the United States. In the United States she achieved fame as secretary of the Chicago branch of the National Women's Trade Union League and then as editor of the League's Journal *Life and Labor*, where for a time Miles Franklin worked as her assistant. Later she became an organiser for the union movement.

Alice Henry lived for thirty years in America, finding greater oppor-

187

tunities and recognition for her work for women and the trade union movement than would have been possible in Australia. Just before the publication of her book *The Trade Union Woman* in 1915 (another book *Women and the Labor Movement* was published in 1924) she was interviewed by the American *Evening World* and described as a 'spokeswoman for the millions of her sex' employed in industry in the United States. She told the interviewer she was campaigning for a shorter working day for women, a minimum wage, wages and advancement to be decided on competence not sex, and neither compulsion for nor prohibition against wage-earning after marriage.[9]

In 1933, when she was seventy-six, Alice Henry returned to live in Melbourne, writing occasional articles. For the *Centenary Gift Book* in 1934 she wrote a chapter on the woman suffrage struggle, 'Marching towards Citizenship'[10] and in 1937 she compiled a bibliography of Australian women writers. The women she included in her list were: Ada Cambridge, Jennings Carmichael, Caroline Chisholm, Lala Fisher, Mary Hannay Foott, Maud Jeanne Franc, Mary Gaunt, Alice Henry, Cecilia Hill, Caroline Leakey, Ida Marriott, Louise Mack, Catherine Mackay (Martin), Louisa Meredith, Agnes Murphy, K. Langloh Parker, Rosa Campbell Praed, C.H. Spence, Agnes Storrie, Jessie Couvreur, Ethel Turner, Lillian Turner, Mary Vidal and Alice Werner.[11]

Alice Henry died in Melbourne in 1943 at the age of eighty-six.

Bella Guerin

'. . . *the women of Australia have solid grounds for rejoicing.*'

Bella Guerin, the first woman graduate in Australia, received the degree of Bachelor of Arts from the University of Melbourne on 1 December 1883. The daughter of the Irish-born Chief Warder of Ballarat Gaol, she was educated at Ballarat but had to wait three years after matriculating before being admitted to the University of Melbourne in the first group of women students. After graduating she taught at the Ballarat convent where she had been educated, gained a Master of Arts degree, and when the Ballarat School of Mines affiliated briefly with the University in the late 1880s she was appointed Lady Principal in charge of matriculation honours students.[12]

In 1891, at the age of thirty-three, she made a rather unlikely marriage to eighty-year-old Henry Halloran, a widower and retired senior civil servant, a poet and literary figure in Sydney. By this time she was writing poetry and after her marriage she began contributing poems and scholarly essays on such topics as 'Modern Woman' and 'Modern Education' to the *Sydney Quarterly*.[13]

188

Bella Guerin became the first woman graduate in Australia when she received the Bachelor of Arts degree from the University of Melbourne. She wrote articles on 'Modern Woman' and 'Modern Education' for a Sydney periodical and in later life was a radical feminist and socialist who spoke on the Yarra Bank. (Bulletin 19 January 1884)

In 'Modern Woman' she termed the availability of university education to women as 'the Second Renaissance':

> ... the women of Australia have solid grounds for rejoicing. In the New World, and in Russia, the pioneers of female advancement are to be found ... the daughters of Australia can share freely in the efforts and consequent rewards which this new social movement so abundantly offers.[14]

Two years after their marriage Halloran died leaving Bella with a baby son, and she returned to Melbourne. She wrote little but later became widely known as a feminist and socialist, and an organiser of labour women. She was a prominent Yarra Bank orator, speaking out against conscription and the restrictions on freedom of speech during World War I.

Mary Gaunt

Unlike Alice Henry and Bella Guerin, Mary Gaunt was not a publicist for women's causes. A woman of conservative background, her overriding ambition was to earn her own living. At this she was successful, being probably the first Australian woman to make a comfortable living by writing books. Born in 1861 at Indigo, northern Victoria, a daughter of police magistrate William Gaunt (later a judge) and his wife formerly Elizabeth Palmer, she was one of a distinguished family. Two of her brothers, Ernest and Guy, became admirals in the British Navy and were knighted, another brother, Cecil, became a colonel in the British Army, and her younger sister, Lucy Archer, became principal of Trinity College Hostel (later Janet Clarke Hall) at the

189

University of Melbourne.

From an early age Mary Gaunt believed that women had the right to follow careers and be financially independent even after marriage. In March 1881 she was the second woman to sign the matriculation roll at the University of Melbourne after legislation made the entry of women students possible. She enrolled that year in an arts course but, after failing several first year subjects, did not continue.[15] In an interview with the *Sydney Mail*, some years later, Mary Gaunt said that at the age of twenty she surveyed her future: '. . . what was to become of me? and not only me, but hundreds of other girls, too, girls of the upper middle class, who have no provision made for them in case they do not marry'.[16]

At the university she had met Edward Ellis Morris, Professor of Language and Literature, who encouraged her to write:

> . . . he, seeing a discontented little girl who felt there was nothing much before her in life save matrimony — that befell every Australian girl — suggested that I should write articles and stories. Not that he saw in me a budding genius.[17]

She began writing by reviewing a book sent to her by Professor Morris, following this with the first of a number of stories based on the experiences of her brothers. The first was rejected by the *Argus* but the *Age* accepted it and paid her five guineas. Soon after the *Sydney Mail* accepted a story, 'Lost in the Bush'. The opportunity to write on a more permanent basis came in 1887 when Professor Morris, as editor of *Cassell's Picturesque Australasia*, arranged for her to write nine chapters of the four-volume work. One of the articles, 'Proclaiming a Protectorate', is about New Guinea, written in a manner that suggests the writer had visited the country. In fact Mary Gaunt had gathered the information from her brother who had been in New Guinea with the British Navy. In addition she wrote on the gold discoveries, Ballarat, Eureka, the Riverina, inland towns of Victoria, and on three explorers.

Her brother Guy provided the information for her articles published in the *Argus* in 1888 on 'Life on board the training ship Worcester. By the Captain of the Maintop Starboard'. Through her ghosting of her brothers' experiences Mary Gaunt gained journalistic experience unavailable on the same scale to most other women writers.

Her own life in goldfields' townships provided material for many other stories which she contributed to Australian and overseas papers and magazines. One, 'The riots at the Packhorse', based on the goldfields riots at Buckland River in 1857, which took place while her father was gold commissioner there, appeared in the *Australasian* during the first three months of 1890. The story was used again in her novel, *Deadman's* published in London in 1898.

Although advanced in her ideas on women's employment, Mary Gaunt

Mary Gaunt came from a distinguished and conservative family background. Her father was a judge, two of her brothers became admirals in the British Navy and were knighted, another brother was a British Army officer and her sister became head of a university college. She took up writing because she believed women had a right to be independent. As a young woman in Australia she wrote several chapters for Cassell's Picturesque Australasia *and several novels. Later she became a successful author of travel books. (Mrs Jill Marshall, Kerang, Victoria)*

had very conservative ideas on social issues. Her story 'Some Australian Paupers' published on 12 May 1890 in *Centennial Magazine* was a very unsympathetic account of poor people who, in the writer's view, could do more to look after themselves.

Her earnings from writing for *Cassell's* and for Australian newspapers and periodicals enabled her to travel to England, Europe and India in 1890 and 1891. When her first novel, *Dave's Sweetheart*, set in a mining camp at Deadman's Creek diggings in north-east Victoria, was published in London in 1894 it received good reviews in England and Australia. The London *Daily Telegraph* said it was 'in every respect one of the most powerful and impressive novels of the year'.[18] Within months a second edition appeared and later it was published in Arnold's 'Library of Australian Authors'.

The same year in which. Mary Gaunt's first novel was published she married, at the age of thirty-three, Tasmanian-born Dr Hubert Lindsay Miller, formerly medical superintendent of Melbourne Hospital (1881–83), whose first wife had died in 1892. At the time of his marriage he was a doctor at Warrnambool. After their marriage Mary continued to write, her experiences at Warrnambool providing her with information for a series of articles on 'Little industries for women', published in the *Argus* in 1897 and 1898. During this period her novels continued to be published in London — *The moving finger*, a collection of short stories, in 1895 and *Kirkham's Find* and *Deadman's* in 1898. In 1900 she contributed 'The Light of Goat Island' to *Childhood in bud and blossom*, a prestigious publication containing a collection of articles and stories published to aid the Melbourne Children's Hospital. The same year, after they had been married only six years, her husband died at Kew Mental Asylum at the age of forty-three leaving her, '. . . penniless, homeless and alone. Of course I might have gone back to my father's house . . . if I stayed quietly in Australia I had exactly thirty pounds a year to

In 1900 Mary Gaunt contributed a short story 'The Light of Goat Island' to a prestigious publication, Childhood in bud and blossom, *published to aid the Melbourne Children's Hospital. Her story was illustrated by a drawing of a bunyip by C. Douglas Richardson. Soon after, Mary Gaunt's husband, Dr H. Lindsay Miller, died and she left to live in London where all her books were published. (Childhood in bud and blossom.)*

call my own'.[19]

In 1901 Mary Gaunt decided to return to London where she had been successful before, and she was never to return to Australia. Determined to make money 'by my pen in the heart of the world', she describes her disheartening experiences:

Oh, the hopes of the aspirant for literary fame, and oh, the dreariness and weariness of life for a woman poor and unknown in London! I lodged in two rooms in a dull and stony street. I had no one to speak to from morning to night, and I wrote and wrote and wrote stories that all came back to me, and I am bound to say the editors who sent them back to me were quite right. They were poor stuff, but how could anyone do good work who was sick and miserable, cold and lonely, with all the life crushed out of her by the grey skies and the drizzling rain? I found London a terrible place in those days; I longed with all my heart for my own country . . . I did not go back to my father, because my pride would not allow me to own myself a failure and because all the traditions of my family were against giving in. But I was very near it, very near it indeed.[20]

She persevered but decided that it 'was simply hopeless to think of writing stories about English life. The regular, conventional life did not appeal to me;

192

I could only write adventure stories'. Partly through a friendship with John Ridgwell Essex, she developed an interest in Africa, for he had lived there, and she began to write of the continent, sometimes in collaboration with him. In 1907 she visited the west coast of Africa, making an adventurous and dangerous trip 400 miles up the Gambia River into country rarely visited by women.[21] Subsequently she wrote a number of African books including *Alone in West Africa*, published in 1912. The London *Daily Telegraph* said of her style:

> She is rich in feminine intuition, in vivacity, and in narrative skill. She aims always at the vivid personal impression; actuality is of the essence of her temperament . . .[22]

In 1910 one of her most successful books, *The uncounted cost*, was published. Set in Africa, it was banned by a chain of circulating libraries in England because the heroine had pre-marital relations with a young man who promised to marry her but eventually broke off the relationship. The ban, of course, focussed attention on the book and sales far exceeded expectations.

In 1910 she published a crime thriller, *The mummy moves*. Although successful in England, its greatest success was to come later in the United States where, in 1919, the Chicago *Daily News* paid $1000 for serial rights. In 1913 she went to China, where she travelled north from Peking by mule cart to visit the hunting palace of the Manchus, recording her experiences in *A woman in China*, published in 1914. She planned an overland journey along the old caravan route to Russia but when this proved to be impossible, because of brigands, she travelled to Vladivostok and across Siberia to Sweden and Norway, learning en route that World War I had begun. This story was told in *A broken journey*, published in 1919.

After World War I Mary Gaunt moved to Bordighera, on the Italian Riviera. In the next twelve years she wrote ten books, including *As the whirlwind passeth*, set in early New South Wales, during the time of Governor John Hunter. She also worked on her memoirs but in 1940, after the start of World War II, she had to abandon most of her belongings and flee to France.[23] By then she was nearly eighty and unable to walk. Before she left she wrote to her niece, Ellinor Archer, in Australia:

> I sort of live from day to day and hope for the best. I haven't succeeded in getting any money yet and am borrowing for a stamp from Anselma [her maid]. I've got to live very economically for the pound has fallen in the opinion of Italy and where I was quite comfortably off I am now very poor.[24]

Mary Gaunt died in Cannes Hospital on 19 January 1942 at the age of eighty-one and unfortunately none of her papers or autobiographical writing have been located.

Frances Gillam Holden

'Teach her when she is young.'

In the latter part of the nineteenth century trained nurses, like university graduates, belonged to an elite group of educated women, some of whom turned to writing to express their views on women's and social issues. Frances Holden, a Sydney hospital matron, became a prolific writer in the cause of better education for women, particularly in raising awareness of health issues.

Frances Gillam Holden was born in 1843 at Gosford, north of Sydney, the eldest daughter of Alfred Holden, police magistrate and his wife formerly Jane Osborne, a member of an old established family in the Illawarra district. When Frances was six the family moved to a large property at Penshurst where, with her brothers and sisters, she was educated at home by tutors (her father did not approve of education in schools) and encouraged to read, particularly poetry. She worked as a governess for some years but at the age of thirty-one, together with her younger sisters Laura, Rosamund and Edith, decided to become a nurse. In June 1874 Frances Holden entered Sydney Infirmary and Dispensary to train under Lucy Osburn who had been sent to Sydney by Florence Nightingale. A woman of strong character, she did not get on with Lucy Osburn and in March 1875 she was dismissed.

After nursing privately for a few months, Frances and two of her sisters went to the Hobart General Hospital to assist the lady superintendent in reforming the administration. After a year of turmoil, during which a Royal Commission upheld their complaints against the management and conditions at the hospital, and a spell as an invalid recovering from typhoid, Frances Holden was in September 1880 appointed Lady Superintendent at the new Hospital for Sick Children, which had been opened at the beginning of that year at Glebe Point.[25]

Although the hospital progressed well, friction developed between Frances Holden and the honorary doctors, four resigning in 1884 and a further three some time later. Whether Frances Holden adopted a 'hostile attitude' to the doctors, as the historian of the early days of the hospital, Dr P.L. Hipsley believed, or whether she just adopted a less subservient attitude than the doctors expected, the situation deteriorated. 'She was a woman who liked to have her own way, and was rather inclined to give orders instead of taking them from the doctors', Dr Hipsley wrote.[26] Problems escalated in June 1887 when Frances Holden wrote to the Board complaining of the treatment of two of the patients by certain physicians. The dispute became public and the *Bulletin* published several cartoons on the subject, describing the Lady Superintendant as '. . . a clever woman with a tendency to overestimate her ability; imperious in disposition, when thwarted she is inclined to become

In 1874 Frances Gillam Holden began to train as a nurse at Sydney Infirmary under Lucy Osburn who had been sent to Australia by Florence Nightingale. Following a dispute with Lucy Osburn she was dismissed but in 1880 she was appointed Lady Superintendent at the new Hospital for Sick Children opened that year in Sydney. Frances Holden was a prolific writer in the cause of better education for women, particularly in health matters. (Town and Country Journal 3 September 1887)

As Lady Superintendent of the Children's Hospital Frances Holden became involved in a long-running dispute with 'irascible medicos' during which she was accused of being imperious and hysterical. The dispute, which made good copy for reporters and cartoonists, ended with Frances Holden's dismissal, although the hospital was said to have had a minimum death rate and a maximum of cures during the time she was Superintendent. (Bulletin 27 August 1887)

195

hysterical and to give vent to wild statements and wilder tears — a woman's common refuge'.[27] At the height of the dispute the *Town and Country Journal* stated that the hospital had been 'a wonderful success, and the minimum death rate within its walls, and the maximum of cures effected, have been remarkable. For these good results the main credit has been admittedly due to Miss Holden...'.[28] After further disputes between an 'irate Lady Superintendent and irascible medicos', Frances Holden was asked by the Board to resign and, when she refused, was dismissed. She refused to move from the hospital and eventually the Government was forced to order a judicial inquiry. Although ill again with typhoid Frances Holden took part in the case. Despite considerable support, however, she failed to prove her charges against the medical staff and was dismissed in October 1887. Several staff went with her.

From the 1870s Frances Holden had lectured and written on nursing, physiology, hygiene and hospital reform, social reform and women's rights and had advocated higher education for women. Under the pseudonym 'Lyra Australia' she contributed poems to the *Sydney Mail* from 1870 to 1897. As 'Australienne' she wrote 'The Captain's Story' for the February 1883 *Literary News*, and she also wrote under that name for the *Sydney Mail*, *Sydney University Review*, *Melbourne Review*, and the *Australian Woman's Magazine and Domestic Journal*. In her own name she contributed to some of these journals and to the *Town and Country Journal*, *Dawn* and *Humanity and Health*, published in New York. Some of her best known articles and pamphlets were written while she was superintendent of the Children's Hospital. *Trained nursing* appeared in 1882 and in 1884 *The travels of Red-jacket and White-cap; or, a history of the circulation of the blood*, a booklet recommended as a textbook in schools.

In 1887 she published *Her father's darling, and other child pictures*, a collection of sentimental, moral poems and short stories about sick children in hospital. In it she pleaded the benefits for children from 'dirty, dingy, crowded, noisy abodes' with 'overworked, anxious' mothers in being cared for for a few months in the Children's Hospital where all that is 'coarse, rude, and objectionable is held in abeyance by the simple presence of gentlewomen'. The *Bulletin* carried a scathing review of *Her father's darling*. The reviewer stated he had looked 'in vain for a slab of inspiration' among the references to 'woman's deft and gentle touch', 'ferny fronds', 'gentle moanings' and 'silken tresses'.[29]

If this had been the extent of Frances Holden's writing she could be overlooked but in her articles for serious magazines she was an effective publicist for the cause of education for women. In one pamphlet 'Women's Ignorance and the world's need' she urged that women should gain more knowledge about health. The *Sydney Morning Herald* said:

At present many of those for whom a pamphlet like this is intended are ignorant of natural laws, which should be guiding principles of their lives. Forced brains and stunted bodies, diseased lungs, and sickly faces, all these are the outcome of that inattention to the laws of health, which too frequently prevails.

The *Woman's World Magazine* wrote:

> The *brochure* treats of 'Women's Ignorance', of sanitary science and domestic hygiene and the 'need' of education with regard to physiology. The earnestness that characterizes all Miss Holden's writings was never more forcible than in the present instance...[30]

To present-day readers the pamphlet presents a contradictory collection of views but at the time it was issued (1883) it was a forward-looking plea for improving women's knowledge of physiology and anatomy as a means of preventing disease. It sprang from Frances Holden's experiences as superintendent where daily she received young children who were the victims of neglect. She saw the cure, not as some others did in reform of the social system, but in better education for women. She deplored the spate of superficial articles on health — '"Health-hints," "health-notes," "popular hygiene"'. Her solution was:

> Teach *her* when she is young. Teach her as well as her brother... I would further with my warmest efforts woman's emancipation from the worse than Egyptian bondage of Physiological darkness.[31]

In a series of papers published in the *Sydney Quarterly Magazine* between 1883 and 1888 she put the case for women's control of hospitals and other care institutions and in 'Institution reform' she pleaded for the employment of capable and cultured women in public institutions. Very conscious of being a 'gentlewoman' herself, she stressed that the women employed should be practical but also 'refined gentlewomen'. In 'Petticoat government' she urged that women prisoners should be under the control of women warders, a theme taken up by many feminist writers. In another article, 'The gospel of physical salvation', she reiterated a theme that runs through much of her writings — the fallacy that lies in caring for spiritual health while neglecting physical health.

One of her most popular pamphlets was *What typhoid is, and how to nurse it. Its simple and successful treatment*. Originally written in 1888, it had reached a print run of 7000 when the third edition was issued in 1889. Strangely, as Frances Holden herself suffered twice from typhoid, the third edition included a new chapter called 'Prevention of typhoid easy'. Frances Holden retired from writing and public life when she was about sixty and she died at Burwood in 1924 at the age of eighty-one.[32]

Grace Jennings Carmichael

Grace Jennings Carmichael was born in Ballarat in 1867 to Archibald Carmichael, a Scots-born miner who had been involved in the Eureka rebellion in 1854 and his Cornish-born wife, Margaret Jennings Clark. When Grace was three her father died leaving his widow with three children to support. Five years later Grace's mother married Scots-born Charles Naylor Henderson and in 1879 the family moved to the Orbost district in east Gippsland where Henderson became manager of a huge station owned by Sir William Clarke. The property was bordered by the Snowy River on the west and the Brodribb River on the east and the town of Orbost was built later on its south-west corner. The beauty of the area, known as the Croajingolong country, with its wild forests, high mountains and fast snow-fed rivers, made a vivid impression on twelve-year-old Grace which she later expressed in poetry and stories. She began writing poetry and at the age of thirteen had her first verse published in the *Bairnsdale Advertiser*.[33]

In 1886 she became a probationer nurse at the Melbourne Hospital for Sick Children and despite contracting typhoid fever in an epidemic among the nurses that took two lives, she passed the newly instituted nursing certificate with credit the following year. During her training she contributed many poems and articles to the *Australasian*, receiving encouragement from editor David Watterston, who recognised her ability.

In 1891 she published *Hospital Children, Sketches of Life and Character in the Children's Hospital, Melbourne*, a collection of articles most of which had been published previously in periodicals. Her aim, she said, was 'to bring the reader a little closer to the realities of child-suffering'. Although the articles were not aimed at reforming the system, they were remarkable in bringing the suffering of children before the public. She wrote of a child victim of a 'terrible hip disease' who wasted away 'with blanched face and emaciated frame... until the cross of flowers is made for another childish figure in its mortuary shrouds'; of typhoid epidemics and of battered children:

> a dear little lad who recounted the history of certain bruises so
> reluctantly, and, after entering into the details of flogging with a rope's
> end, while strapped to a table, added wistfully — 'But don't tell the
> other nurses; I don't want to disgrace my father'.

She wrote of child patients with hair so matted it had to be cut off, clothes so filthy they had to be burned and bodies so ingrained with dirt that they defied the best efforts with soap and water. She wrote also of the despair of seeing children return to hospital with a recurrence of illness after being neglected and allowed to roam cold, windy streets in ragged, thin clothing while their mothers were out earning a pittance washing, or out drinking.[34]

Through a friendship with philanthropist Lady (Janet) Clarke, wife of Sir William Clarke, owner of the east Gippsland station where she had spent some years of her childhood, Jennings Carmichael met wealthy people who subscribed to the publication of her first book of poems and later, in 1895, to the English edition, the first selection of poetry published in London by a Victorian-born woman. Ada Cambridge, the best-known woman writer in Australia at the time, wrote to Jennings Carmichael (the name she used for publication), 'At your age I could never have written as you do'.[35]

After completing her training at the Children's Hospital, Jennings Carmichael went to Barunah Downs station near Geelong to nurse a small boy who had had his legs amputated. Later she met Henry Francis Mullis, an Edinburgh-born architect, and they were married at Fitzroy in 1895, soon after going to live in Adelaide where their son Geoffrey was born in 1896. Later they left for England where two more sons and a daughter were born. Jennings Carmichael continued to write verse which was published in the *Australasian* but the quantity diminished during a time when the family's finances deteriorated and they lived in poverty in the East End of London. Deserted by her husband, Jennings Carmichael became ill and died in February 1904, at the age of thirty-seven, only a short time after the death of her daughter. Her funeral was arranged by Australian authors living in England. Her young sons were put into the Northampton Workhouse where they remained for six years until some Australian writers, including Alice Grant Rosman, became interested in them. In 1910 C. Hay Thomson, in an article in the *Argus*, called for funds to be raised 'to rescue these children from "the pauper taint", so that they may be brought to their mother's country...'[36] A committee was formed at a public meeting held in the Melbourne Town Hall on 11 May 1910 to raise money for the children's welfare and the Victorian Government granted free passages to Australia for the boys by then aged eight, eleven and fourteen. After they arrived in Australia the boys dropped their surname of Mullis and reverted to their mother's name of Carmichael.

Grace Jennings Carmichael's fame as a poet survived through a generation. In 1937, an admirer of her poetry, Mrs G.A. Hunter, arranged for a sculpture of her by Wallace Anderson to be placed in the Shire Hall at Orbost. In other commemorative moves, a portrait was placed in the nurses' room at the Children's Hospital and a memorial, in the form of an open book of marble engraved with a spray of wattle, was sent from Melbourne to be placed on her grave in London.[37]

199

Mrs Bessie Harrison Lee

*'... we ... could only stand helplessly by and mourn the patient victim
of degraded marriage.'*

Bessie Lee was born at Daylesford, Victoria, to Emma and Henry Vickery in
1860. Her mother died when she was eight and, unable to look after his five
children, her father farmed them out among relatives. Bessie was sent to an
uncle and aunt in Footscray, Melbourne where she was loved one day but
'bruised and blackened' the next, during her relatives' bouts of drunkenness.
Later she was sent to an uncle and his wife at Railway Creek, three miles from
Enoch's Point, a small mining settlement in north-eastern Victoria. Her aunt,
a hard and unsentimental woman, continually stressed the need to remain
pure. 'One slip and everyone will scorn you', she told Bessie.[38]
   Despite attending school only intermittently Bessie taught herself by
reading constantly and she began writing verse at an early age, her first poem
being published in the *Australian Journal* when she was twelve. At the age of
nineteen she married Harrison Lee, a railway worker from Melbourne. Their
first homes were cottages in the poor, inner Melbourne suburbs of Footscray
and Richmond, where Harrison Lee was sometimes without work. Bessie,
distressed by the conditions around her, started Sunday School classes, visited
the sick and toured slums, refuges, opium dens and gaols, sometimes in the
company of philanthropist Dr John Singleton. In the slums she learnt, she
wrote, of 'sin and suffering and poverty'.
   In 1883, following the visit to Australia by leaders in the temperance
movement, she was elected president of the Women's Christian Temperance
Union and began a career of public speaking and of writing for daily
newspapers and temperance journals.
   In 1890 she wrote letters to the Melbourne *Herald* on marriage, advocating abstinence from intercourse to prevent the birth of unwanted children, and then published her views in articles and in a pamphlet entitled
Marriage and heredity (called *Marriage and the social evil* in another edition)
which reached its fourth edition in four years. *Marriage and heredity*, written in
a popular style, included sensational stories of young girls in opium dens,
prostitutes, girls and men dying from venereal disease, and mothers overburdened with numerous children they were unable to feed and clothe.
Typical of her writing was the story of a woman who had been warned that
further child-bearing would cause her death:

> ... our bitter tears fell on the grave of that gentle woman, who had been
> as surely murdered as any other victim of man's passion. Had she not
> been his wife, he would have been arrested for outrage and murder: being
> his wife, the law could do nothing, and we, who loved her, could only
> stand helplessly by and mourn the patient victim of degraded marriage.[39]

This photograph of Bessie (Mrs Harrison) Lee appeared in her autobiography One of Australia's daughters *published in London in 1900. She had risen from a poor, deprived background to be a renowned temperance speaker who made many trips abroad promoting the temperance cause. After seeing the effects of frequent pregnancy and childbirth in the slums of Melbourne, she had also become an advocate of 'ideal' or celibate marriage for women who did not want more children. (*One of Australia's daughters*)*

201

Bessie Lee designated her ideas on sexual abstinence, if children were not wanted, as 'ideal marriage' but admitted 'My ideal marriage is perhaps too lofty a standard to be reached by all'. Her writing always carried a message. From February to July 1888 the *Australian Journal* ran a serial by her entitled, *Tempted and Tried: the story of two sisters, an Australian tale* containing a character modelled on a woman of simple faith and great sweetness of disposition whom she had met in the slums of Collingwood.

By 1896 Bessie Lee had become a well-known figure and began to make the first of many trips abroad promoting the temperance cause. Through her involvement in temperance movements and her experiences among under-privileged people she became an advocate of women's rights, advocating the right to vote and the right to freedom from male exploitation, either through prostitution or in marriage.

Her husband, Harrison Lee, died in January 1908. He is mentioned little in her autobiography and this, together with her views on intercourse in marriage and the fact that she did not have children, may indicate that her own marriage was 'ideal'. Eleven months after Lee's death she married a well-to-do New Zealand sheep farmer widower Andrew Cowie, who had first contacted her by letter after reading of her campaigns. In later life, after her second husband's death, she settled at Pasadena, California where she became a national figure through her temperance campaigns. She died at Pasadena in 1950.

12

Women's Pages, Slightly Fanciful

'Feminine Facts and Fancies'
Age 3 July 1897

The earliest women writers for newspapers in Australia were employed in all aspects of journalism, although in small numbers, as was noted in the *Illustrated Sydney News* in 1891:

> Nearly every newspaper of standing has one lady, or more, on its staff or among its contributors. Many of these also correspond with intercolonial, American, and English periodicals, and all are doing widely varied, and I may safely say arduous, journalistic work. The demands made upon them embrace not only social matters, which are supposed by some of the uninitiated to be the peculiar and limited sphere of women's efforts in newspaper writing; but leader writing, critiques on art, music, and the drama, biographical sketches, and, indeed, a facility for putting pen to any and every topic under the sun that may happen to crop up and absorb, for the moment, the attention or curiosity of the news reading public.[1]

This employment of women reporting on a wide range of topics was not to remain typical of the later involvement of women in journalism, however. The change began with the proliferation of women's columns and women's pages in newspapers and periodicals.

Responding to a perceived demand, proprietors and editors of one Australian periodical and newspaper after another began from 1870 to publish articles and items aimed at women readers. At first these columns were comprised of pieces culled from other sources, such as books of recipes or overseas newspapers, and there was no necessity to employ women journalists to cobble together such collections. One man who did this work was E. P.

Field. Trained for the bar, he took up journalism while waiting for clients. The *Bulletin* writing of the 1880s described him:

> To bring in a few guineas he took up journalism of a kind, and a very remarkable kind for his sex . . . Woman's needs in the way of gossip and modes were not catered for as they are to-day . . . Field with the suave smile and polite manner that suggested 'Gentle Annie', took up this branch with quite remarkable success.[2]

Once newspapers and periodicals began printing local news for and about women, however, editors began to see the advantage in employing women writers to write and edit these pages. Thus a larger and more regular, although still small, avenue of permanent employment opened to women journalists. Although an advance in terms of employment, this proved a backward step for their involvement in general reporting. Catherine Spence was proud, when in America in 1894, to be writing on general topics for Australian newspapers, in contrast to American women journalists who, she found, were confined to women's page material. Her experience, however, was not by then typical of Australian women journalists.[3]

Male antagonism to women entering this previously almost all-male profession was evident after a number of women had been employed on newspapers in positions of some permanence, even though perhaps not as full staff members. (The notorious disregard for records in the newspaper world has meant that little has survived concerning staff in the nineteenth century.)[4] In a review of a book *Ladies at Work*, which consisted of a collection of papers on the avenues of employment open to women reprinted from the English *Monthly Packet*, the Melbourne *Argus'* male reviewer said:

> Doubtless there are some departments of journalism in which women may advantageously enter into competition with men, though we do not like the idea of any competition between the sexes. A very useful function is discharged by those who in the daily newspaper and elsewhere discourse of skirts and of sleeves, and tell us the latest novelties — hats and cloaks. There are those who give themselves up to the adornment of households, whose word is law in the artistic arrangement of furniture and in the due balance of colour in wall-paper. Fanny L. Green (author of the chapter on journalism), however, is not content thus to put the field of the lady journalist. She gives us a glowing picture of the large incomes made by leader-writers (a picture not without colour from fancy) of the luxurious lives led by the foreign correspondents, of the gay times enjoyed by the descriptive reporters and the interviewers, and asks why these departments also should not be included within the sphere of woman. Why not, indeed? The female reporter might greatly enliven our news columns. A new and agreeable turn might be given even to the dreary Parliamentary debate by the light touch of the female hand. We may be sure that henceforth nothing will be sacred to man alone.

Doubtless there is here, as elsewhere, an ample field of feminine employment. To literature proper woman needs no special invitation. Already the greater part of books are written by women, including nine-tenths of all the novels. The magazines are almost entirely monopolised by women, and there is no editor who has not become prematurely aged by the piles of feminine 'copy' he is called upon to peruse under threat of being exposed in *The Author* if he is slow to accept or backward with the remuneration.[5]

As remarked earlier, there was similar male opposition to the employment of female compositors. When other printers followed Louisa Lawson's lead in employing female compositors, a correspondent, T. E. Colebrook, wrote to the *Sydney Morning Herald* defending the recent decision of the New South Wales Typographical Association to oppose entry into the industry of female compositors. He pointed to advertisements in the Positions Vacant column showing vacancies for a hundred female servants, work for which females were 'naturally adapted'.[6] There was similar opposition when the *Sydney Morning Herald* in 1895 employed females to distribute type for the new Hattersley machines.[7]

In 1870 the weekly *Town and Country Journal* began to publish a 'Ladies' Column'. The issue of 8 January that year was typical, consisting of a long article, apparently taken from an overseas paper, entitled 'Paris fashions for December' and a section called 'Domestic Recipes'. In the middle of recipes for stewed tomatoes, lemon sugar, walnut catsup, anchovy sauce, muffins, short crust pastry and 'a good gravey' there were remedies for sore throats, headache and cold feet.

Fashions and household hints remained constant features of the column. Sometimes a poem or an article, particularly on a facetious theme regarding women, was added: the issue for 13 August 1870 included an article entitled 'Should women vote or darn stockings?' In the 24 December 1870 issue the 'Ladies' Column' consisted of a homily on wifely devotion, a reply to a correspondent on what to do with a spoilt daughter, a poem 'Why can't girls propose?' and household hints. Two examples of the few articles of any significance to women's thought printed during the year, both apparently taken from overseas newspapers, were 'Mr. Greeley on Woman's Rights' by Horace Greeley, founder of the *New York Tribune*, and a short piece on 'Women and the press'. The latter represented a view on women writers current overseas and drew attention to the fact, important for women, that much casual journalistic work could be done at home:

With the growth of the press has grown the direct influence of educated women on the world's affairs. Mute in the senate and in the church, their opinions have found a voice in the sheets of ten thousand readers.

205

First in the list of their achievements came admirable novels; not because fiction can be written without knowledge, but because it only requires that knowledge which they can most easily attain, the result of insight into humanity. As periodicals have waxed numerous so has female authorship waxed strong. The magazines demanded short graphic papers, observations, wit, and moderate learning — women demanded work such as they could perform at home, and the ready pay upon performance which they invariably obtain; the two wants met, and the female sex has become a very important element in the fourth estate.[8]

Few would, even now, consider women to be 'a very important element in the fourth estate' in Australia. They certainly were not in 1870 and it is doubtful if at that time the *Town and Country Journal* was accepting much material, if any, from Australian women writers.

By 1881 the *Town and Country Journal* had expanded its 'Ladies' Column' to a page which included a collection of items on social events such as races, balls and band recitals, headed 'Gipsy's Notes'; some items reprinted from other sources; fashion notes; and household recipes. The dichotomy between the innocuous material regarded as suitable for women readers and the reporting of the 'real' often violent world on other pages of the same publication was pronounced. In an issue in which a woman reader's information needs were supposed to be satisfied by reports of society events and household hints, she could on other pages read of the hanging of a man found guilty of repeated and violent incest on his young daughter, of pathetic cases of abandoned babies, of a coroner commenting on the extraordinary amount of child killing, or of a woman described as a 'vagrant' found dying on a railway line.

Women's successes in unusual careers were sometimes reported, as in the 2 April 1881 issue which announced that the London *Morning Post* was sending a 'lady war correspondent', Lady Florence Dixie, to Cape Town to report 'war incidents'. Accompanying her was Elizabeth Thompson as a 'paintress of battle scenes'. Australian women journalists had some time to wait for similar assignments! By 1890 the *Town and Country Journal's* 'Ladies' Pages' had expanded to two pages consisting of an agglomeration of small items, some of them fillers.

Following the *Town and Country Journal's* example, the *Sydney Mail* in 1871 began to include similar material for women. The 25 March 1871 issue had an item 'Fashions for January', reprinted from the London *Graphic*. After a few months, although still not labelled a ladies' column, the *Sydney Mail* was including in each issue a few items designed for women readers. Regular items included one on domestic economy, containing recipes and household hints, and another entitled 'ladies' worktable' consisting of sewing and knitting directions. None of these items showed any sign of local authorship, appearing to have been lifted from other publications without acknowledgement. In the 1880s the *Sydney Mail* employed Mrs Carl Fischer to conduct the women's section, the main feature of which was her column 'Hausfrau's Lucky Bag' in which she replied to readers' questions (see Chapter 7).

The *Illustrated Sydney News* made several attempts at a column for women. Early in 1880 it included an unsigned 'Ladies' Column', and at other times there were reports entitled 'Sydney Society' signed by 'Uralla'. In 1881 the paper carried the regular series 'Silverleaf Papers' by Jessie Lloyd, which would have appealed to its mainly country readers (the full name of the publication at this time was *Illustrated Sydney News and NSW Agriculturalist and Grazier*). This was supplemented by 'What a London Lady says' by 'Felicia'. Later the paper included a page consisting mainly of fashion news under the title 'Our Ladies Corner'. Answers to correspondents were by 'Lusi'.

Almost all periodicals were ahead of daily newspapers in introducing columns for women readers. In Melbourne the *Australasian* had 'The Lady's Column' running in 1878; in Brisbane the *Queenslander* included a women's column in the 1870s and employed an editor, Mary Hannay Foott, in 1886; the *Bulletin* began its Women's Letter in 1888 and Melbourne *Punch* had a 'Lady's Letter' running by the 1890s.

Lucinda Gullett

> '... the "father," or, should we say, "mother" of Australian woman journalism.'
> Newcastle Morning Herald 26 June 1900

In 1872 at Williamstown, Victoria, Lucinda (Lucy) Willie had married her cousin, Henry Gullett, recently appointed editor of the *Australasian*. She probably began writing for the paper soon after her marriage and she later adopted the name 'Humming Bee' for her contributions. She is known to have been responsible for 'The Lady's Column' from 1880. She was a competent writer and her columns, although similar in content to other early women's columns, were much more readable.

Lucy Gullett continued to work for the *Australasian* until 1885. In that year the family moved to Sydney where Henry Gullett became a joint editor of the *Daily Telegraph*, in which he had bought an interest. In Sydney Lucy Gullett continued the work she had done in Melbourne, writing for the *Daily Telegraph* still under her pseudonym, 'Humming Bee'. She also played a public role as a journalist, encouraging other women to take up journalism as a career, and her home became a meeting place for intellectuals. One of her protegées was Zara Aronson, who became social editor of the *Sydney Mail* after the death of Mrs Carl Fischer.

207

When she died in 1900 Lucinda Gullett was described as one of the pioneer women journalists and the 'mother' of women journalists. She began writing for the Australasian *under the name of 'Humming Bee' in Melbourne in the 1870s and used the same name when she began writing for the Sydney* Daily Telegraph *in 1885. When she left the* Telegraph *Dame Mary Gilmore's mother, Mary Ann Cameron, took over as 'Humming Bee'. (Painting by Madam Mouchette, reproduced by permission of John S. Drury, Port Melbourne, Victoria)*

When Henry Gullett left the *Daily Telegraph* in 1890, following a disagreement on policy, and became associate editor of the *Sydney Morning Herald* (later acting editor), Lucinda Gullett left the *Daily Telegraph* also and during the early 1890s wrote for the *Sydney Morning Herald*. Her place as 'Humming Bee' on the *Daily Telegraph* was taken by Mary Cameron, mother of Mary Gilmore.[9] As in other women's pages, the most valued contribution by 'Humming Bee' was a column replying to readers' queries on a great range of topics.

In the 1890s at least two other women joined the *Daily Telegraph*. Susan D'Archy who had grown up on an outback station was in charge of the social and fashion columns for some years. She later wrote for several newspapers, including the *Maitland Mercury*, and was a contributor to a Paris paper. The other woman social reporter was Eliza Ann Ashton, wife of painter Julian Ashton. She was a feminist with literary and musical interests and had created a furore when she expressed critical views on marriage. She was a member of the Womanhood Suffrage League of New South Wales and a committee member of the Women's Literary Society. When she died in 1900, aged less than fifty, Louisa Lawson wrote that her death left 'a terrible gap in

After Lucinda Gullett left the Melbourne Australasian *in 1885 her place as editor of 'The Lady's Page' was taken by Mrs Tom Carrington who wrote under the name of 'Queen Bee'. Over the next few years Mrs Carrington developed the page into a section covering a number of pages, the first of which was nearly all taken up by advertisements. The fact that women's pages attracted advertising revenue was one of the main reasons for their inclusion in newspapers and periodicals.* (Australasian 16 May 1891)

the literary world'.[10]

After Lucinda Gullett retired from journalism she was prominent in many philanthropic movements in Sydney until her death after a short illness in June 1900. The *Sydney Morning Herald* described her as 'one of the pioneer women journalists' and the *Newcastle Morning Herald* said:

> Mrs. Gullett used to do 'ladies stuff' on her husband's paper in Melbourne, but her best known work is that which she contributed for so long, week by week, to the columns of a Sydney morning daily. This was a few years ago, when the 'women's page' in the broad sheet referred to was one of the features of contemporary journalism.[12]

One of Lucy and Henry Gullett's four daughters, Amy, married Thomas Heney, Henry Gullett's successor as editor of the *Sydney Morning Herald*.

When Lucinda Gullett moved to Sydney in 1885 her column on the *Australasian* was taken over by Mrs Carrington, wife of Tom Carrington, the paper's art editor, who wrote under the name of 'Queen Bee'. During the editorship of David Watterston from 1885 to 1903 Mrs Carrington developed the 'Lady's Page' into a section.[13] It appears to have become the most effective of the women's pages in attracting advertising, almost all of the first page being taken up with advertisements. Attracting advertising revenue would have been an important factor in deciding to include women's material in newspapers and periodicals.

Mary Hannay Foott

'... we want a lady to represent us at lady-meetings.'
C. H. Buzacott, Queenslander

Mary Hannay Foott's work as a journalist is less well known, but her involvement was at least as important as Lucinda Gullett's in early women's journalism. She was born Mary Hannay Black in Glasgow, Scotland, in 1846, the daughter of James Black and Margaret (née Grant). She is believed to have been related to James Hannay, a Scottish author, who after five years in the navy, became a journalist on the Morning Chronicle which was edited by Black, believed to have been another relative. Her father, James Black, contributed a weekly column to the Glasgow Herald. Mary Black arrived in Melbourne as a child of seven with her family, living at first at Mordialloc, then a bayside settlement outside Melbourne, where she was educated at a private school. As a schoolgirl a poem she entered won a medal in a competition run by the Victorian Caledonian Society. She trained as a teacher and from 1862 to 1868 taught at the Common School in the inner suburb of Fitzroy, but resigned in 1869 to spend the next five years at the National Gallery School. She studied under von Guerard, gaining a First Certificate in 1874, the highest award then granted. She also studied under Louis Buvelot.[14]

During these years Mary Black supported herself by contributing articles, society notes and poems to the Melbourne and Sydney Punch, the Australasian, the Town and Country Journal and the Australasian Sketcher. She was later to remark that Samuel Bennett, proprietor of the Town and Country Journal, was one of only two newspaper proprietors who ever paid her for verse—an interesting comment which may indicate that many women writers who had verse published in the nineteenth century did not get paid for their efforts. (The other proprietor who paid her was C. H. Buzacott of the Queenslander.) A letter dated 18 August 1873 written by Mary Black to the editor of the Australasian Sketcher indicates that she was an established correspondent. The letter sought to clarify some difficulty about submitting material in time for the Town edition. She added that she would be attending the Mayor's Ball

Mary Hannay Foott, well known as the author of the outback poem 'Where the pelican builds', was one of the first women staff journalists in Australia. As an art student in Melbourne in the early 1870s she had kept herself by contributing articles, society notes and poems to periodicals. After her husband died at their far western Queensland station in 1884, she took her two young sons to Brisbane and became editor of the Queenslander's *women's page, writing as 'La Quenouille'. (Book-fellow 15 May 1914)*

and would send a description which should be inserted at a particular page in the material already with the editor.[15]

Soon after this Mary Black left behind the social life of Melbourne and in 1874 at Dubbo married a family friend Thomas Wade Foott, son of James Foott and writer and artist Henrietta Foott. They lived at first at Bourke in western New South Wales where Thomas Foott was Inspector of Stock and where he had lived as a boy on the Foott's station, Jandra. In 1877 they took up Dundoo, a station of 339 square miles on Yowah Creek, a tributary of the Paroo in the far west of Queensland. There they lived in great isolation — the nearest station was 35 miles away and the nearest market town, Bourke, was 200 miles to the south. Their house, built by Thomas Foott, was of pisé construction with a thatched roof and a clay floor covered with carpets made from bullock hides. The seats of the chairs and the decks of the beds were made of greenhide thongs and the only footwear worn by the children was made by Mary Hannay Foott from greenhide.[16] But despite the isolation and hardships Mary Hannay Foott was fascinated and inspired by the harsh country and while there wrote many of the poems that made her a popular poet of the outback.

After some good seasons drought enveloped western Queensland in 1883. The Footts lost 25 000 sheep and faced ruin. The following year Thomas Wade Foott died and was buried at Dundoo leaving Mary Hannay Foott with two young sons. Her father, James Black, who owned large land holdings stretching from Victoria to Queensland, and who had been a partner in Dundoo, sold the station but the stock losses from the drought had been so great that he barely got back the money he had put into the property. He had already given Mary Hannay Foott £2000 and was unable to do more to help her as his other children were also in need of assistance. Ironically the drought broke as Mary Hannay Foott and her children were packing to leave

Dundoo and on the long journey to Brisbane their wagons were bogged many times.

In Brisbane Mary Hannay Foott took a small cottage at Rocklea where she attempted to earn enough money to keep herself and her children by running a small school, advertising in the *Queenslander*: 'Mrs Foott, The Hermitage, Rocklea, wishes to receive boys under 13 as pupils. Studies and terms same as in Govt. Schools.'[17]

During any time she could spare from the school she wrote poems and articles for the *Queenslander* and other papers. Among them was the haunting 'Where the pelican builds' based on a true story of Alfred and Sylvester Prout, whom Mary had known in western Queensland. Just before Christmas 1877 the Prouts had left Davenport Downs on the Lower Diamantina to search for new land to the west over the South Australian border, and were believed to be aiming for the new overland telegraph line linking Adelaide and Darwin. Although one at least of the Prout brothers was renowned as a first-class bushman it was assumed after they had been lost for months that they had perished from thirst in the sandhills and salt lakes of the Simpson Desert. After they had been missing for over two years, the explorer and prospector, William Carr Boyd, who wrote for the *Queenslander* under the name of 'Potjostler', set out in charge of an expedition to search for them, but he was unsuccessful.[18] In her poem Mary Hannay Foott wrote of the Prouts' departure:

> The horses were ready, the rails were down,
> But the riders lingered still —
> One had a parting word to say,
> And one had a pipe to fill . . .
> 'We are going,' they said, as they rode away —
> 'Where the pelican builds her nest.'

and of the years of waiting:

> The creek at the ford was but fetlock deep
> When we watched them crossing there;
> The rains have replenished it thrice since then,
> And thrice has the rock lain bare.

At the top of the poem she had the explanation:

> The unexplored parts of Australia are sometimes spoken of by the bushmen of Western Queensland as the home of the pelican, a bird whose nesting place, so far as the writer knows, is seldom, if ever found.[19]

Where the pelican builds and other poems was published in Brisbane in 1885 and *Morna Lee and other poems*, containing some of the same poems, was published in London in 1890. A. G. Stephens said of her poems:

They are the sincere reflections of a sweet woman's soul, often poetically inspired and poetically phrased, and for the most part seizing a momentary emotion, or idea, or picture, and stating it lyrically and straitly [sic].[20]

After she had been running her school for two years, at the same time contributing to the *Queenslander*, Mary Hannay Foott late in 1886 received a letter from W. Butterfield of the *Queenslander*, in which, on the instructions of the editor C. H. Buzacott, he suggested a permanent position on the paper. He enclosed a note from Buzacott:

Our present arrangement with Mrs. Foott does not work quite satisfactorily. She does not get her letters promptly enough, and is not sufficiently 'in touch' with the office. She has a few scholars, but I think it might be well to ascertain whether she would be willing to give them up in order to our getting more of her services. My idea is that we want a lady to represent us at lady-meetings. In April I hope to have a lady's room ready in our new offices, and where Mrs. Foott, if so disposed, could look through letters, and papers, etc., whenever she was able to come to Town, and where she could receive lady visitors.[21]

As a result she became not only editor of the women's page but wrote most of its contents, including serials, articles and poems. One serial, 'Like Mist on the Mountains', was described as 'written for the *Queenslander*'. Under the pen-name of 'La Quenouille' (distaff—the female side) she ran a column 'The Housekeeper' which contained household hints, such as 'Good sauces improve good food and make even that which is indifferent palatable'. Under this name she also wrote a series of articles on topics such as 'At the Children's Hospital' in which she offered to send a pattern to any readers who volunteered to make some bed jackets for the small inmates.[22]

After she took up full-time journalism, Mary Hannay Foott's sons attended Sherwood State School and from there Cecil Foott won a scholarship to Brisbane Grammar in 1889, Arthur Foott following in 1890. Cecil Foott after becoming an engineer went on to an outstanding career in the Army, eventually becoming a Major General. The younger son, Arthur Foott followed his mother into journalism and at one stage in the early 1900s both mother and son were working on Brisbane newspapers. Both would return home at midnight by the last train and sit down at the kitchen table and talk about their work. In 1907 Arthur Foott joined the *Bundaberg Mail* and his mother, who for some years had interspersed writing with teaching (she had held positions at girls' grammar schools at both Wagga and Rockhampton) followed him there. At Bundaberg she wrote for the *Mail* and also did some teaching. Arthur Foott joined the Army as a private during World War I and was killed as a Lieutenant at the battle of Passchendaele in 1917.

Mary Hannay Foott was also a dramatist. Her 'More than Kin', a

Mary Hannay Foott supported her two young sons by her work as a journalist. The elder, Cecil, (left) beame an engineer and had an outstanding career in the Australian Army. The younger, Arthur, followed his mother into journalism, at one time in the early 1900s both mother and son being employed on Brisbane newspapers. (Annals of Brisbane Grammar School)

comedy, was produced at Government House, Brisbane in 1891 and 'Sweep', a three-act comedy for children, was a popular play and was printed in booklet form.[23] She died in 1918.[24] Her many essays, tales and sketches published in the Australian press have never been collected in book form.

Agnes G. Murphy

'. . . a year's connection with the Press gave her a new confidence . . .'

Two of the women who wrote for Melbourne *Punch* were Sophy Osmond, later a successful novelist in London, who contributed drama criticism, and Agnes G. Murphy, who was employed as social editor. Agnes Murphy appears, from an apparently semi-autobiographical novel *One Woman's Wisdom* published in London in 1895, to have been born in Ireland and migrated to Victoria (Giltland in the novel) as a young adult. The heroine of the novel, Mary Hewson, at first got a job copying legal documents in a lawyer's office, one of the first women to work in this field in 'Bourneville' (Melbourne). Soon after she became a contributor to the 'Giltland Times'

214

and then took up journalism as a profession. The author continued:

> Her literary venture prospered most kindly; and a year's connection with
> the Press gave her a new confidence in herself, and wholly transformed
> her one-time diffidence into the most charming independence.[25]

The novel contains probably the only contemporary fictionalised account,
although idealised and romanticised, of the life of a newspaperwoman. In the
novel the heroine, through her work as a reporter, becomes a member of the
higher levels of society centred on the vice-regal representatives, and uses her
friendship with the Governor to further the cause of higher education for
women. When the 'Giltland Times' changed hands, however, the new
owners made many staff changes, 'several clever journalists being displaced',
including Mary Hewson who, to the 'surprise of the whole staff', was
superseded by a sister of one of the new directors, a woman 'utterly common-
place in appearance and manner, original only in orthography, eccentric in
grammar, and not even witty...'[26]

When Hume Nisbet reviewed the book in the *British Australasian* he
wrote of the heroine:

> She becomes one of the Fourth Party, and gives with curious nicety the
> working methods of some of the Press; indeed her character studies in
> this department, as well as her side lights on fashionable society over the
> seas, rank amongst the most felicitous of her efforts, the details being put
> in lightly and humorously, yet with an exact precision that is
> admirable.[27]

After her dismissal the heroine of the novel is unable to find a suitable
permanent position on any 'Giltland' journal but several accept contributions
from her. Eventually she returns to England where, predating Alice Henry's
real-life success in the American trade union movement, she becomes Secretary of the Women's Labour Union and 'one of the most earnest and
seductive platform speakers in Great Britain'.[28]

It is not clear to what extent Agnes Murphy's life paralleled her heroine's
but she was certainly the social editor of Melbourne *Punch* ('the premier
society journal of Australia') for a considerable time. The women's page,
following the pattern adopted by many weeklies, was in the form of a letter.
Called 'The Lady's Letter' it was a gossip column with a touch of satire
written by 'Rhoda' from Holmsby House, Toorak to 'My dear Esme', plus
columns headed 'Gossip' and 'Social'. By 1895 the letter-writer was 'Minetta'
and she wrote to 'Mab', while 'Rhoda's Letter' came from Brunswick Square,
London. This may have coincided with Agnes Murphy's return to London for
the publication of *One Woman's Wisdom*.

In the early 1890s when E. Jerome Dyer edited a book about Victoria
and its resources for the Victorian Government, Agnes G. Murphy, described
as social editor of *Punch*, wrote an article for the work entitled 'Social Life in

Holmsby House, TOORAK, WEDNESDAY.

MY DEAR ESME,—One would never have thought that Sir Henry Loch would have recourse to hair-dye as a means of hiding the signs of advancing years. But yet, be for in Saturday's *Argus* the London ... of that journal says:—"Sir Henry ...king younger and more spry than the ft Melbourne— not a grey hair in the ... of his ample beard, and no trace of ... gait or carriage." On the day Sir ... Melbourne every hair of his ample ... was hot white was decidedly grey, and ...ough he was, folks will hardly believe ...bl patronise gold-wash. The paragraph ...plained in another way—the writer ... Sir Henry Loch the day he left Melbourne ... ...ling to his description I should ... ... a hundred to one that he ... him on the day he returned to ...

looked so absurd to see the rows and rows of empty seats, while all round the barrier the people were packed liked sardines. After a patient wait, however, the " great unwashed " found their way in and divided the crushing.

A LADY sitting near me was full of wrath on seeing that very few men took their hats off during the singing of the National Anthem. She was still further horrified when it was pointed out that clergymen were among the offenders. " Ah, well," exclaimed the lady, fixing her eyes on the two clerics near her, " they are only priests." The joke was that they were two prominent and moustached Church of England ministers. Because their choir was composed of Sunday School children they were perforce the noisiest and most unruly choristers that ever sang. People had to put their fingers in their ears to shut out the din, which was deafening. The Governor, who was well received, was looking particularly well.—Yours ever, RHODA.

MR. GEORGE JENKIN, a director of a number of land companies, leaves for a trip to Europe on Saturday next, by the s.s. *Ormuz*. Mr. Jenkin has gone for a much-needed holiday, and also to obtain a fortune lately left him.

MRS. ANNE C. FALL, the third woman lawyer in Boston, has just been admitted to the Suffolk Bar. She will practise law with her husband, but there will be no legal partnership, on account of the law forbidding contracts between husband and wife.

THE brilliant success of the Clara Merivale Opera Company is in no small measure due to the splendid chorus of sixty voices and full orchestra. In one scene one hundred and twenty persons appear on the stage, the spectacle being extremely fine.

AT Bathurst the other day the younger son of a titled family was charged with illegally using a horse, the property of a local magistrate. It was pleaded that the gentleman being short-sighted, he merely mistook another horse for his own, so the case was withdrawn.

" ONE of the most distinguished of Australians," says the *World*, " is now on a visit to England— namely, Mr. J. B. Patterson, of Victoria, the most prominent member of the Gillies-Deakin Government of Victoria, who is said to have put down the recent Australian strike by his courage and ability. Mr. Patterson is a Northumberland man, and has been in Australia for over thirty-nine years." Most distinguished of Australians is good; but we wonder what Gillies and Deakin think of J. B.'s alleged place in the Cabinet.

LORD BRIDPORT and the Hon. Alexander Yorke went to Windsor Castle the third week in February as Lord and Groom-in-Waiting to Her Majesty the Queen. The former is a cousin of Captain Acland Hood, and Mr. Yorke made a long stay in Melbourne as the guest of Sir Henry and Lady Loch.

A CURLING match, or bonspiel, took place early in February on the lake in the policies of Keith ...

Gossip.

THE takings at the People's Palace on Easter Monday, the opening day, were £700.

THE late Lady Rosebery has bequeathed to her secretary, Miss Moick, the handsome sum of £300 a year.

MR. and MRS. Brough will be entertained at a river picnic on Saturday by the Johnsonian Club, Brisbane.

MISS MYRA KEMBLE is doing tremendous business with " Dr. Bill " at the Theatre Royal, Adelaide.

DR. THORNTON, Bishop of Ballarat, visited Hamilton on Thursday to christen the son of the Rev. Mr. Siggers.

MR. DAVID KERCK, of Chiltern, now bound for England is said to ...

Writing women's page material in the form of letters was a popular device with many periodicals. Melbourne Punch's 'Lady's Letter' followed this pattern in the 1890s with letters addressed from 'Rhoda' at the very social address of Holmsby House, Toorak to 'Esme'. Like the Bulletin's women's letters 'Rhoda's' letters consisted of gossip with a touch of satire. Agnes Murphy, author of a novel with a woman journalist as heroine, was social editor of Punch. (Melbourne Punch 2 April 1891)

Victoria'. Perhaps the propaganda style of the publication encouraged her to abandon her satirical touch, for she wrote fulsomely of Melbourne society.[29] In 1909 her second book, a biography of Melba containing chapters written by Nellie Melba on the selection of music as a profession and on the science of singing, was published in London.[30]

Ada (Kidgell) Holman

From about the mid-1890s the Sydney contributor to Melbourne *Punch's* 'Lady's Letter' was Ada Kidgell, later Ada Holman, wife of W. A. Holman, New South Wales Labor politician and Premier. Ada Augusta Kidgell was born in 1869 at Ballarat, Victoria, daughter of an English-born journalist Ebenezer Kidgell and his Irish wife, formerly Agnes Martin. Her childhood and youth seem to have been spent in poor circumstances in the places where her father obtained journalistic positions—on the *Clunes Guardian*, near Ballarat, in suburban Melbourne on the *Hawthorn and Borroondara Standard* and on the *Sunday Times* in Sydney where he worked as sub-editor from 1895 until his death in 1902.

The move to Sydney gave Ada Kidgell the opportunity to take up writing herself and by 1896, in her late twenties, she was placing short stories, reviews, and political and literary items under her own name and the pseudonyms 'Marcus Malcolm' and 'Nardoo'. As 'Myee' she sent 'Our Sydney Letter' to Melbourne *Punch*. She also contributed to the *Sydney Mail, Sydney Morning Herald* and the Catholic *Freeman's Journal*, and she edited and wrote most of the copy for the *Co-operator*, a trade journal for rural producers.[31]

After her marriage in 1901 Ada Holman had some success in continuing her writing career, but she resented the limits placed on her freedom to work by the fact that she was married to a prominent politician and public opinion expected her to conform to the conventional roles of wife and mother.

As a further development in publishing specifically for women, on 7 January 1888 the *Sydney Morning Herald* began a weekly 'Woman's Column', sometimes sub-titled 'Woman's Talk to Women', in its Saturday edition. The column differed from conventional women's page material in containing no household hints or society or fashion news. Instead there were long essay-style articles dealing with serious topics of interest such as female suffrage and female employment opportunities. The column often consisted solely of one long essay on a topic such as 'The Amiable Woman' (14 July 1888); 'Women's Clubs' (4 August); 'Rinking' [roller-skating, the latest craze] by 'Moree Bealiba' (18 August); 'A College for Cookery' by 'E.T.A.' (13 October); and 'Women of the Nineteenth Century' by 'Liberta' (17 November). On 10 May 1890 there was a larger section than usual on the subject 'The Enfranchisement of Women. Two Views of the Question'. The negative was argued by 'Semper Fidelis' and the affirmative by 'Eucalypta'. On 12 July there was an article on women's suffrage entitled 'Something on the other side' signed by 'A MAN'.

When a second article was added to the column it was almost invariably about the Women's Industries and Centenary Fair held in 1888. It seems likely that it was the heightened awareness of women created by this Fair that actually provided the motivation for starting the column. It also seems likely that Emily Manning who had, by this time, been writing for the *Sydney Morning Herald* on many topics, including the writing of editorials, was the editor and perhaps main writer of the column. The regular appearance of the column ceased in the second half of 1890, coinciding with her illness and death. Apart from Emily Manning the *Herald* at this time had Mrs Carl Fischer, Miss Moon and 'Rose de Bohème' as semi-permanent writers or contributors. Miss Moon obtained the position of book reviewer in the late 1880s. She is believed to have been the first woman to hold such a position in Australia, as distinct from those women who occasionally contributed reviews. She was responsible for most of the reviews in the *Herald* until the appointment of Thomas Heney (later editor) as literary editor in 1893.[32]

Agnes Rose-Soley ('Rose de Bohème')

The disappearance of the 'Woman's Column' did not altogether stop the publication of the type of articles it had featured. By the time of its demise 'Rose de Bohème', who was to remain with the *Sydney Morning Herald* for many years, had joined the paper's staff as a regular contributor. In fact the disappearance of the 'Woman's Column' provided the opportunity for her to write on a wider range of general topics than had been published in the column. One of her first articles after the column ceased, published on 26 July 1890 under the heading 'A Woman's View', was on the topic that had Sydney in a ferment of discussion at the time — the performance of Ibsen's 'Doll's House' which brought the subject of the liberation of women to the fore. 'Rose de Bohème's' later articles were as often on general topics as on those specifically related to women, one being 'Fossicking round the fossils' about Jenolan Caves.[33]

Agnes Rebecca Rose, born in Scotland about 1847, was a well educated woman. She had studied in France and at Newnham College, Cambridge,

Agnes Rose-Soley began writing for the Sydney Morning Herald as 'Rose de Bohème' when its first 'Woman's Column' was being published between 1888 and 1890. When the column ceased she continued to write feature articles and was still a Herald writer many years later. Born in Scotland she was educated in France and at Newnham College, Cambridge. A member of the London Lyceum Club, she was a founder of the Lyceum Club for university educated women in Sydney. (Stray chords)

FEMININE FACTS AND FANCIES

The popularity of painted gauze was never greater than it is at present. Mounted on sunshades of white silk or satin it was never culiarly effective, and to gala gowns it lends a touch of individuality none too easy to obtain in these days when any woman with artistic instincts has such a plethora of exquisite materials to choose from. At the last great race meeting in Paris one of the most beautiful gowns worn was in rose silk, covered with pale green gauze, on which was painted a design in roses. The bodice was tabbed and ornamented with small pearl buttons on either side of an ecru embroidered front, beneath which was a full silk vest. Pale green—harmonising with the lighter shades of the foliage of the roses—was worn round the waist and the neck-band, and also formed a little ruffle just above the hem of the skirt. These gauzes are frequently painted by well-known artists, whose work commands prices so large that anything coming from their brush is treated even by the frivolous with marked consideration. In these circumstances, the gauze is subjected to a very little cutting, and is cared for in a manner that will probably ensure its being handed down to future generations after the fashion of the stately brocades of days gone by.

To provide something in the way of novelty is invariably the aim of those interested in promoting garden fetes and such like entertainments. To these may be recommended the bicycle tortoise race—an institution that is creating great diversion in such entertainments in England just at present. The wild efforts of the riders to maintain their balance while hardly moving is specially entertaining to those who know the extreme difficulty of riding "dead slow." Not so novel, but equally amusing, is the hat trimming contest, in which men alone compete. They cycle to a given point, where they find hats and the means of trimming them—the crowd naturally centres about...

happy hunting grounds of pilferers, but lately quite a distinguished burglar of the female persuasion has been making things unpleasant for bathers. Her identity was for long a secret, and the pretty little woman in a very "swagger" bathing suit was never for an instant suspected. She herself was a victim as often as anybody else, so of course came in for the public sympathy. More than once she had gone—quite accidentally, of course—into the wrong machine, and if it was occupied she apologised so profusely and sincerely for her very "silly" intrusion that people got quite fond of her both in the water and out of it. One unhappy day, however, she visited a machine apparently empty—and after a careful survey, began to stock the crown of her dapper little rubber cap with such small souvenirs as it was worth her while to take possession of. It was a sad moment when another bathing dressed figure rose from a corner in whose recess it had been hidden by a careful arrangement of towelling. This was nothing less than the female detective who had been "put on the job," and the dainty little bather is now missing from her wonted haunts. The circumstance created a little stir as going to show how things have changed since Bill Sykes was accepted as a typical burglar. Poor Bill is practically not "in it" these times, and a leading English paper very wisely points out how greatly the old order has changed. The modern burglar no longer depends on dark nights and lanterns, and only in one sense of the word are his deeds deeds of darkness. He is nothing if not up to date, and the telegraph enters into his service. He may come as a rate collector, a plumber, an insurance man, or a piano-tuner, and the safest time for the wary housekeeper is really when the lights are out and the world is wrapt in slumber—the very time in which the burglar of bygone days was most industriously plying his trade.

The English language as "made in Germany" can hardly be considered an improvement on the domestic production. Upon a...

WOMEN IN POLITICAL STRIFE.

THE ROWDY SCENES IN NEW ZEALAND.

"FREE SHOW" AND AN APPRECIATIVE AUDIENCE.

[FROM OUR CORRESPONDENT.]

WELLINGTON, 3rd September.

For the first three decades of its existence the New Zealand Parliament was remarkable amongst colonial legislatures for its high tone, and the orderliness and decorum with which its proceedings were conducted. Not the past week's record in the House of Representatives has been that of "scenes," one after another, of members named, of personal abuse in the choicest Billingsgate, and of occurrences which threatened to terminate in a resort to fisticuffs. If rumor be true, more than one member has been known to take his coat off in the lobbies, and a pugilistic encounter has only been prevented by the timely interference of less belligerent legislators. Party and personal animosity is at such a high tension that there is no knowing when the cord will snap asunder. Mr. Taylor has been named, but let off with an apology, for calling the ex-Treasurer a "miserable coward"; and Mr. Taylor was told by Mr. Fisher that his father was a notorious drunkard, and that he got seven days' in gaol for stealing beer. Of course there was not a word of truth in these assertions, Mr. Taylor's father never having been a drunkard, and never having served a term in prison for anything—in fact Mr. Taylor, sen., is as great a teetotaller as his son, who is the uncompromising apostle of prohibition—but under the shelter of Parliamentary privilege these random shots were fired against a man who had no other remedy against his slanderer except shooting at sight, as they do in Texas, or bodily castigation with a stockwhip. These are specimens of the extent to which personal abuse is now carried in our House of Representatives, and...

Daily newspapers were behind the periodical press in introducing women's columns. The Melbourne Age began its weekly column 'Feminine Facts and Fancies', on Saturday 3 July 1897. It was written in essay style and ranged over many topics from manners to international events. Other items of interest to women were often printed on the same page. (Age 10 September 1898)

---

before emigrating to Australia for health reasons. In 1891 she married John Fisher Soley, a leader-writer on the *Sydney Morning Herald*, and after their marriage they used the name Rose-Soley. Agnes Rose-Soley had been a member of the London Lyceum Club and was a founder of the Sydney branch of the Lyceum Club. During World War I the Club printed a collection of her poems, *The Call of the Blood and other War Verses*, as a money-raising effort. Some of her poems had been printed previously in the *Sydney Morning Herald, Sydney Mail, Daily Telegraph* and the *Bulletin* and others in London, San Francisco and Honolulu papers. Another collection, *Stray Chords*, was issued by the Lyceum Club in 1923. Agnes Rose-Soley was also a novelist, writing with her husband as joint author, *Manoupa*, a novel set in the South Seas.[34]

Agnes Rose-Soley was still writing for the *Sydney Morning Herald* when the paper re-started a women's section in 1905. Although the *Herald* and its associate paper, the weekly *Sydney Mail*, employed more women earlier than probably any other paper in Australia (Isabelle Le Patourel, Florence Baverstock, Theodosia Britton, Zara Aronson and Agnes Mowle were numbered among them) the paper was among the last to have a regular women's page (see Chapter 13).

On Saturday 3 July 1897 the Melbourne *Age* began a weekly column headed 'Feminine Facts and Fancies' written by 'Viola'. The writer may have been Henrietta McGowan (later Mrs Frank Walker) who was later a prominent *Age* journalist. The contents usually ranged from the reporting of local events to reflective comments on a great variety of topics such as manners, overseas royalty and table settings. This column, which was superior in quality to other women's columns, continued into the twentieth century. On the same page there were often other items of interest to women. One issue included an item headed 'Ladies as Reporters' and another reprinted a piece from the English *Spectator* on 'Women as Stockkeepers'.[35]

Stella Allan

'Thou art a woman,
And that is saying the best and the worst of thee.'
Argus 16 April 1898

Although the *Argus* had printed many of Alice Henry's articles from 1884 on, these were aimed at the general reader and it was not until 16 April 1898 that the paper began to publish a regular women's column. The heading was 'Woman's Realm' (sometimes called 'Women's Realm'), with the quotation above, (hardly likely to have been chosen by a woman) attributed to British poet P.J. Bailey as a sub-title.

The first columns were written by contributors, Marian Jones and later Florence Baverstock. The first woman appointed to the staff of the *Argus* was Miss Frances F. Elmes who was engaged in 1898 to write and edit 'Woman's Realm', being followed by Miss A.A. (Bunchy) Wheeler in 1905.[36] Frances Elmes was a short story writer whose work appeared in the *Bulletin*, and in the *Bulletin Story Book*, and was the author of *The Melbourne Cookery Book*. At first the column seemed to lack any direction, usually consisting of a collection of odd items which could range from the latest gossip about actress Mrs Patrick Campbell to articles on kissing and on women as handlers of guns and rifles.

WOMAN'S REALM.

"Thou art a woman,
And that is saying the best and worst of thee."
—Bailey.

Who would imagine that danger lurked hidden in such a simple article of apparel as a collar or a comb? Life, we know, is full of pitfalls, and if we were always detecting the gooseberry in our champagne and the turnip in our conserves it would simply become intolerable. If all that has been said in the "Lancet" against the use of celluloid be true, no insurance office would possibly undertake the life of a wearer of ornaments made from this fashionable material. A warning is given against the dangerously combustible and inflammable properties of celluloid, which, it is said, is utterly unsuitable for ornamental or useful purposes on the person, since it exposes the wearer to such serious risks. Perhaps the danger is somewhat overstated. Of course fumes given off by hot curling-tongs being applied to celluloid hair-combs will cause them to ignite; so also will a lighted match ignite the smoke puffed out of a cigar and cause it to take flame readily.

We hear of women nowadays taking to all sorts of unlikely trades and professions. The novel business of a hair farm has lately been started in the south of France. Hitherto prisons, convents, and private people have supplied the enormous quantity of hair which is sold to give artificial charm to those who require additional locks and coils or plaits to assist their scanty tresses to vie with others of the fair sex more blessed in this respect. The farm is said to afford employment to girls with a superabundant supply of hair whilst their locks are being cultivated to the required state of perfection. They are then shorn, and either retained whilst their hair grows again, or, if the second crop is not promising, they are dismissed, and other maidens take their places. An English newspaper says that a few weeks ago a Paris hairdresser received an offer of 80lb. weight of hair from a convent near Tours. This represented the tresses of 300 novices who had lately entered the convent, for on taking the veil of course the head is shorn.

The Melbourne Argus began a weekly women's column, called 'Woman's Realm' on 16 April 1898. The paper's first women writers included Marian Jones, Florence Baverstock, Frances Elmes and A. A ('Bunchy') Wheeler and in 1908 Stella Allan (above) began her 'Women to Women' feature under the name of 'Vesta'. Before her marriage she had a remarkable journalistic career in New Zealand, succeeding against a great deal of male opposition in joining the parliamentary press gallery in Wellington. (Mrs Isobel Keep, Hawthorn, Victoria)

The Argus women's page was not to develop its true character until it was taken over in 1908 by Stella Allan. Stella Allan's remarkable journalistic career had begun in New Zealand in 1898 when, after a great deal of opposition, she was accepted as the correspondent of the Lyttleton Times in the parliamentary press gallery. Born Stella Henderson in 1871, at Kaiapoi on the South Island, she graduated Bachelor of Arts with first class honours in 1892 and Master of Arts in 1893. After she qualified as a lawyer special legislation was passed by the New Zealand Parliament to allow her to practise,

221

but she preferred to take up journalism. When she first applied to join the parliamentary press gallery objections were raised that separate accommodation from the male pressmen and a special 'retiring room' would have to be provided. The underlying objection was the fear that the introduction of women into a previously all-male section of the profession would lead to a lowering of wage rates, as had happened in several other occupations.[37]

In 1900 she married Edwin Frank Allan, senior leader-writer for the Wellington *Evening Post*, and in 1903 they settled in Melbourne when Allan was appointed foreign affairs leader-writer for the *Argus*. Soon Stella Allan was writing for newspapers in Melbourne including contributing regular 'Fiction of the Day' reviews to the *Argus*, beginning in April 1904. In 1907 the *Argus* commissioned her to write a series of articles on the first Australian Women's Work Exhibition held in October that year. These were a great success at the time and still make interesting reading. On 19 February 1908 she began to contribute a regular Wednesday feature, and on 13 May 1908 her regular 'Women to Women' feature signed 'Vesta' (Roman goddess of hearth and household), which was to be a feature of the *Argus* for many years, began.[38] Vesta's pages covered every aspect of women's affairs and community welfare issues and for the next thirty years they provided a haven of common sense for people requiring information, advice and help. She wrote her stories first hand, travelling extensively by train and horse and buggy to report on women on outback farms and in country towns in droughts, floods, mice plagues and bushfires.[39]

When the Australian Journalists' Association was formed in 1910 Stella Allan was a foundation member and in 1924 she was substitute Australian delegate to the League of Nations. After her retirement in 1938 she continued to write for the *Argus*. She died in Melbourne in 1962 aged ninety.

Janet Nanson

'. . . *she took surreptitious notes on her white shirt cuffs while seated in the "ladies gallery"* . . .'
West Australian 15 December 1943

Janet Nanson's career began with the *West Australian* when she was appointed social editor in 1897, the first woman to join the staff. Formerly Janet Drummond Durlacher, she was born in 1868 and in 1887 married journalist John Leighton Nanson, who after holding other positions on the *West Australian* became associate editor and chief leader-writer in 1897. Janet Nanson wrote under the name of 'Sigma' in the *West Australian* and was the original 'Aunt Mary' of the *Western Mail*, the weekly run by the *West*

222

Janet Nanson was probably Australia's first woman political journalist. Before she was admitted to the press gallery in the Western Australian Parliament she sat in the ladies gallery taking notes on the white cuffs of her blouse so that she could get her story out to readers of the Perth Morning Herald. *Earlier she was the first woman to join the staff of the* West Australian *writing social notes as 'Sigma' and the children's page of the* Western Mail *as 'Aunt Mary'. (Courtesy The J. S. Battye Library of West Australian History [3326]* West Australian *15 December 1943)*

Australian for country people.

In 1901 her husband won a seat in the Western Australian Parliament. In 1902 he resigned from the *West Australian* and bought a controlling interest in the *Morning Herald*, launched by the owners of the *Daily News* to compete with his old paper. Later Janet Nanson left the *West Australian* to become a political reporter for her husband's new paper, becoming probably the first woman political journalist in Australia. Like Stella Allan in New Zealand she had some trouble being admitted to the parliamentary press gallery. Before gaining admission she used to take 'surreptitious notes on her white shirt cuffs while seated in the "ladies gallery" '. Her political reports were always widely read. When Leighton Nanson sold his interest in the *Herald* Janet Nanson left the paper and did no more regular newspaper work. After her husband's death in 1916 she lived in alternately London, the home of her only daughter, and Perth, until her death in Perth in 1943.[40]

In 1901 the *West Australian* had engaged Mrs A.G. Curthoys as music critic and soon after Mrs Emily Pelloe founded the *West Australian*'s women's page, using the pen name 'Ixia'. During this time Mrs Muriel Chase, who was related through her mother's family to the great English social worker, Elizabeth Fry, began writing for the paper and in 1903 she became social editress of the *West Australian* succeeding Janet Nanson, writing under the name of 'Adrienne' and she also succeeded Janet Nanson as 'Aunt Mary' on the *Western Mail*. She continued in these positions until her death in 1936. Like many other women journalists she was prominent in organising an association of women writers, being a foundation member of the Women Writers' Club.[41]

Margaret Baxter, *Hummer* and 'Lucinda Sharpe', Mary Ann Cameron, Jeannie Lockett, Dame Mary Gilmore

The inclusion of women's columns in specialised journals, particularly in trade union and labour papers, began in the early 1890s, but other types of periodicals also ran these columns. The Catholic *Freeman's Journal* had a women's page in the 1890s, its editor being Margaret Agnese Baxter, a daughter of John Baxter, Collector of Customs. In 1904 she left for London to become a correspondent for the Sydney *Daily Telegraph* and she contributed to many British publications.[42]

In 1892 the *Hummer*, the journal of the Amalgamated Shearers' Union, published at Wagga, New South Wales, began 'Our Sisters' Column', a far more down-to-earth women's section than those appearing in other newspapers and periodicals. To a great extent it was kept going by readers' letters on subjects such as unfair treatment of servants, women's suffrage and women's employment. Typical of these was a letter from Ellen B. published on 28 May 1892 beginning, 'DEAR HUMMER, Don't you think it is about time we women had a Union?'. It detailed an instance of the unfair treatment of two girls looking for work as servants and concluded 'Women want more protection. This can only be brought about by themselves. Yes, we want a union'.

The paper also ran a series of radical articles by 'Lucinda Sharpe', a pseudonym used by journalist and trade unionist William Lane who later led a group of Australians to form the 'New Australia' socialist settlement in Paraguay. Under headings such as 'Lucinda Sharpe on Color, . . . on Thrift, . . . on Schooling', and many other subjects, these articles elicited considerable response from readers.

When the *Hummer* was amalgamated with the *Worker* in October 1892, 'Our Sisters' Column' continued for a short time and then lapsed. A women's column was not to appear again until Mary Gilmore became women's editor in 1908.

Twenty years before Mary Gilmore joined the *Worker* to become a great

224

advocate for social and economic reforms, her aunt Jeannie Lockett was writing on labour questions for a London magazine and her mother, Mary Ann Cameron, was writing for the *Town and Country Journal* and the *Daily Telegraph* in Sydney. The two sisters Jeannie (Jane) and Mary Ann were born in the Bathurst district, daughters of a farmer, Hugh Beattie, who had emigrated from County Antrim, Northern Ireland. Mary Ann Beattie married Donald Cameron, son of a farmer on adjoining land.

Jeannie Beattie became a teacher before marrying Thomas Lockett in Wagga. Later in Sydney she was headmistress of several public schools, preparing her pupils for university exams and being highly praised in a school inspector's report. While teaching she was also a writer of romances and a contributor to English magazines including *Nineteenth Century, Westminster Review* and *St James's Gazette*, as well as the Australian *Town and Country Journal*. Her articles on labour questions published in the *Westminster Review* were on a subject that set her apart from most women journalists of the time. They included 'The Labour Question in Australia. From an Australian Point of View' published in 1889 and 'The Labour Battle in Australia' on the great maritime strike, published posthumously in 1891.

Jeannie Lockett was also the author of several serials and stories published in the *Town and Country Journal* and the *Evening News*. The last, 'The Case of Dr Hilston', was completed only a few weeks before her death in November 1890 at the age of forty-three. In her short life she had combined a range of activities unusual for a woman at the time. She had been both a serious writer and an author of lighthearted entertainment, combining her writing with a successful career as a teacher and bringing up a family of three children.[43]

Her niece, Mary Jean Cameron, later became famous as Dame Mary Gilmore. In 1887 while she was teaching at Illabo near Bethungra, north of Wagga, she began to contribute to newspapers in Albury and Wagga. She continued these contributions when she transferred to Silverton Public School near Broken Hill, her articles always appearing under a nom de plume because school teachers were not allowed to write for the press. Some of her verses were signed 'Em Jaycee' derived from her initials. In 1890 she transferred to Sydney, then a ferment of political and literary activity where she continued writing and working for radical trade unionist causes.

Her writing career was interrupted by the years she spent at the 'New Australia' settlement in Paraguay, South America, where she married fellow colonist, William Gilmore. After her return she lived on a property near Casterton in western Victoria where her husband worked on the land. At Casterton she began contributing verse to the *Bulletin*, the *Worker* and to Vida Goldstein's *New Idea* in Melbourne. Her long connection with the *Worker* began in 1908 when she began the 'Women's Page' with an article 'For worker women'. She was to edit the page until 1931, the story of her fame as a writer and women's page editor belonging mainly to the twentieth century.

13

Newspaper Women and Social Ladies

'Most of the women inky wayfarers of today had never met Mrs.
Le Patourel . . .'

Bulletin 12 July 1933

Until the 1890s most women engaged in writing for newspapers had stumbled in haphazard ways into their positions, usually either through their interest in some other form of writing, because they had a strong urge to convey their views to the public or because they had special expertise (i.e. as music or theatre critics).

As positions in women's pages journalism expanded it becomes possible to classify broadly the women who took such jobs. Many were, as some of their predecessors had been, women who combined the writing of novels, serials, poetry.or short stories with journalism. Others were natural leaders (the women who later became prominent members of women's clubs and women's movements) attracted to an out-of-the-ordinary occupation. Another group came to newspaper work through their family associations with journalism. Two other types were also attracted to journalistic work. Because so much women's page journalism involved the reporting of society events, women with an upper-class background and an entrée into society circles centred on the various government houses had some advantages. Mrs Le Patourel was the epitome of this type of reporter, having married a governor's aide-de-camp. Others came from the newly emergent group of young women later to be known as flappers. They moved in slightly Bohemian circles and were attracted to work that was apparently more glamorous than the regular standbys of teaching, nursing and office work. Louise Mack was a perfect example, even when past middle age she retained the glamour of a flapper, but she was as well a competent journalist and author.

The *Bulletin* was to be the training ground and outlet for some of the more important of Australia's early women journalists, but it was some years after the *Bulletin* began in 1880 before a women's section was included. By 1886 there was a social column, sometimes signed 'Mab'. This was the pseudonym of Mrs Pattie Fotheringhame, the first woman writer employed by the *Bulletin*, who later started and edited a children's paper *Young Australia*.[1] The social column, later called 'Society', was to continue simultaneously with the publication of a different kind of women's column which began in July 1889. This column, in the form of a letter, took a lighthearted, satirical look at society. Some very accomplished and later famous women were attracted to writing the column which at first covered only Sydney news but was later expanded to take in 'letters' from women correspondents in Melbourne, Adelaide and other capitals.

The writer of the Women's Column for the *Bulletin* was Alexina Maude (Ina) Wildman, a brilliant young woman who, under the name of 'Sappho Smith' began a regular column on 13 July 1889. She was succeeded in 1896 by Florence Blair (later Baverstock) who wrote under the name of 'Cleo' to 'My dear Myee'. In 1898 Louise Mack continued to write to 'Myee' under the pen-name of 'Gouli-Gouli', and in 1901 Conor O'Brien used the pseudonym 'Akenehi' to write to 'My dear Arini'. The technique of writing women's columns in the form of letters was widespread and many imitated the *Bulletin*'s satirical style, not always successfully.

Alexina Maude Wildman

'. . . *the incomparable Ina Wildman ("Sappho Smith").*'
W. E. Fitzhenry

Ina Wildman's column in the *Bulletin* was headed by a Phil May drawing of a very stern, elderly dowager-type female disapprovingly peering over her pince-nez, holding a fan in front of her spare, rigid figure. Nothing could have been more unlike the actual columnist herself.

Ina Wildman first came to the notice of the *Bulletin* when in 1885 at the age of thirteen she arrived by tram from her home in Waverley to complain to a sub-editor about his reply to some verses she had submitted. Many years later the anonymous sub-editor described the incident:

'You are the sub-editor, aren't you,' she said, 'so I suppose you wrote this?' 'This' was an answer to a correspondent — 'Ina M. W.: Delightful verses but why not send something of your own?' an impertinence prompted by the fact that verses emulating those of Dante Gabriel

Rossetti were written in the crude pothooks and hangers of childhood. 'You don't think I could write verses like those? Well, look at this one that I wrote in the tram coming in.'[2]

Ina Wildman convinced the sub-editor of the authenticity of her verse and soon she was a regular contributor of prose and verse. The sub-editor described her at the time:

> ... she was apparently under 16 and wore a pigtail. She was very slender, not either pretty or beautiful, but in feature attractive and in manner charming. In some respects she was strangely child-like. When she received her first payment at the counter on the ground floor she ran upstairs to the sub.'s room and, holding out the money, said 'Look at this? They gave me all that for my verses! Fancy! Some day I'll go all the way home in a cab, but not this week. Won't it be wonderful!'[3]

Her literary success was chequered, however, as the *Bulletin* editor, J. F. Archibald, believed women could not write poetry. Only a very small proportion of the poems she submitted were published until:

> ... Archibald once went on a holiday and the sub. was left in charge. Two columns of her verse appeared in the next issue, and Archibald wired from Rockhampton. There were two more columns in the next and following issues. Archibald wired from Townsville and started for home![4]

Alexina Maude Wildman was born in Paddington in 1872, a daughter of Edwin Wildman, a clerk, and his wife Elizabeth (née Stevens). About four years after her first encounter with the *Bulletin* Ina Wildman, under the name 'Sappho Smith', began a regular weekly column writing to 'My dear Mooribunda'. It provided readers with all the news on governor's balls, race meetings and the latest society marriages but in a facetious way that attracted readers ready to be amused at pomposity. Her pseudonym was itself ironic, combining Sappho, the name of the most famous woman poet, leader of a band of young women poets in Greece in 600 BC called by Plato the 'Tenth Muse', with the utterly ordinary name of Smith.

'Sappho Smith' quickly became a model and an inspiration for the many young women attempting to break into journalism, although she herself was not an uncritical observer of some of the women's issues of the time, or at least of some of their proponents. On women's suffrage supporters she wrote:

> If there is one thing in the world that makes me smile behind my gauze fan ... it is to hear the Sydney she-Suffragists crying aloud in the wilderness, proclaiming their 'advanced opinions' ... their stern contempt for the everyday woman who has no Ideas, a six-foot I. Because, in sober truth, the Suffragists are a sheepy mob — one woman's opinion is their opinion, as anybody knows who attends a Rights seance and watches the way the applause goes. You have only to be 'Lady' So-

Although the women's letter she wrote for the Bulletin appeared under a Phil May cartoon depicting an elderly dowager, the writer Ina Wildman was only seventeen when she began her column in 1889. She wrote her letters in a flippant, satirical style under the name of 'Sappho Smith' her writing becoming a model for many other women journalists who were not always successful in imitating her. (Bulletin 21 September 1889)

an'-So, and the meeting lifts up both feet and its brass-shod gamp to
drive your namby-pambyisms home every time you open your mouth —
and what a Title disapproves of, the whole surge of untrammelled
feminine intellects disapprove of at sight without asking any questions. It
is pitiable. More it is sickening.[5]

During the seven years she wrote the column, Ina Wildman became an
admired figure, afterwards referred to as 'the incomparable Sappho Smith'.[6]
Mrs R. H. Todd, wife of lawyer Dr Robert Todd, and a journalist on several
Sydney papers including Louisa Lawson's *Dawn*, the *Echo*, *Illustrated Sydney
News* and later first editor of *Women's Budget*, received great help from her.
'She was known and rather dreaded by smart society', Mrs Todd said. In a
book of reminiscences written many years after Ina Wildman's death, Mrs
Todd wrote:

> Apart from her somewhat caustic writings, Miss Wildman was a
> sympathetic soul, and was always encouraging to me as a shy and rather
> self-conscious beginner. I happened to meet her one day at a Town Hall
> reception, and was describing to her some of the humours of the last
> Government House ball. The wife of a prominent politician had fastened
> her sparkling diamond necklace with a particularly dingy piece of white
> tape, while her daughter, when I asked her how she was enjoying herself,
> replied rather tartly: 'One doesn't come to Government House to enjoy
> oneself.'
> To my surprise, instead of being amused at my frivolous chatter, she
> remarked wistfully, 'I should so love to go to a Government House ball.'
> In an effort to console her I said, 'But if you did, you could hardly
> write as frankly as you do about the vice-royalties.'[7]

Ina Wildman assured her that she would write in exactly the same way should
she be invited to Government House functions. Part of this story originated in
Ina Wildman's last column published on 22 August 1896. Reporting a
Government House event she wrote of a 'Sydney woman at a Vice Regal
shivoo' who when asked if she was enjoying herself replied 'One does not
come to Government House to enjoy oneself, Mrs Blank!'.

In 1894 Ina Wildman developed Bright's disease. She continued her
regular column for two years, leaving to travel to Queensland in the hope that
the journey would improve her health. She also planned a trip to Europe but
was too ill to leave and she died at Waverley on 15 November 1896 at the age
of twenty-four.[8] After her death she was referred to as 'incomparable', 'never
equalled', 'lamented' and as a writer with 'a wonderful eye for bizarre effects
and a mind like a scintillating surface of light'.[9] Sadly her style and her
subjects were ephemeral; just over ten years after her death the *Bookfellow*
praising the style of one of her successors said:

> One hears people talking of 'Sappho Smith' as the bright star among the
> *Bulletin*'s contributors; but the standard of work has been raised so greatly

230

that much of her work would be unprintable today and this isn't meant by any means in disparagement of clever 'Sappho'.[10]

Florence Baverstock

'All Sydney may know it, but Thursday Island wouldn't understand what it was all about . . .'

J. F. Archibald

On 26 September 1896 six weeks before Ina Wildman's death, a woman then in her late thirties who had been a pioneer journalist and was to become a leader in women's organisations, took over the *Bulletin*'s women's column. She wrote under the name of 'Cleo' (one of the nine Greek muses, at first of epic poetry and later of history) and addressed her letter to 'My dear Myee'.

The writer was Florence Blair, born in 1861, daughter of journalist and politician, David Blair, the first editor of the Melbourne *Age* and before that a staff journalist on the Melbourne *Argus*. In her youth in Melbourne she assisted her father in the writing and production of his two works of popular history *The history of Australasia* (1878) and *Cyclopaedia of Australasia* (1881) and in the early 1880s she became a regular contributor to the Melbourne *Argus* at time when women were rare in journalism. On one occasion when she handed the editor, Edward Cunningham, an article he had commissioned, she said, 'The day will come when women will be employed as regular staff writers on newspapers'. 'God forbid', replied Cunningham.[11]

Florence Blair wrote leaders as well as features for the *Argus*. She was also among the first women writers to send despatches back to Australia from overseas. In the 1880s she visited Tonga and Samoa and from there wrote vivid descriptions of her impressions, including a visit to R. L. Stevenson's family at Vailima and an overnight stay in a Samoan chief's tribal camp. All were signed 'Victorian Girl'.

Back in Melbourne she and her sister, Lily, (later Mrs Percy Hunter) joined a few *Argus* journalists including Donald Macdonnell, John Sandes and Davison ('Peter') Symmons, described as 'the brightest wits on the Melbourne press', in writing for an entertaining weekly of musical, theatrical, social and general news and comment called *Bohemia*, edited by E. Jerome Dyer. This involvement did not last long as *Argus* proprietor Lachlan Mackinnon decided that the journalists he employed should support the *Argus*'s stablemate the *Australasian* with contributions rather than spend their time on an independent production. Macdonnell, Sandes and Symmons accepted a 50 per cent rise and agreed to drop *Bohemia* and start a column under the name of 'Oriel' to be published in the *Argus* each Saturday.[12] There is no indication of any

Florence Baverstock was one of Australia's first women journalists. A daughter of Melbourne newspaperman and editor, David Blair, she began writing in the early 1880s, later sending despatches from overseas which were published under the name of 'Victorian Girl'. In 1896 she became editor of the Bulletin's Women's Letter, regarded as the 'blue ribbon' job of its kind in Australia. This photograph was taken during the time she was editor of the women's section of the Sydney Morning Herald *from 1914 to 1918. (Photograph Fleur Harmsen, Snug, Tasmania)*

such inducement to Florence and her sister, but they were employed on the *Argus* only as casual contributors not staff members.

Florence Blair made another overseas trip in 1895 and again using her byline 'Victorian Girl' wrote a series of popular articles describing British and European life and events from a woman's viewpoint. While in London she developed a lifelong interest in the theatre and she was later to use the knowledge she acquired as drama critic for Sydney publications.

Not long after her return to Australia, J. F. Archibald, editor of the *Bulletin*, offered her the blue ribbon job of the 'Women's Letter'. An indication of the adventurousness of her move can be seen from her brother's comment when he called for her at the *Bulletin*, then a gathering place for Sydney's Bohemians and a paper with a radical policy, to take her to visit friends. 'Please don't tell them you're on the *Bulletin*,' he begged, 'they might be shocked'.[13]

Florence Blair's writing style was a little heavier handed than Ina Wildman's but the satire remained. Reporting on a new club, she wrote:

> The new ladies' club has taken unto itself new premises in Phillip-street, and, of course, has called itself the Victoria. Who was it that originally said that all women were King-worshippers, Queen-worshippers, and lord worshippers?[14]

Her comments on the dressing of society figures could be biting: 'Lady T. was simply dressed in a blue alpaca skirt and grass-lawn blouse, and walked ungloved, which — if you have nice diamond rings — is now the correct snap'.[15]

Archibald advised her against being allusive. After cutting out one of her pars he said:

> 'All Sydney may know it, but Thursday Island wouldn't understand what it was all about. . . . A par must be thistledown to be light enough to blow across a continent, but it must convey a tiny seed of fact to be worth the sending.[16]

When Florence Blair left the *Bulletin* in 1898 just before her marriage to Captain Archibald B. Baverstock, an English sea captain she had met on her voyage to London in 1895, her *Bulletin* colleagues presented her with a gold bracelet set with a ruby, a pearl and a sapphire edged with small diamonds. She returned to Melbourne to live and worked for a time for the *Argus'* recently begun 'Woman's Realm' column. After the birth of her third child she returned to Sydney in 1907 to take over the *Daily Telegraph's* women's page. In describing how she transformed it, the *Bulletin* gave a good description of most women's columns:

> . . . her informative nib lifted the TELEGRAPH'S women's columns for a time out of the deadly, dreary ruck of long dress reports and the lists of those who 'also ran' at miscellaneous functions. But the ruck resumed business, as presumably better suited to the genteel lady reader, who eagerly chases the tales of interminable tea-fights at the breakfast table, and reads with starting eyes that 'Miss Jones looked pretty as usual,' and that Miss Robinson wore a garniture of brown bombazine trimmed with pale black, and was so tightly laced that she could only breathe by deputy.[17]

In 1914 Florence Baverstock moved to the *Sydney Morning Herald* to run the women's section. Although restricted by the bounds of what were regarded as subjects of interest to women, she wrote articles on general topics and music and drama criticism in a graceful and entertaining style. After her retirement from full-time work with the *Sydney Morning Herald* in 1918 she continued to contribute to many publications. She was an early member of the New South Wales Institute of Journalists (one of the predecessors of the Australian Journalists' Association) and when the Society of Women Writers was formed in 1925 she was elected first president.

Florence Baverstock died at Mosman at the age of seventy-six in 1937. Both her daughters, Sheila Wigmore and Dolly Baverstock, and her son Bill became well-known journalists. A few months before her death Dame Mary Gilmore had written to her: 'If ever one woman admired another, I admired you. I love character, I love strength and I love the definite. And then there is intellect and toleration'.[18]

233

Louise Mack

'. . . the Bible of all the bright young things who did not then know they were "flappers".'

Ada Holman

One of the brightest and most appealing characters among the early women journalists in Sydney succeeded Florence Baverstock as writer of the *Bulletin's* women's column in 1898. Writing as 'Gouli Gouli', her real name was Louise Mack. From a frugal background Louise Mack emerged as the true Bohemian of the women writers of the period. Starting her writing career as editor of a schoolgirl magazine, she later starved in a garret while writing a novel in London, made a great deal of money writing potboilers for the Harmsworth press, spending it all extravagantly, and was one of the very few women war correspondents in World War I.

Louise and her sister Amy, also a writer, were two of the thirteen children of Rev. Hans Hamilton Mack, a Wesleyan minister, and his wife, both born in Northern Ireland. In Australia Rev. Mack ministered in many places. Louise (Marie Louise Hamilton) was born while he was a minister in Hobart in 1870 and Amy while he was ministering at Port Adelaide in 1876. In 1882 the family moved to Sydney and Louise became a pupil at Sydney Girls' High School where she wrote verse and edited 'The Girls' High School Gazette'. Ethel Turner, a pupil at the same time, was editor of a rival paper 'The Iris'.[19]

After failing to matriculate Louise Mack worked briefly as a governess and in the early 1890s sent her first contribution to the *Bulletin*. She described her elation at the result in an interview with Mrs Charles Bright, editor of *Cosmos*:

> Everyone has red-letter days in his or her experience, and one of mine is a memorable morning when the postman brought a letter addressed Mr. L. Mack, asking that gentleman to call on the editor of the *Bulletin*.[20]

She searched for the *Bulletin* office, eventually finding the stairs and walking up with a 'most violently beating heart'. J. F. Archibald, thinking a man had written her poem 'Soul Flight', was surprised to see a blue-eyed, golden-haired young girl. He advised her on writing and accepted 'Soul Flight' which appeared under the initials M.L.M., the first writing for which Louise Mack was paid. Encouraged, she wrote a short story and when this was accepted also she decided to adopt literature as a profession. In the following years she wrote short stories and verses for the English *Cassell's Magazine*, and for nearly all the Sydney papers, including the *Bulletin, Sydney Mail, Town and Country Journal, Illustrated Sydney News, Daily Telegraph* and *Sunday Times*.[21]

Louise Mack was the author of three books and a scintillating figure in the Bohemian world of literary Sydney when she took over as the writer of the Bulletin's women's letter in 1898. She left Australia in 1901 for London where she wrote pot-boilers for the Harmsworth Press, sometimes writing three at the one time. After the start of World War I she defied a ban on women war correspondents, travelling to Holland and Belgium and reporting on the fall of Antwerp. (Cosmos 31 October 1895)

In 1895 she sent the manuscript of a novel *The world is round* to London publishers Fisher Unwin and Co, and by return post received news of its acceptance and proposals for all her future work. 'The letter dropped from my hands with incredulous delight,' she said. 'Here, at last, was the fulfilment of my waking dreams, and for days I walked as on enchanted ground.' The publisher's reader described it as 'a brilliant little study . . . sparkling and witty, told in a graphic style'.[22] With the publication of this book, followed by *Teens* and *Girls Together*, both based on her schoolgirl experiences at Sydney High, she became a famous and admired young author.

In 1896 in Sydney she married Percy Creed, a barrister from Dublin. Marriage did not interrupt her literary career and in 1898 she joined the *Bulletin* staff to take over the 'Women's Letter' under the pen-name of 'Gouli Gouli'. Her column was brightly written but the satiric touch so noticeable when the column was written by Ina Wildman was not so much in evidence. She continued with other writing, the *Bulletin* in 1901 publishing her poems, *Dreams in flower*. Although A. G. Stephens said 'in their quality of poetry they form a most distinguished body of verses written by a woman in our own country',[23] their reputation did not last and she is remembered chiefly as a writer of juvenile fiction and a journalist rather than as a poet.

In 1901 Louise Mack, having apparently separated from her husband, left Sydney to seek wider opportunities in London. She left with a gift presented by fellow journalists Zara Aronson and Ethel Turner on behalf of her friends and an address designed by Norman Lindsay which included a verse 'Will You Remember' written by A. G. Stephens.[24] Arriving in London practically penniless she wrote a novel, *An Australian girl in London*, which was published in 1902. It was well received and she became a protegée of W. T. Stead, writing for his *Review of Reviews*.[25] Success in London was not enough for her restless nature, however. In the following years Louise Mack travelled widely and for some time lived in Florence, where she edited the *Italiano Gazette*, an English paper, from 1904 to 1907.

Later back in England, again without money, she applied for a vacancy on the *Daily Mail* run by Alfred Harmsworth (later Lord Northcliffe) and had to take a taxi to the interview because her shoes were so worn she could not walk in them. She got the job and on the way out told the commissionaire to pay the taxi and put the cost down to the boss. Ada Holman wrote, 'The man, probably dazzled by the blue eyes and baby face, meekly obeyed... Lord Northcliffe recognised her light touch in journalism as just what he wanted'.[26] She was to write many successful serials for the Harmsworth Press, probably diluting her literary talent in the process. By 1913 she was reported in the Australian press as being one of the most popular writers in London, her serials reaching millions of readers. Published first in the *Daily Mail, Daily Mirror* and other Harmsworth newspapers, they were published subsequently in book form. *The Music Makers* appeared serially in the London *Daily Mirror* and in translations in the *Hebdomadaire* Paris, *Morgen* Berlin, and *Courier* Milan, and then was published as a book. Later she also wrote a dramatic version for the stage.

For four years running there was never a time when she did not have one serial running in one of the Harmsworth publications and at one time she was writing three simultaneously. She described it as exciting work keeping three sets of printers going, one of them alone absorbing 2500 words a day. She told the *Lone Hand* she enjoyed the work describing it as 'the most delightful thing in the world'[27]. A *Lone Hand* interviewer wrote:

> Her wonderful vitality seems to gain force under pressure, and she finds that the heavier the work the more capable she is of expressing herself. She never actually writes a line, but dictates direct to the type-writer, except when she is in a very rapid mood, and then the secretary has to resort to shorthand. The actual composing of a story only occupies three hours a day; but during this space of time the novelist dictates without a stop.
>
> Louise Mack's interesting experiences in journalism have been of considerable service in writing serials, for the feuilleton[28] requires a condensed method, and each instalment must end with a quick curtain. Even when she was editor of a rival journal to one conducted by Ethel Turner at the Sydney High School, she was learning the art of rounding

off a paragraph.[29]

By 1913 Louise Mack was homesick and she intended to return to Australia in 1914 but was prevented by the start of World War I. This was a wonderful opportunity for a journalist on the spot and defying the rule that no woman was to go to the front as a correspondent, she managed to get to Belgium as the first woman war correspondent, reporting for the *Evening News* and the *Daily Mail*. Her eye-witness account of the German invasion of Antwerp and her adventures were published in a book, *A woman's experiences in the Great War* in 1915. She was described at the time as: 'the only Englishwoman to stay in Antwerp during the German occupation, the only Englishwoman to enter Brussels while the Germans were actually in possession, and the only woman writer to visit Aerschot after the sacking of that town'.[30] She narrowly escaped capture by the Germans, at one stage adopting the disguise of a Belgian serving-maid employed cutting sandwiches for German soldiers in one of the restaurants of Antwerp. Risking being shot as a spy, she escaped eventually by being driven in a cart by a suspicious Belgian.[31]

Later in the war she returned to Australia and toured the country speaking of her war experiences and raising money for the Red Cross. In 1924 at the age of fifty-four, she married Captain Allen Illingworth Leyland, a New Zealand Anzac aged thirty-three. Unable to get a permanent journalistic job in Australia, she worked as a freelance journalist and often visited the *Bulletin* office where W.E. Fitzhenry frequently talked with her:

I wish now that I had recorded her amusing recollections of some of her sister writers: Constance Clyde, Barbara Baynton, Ethel Mills, Maud Light, Ethel Castilla, Tarella Quinn, the Turner sisters and the incomparable Ina Wildman ('Sappho Smith').[32]

Louise Mack published two more novels but they made her little money and she died in poor circumstances in 1935 at the age of sixty-five. Her second husband had died three years earlier. After her death Ada Holman wrote:

The never-to-be forgotten 'Teens', the apotheosis of the Sydney High School girl, became the Bible of all the bright young things who did not then know they were 'flappers'. They worshipped their spokeswoman. A few years ago when I was on holiday with Louise in Queensland, important matrons were constantly introducing themselve as prototypes of her characters and demanding her autograph . . .

Courage was the keynote of her character, and 'Darkest before Dawn' peculiarly her motto. She had, her friends are glad to know, years of success and happiness in England, and again, in Italy — the country of her instinctive adoption; even if they are saddened by the knowledge that life was not as kind to her as it should have been in her later years.[33]

Her sister Amy Eleanor Mack, a less temperamental and effervescent character than Louise, lived a more sedate life while achieving great distinction as a
journalist. Soon after leaving school she began work as a reporter and from
1907 to 1914 was editor of the 'Women's Page' of the *Sydney Morning Herald*.
In 1908, when she was thirty-two, she married Launcelot Harrison, a
zoologist, later Professor of Zoology at Sydney University, and wrote several
popular children's books. Amy Mack and her husband went to England in
1914 and when her husband was posted to Mesopotamia on war service she
worked as publicity officer for the welfare section of the Ministry of Munitions
and later for the Ministry of Food. Back in Australia she contributed regularly
to the literary page of the *Sydney Morning Herald*. She was credited with an
amazing memory and in the years before her death in 1939 she regaled her
friends with anecdotes of her life as a journalist and publicity officer.[34]

Conor O'Brien

When Louise Mack left the *Bulletin* and Australia, the women's page was
taken over by (Agnes) Conor O'Brien, a New Zealander, described by Zara
Aronson as 'one of the most notable women journalists of Australia'.[35] While
living with her mother and brothers in Melbourne she became a frequent
contributor of short stories and prose sketches to the *Argus*, the *Australasian*
and the *Evening Standard* using the name of 'Lynette'. Her first *Bulletin* column
was written on 20 April 1901 but she had previously stood in for Louise Mack
when she went on holidays. When she took over on a permanent basis she
tried to talk to J. F. Archibald about the 'Letter' but, she wrote, 'he lowered
himself back into the proof he was "mending," and I got no help from him
except a remark that "the people are famishing for York ham" ' (the Duke and
Duchess of York were visiting Australia).[36] Conor O'Brien was doubtful of her
ability to keep up the standards of her famous predecessors but after she had
been in the position for nearly six years, the *Bookfellow* commented:

> ... it is her literary sense that makes her work especially good. She
> comes in succession to a long line of clever writers: to Mrs. Creed,
> distinguished both in verse and prose ...; to Mrs. Baverstock, now in
> charge of the 'Women's Column' of *The Daily Telegraph*, Sydney; and to
> Miss Ina Wildman, 'Sappho Smith,' whose too early death was lamented
> some years ago. Each of these ladies had their particular value; but none
> of them ever gave *The Bulletin* such a brilliant page as Miss Conor-
> O'Brien has written in recent years.[37]

In 1911 Conor O'Brien married William Macleod, the manager of the
Bulletin. Her book about him, *Macleod of "The Bulletin"*, published in 1931
contains accounts of many *Bulletin* writers and artists. She died in 1934.

238

Alice Grant Rosman worked as a journal-ist on every paper in Adelaide as a writer of women's page material and also as a sub-editor. For some years she was the Adelaide correspondent for the Bulletin, writing under the name of 'Rosna'. In 1910 she went to London to report the Coronation for Australian papers and later was a very successful writer of pop-ular novels, eight in succession becoming best sellers in the United States. (Lone Hand 1 April 1914)

Alice Rosman

Correspondents of the *Bulletin's* Women's Letter in other states included Eugenia Stone in Melbourne, Alice Rosman in Adelaide and Mrs Marie Irvine in Brisbane. Mrs Irvine later joined the Sydney *Sun*.

South Australian-born Alice Grant Rosman who became a best-selling novelist in the English and American market, began her writing career as a journalist and for three years was *Bulletin* correspondent in Adelaide writing as 'Rosna'. She was born at Kapunda, South Australia, in 1881, a descendant of an old-established family and inherited her writing ability from her mother, Alice Mary Bowyer Rosman, a poet and song-writer. Educated at the Domini-can Convent, Cabra, she began writing while a child, having stories accepted by the Adelaide *Observer*, *Chronicle* and *Southern Cross*. Described later as a 'flapper', she gained experience writing, at one time or another, for every paper in Adelaide as well as the *Bulletin*, *Native Companion*, *Lone Hand* and other periodicals. A contemporary woman journalist in Adelaide was Eva D'Arenberg who was social reporter on the *Register*.

For three years Alice Rosman was on the staff of *Gadfly*, launched in Adelaide in 1906 by C. J. Dennis of 'Sentimental Bloke' fame and A. E. Martin, and she was a writer and sub-editor on the *Evening Post*. In 1911 she went to London to report the Coronation for several Australian papers. She wrote a very successful series on economical travelling for the Melbourne *Everylady's Journal* and continued to send interviews, articles and pars to the *Bulletin* and other Australian papers. While writing novels she also worked on the staff of the *British Australasian* and from 1920 to 1926 was assistant editor of the *Grand Magazine*. Her novel *The Window*, written in 1926, was marketed in England and the United States and went into twelve editions in five months. From then on she produced popular novels, some published in the Mills and Boon series, at the rate of one or two a year, eight in succession becoming best sellers in the United States. In 1936, when she was interviewed for *A book of South Australian women*, she was unmarried and living with her sister in a flat in Bloomsbury. She died in 1961 at the age of eighty.[38]

Eugenia Stone

> '*The* Bulletin *staff fell for her as one man.*'
> Norman Lindsay

The Melbourne 'Women's Letter' of the *Bulletin* was written for some years by a very competent journalist, Eugenia Stone, who wrote under the name of 'Tryphena'. A daughter of John Stone, of Melbourne, she began her journalistic career on *Table Talk*, a light and lively social, political and literary journal edited and published in Melbourne by Maurice Brodzsky.[39] While writing for the *Bulletin*'s 'Women's Letter' from Melbourne, Eugenia Stone created a stir among the staff when she visited Sydney. Norman Lindsay wrote that 'the *Bulletin* staff fell for her as one man, each member taking her out to lunch or dinner'. He described her, in true Lindsay style, as 'a big handsome girl even for those days, when big girls were the mode, and she dressed in its rich stylisms which emphasized an opulent femininity in breasts and bottoms'.[40]

When she left for England in 1907, the *Bookfellow* said 'a small syndicate of paragraphers' was required to take over her work: 'It is difficult to find among local women writers one who combines with personal popularity, tact and wit, a ready pen and a nose for news, and all these qualities are demanded'.[41]

While travelling overseas Eugenia Stone met Sir George Doughty, a Liberal Unionist Member of the House of Commons and twice Mayor of Grimsby, who was then a widower aged about fifty. They were married in 1907 and returned to Australia in 1913. Her husband died in April 1914.

Isabelle Le Patourel was part of Sydney's social life centred on Government House during the time her husband was aide-de-camp to the Governor, Lord Loftus. This experience was to be invaluable when she took up journalism. At first she reported the Sydney social scene for the Melbourne Australasian *and later was social editor on the* Sydney Morning Herald *for twenty years. (Sydney Morning Herald 5 July 1933)*

Isabelle Le Patourel

Mrs Le Patourel was another early woman journalist who to some extent owed her success to the fact that she was part of the social milieu about which she wrote. Born in England in 1856, a daughter of Charles Durham, a merchant, Isabelle Sarah Tempest Durham was brought to Australia as an infant but later returned to England to complete her education. She married Captain Henry Le Patourel and when her husband was appointed aide-de-camp to Lord Loftus, Governor of New South Wales, she returned to Australia with the vice-regal entourage in 1879. By then she had one daughter and she had another in 1881. For the six years Lord Loftus held the position of governor she was closely connected with vice-regal life, an experience that was to prove invaluable when she entered journalism. At the completion of Lord Loftus's term, Captain Le Patourel took up a commission with the Garrison Artillery so the family remained in Sydney.

In the 1880s, when she was about thirty, Mrs Le Patourel began reporting the social scene from Sydney for the Melbourne weekly, the *Australasian*, later joining the *Sydney Morning Herald* as social editor. When she died at Woollahra, Sydney, aged seventy-seven on 4 July 1933, the *Bulletin* wrote:

> Most of the women inky wayfarers of today had never met Mrs. Le Patourel, but all had heard of her. It was her pen that recorded the social

happenings of Sydney at the end of last century and the beginning of this
... For 20 years or more, she ran the social pages of 'S. M. Herald'.[42]

One of her daughters, Vera, became the wife of Sir Charles Bickerton
Blackburn, later Chancellor of the University of Sydney.[43]

Theodosia Britton

Theodosia Britton, a bright young Sydney University graduate, was a contemporary of Isabelle Le Patourel's on the *Sydney Morning Herald*. When the
paper decided to restart a women's page in 1905, after allowing its women's
column to lapse in 1890, Theodosia Britton was given the formidable task of
editing 'A page for women'. Like a number of other early women journalists,
Theodosia Britton came from a newspaper family. Her father was Alexander
Britton, at the time of her birth in Melbourne a journalist on the *Argus*, and
her grandfather, also Alexander Britton, had been proprietor of the *Castlemaine Mail*. Her mother, formerly Ada Willoughby, was a sister of Howard
Willoughby, editor of the *Argus* and a cousin Miss A. A. (Bunchy) Wheeler,
a well-known early woman journalist in Melbourne. As a young child
Theodosia attended a kindegarten school in Jolimont run by the Misses Budd.
Following the family's move to Sydney, when her father was appointed chief
sub-editor (later associate editor) on the *Sydney Morning Herald*, she was
educated at home. She matriculated and graduated BA from Sydney University in 1891 at the age of twenty.

*Theodosia Ada Britton came from a news-
paper family on both her father's and her
mother's side. After she graduated from
Sydney University in 1891 at the age of
twenty she began contributing to the Melbourne* Argus *and* Australasian *and then
to the* Sydney Morning Herald *where her
father was associate editor. Later she joined
the staff of the* Herald *and when the paper
began a page for women in 1905 she was
appointed editor. (Althea Farr, Double
Bay, New South Wales)*

In the 1890s she wrote for the *Australasian* under the pseudonyms 'Biddy B. A.' and 'Ino' and also for the Melbourne *Argus*. Probably through the influence of her father she also became a regular contributor to the *Sydney Morning Herald* at about the same time, later joining the staff. In her writing she was a champion of temperance and of feminist causes, such as the passing of the Married Women's Property Act, free kindergartens and changes to the laws on prostitution.[44]

Theodosia Britton's first attempt as editor of 'A page for women' resulted in a rather dull collection of small items but the page soon settled down to a more interesting format. In 1905 she married Albert E. N. Wallace and her career with the *Herald* ended before the birth of her first child in 1907. She took time out from reporting to write a book, *The Etiquette of Australia*, and then resumed journalistic work. While raising young children she worked on several papers including the *Bystander* where her salary was £3 per week. In later years Theodosia Wallace wrote syndicated letters for country papers and was first head of the Country Press press-cutting service. She died in 1953 aged about eighty.

Zara Aronson

'. . . *certainly one of Sydney's most capable journalists.*'
Table Talk 5 September 1901

Like Mrs Le Patourel, Zara Baar Aronson was a very competent journalist who made use of her social contacts. In 1897 when she was thirty-two and married to a Sydney merchant she succeeded Mrs Carl Fischer as editor of the women's page in the *Sydney Mail*. She was already well known as a worker for charitable causes and prominent in literary and feminist circles.

Zara Aronson was born in Sydney in 1864 into a Jewish family. Her father was German-born Moritz Baar, who had been a merchant in Hanover and London and her mother was the former Zillah Valentine. Taken to Europe at three, Zara was educated at Bradford Girls' Grammar School in Yorkshire and later at Weisbaden, Germany. She had a family background in writing both on her mother's and father's sides, her maternal uncle being Mr B. B. Valentine, a senior journalist on the staff of the *New York Herald*. She returned to Sydney in 1879 and in October 1882 at the age of eighteen married Frederick Aronson. In her early married life she worked for charitable organisations and in the 1890s turned to feminist activities, becoming an original member of the Women's Literary Society and a founder of the National Council of Women. Encouraged to write by Lucinda Gullett she

Zara Baar Aronson was already well known as a worker for charitable causes and prominent in literary and feminist circles when she joined the Sydney Mail *in 1897 to write the 'Ladies' Page'. She wrote under the pseudonym of 'Thalia', one of the nine Greek muses. When her husband's jewellery business took them to Perth she wrote for the* Western Mail. *In later life she received an OBE for her work for charity.* (Table Talk 5 September 1901)

contributed to the *Town and Country Journal* and the *Illustrated London News* before joining the *Sydney Mail* as 'Thalia' (one of the nine Greek muses, representing pastoral poetry and comedy). Her page, which continued until 1901, consisted mainly of replies to readers' queries and a fashion section, and would hardly have tested her ability.

In 1899, as *Sydney Mail* representative, she ran the Press Stall during a Monster Fair in aid of the Queen Victoria Consumptives' Homes. While the Fair was on she was one of those responsible for the publication of five issues of *Press News* to which writers such as Ethel Turner, Louise Mack, Roderick Quinn and Rolf Boldrewood contributed. Bound together, these issues became a collector's item.

By 1899 her husband had set up as Frederick Aronson and Co, wholesale jewellers and importers and in 1901 she resigned to accompany him to Melbourne where he took charge of the Melbourne branch of the firm. Before leaving Sydney she was entertained by friends and presented with a silver-framed address signed by more than seventy well-known Sydney people, and a sixteen-piece silver toilet set testifying to the value of her literary and charitable work in Sydney.[45]

In 1903 when she returned to Sydney, for about a year she edited the *Home Queen*, a paper for country women, writing much of it herself, including the theatrical and fashion columns. In the following years she edited the fashion pages of the *Town and Country Journal* and the Sydney

132 THE SYDNEY MAIL, SATURDAY, JULY 17, 1897

Novel Style for Evening Dress.

New Ball Headdress.

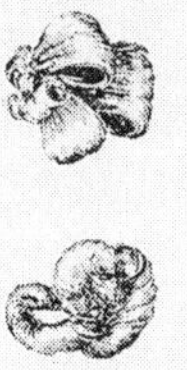

Two Novel Coils for the top of the head, as the hair is now worn.

Marie Stuart.

Pompadour.

NEW STYLES OF HAIRDRESSING.

THE LADIES' PAGE

Answers to Correspondents.

By Thalia.

Cinderella.—What a kind correspondent you are becoming, and how good to send me the recipe for the cakes. Many thanks. 1. Sponge cake will not stick to the tin when baking if you butter your dish well before cooking. 2. You do not say if the judge's wig that you want is to be knitted or crochet. Kindly write and let me know, and I will then procure it for you.

Ceris.—Why do you want a second-hand bag? They are to be procured so cheap at Messrs. Anthony Hordern's and Messrs. Farmer and Co.'s, that I would strongly advise you to write and get their price lists. The only place you can buy a second-hand bag is at a pawnshop, and then you would have to get some one to purchase it for you.

Mary Webb.—I cannot think what prevents the creases coming out of your sister's dress, and under the circumstances would suggest your sending it to a tailor's to be properly pressed with tailors' irons, and I think that the skirt will then look quite as good as new, for it is wonderful what professional irons can remedy. Let me know if you follow out my advice.

Just Dressmaker.—All the plates used in the "Mail" hail from London, so their paper patterns are unprocurable. The bodice of the half-mourning gown of May 29th is cut exactly the same at the front, therefore of full silk, disappearing into the waistband. The back of the walking dress of March 6th has a yoke the same as in the front and the bodice is cut plain, with the velvet collar to finish it off.

Pansy.—Many thanks for the recipe for "ammonia cakes," and herewith give it to my readers: Put three coffee cupfuls of white sugar into a vessel with a lump of ammonia about the size of a large hen's egg (the vessel must be large, as the contents will effervesce when the water is added), and pour over it five pints of boiling water, and stir till the sugar and ammonia are melted. Put 6lb. of flour into a dish, and mix with it thoroughly 1½lb. of butter, then mix this up with the ammonia water, knead very stiff and roll out thin, cut into shapes, and bake to a light brown. When properly made these biscuits should be thin and crisp.

Herenia.—I am afraid that I do not see my way very clear to send you much information for decorating your house, as your letter is not explicit enough for me to understand what you really want. Kindly answer my questions, and I will then see what is to be done. 1. Do you wish me to suggest what wall papers would look well, and what paint? 2. Have you purchased any furniture as yet for your bedroom, and if not, what do you want? 3. Perhaps, your best plan would be for you to write again to me with a distinct list of your proposed requirements, as your last letter does not assist me at all. Why did you start to address me as Cleo, and then change it to Thalia. Have you ever written to Cleo before?

Indiana.—Thanks for your kind wishes. As far as your first question is concerned, I am afraid I cannot help you, as law questions are hardly within the ranges of a ladies' page. I should, however, advise you to consult the nearest magistrate, and he would be able to advise you who to write to in Sydney. Your good wishes on my behalf are most acceptable. I really feel I have several interested friends among my correspondents. I see your letter is dated June 1, but it has only just come to hand, and in re-reading it I find that all your questions can only be answered by some one belonging to the legal profession. Perhaps you have a friend whom you could consult without going to a stranger.

Rustic.—I am delighted that the wall paper was satisfactory, and hope that your friends will also approve of my taste. 2. I think that you can teach yourself photography in a simple form, and advise you to write to Messrs. Baker and Rouse, George-street, Sydney, for all information on the subject. They will tell you every detail necessary for your trial efforts, and also the price of an inexpensive outfit. 3. I hardly like to give you an opinion about your handwriting, as I do not consider I am capable of judging. I think, however, that you use a thin pen, and if you tried a broader nib your letters would be formed with more character than they are at present. Try to practise to write on paper that is not lined, as the latter in a measure retards the fluency of your hand. I am always pleased to help, so hope to hear from you soon again.

Leah the Forsaken.—What an extraordinary nom de plume you have chosen, and why did you select it? In reference to your little niece's eyes, I would not advise you to do anything until a medical man had seen her; in fact, an eye specialist is what I would recommend, as no one could give an opinion until her sight had been tested. Write to Miss Van Brakkel, the Strand Arcade, Sydney, and she will advise you what to use for your hair. The only recipe for citron preserve that I have is as follows:—Cut the citron in thin slices, boil in water with a small piece of alum until clear and tender, then rinse in cold water. Make a syrup of ¾lb. of sugar to 1lb. of citron; boil a piece of ginger in the syrup, and then pour the citron in and let it boil for a few minutes. Put in one lemon to five of the fruit.

Ita.—To sautez carrots boil some small ones till tender in some stock, then sautez them in hot butter, season, sprinkle with finely chopped parsley, and serve very hot. Older carrots can also be prepared in a way to make them quite as palatable as the younger vegetable. Cook them in the stock pot, and when quite tender cut them in thin slices, and fry or sautez them; or make a white sauce with a little broth, butter, flour, seasoning to taste, and a tiny pinch of caster sugar. They are also very good if they have been previously boiled with a piece of bacon, or pickled pork. The same kind of recipes can be applied to young turnips and parsnips, but these are generally preferred en puree, which is done in the usual manner. A good way to cook cauliflower is to serve it in the plainest way, trim the leaves off, be careful to break none of the sprigs, rinse in fresh water, and cook them till tender, putting them straight into boiling water and plenty of it. Serve with plain hot butter, or with oil and vinegar; or, again, with a parsley, and served as hot and crisp as possible they make a most sightly and acceptable dish. Finally, try this method: Boil the cauliflower until three parts cooked; butter a baking dish that can be sent to table, sprinkle it with bread crumbs, and fill with alternate layers of cauliflower and Parmesan cheese; season between the layers with salt and plenty of pepper, pour a few tablespoonfuls of cream over the whole, and either cover with cheese and bread crumbs or with a layer of light puff paste. Whichever way one chooses the result is excellent.

Fashion Notes.

Much as I favour French dishes, French charms, and French frocks, I own with the usual power of independence that I love the English more, and the thrill of joy that I experience when I hear of an English dressmaker competing successfully with a French one is quite too delightful.

The great couturieres of Paris have but small faith in "le gout Anglais." This, perchance, accounts for their first endeavour of disposing of all their bizarre and impossible models to the English and colonial markets. This they, alas, are too often able to do, as witness the atrocious monstrosities in the shop windows labelled Paris models.

Experience teaches much, and it is only by judgment, perseverance and an unerring eye for effect, good taste, and imagination that we are capable of ... modes are in every way suitable, perhaps, for carriage wear, but, on the other hand, utterly out of place if worn amidst the crowded streets of Sydney, where a well-dressed woman has, unfortunately, often to bear the brunt of being stared at, chiefly through her individuality of smart dressing being too pronounced by simplicity.

My London letters tell me of forthcoming visions of lace, of insertion, of canvas in all shades, and of grass lawn in every possible variety for trimmings. The canvas is being made in a variety of colours and will be much en evidence as hat ruchings all along the brims, or sometimes folded to form the crown of the hats. All flowers are to be set up very high, and will in consequence nod and waggle about in a most lunatic manner, while all the newest straws are very rough in texture and well to the fore in bright colouring.

A very new idea is the rucked bow, where the ribbon is really rucked like the fashionable sleeves, a row of piping cord being run in at each side and another down the centre of the ribbon employed.

I have already had a few details of fashion's fancies as seen at recent church parade in London from reliable information, and gather that all the smartest gowns are either tucked or corded, and pouched either back and front, or in front only. Tucked skirts could ever enough to make ... straight trimmings from waist to hem or in frills put on in sharply pointed panier shape.

There are many new and pretty items in the adjuncts of dress, such as boleros made in gimp and edged with kiltings of lisse bordered with black satin. Kiltings of every sort and size are being eagerly adopted both for the inevitable ruffs and also for the boleros and bodice trimmings. I hear of a new gold and buttercup colour, which mingles with white and ecru in the thickest makes of guipure, and this is alone to constitute many of the short boleros which simply surround the armhole.

Belts of the Swiss form accompany many of the boleros, and are made of lace braid tinted by silk stitching. We are not only going to wear coloured belts of kid, but white ones, which indeed are the most favoured, and also a number of belts are prepared of Petersham, with bands of kid stitched down the centre. We must also consider the subject of ruffs more closely, for they appear to have returned with renewed popularity. There is a novel kind of kilting, known as the Fedora, which shows a sort of fancy pleat. Sometimes this is box-pleated or treble box-pleated, with a band of feather trimming in the middle. Occasionally the black is blended with colour. Most of them are much wider at the back of the neck than in the front, and are supported by large black satin bows.

The most exquisite devices are being employed for parasol handles. Some are white enamelled, others green, and sprays of delicately modelled flowers ornament the handles. A sprig of buttercups on a white parasol is charming. The cherries, so much in vogue last year, are not so fashionable for parasol handles this season, but instead of this they are finding their way into the hats. Ultra-Parisian is a small crinkled capote of dull gold straw, with a twist and rosettes of black chiffon, and a cachepeigne and upstanding bunch of cherries.

Shepherd's plaid is to be the sign of the approach of spring, and one gown just being produced by a leading modiste shows by its simplicity that over-trimming is not by any means to the fore in the forthcoming modes. The one I have seen has a plain skirt and a pouched bodice fastening on the left side into a sash of cerise-coloured glace silk. The side fastening was adorned with a full frill of white chiffon and white silk braiding, while a tucked chemisette collar-band of cerise silk completed a gown certainly claiming "pure and simple" as its trade mark. The hat to be worn with it was of cerise straw with a beefeater crown of white glace silk veiled in ecru lace and high bows of pink glace and pink roses on one side.

The new linens this year contain shades of green, china blue, daffodil, and rich brown, the tone of the bulrush. It will be correct to wear coat and skirt and bolero skirt costumes of these with linen waistcoats in some contrasting shade, but to give the desired perfect fitting effect the costume must be manipulated by a tailor, and not as many think only necessary a "home-made dressmaker." Pink vests would look well on a blue gown, and perhaps yellow for ivory white or green with pink or lemon yellow.

For visiting frocks no smart gown is complete without a touch of black somewhere in its composition.

Satin cloth is a novelty in the materials for the season, and in conclusion this week I will give an idea for a gown worthy of all due consideration by its charm and originality. Edge the bottom of the skirt with a 3in. wide shepherd's plaid ribbon, piped at the upper and low edge with cerise ribbon, and have a full pouch bodice of shepherd's plaid silk caught by a deep black satin belt.

I have just heard of some very dainty fancy dresses to be worn by some pretty boys and girls at the Children's Ball to be held this week at the Sydney Town Hall, and I hope to be able to give a full description of their charms very shortly. Messrs. W. T. Waters, of King-street, are undertaking the responsibilities of the frocks, and, from what I am told, the success of the little gowns is quite assured.

THALIA.

A SMART VISITING GOWN.

Smart Visiting Dress.

It is made in pale biscuit-coloured moire, the skirt quite plain, and the bodice of chiffon, in that lovely shade of turquoise which is almost green, while over it falls a transparent saque bolero of the fashionable black net, edged with an applique of turquoise glace and cream lace, and further trimmed with an embroidery of steel and jet beads. The deep waistband is of black satin, fastened with turquoise and steel buttons at either side of a central fold of embossed silk with a cream ground, which continues its career between the soft fullness of the chiffon, and finally composes the collar. There is a separate foundation of turquoise-blue silk to complete the lovely scheme of colour, when the overskirt is held up. Hat of dark-blue straw, trimmed with pleated green chiffon and plumes.

Zara Aronson wrote the Sydney Mail's 'Ladies' Page' for four years from the beginning of 1897 when she was appointed following the death of Mrs Carl Fischer. She was regarded as an unusually competent journalist but the content of the 'Ladies' Page' would not have taxed her ability. Like many other women's pages it consisted of answers to correspondents' queries and fashion notes. (Sydney Mail 17 July 1897)

Sunday Times and was Sydney correspondent of the Brisbane *Telegraph*. About 1912 Frederick Aronson set up a branch of his jewellery business in Perth and Zara joined the staff of the *Western Mail*, whose editor described her as a 'most capable journalist'.[46] *Table Talk* in a feature on her in 1901 said she 'entirely discards "notes," and dictates all her work "straight off the reel" to her typewriter.': 'Added to her facile pen, this popular writer possesses a charming personality, is a bright conversationalist and was certainly one of Sydney's most capable journalists'.[47]

From 1914, when she returned again to Sydney, Zara Aronson became more involved in charity and committee work and her journalism as a full time career lapsed. From 1930 to 1937, however, she was a contributor to the *Sydney Morning Herald*. In 1925 she was a foundation secretary of the Society of Women ·Writers of New South Wales. When she was awarded an OBE in 1936 the *Sydney Morning Herald* said she had 'helped with every big charitable project in Sydney since 1879'[48] She died in Sydney in 1944.

Ethel Turner

Another field of employment for women writers was on the children's pages of newspapers. Two women who later became famous as writers of books for young people began their writing careers in this way. Ethel Turner in Sydney wrote for the *Illustrated Sydney News* and the *Town and Country Journal* and in Melbourne Mary Grant Bruce wrote for the *Leader* and the *Age*.

Ethel Sibyl Turner, born at Doncaster, England in 1872 arrived in Sydney at the age of nine with her mother and sisters. With her sister Lillian ·she was educated at Sydney Girls' High School where they were contemporaries of Louise Mack who edited the school paper. When Ethel Turner's contributions to this paper were rejected, she and her sister Lillian and some friends decided to start a rival paper, the *Iris*.

Ethel Turner reacted similarly when the first contributions she sent to a Sydney newspaper after leaving school were returned. Again, with the aid of her sister, she started a magazine of her own, the *Parthenon*. The sisters wrote almost the entire contents of this monthly magazine, canvassed for subscriptions and advertisements and kept the accounts. The *Parthenon* lasted for three years and paid a small dividend. Part of Ethel Turner's work on this paper was the Children's Page, which attracted the attention of the editor of the *Illustrated Sydney News*. When the *Parthenon* ceased he offered Ethel Turner £100 a year, a salary she regarded as 'magnificent',[49] to supply similar matter for his paper. When the *Illustrated Sydney News* ceased in 1895 her children's column, described at the time as a 'fanciful, conversational commentary on little people's ways',[50] written under the name of 'Dame

Apart from the women's pages, another avenue of employment for women on newspapers was on the children's pages. Two of Australia's most popular children's authors of former years, Ethel Turner and Mary Grant Bruce, edited children's pages. Ethel Turner, famous as author of the best-selling Seven little Australians, *ran her own monthly magazine the* Parthenon *for three years then took her children's column, written under the name of 'Dame Durden', to the* Illustrated Sydney News *and then to the* Town and Country Journal. *(*Bookfellow *25 March 1899)*

Durden', was transferred to the *Town and Country Journal*. She also wrote stories for other magazines, including several for the *Windsor Magazine* published in London.

Late in 1893 Ethel Turner finished what was to become one of the most popular of Australian stories, *Seven little Australians*, and sent it to the Melbourne office of publishers Ward, Lock and Co. William Steele, the Australian representative of the firm, said of the arrival of the manuscript:

It made such a good impression that I read on with increasing interest until lunch time. I hurried through my meal and resumed the story as quickly as possible, and when I finished it in the afternoon I felt certain that I had a good thing. Though supposed to submit everything to London I decided to write to Miss Turner on my own responsibility and offer a price. We agreed about the terms and I then sent the MS. to London . . . and in due course — about the middle of 1894 — the book came out. Its success was immediate. The press was enthusiastic. George Meredith, Miss Frances Hodgson Burnett, Mark Twain and many other people wrote appreciatively to Miss Turner. Ada Cambridge had a nice article about it in the *Review of Reviews*. And the book sold and kept on selling splendidly. It is still selling, and is now in the sixteenth edition, and the author has been drawing a royalty on sales. Since then we have published seventeen other books by Ethel Turner, and it has been a labor of love to me to help them along.[51]

Ethel Turner followed *Seven little Australians* with *The Family at Misrule* and over the years wrote nearly thirty other books for girls and several plays. For some years she wrote books at the rate of one a year, usually having a new book out for the Christmas trade. In the five years from the publication of her first book in 1894, 115 000 copies of her books had been sold.

In 1896 Ethel Turner married Herbert R. Curlewis, a Sydney barrister and one-time contributor to her girlhood magazine, the *Parthenon*, who later became a New South Wales District Court judge. One of her daughters, Jean Curlewis, edited the children's magazine pages in the *Daily Telegraph* and published several books for children. Lillian Turner also wrote twenty or so books for children. Her first novel, *The lights of Sydney* published in 1896, won first prize of £50 in Cassell's novel competition in London.

Mary Grant Bruce

Mary Grant Bruce, later famous as the author of the 'Billabong' series of children's books, got her start in journalism by winning, at the age of sixteen, a prize offered by the Melbourne Shakespeare Society. Her entry was regarded as the best ever received by the Society and as a result the Society's President, Dr J. Nield, kept in touch with her, criticised her writing, sent her books and guided her reading. Later he recommended her for a job on the *Leader*, the weekly country paper run by the *Age*.

Mary Grant Bruce was born at Sale, Victoria in 1878, a daughter of a pioneer surveyor who had surveyed the New South Wales–Victorian border from the head-waters of the Murray east to the sea. While surveying he had met and married Minnie Whittakers, who lived with her pioneer parents on an isolated property in the Australian Alps. From an early age Mary Grant Bruce enjoyed reading and when a local bookshop owner ran a competition for the best story from local children, she won the trophy.[52]

By the time Mary Grant Bruce was twenty in 1898, the family's finances had deteriorated. Although at that time it was unusual for unmarried middle-class girls to leave home, she left for Melbourne taking £5 with her. At first she worked in poorly paid temporary secretarial jobs, making a little extra money by writing stories, one of which, 'Her little lad', was run by the *Leader* as its main Christmas story in 1898. Through Dr Nield she came to know the editor of the *Leader*, Henry Short, and when a vacancy occurred she was appointed editor of the children's page, writing under the name of 'Cinderella'. During the decade she edited the page it became livelier and she included

Mary Grant Bruce began her writing career as editor of the children's page of the Melbourne weekly Leader, writing as 'Cinderella'. After she became famous as the author of the very popular 'Billabong' series of books for young people, she returned to journalism several times. She was editor of Woman for two years from 1910 and also editor of Woman's World for a short time. (Lone Hand 2 December 1912)

more competitions and illustrations. Her wage was small but as the work was not demanding she had time for freelance writing. By the end of the decade she had written for nearly every newspaper in Australia, including the Age, Table Talk, Lone Hand, Woman's World, and Woman, on a wide variety of topics including baby welfare, education, agriculture, fishing, sport, theatre and book reviews. Later she became a member of the literary staff of the Age and the Leader and for two years from 1910 edited Woman. By then her first book, A little bush maid had been published, first as a serial in the Leader and then in London in book form in 1910. This was followed by Mates at Billabong in 1911.

Mary Grant Bruce's fame rests on her very popular 'Billabong' series of children's books, published over the next thirty years, but intermittently she returned to journalism. In 1913 in England she wrote for Lord Northcliffe's Daily Mail and in 1926, after her return to Australia she took over as editor of Woman's World for six months.

While working in England she met a distant cousin, Major George Evans Bruce, also an author. They returned to Australia and were married in Melbourne in 1914 but sailed almost immediately for England following the start of World War I. While her husband trained army recruits Mary continued writing books and magazine articles. After the war they moved to Australia with their two young sons living for some years at Traralgon, Gippsland. In 1927, however, they left Australia intending to settle permanently in Ireland but the death of their younger son who accidentally shot himself soon after their arrival caused them to abandon this plan and they spent the next twelve years in the south of England and the Continent. They returned to Australia in 1939 but following the death of her husband in 1948 Mary Grant Bruce again returned to England and died there ten years later.

14

Postscript

Some of the women writers whose careers began in the latter part of the nineteenth century continued to be successful after the turn of the century, being joined by others, beginning with Miles Franklin and Henry Handel Richardson, whose fame and achievements now overshadow them. The earlier writers deserve acclaim, however, for their pioneering efforts. Often in odd moments snatched from housework or caring for families, they toiled laboriously over their handwritten manuscripts, and this was at a time when books were sometimes two or three volumes in length, serials ran to sixty chapters or more and newspapers commonly printed very lengthy articles. In 1893 Ethel Turner recorded that she had written 23 000 words by hand to add to 7000 words already written, then had made a handwritten copy of the entire manuscript of 30 000 words in five weeks.[1]

By 1900 typewriters were coming into use, one aspect of the changes that would take place in the writing profession. Journalism certainly did change. In the early years of the twentieth century women's columns expanded to pages, and pages spread into sections. This was partly as a result of the publicity attached to the women's suffrage campaign and other women's issues which made women more newsworthy. Social changes including the expansion of shops into department stores and the increasing availability of new household equipment and ready-made clothing ensured an increase in advertising revenue to support these pages.

Although confined in content, the layout of women's pages improved and more jobs became available to women reporters. As in previous years, however, the entry of women into journalism remained a haphazard matter until the beginning of the cadetship system. (By the early 1920s there were a few women cadets on most metropolitan newspapers but the scarcity of such positions is shown by the fact that the Perth *Daily News* did not engage its first female cadet until 1928.[2]) Before this formal method of training was available, women trying to obtain positions as reporters usually began with a hopeful bombardment of newspaper offices with unsolicited contributions. This method was recommended by Melbourne journalist Henrietta McGowan in a book on the work available to women early in the twentieth century. 'The woman who comes to be recognised as an occasional contributor of merit naturally stands the best chance of obtaining permanent employment,' she wrote.[3] Once entered, it was a well paid profession. Women received the same rates as men, although this was undermined by the fact that women were rarely promoted to the higher graded positions.

Whether the standard of writing improved over the years is debatable. Certainly the subjects of women's page journalism continued to remain stereotyped. Henrietta McGowan, in a passage ostensibly describing the adaptability required of a woman journalist, gave a depressing impression of the women's pages rounds on a newspaper:

> She must be sufficiently adaptable to convince a Salvation Army officer of her interest one hour, and give a sympathetic report of a shop show an hour after. She will probably be called on to furnish information on every subject, from pickling gherkins to managing a bank account . . .[4]

A male observer was critical of the standard of their writing. Writing in 1907, he thought Australian women journalists had joined the 'flippant school' in their efforts to emulate 'Sappho Smith's' brilliant style:

> Over all the larger Melbourne and Sydney journals there is now the trail of the flippant woman writer. Not a line of the product rings true. Every word of it is imitation. Whether it is a wedding, or an engagement, or an infant baptism, or a crush at Government House, or a Lady Mayoress's reception or an afternoon tea-party, or a display of new millinery, or a theatre, or a football match, the Sappho Smiths of these times bring to bear the same set of phrases, the same slap-dash methods, the same cynical suggestion of a *roué* of seventy in a garden of growing girls.[5]

Perhaps when faced with an endless round of reporting such events, cynicism was inevitable.

Many of those who took up journalism were outstanding women of great ability, yet they remained confined to a great extent to the writing of superficial news, innocuous social notes and household hints. A poem published in the *Bulletin* in 1918 described the life of the 'newspaper girl':

> Oh, isn't it wearisome, Newspaper Girl
>   (I know that at heart you're a sport),
> To chronicle brassard, and slip-on, and curl,
> The piffle and drivel of fashion's gay whirl —
>   The sex's sole small talk, in short?
>
> And what is the use of it, Newspaper Girl,
>   Though no reputation it wrecks?

I've heard you in private, your knowledge unfurl,
And if you could print 'em, they *would* cause a skirl —
The things that you know of the sex![6]

Most women journalists were not to break out of the social reporting role for many years, many not until the 1970s.[7] Not only they suffered, but their readers also. What they wrote appeared to be what was regarded as the news that was fit to print for a woman reader, or what women wanted to read. It was a diet that was to continue for many years. Yet the contrast remained between what was provided for women readers on the women's pages and a world that included violence, hunger and domestic suffering, often portrayed in news stories on other pages. There was to be little serious attempt in women's page journalism or in twentieth century women's papers, for many years, to come to terms with fundamental social and feminist issues.

Notes

1 A Blank Page

1 Quoted in Ida Beatrice O'Malley *Women in Subjection* London: Duckworth, 1933 p. 66
2 *Bulletin* 30 December 1926
3 *Australian Dictionary of Biography* (ADB) Carlton, Vic.: Melbourne University Press, 1966–86 Vol. 1 (Forster)
4 Thérèse Huber *Adventures on a Journey to New Holland* with an introduction by Leslie Bodi. Melbourne: Lansdowne Press, 1966. Leslie Bodi's introduction has details of Thérèse Huber's life.
5 Arrival, Tasmanian State Archives: CSO 1/228/5593, p. 240; departure Hobart *Town Courier* 21 February 1829
6 Sidney Lee (ed.) *Dictionary of National Biography* London: Smith, Elder, 1897 (Rede)
7 *British Library General Catalogue of printed books* London: K. G. Saur, 1985
8 London *Morning Herald* 27 September 1827. The article was reprinted in the *Colonial Advocate* 1 May 1828.
9 Mary Leman Grimstone *Woman's Love* London: Saunders & Otley, 1832. Foreword and postscript obtained from State Library of Tasmania, believed to hold the only copy of the book in Australia.
10 E. Morris Miller 'Australia's first two novels' Tasmanian Historical Research Association *Papers and proceedings* Vol. 6, No. 2, September 1957; Vol. 6, No. 3, December 1957. This article contains some biographical details of M. L. Grimstone; also E. Morris Miller *Pressmen and Governors* Sydney: Angus and Robertson, 1952, pp. 58–61
11 Postscript to *Woman's Love* p. 360
12 ibid. pp. 369–70
13 *Tasmanian and Austral–Asiatic Review* 21 February 1834
14 Copies from W. L. Crowther Library, State Library of Tasmania
15 Miller 'Australia's First Two Novels'

2 Pioneers in Publication

1 Information on Ann Howe from J. A. Ferguson, Mrs A. G. Foster and H. M. Green *The Howes and their press* Sydney: Sunnybrook Press, 1936; C. Brunsdon Fletcher 'Centenary of "The Sydney Morning Herald"' *Royal Australian Historical Society (RAHS) Journal* Vol. XVII, Part II, 1931; R. B. Walker *The Newspaper Press in New South Wales 1803–1920* Sydney: Sydney University Press, 1976; ADB Vol. 1 (Howe)
2 Gwendoline Wilson *Murray of Yarralumla* Melbourne: Oxford University Press, 1968, p. 89
3 National Library of Australia (NLA) MS 565/135, Murray papers. Letter August 1884, St Omer, Braidwood from Anna Maria Bunn to her godson. Anna Maria Bunn also spent a short time at Miss Dodd's school at Limerick.
4 Information on Anna Maria Bunn from Dr Terry Bunn, Thirroul, NSW; ADB Vol. 1 (Bunn)
5 Information from Dr. T. Bunn

6 'An Australian' [Anna Maria Bunn] *The Guardian* Sydney: J. Spilsbury, 1838, p. 14
7 ibid. p. 187
8 ibid. pp. 215, 217
9 ibid. p. 398
10 ibid p. 405
11 Miller *Pressmen and Governors* pp. 52–3
12 Preface of Fidelia S. T. Hill *Poems and recollections of the past* Sydney: T. Trood, 1840. Information on Fidelia Hill is also contained in the preface and footnotes in Louise Brown *A Book of South Australia: women in the first hundred years* Adelaide: Rigby, 1936, p. 66
13 Marcie Muir *Charlotte Barton: Australia's first children's author* Sydney: Wentworth Books, 1980, p. 13
14 ibid. p. 20
15 Dorothy Walsh (ed.) *The Admiral's wife, Mrs Phillip Parker King, a selection of letters 1817–56* Melbourne: The Hawthorn Press, 1967, p. 48
16 James Jervis *A history of the Berrima district 1798–1873* Berrima: Berrima County Council, n.d.; ADB Vol. 1
17 James Atkinson *An account of the state of agriculture in New South Wales* London: J. Cross, 1826. Atkinson's book is remarkable for its early use of coloured plates as illustrations. The three coloured plates depict 'An exploring party in NSW'; 'Party preparing to bivouac' and 'Party bivouac'd for the night'. A black and white illustration shows the ground plan and elevation of a typical early homestead and the ground plan of a milking yard.
18 *Sydney Morning Herald* 27 December 1841
19 *Sydney Gazette* 23 December 1841
20 NLA, MS 289, Journal of Earl Grey A. W. Manning
21 NSW Birth records
22 Faith Compton Mackenzie *As much as I dare* London: Collins, 1938, p. 77
23 ibid. p. 76
24 Mrs Francis [Mary] Vidal *Tales for the bush* 4th edn. London: Francis and John Rivington, 1846, p. 21
25 ibid. p. 64
26 ibid. p. 74
27 A. E. Shipley *'J.' A memoir of John Willis Clark* London: Smith, Elder, 1913, p. 57
28 E. Morris Miller *A history of Australian Literature* Vol. 1 Sydney: Sydney University Press, 1973, p. 401
29 Mrs [Mary] Vidal *Bengala: or, some time ago* London: John W. Parker, 1860. Preface

3 A Degree of Professionalism

1 First used by Alice Henry; heading of obituary in Adelaide *Observer* 9 April 1910; Will J. Sowden, editor of the *Register*, in address to the Adelaide Destitute Asylum, 29 October 1910
2 'Catherine Helen Spence 1825–1905' pamphlet reprinted from the *Register* 31 October 1905 on occasion of her 80th birthday, p. 33
3 ibid. p. 17. Tribute by R. Kyffin Smith, journalist
4 Adelaide *Observer* 9 April 1910
5 Catherine Helen Spence *An Autobiography* Adelaide: W. K. Thomas, 1910, reprinted from the *Register* p. 22
6 ibid. p. 23
7 'The fiction fields of Australia' *Journal of Australasia* September, October 1856

8 Spence *Autobiography* p. 23; *Tender and true* was reviewed in the *Advertiser* 5 September 1857

9 Spence *Autobiography* p. 25

10 ibid. p. 25

11 ibid. p. 52

12 ibid. p. 55

13 Adelaide *Advertiser* 13 November 1931

14 Spence *Autobiography* p. 56

15 ibid. p. 56

16 ibid. p. 63

17 ibid. p. 55

18 ibid. p. 79

19 C. Hay Thomson 'Women writers of Australasia' *Cassell's Magazine* January 1909. Obituaries: *Observer* 9 April 1910, 5 November 1910; *Advertiser* 4, 6, 11, 13 April 1910; *Register* 4, 11 April 1910

20 Vivienne Rae Ellis *Tigress in exile* Hobart: Blubber Head Press, 1979 contains details of Louisa Meredith's early life; ADB Vol. 5

21 ibid. pp. 37–8

22 Mrs Charles [Louisa Anne] Meredith *Notes and sketches of New South Wales during a residence in that Colony from 1839 to 1844* London: John Murray, 1844, contains details of Louisa Meredith's life in her first years in Australia

23 ibid. pp. 161–2

24 *Sydney Morning Herald* 1 March 1845

25 *Argus* 22 October 1896

26 Mrs Charles [Louisa Anne] Meredith *My home in Tasmania; or, nine years in Australia* [called *My home in Tasmania, during a residence of nine years* in English edition] New York: Bunce and Brothers, 1853. Preface

27 Louisa Anne Meredith *Tasmanian friends and foes, feathered, furred and finned* Hobart: J. Walch & Sons, 1880. London: Marcus Ward and Co. Preface

28 Louisa Anne Meredith *Bush friends in Tasmania* Last series. London: Macmillan, 1891. Title page

29 London *Times* 4 December 1895. Obituaries: *Argus* 22 October 1895, Launceston *Examiner* 22 October 1895

30 Margaret Swann 'Mrs. Meredith and Miss Atkinson. Writers and naturalists' *RAHS Journal* Vol. XV, Part 1, 1929, p. 18

31 G. B. Barton *Literature in New South Wales* Sydney: Government Printer, 1866

32 Swann 'Mrs. Meredith' p. 21

33 Alec H. Chisholm *Strange journey. The adventures of Ludwig Leichhardt and John Gilbert* Adelaide: Rigby, 1973, contains details of Calvert's journey with Leichhardt; ADB Vol. 5

34 Swann 'Mrs. Meredith' p. 22

35 The University of Kiel has been unable to trace any record of a publication containing illustrations by Louisa Atkinson. (Letter dated 2 October 1987)

36 *Sydney Morning Herald* 2 May 1872; death notice 30 April 1872

37 *Sydney Mail* 31 August 1872

4 Visitors and Lady Travellers

1 Alexandra Allen *Travelling Ladies* London: Jupiter, 1980. Preface

2 Clara Aspinall *Three Years in Melbourne* London: L. Booth, 1862

3 Emily Leakey *Clear shining light: A memoir of Caroline W. Leakey* London: J. F. Shaw, n.d. contains details of Caroline Leakey's life

4 ibid. pp. 23–5
5 ibid. p. 42
6 Oline Keese [Caroline Leakey] *The broad arrow: being passages from the history of Maida Gwynnham, a lifer* London: Richard Bentley, 1859. Preface pp. v–vi
7 *Athenaeum* quoted in Emily Leakey, p. 54
8 *Australasian* 5 February 1887
9 Caroline Leakey *The broad arrow* Vol. 2, pp. 267–8
10 Emily Leakey *Clear shining light* pp. 90, 98, Chapter XV
11 Charlotte Haldane *Daughter of Paris. The Life Story of Celeste Mogador* London: Hutchinson, 1961 contains biographical details of Celeste de Chabrillan's life; Celeste de Chabrillan, *The Gold Robbers* [English translation of *Les Voleurs d'Or* by Lucy and Caroline Moorehead] Melbourne: Sun Books, 1970
12 Haldane *Daughter of Paris* p. 146; arrival of *Croesus Argus* 10 April 1854; Count de Chabrillan's appointment as Consul *Argus* 20 April 1854
13 Haldane *Daughter of Paris* p. 187
14 ibid. p. 188
15 ADB Vol. 3, pp. 367–8
16 *Argus* 30 December 1858
17 Victorian marriage records. A search of newspaper shipping records also revealed nothing of arrival and departure at dates that may be deduced from her book: Mrs Charles [Ellen] Clacy *A Lady's Visit to the Gold Diggings of Australia in 1852–53* London: Hurst and Blackett, 1853
18 Reviews quoted at end of Elizabeth A. Murray *Ella Norman; or, A Woman's Perils* Melbourne: Hill of Content, 1985. The foreword by Sir Brian Murray contains biographical details
19. Mrs R. [Sarah] Lee *Adventures in Australia; or the Wanderings of Captain Spencer in the Bush and the Wilds* London: Grant and Griffith 1851. Preface to first edition
20 ibid. p. 284
21 DNB Vol. VI, pp. 41–3 [Bowdich]
22 Anne Bowman, *The kangaroo hunters; or, Adventures in the Bush* Philadelphia: Poter and Coates, 1858. Preface
23 ibid. p. 440
24 Dorothy Middleton 'Isabella Bird Bishop 1831–1904; Alexander op. cit. contain details of Isabella Bird's life
25 *Australia Felix. Impressions of Victoria* Articles from unknown [English] periodical bound together in NLA copy
26 Lady [Mary Anne Broome] Barker *Letters to Guy* London, Macmillan, 1885. Biographical details in *Remembered with Affection, a new edition of Lady Broome's 'Letters to Guy' with notes and a short life by Alexandra Hasluck* Melbourne: Oxford University Press, 1963

5 Eccentric Entrepreneurs

1 Alison Adburgham *Women in print. Writing women and women's magazines from the Restoration to the accession of Victoria* London: George Allen and Unwin, 1972, p. 57. This and Cynthia L. White *Women's magazines 1693–1968* London: Michael Joseph, 1970, contain accounts of early women's magazines in Britain
2 *Spectator* 17 July 1858
3 ibid. 3 July 1858
4 *Empire* 19 July 1858
5 ibid. 20 July 1858

6 Jeremy Diddler was the chief character in a farce by Kenney called 'Raising the Wind', first produced in 1803. His main characteristic was continual borrowing of small sums of money which he did not repay ('raising the wind'). The surname became part of the language — a diddler meaning a mean swindler or cheat, one who diddles people out of what belongs to them. OED

7 *Sydney Morning Herald* 20 July 1858 quoting the *San Francisco Herald* 20 April 1858

8 In his letter George Weekes claimed that he and his wife had left America openly under their own names on the *Glimpse*. The list of passengers when the ship arrived in Sydney on 9 June 1858 (*Sydney Morning Herald* 10 June 1858) did not include any passengers named Weekes but did include 'Mr and Mrs Purceval', a name similar to one under which an American paper claimed they had travelled

9 *Age* 27 July 1858

10 *Spectator* 31 July 1858

11 ibid.

12 ibid.

13 ibid. 1 September 1858

14 The *Empire* ceased on 28 August 1858 and resumed under new proprietors on 23 May 1858

15 *Spectator* 18 September 1858

16 ibid. 2 October 1858

17 ibid. 13 November 1858

18 ibid. 11 December 1858

19 ibid. 30 December 1858

20 ibid. 22 January 1858

21 William Howitt *Land, Labour and Gold* Vol. 1, London: Longmans, Green, 1855, p. 406; also *Age* 15 December 1857. In a letter to the *Age* dated 17 December Caroline Dexter appeared to deny that she was a 'Rights of Women Advocate' or a 'Lecturer on Bloomerism and kindred subjects' but this was in the context of a letter in which she was mainly denying that she was the author of 'the late notorious reprint of a *crim. con.* case'.

22 Howitt *Land, Labour and Gold.* Howitt heard Dexter speak to the miners on 15 August 1853 at White Hills, Bendigo

23 William Moore *The Story of Australian Art* Sydney: Angus and Robertson, 1934, p. 28–9

24 William Dexter's authorship of these drawings can be deduced from the fact that 'Opposum by Moonlight' was in his 1857 Melbourne Exhibition (Melbourne *Punch* 10 December 1857) and also 'Native Camp, Gippsland', both of which are reproduced in the *Spectator*; Moore op. cit

25 Latrobe Library, Box 1834/3 MS11630. Leaflet advertising the *Ladies' Almanack*

26 ibid. Letters from Caroline to William Dexter

27 ibid. Leaflet advertising Madame Carole's Mesmeric Institution at 114 Collins Street, corner of Russell Street, late of 190 Collins Street

28 'Old Colonist' *Colonists, Copper and Corn in the Colony of South Australia 1850–51* (ed.) E. M. Yelland, Melbourne: Hawthorn Press, 1970

29 Harriet Clisby's life later formed the basis for a book — Shirley Darbyshire (Mrs Laurence W. Meynell) *Henrietta Condon MD*, London: Ivor Nicholson and Watson, 1936

30 *The Interpreter. An Australian Monthly Magazine of Science, Literature, Art &C.* Melbourne: Gordon and Gotch. Two numbers published January and February 1861

31 Henry Gyles Turner 'Some More Victorian Magazines' *Library Record of Australasia* Vol. 1, No. 3, p. 89

32 Interviews with Harriet Clisby containing material about her life appeared in several English and Australian papers at the time of her hundredth birthday on 31 August 1930 including *Sydney Morning Herald* 14 October 1930; *Adelaide Advertiser* 18 October 1930. Also London *Sunday Times* 7 October 1928

33 Dora Wilcox and William Moore 'The Wife of the Artist' *Art in Australia* 3rd series, No. 36, 15 February 1931. This article contains details of Caroline Dexter's life.

6 Mostly Moral and Earnest

1 [Elizabeth Selby—Mrs E. Wild] *Long Bay, by Bess of the Forest, the Lancashire Lass* Sydney: J. G. O'Connor, 1865

2 Cecilia H. W. Hill *Checkmated* Melbourne: W. H. Marshall, 1878, was reviewed by H. G. Turner in *Melbourne Review* Vol. 4, 1879, p. 111–12

3 Rev. W. Gray 'Mount Barker Pioneers. The Authoress Maud Jean Franc' *Mount Barker Courier and River Murray Advocate* 22 June 1930. This article contains information about Matilda Evans' life

4 Maud Jean Franc [Matilda Evans] *Marian, or, The Light of Some One's Home* 4th revised edition, London: Sampson Low, 1868, p. 377

5 *Register* 25 April 1863

6 Maude Jeanne Franc [Matilda Evans] *Beatrice Melton's Discipline* London: Sampson Low, 1880, pp. 3–4

7 Gray 'Mount Barker Pioneers'

8 *Kapunda Herald* 8 November 1867, Chapter XXII of 'Golden Gifts'

9 *Advertiser* 23 October 1886; *Register* 25 October 1886

10 Adelaide *Observer* 30 October 1886

11 *Quiz* 1890 issues

12 Gray 'Mount Barker Pioneers'

13 Unpublished material ADB files under Maria Scott; ADB Vol. 1 (Barney)

14 Ellen Liston *Pioneers* (comp.) E. A. Harwood, Adelaide: Hassall Press, 1936. Preface p.x

15 ibid. The Preface contains details of Ellen Liston's life

16 [Henrietta Foott] *Sketches of Life in the Bush: or, Ten Years in the Interior* Sydney: Gibbs, Shallard, 1872, p. 80

17 Information on Henrietta and James Foott from Gladys Cooney, Broadbeach Waters, Queensland, Bethia Foott 'Of Henrietta Marooned' *Bulletin* 4 October 1958; Bourke and District Historical Society

18 [Henrietta Foott] *Sketches of Life* p. 18

19 ibid. p. 30

20 Bethia Foott 'Of Henrietta Marooned'

21 Frank C. Brewer *The Drama and Music in New South Wales* Sydney: Government Printer, 1892, p. 9

22 *Bow Bells* reprinted in *Truth* 13 June 1920

23 *Truth* 9 November 1919, 13 June, 25 July 1920 ('Old Chum's' column in Forde, J. M. Q991.1 ML) contains details of Eliza Winstanley's life and career; ADB Vol. 2 (O'Flaherty); theatrical references in *Australian*

24 Sarah Susannah Perry *'Durable Riches'; or a Voice from the Golden Land* (ed.) Rev. Alfred J. Perry, London: Partridge and Co., 1857. Memoir by Emma Falkner. The memoir contains biographical details

25 ibid. pp. 43–4

26 Rae Webling 'A Song of Australia. Caroline Carleton. Her Poems and biography', Adelaide, 1977 typescript in ADB unpublished files contains details of Caroline

Carleton's life
27 The copy of the words and music of the 'Song of Australia' held in the National Library, Canberra came from Richard Copp who as bandmaster of the 13th Battalion carried the copy in his military pack through his service from 1914 to 1918 in Egypt, on Gallipoli and in France. He had charge of the only band to play on Gallipoli and played three Australian marches prior to the evacuation.
28 Newspaper cutting, undated [?18 June 1936] referring to ceremony, pasted in book containing original copy of 'Song of Australia' in National Library of Australia
29 H. A. Kellow *Queensland Poets* London: Harrap, 1930; ADB Vol. 5 (O'Doherty)
30 'Eva' of 'The Nation' [Eva O'Doherty] *Poems* San Francisco: P. J. Thomas, 1877, p. 265
31 R. Spencer Browne *A Journalist's Memories* Brisbane: Read Press, 1927, p. 108
32 ADB Vol. 4 (Hopkins)
33 F. R. C. Hopkins (ed.) *The Australian Ladies Annual* Melbourne: McCarron Bird, 1878. Preface
34 *Melbourne Review* Vol. 4, 1879, pp. 108–10
35 ibid. pp. 111–12
36 Miller *Pressmen and Governors* pp. 688

7 Early Journalists and Country Editors
1 *Athenaeum* May 1867 quoted in Janine Burke, *Australian Women Artists* Melbourne: Greenhouse Publications, 1980, p. 20
2 *Town and Country Journal* 14 January 1871. This article, based on letters and information in Dr J. D. Lang's possession, contains many biographical details of Adelaide Ironside
3 ibid.; Cyril Pearl *Brilliant Dan Deniehy: a forgotten genius* Melbourne, 1972, p. 4
4 E. A. Martin *Life and Speeches of Daniel Henry Deniehy* Melbourne: George Robertson, 1884, p. 4
5 ibid. p. 4
6 Elinor Rice Hays *Those Extraordinary Blackwells* New York: Harcourt, Brice and World, 1967. This book contains details of Anna Blackwell's life.
7 *Sydney Morning Herald* 18 December 1860
8 *Sydney Morning Herald* Archives. Letters, James to John Fairfax, 31 January 1865; 29 August 1865
9 *Sydney Morning Herald* 31 October 1870
10 ibid.
11 Hays *Those Extraordinary Blackwells*
12 *Sydney Morning Herald* Archives. James Fairfax letter 4 June 1881
13 Hays *Those Extraordinary Blackwells*
14 *Sydney Morning Herald* 4 June 1910
15 G. D. Richardson 'David Scott Mitchell' *Descent* Vol. 1, Part 2, 1961
16 William L. Curnow 'Emily Australie Heron' *Centennial Magazine* Vol. 3, No. 2, September 1890. Most of the biographical details on Emily Manning are taken from this article
17 Curnow *Centennial Magazine*; *Sydney Morning Herald* 26 August 1890
18 [Emily Manning] Australie *The Balance of Pain and other Poems* London: George Bell, 1877; *Illustrated Sydney News* 18 August 1877
19 Curnow *Centennial Magazine* p. 135
20 *Illustrated Sydney News* 30 August 1890
21 Curnow *Centennial Magazine* p. 135
22 *Sydney Morning Herald* 26 August 1890
23 Gavin Souter *Company of Heralds* Carlton, Victoria: Melbourne University Press,

1981, p. 104
24 Biographical material on Mrs Fischer: *Sydney Mail* 17 October 1896; Victorian Marriage Records; Letter from Dr Ailsa Zainu'ddin, Monash University, Mrs Fischer in Victoria (7 May 1987)
25 *Bulletin* 19 March 1925
26 *Sydney Mail* 17 October 1896
27 *Sydney Morning Herald* 8 October 1896, 2 January 1897; *Sydney Mail* 10 October 1896
28 *Bulletin* 6 January 1927
29 Letter from David Andrews, Chief Librarian, West Australian Newspapers, 23 July 1986; West Australian Newspapers *Quarterly Bulletin* 1963 issues
30 *Bulletin* 21 March 1907
31 ADB Vol. 4 (Gill)
32 ADB unpublished material (Falls and Jones); *Sydney Morning Herald* 3, 12 January 1877
33 *Bulletin* 7 February 1880
34 The Kyneton Historical Society (letters 19 August, 4 October 1987) has been unable to locate a reference to the female editor referred to but is hopeful that the information will be found
35 Information from Norm Bloomfield, editor, *Molong Express*; David Rutherford, Molong historian, Forster, New South Wales; *Molong Express* 9 August 1919; 'Molong Historian' Molong Historical Society, Vol. 1, No. 17, December 1974
36 *Molong Express* 9 August 1919, reprinted in *Molong Express Centenary Special* November 1976
37 *Bulletin* 12 November 1925
38 *Bulletin* 16 July 1881; information from Rod Kirkpatrick, Orange, New South Wales
39 ibid. 5 November 1881
40 ibid. 18 February 1882
41 ibid. 19 February 1882
42 ibid. 7 July 1904
43 *Sydney Morning Herald* 9 January 1930
44 *Port Denison Times and Bowen Advocate* 16 February 1901 contains biographical details. Also Rod Kirkpatrick *Sworn to no Master* Toowoomba: Darling Downs Institute, 1984, pp. 169–170; James Manion 'History of Newspapers in North Queensland' *Journal of the Royal Historical Society of Queensland* Vol. 11, No. 4, 1983
45 *Port Denison Times* 1 September 1900
46 ibid. 8 January 1901
47 *Worker* 2 March 1901
48 ibid.
49 *Port Denison Times* 5 February 1901
50 Kirkpatrick *Sworn to no Master*

8 Voices from the Bush
1 B. N.S.W. [Barbara Baynton] 'To my country' *Bulletin* 15 March 1902
2 *Chambers's Miscellany of Useful and Entertaining Facts* Edinburgh: William and Robert Chambers, 1847
3 [Annie (Baxter) Dawbin] *Memories of the Past by a Lady in Australia* Melbourne: W. H. Williams, 1873; Lucy Frost *No Place for a Nervous Lady* Melbourne: McPhee Gribble/Penguin, 1984, pp. 97–150
4 Mrs Dominic D. [Harriet] Daly *Digging, Squatting, and Pioneering Life in the Northern Territory of South Australia* London: Sampson, Low, 1887
5 Mrs Edward Millett *An Australian Parsonage; or, the Settler and the Savage in Western*

Australia 2nd edn London: Edward Stanford, 1872

6 'The Silverleaf Papers. Seasons of Drought' *Illustrated Sydney News* 23 April 1881

7 'The Silverleaf Papers. Poor People' *Illustrated Sydney News* 13 May 1882

8 Joan M. McKenzie *Silverleaf. The Story of Jessie Lloyd, pioneer writer of north western New South Wales* Dubbo: J. M. McKenzie, 1986. This book and information from Joan McKenzie, Coonamble, NSW are the sources of information on Jessie Lloyd's life

9 Silverleaf [Jessie Lloyd] *The Wheel of Life: a Domestic Story of Bush Life in Australia* Sydney: George Robertson, 1880; *Echo* 17 January 1880

10 *Illustrated Sydney News* 29 August 1885

11 ibid.

12 *Coonamble Independent* 22 August 1885

13 Marcie Muir *My Bush Book: K. Langloh Parker's 1890s Story of Outback Station Life* Adelaide: Rigby, 1982

14 *Pastoralists' Review* 17 August 1903

15 Adelaide *Observer* 16 December 1905

16 *Town and Country Journal* 4 November 1876

17 K. Langloh Parker *The Euahlayi Tribe: A Study of Aboriginal Life in Australia* London: Constable, 1905

18 'My darkie friends' *Sydney Mail* 16 December 1899

19 *Lone Hand* 2 December 1912

20 K. Langloh Parker *Australian Legendary Tales. Folk-lore of the Noongahburrahs as told to the Piccaninnies* London: David Nutt, Melbourne: Melville, Mullen and Slade, 1896

21 'My tame wild birds' *Emu* Vol. 1, Part 3, April 1902

22 *Pastoralists Review* 17 August 1903; *Sydney Morning Herald* 23 July 1903

23 Adelaide *Observer* 16 December 1905

24 Josephine Margaret Bagot *Reveries in Retrospect* Adelaide: Hassall Press, 1946

25 Laura Palmer-Archer *A Bush Honeymoon and other stories* London: T. Fisher Unwin, 1904. Foreword by Rolf Boldrewood

26 C. Hay Thomson 'Women Writers of Australasia' *Cassell's Magazine* January 1909

27 Sally Krimmer and Alan Lawson (eds) *Barbara Baynton* St Lucia, Queensland: University of Queensland Press, 1980. Introduction; H. B. Gullett 'Memoir of Barbara Baynton' *Bush studies* Sydney: Angus and Robertson, 1965; ADB Vol. 7 (Baynton)

28 Information from H. B. Gullett, Griffith, ACT

29 *Bulletin* 4 February 1903

30 *Sydney Morning Herald* 10 June 1911

31 *Argus* 29 May 1929

32 *Bulletin* 4 April 1907

33 *Home* September 1920

34 Information from H. B. Gullett

9 Renown, Mostly Abroad

1 Ada Cambridge *Thirty Years in Australia* London: Methuen, 1903, p. 87

2 Victorian death records

3 Cambridge *Thirty Years* p. 86

4 *Bookfellow* 1 May 1912, p. 130

5 Box 169/1 Latrobe Library. Letters to William P. Hurst 15, 23 December 1874

6 Cambridge *Thirty Years* pp. 132–3

7 Desmond Byrne *Australian Writers* London: Richard Bentley, 1896, p. 137

8 *Melbourne Review* No. 26 April 1882 p. 225

9 A.C. [Ada Cambridge] *Unspoken Thoughts* London: Kegan Paul, 1887

10 *Bookfellow* op. cit
11 A. W. Barker *Dear Robertson. Letters to an Australian Publisher* Sydney: Angus and Robertson, 1982, pp. 6–7, 131, 132
12 *Argus* 21 July 1926
13 *London Times* 21, 24 July 1926
14 Pandora Press: Ada Cambridge *A marked man*; Rosa Praed *Lady Bridget in the Never-Never Land* and *The bond of wedlock*; Catherine Martin *The incredible journey*
15 E. A. Huybers 'From Birth to Borderland' 1941. ML MSS 1423
16 ML Mfm FM 4/447
17 *London Times* 25 October 1897; Women's Executive Committee and Advisory Council 150th Anniversary Celebrations *Peaceful Army. A memorial to the pioneer women of Australia 1788–1938* Sydney: 1938 contain details of Jessie Couvreur's life
18 *Argus* 14 December 1883
19 *London Times* op. cit
20 Quoted in Raymond Beilby and Cecil Hadgraft *Australian Writers and their work. Ada Cambridge, Tasma and Rosa Praed* Melbourne: Oxford University Press, 1979, p. 21
21 *Illustrated Sydney News* 25 April 1891
22 *London Times* op. cit
23 *London Times* 20 May 1895
24 *Peaceful Army* op. cit.; Colin Roderick *In Mortal Bondage. The strange life of Rosa Praed* Sydney: Angus and Robertson, 1948; *Illustrated Sydney News* 11 April 1891; *London Times* 15 April 1935 contain details of Rosa Praed's life
25 *Sydney Morning Herald* 16 April 1935
26 ibid.
27 *Peaceful Army* op. cit. p. 119
28 *Sydney Morning Herald* op. cit
29 M.C. [Catherine Edith Macaulay Mackay {Martin}] *The Explorers and other poems* Melbourne: George Robertson, 1874
30 Catherine Spence *Autobiography* p. 55
31 ibid.
32 Miles Franklin *Laughter, Not for a Cage* Sydney: Angus and Robertson, 1956, pp. 86–7
33 John V. Byrnes 'Catherine Martin and the Critics' *Australian Letters* Vol. 3, No. 4, June 1961
34 [Catherine Martin] *The old roof tree. Letters of Ishbel to her half brother Mark Latimer* London: Longmans Green, 1908
35 South Australian death records
36 *Sydney Morning Herald* 23 May 1891
37 *London Times* 9 February 1926
38 *Australasian* 7 April 1894
39 *Australasian* 23 June 1894; Mrs Hirst Alexander 'Women of Australasia' in *Australasia* London: Kegan Paul, 1900, p. 307
40 *Bookfellow* 1 March 1912, p. 88
41 H. A Kellow *Queensland Poets* London, Harrap, 1930; ADB Vol. 8 (Fisher)
42 *London Observer* 10 April 1898, published as an advertisement in *By creek and gully*

10 New Women in Print

1 Gertrude Lawson 'The mother of Henry Lawson' *Aussie* 15 July 1922
2 *Dawn* 15 May 1888
3 *Bulletin* 24 October 1896
4 *Dawn* May 1899

5 *Dawn* January 1889 (reprint from *Boomerang*); August 1889; October 1889
6 ibid. November 1889
7 ibid. September 1890
8 ibid. July 1889. Two years later the 'Dawn' Club became part of the Womanhood Suffrage League
9 ibid. February 1892
10 ibid. March 1891
11 ibid. August 1900
12 ibid. May 1898
13 *Bulletin* 24 October 1896
14 *Dawn* April 1905
15 ibid. July 1905
16 *Australian Woman's Magazine* February 1884
17 *Woman's World* July 1886
18 ibid. May 1886
19 *Daily Telegraph* 21 April 1915 (This article has details of M. Wolstenholme/Anderson's life); ADB Vol. 7
20 *Sydney Morning Herald* 11 November 1892
21 *Daily Telegraph* op. cit
22 *Woman's Voice* 9 August 1894
23 ibid. 23 August 1894
24 ibid. 22 September 1894
25 ibid. 17 November 1894
26 ibid. 1 December 1894
27 ibid. 27 July 1895
28 ibid. 19 October 1895
29 ibid. 2 November 1895
30 *Daily Telegraph* op. cit.; *Lone Hand* 2 February 1914
31 Lurline Stuart *Nineteenth Century Australian Periodicals* Sydney: Hale and Iremonger, 1979, contains details of magazines; also Frank S. Greenop *History of Magazine Publishing in Australia* Sydney: K. G. Murray Publishing Co., 1947
32 *Argus* 7 July 1881
33 The 'Vagabond Papers', a series on social issues written anonymously by John S. James from information obtained by personal experience appeared in the *Argus* in the late 1870s.
34 *Bulletin* 16 April 1886
35 Farley Kelly 'The Woman Question in Melbourne 1880–1914' NLA Mfm G2025
36 *Cassell's Magazine* January 1909
37 *Sydney Mail* 11 July 1896
38 *Cassell's Magazine* op. cit
39 *Dawn* August 1891
40 *Dawn* 1 July 1895
41 Zara Aronson 'The early days' *Sydney Morning Herald* 4 April 1935. Zara Aronson refers to Mrs Fotheringhame (she spelt the name without an 'e') as the editor of *Young Australia* and her sister-in-law, Miss Josephine Fotheringham[e] as another journalist.
42 Frank S. Greenop *Magazine Publishing* p. 200

11 Women's Voices, Very Diverse
1 Nettie Palmer (ed.) *Memoirs of Alice Henry* Melbourne: 1944, pp. 5–6. Alice Henry's account of her life in these memoirs is the basis for information about her.

2 ibid. p. 10
3 ibid. p. 13
4 ibid. p. 14
5 ibid. p. 15
6 Jeanne Young *Catherine Helen Spence* Melbourne: Lothian Publishing Co., 1939, p. 132
7 *Woman's Sphere* February 1901; NLA MS 1066 Alice Henry Papers
8 *Bulletin* 14 November 1896
9 NLA MS 1066 The undated cutting from *Evening World* is in Alice Henry's papers
10 Frances Fraser and Nettie Palmer (eds) *Centenary Gift Book* Melbourne: Robertson and Mullen, 1934, pp. 101–7
11 ML QA 820.3H Alice Henry 'Bibliography of Australian Women writers'
12 Farley Kelly *Degrees of Liberation* Melbourne: Women Graduates Centenary Council of University of Melbourne, 1985; ADB Vol. 4
13 *Sydney Quarterly Magazine* 1887, 1888, 1889
14 ibid. 1887, pp. 324–6
15 Ian F. McLaren *Mary Gaunt Cosmopolitan Australian. An Annotated Bibliography* Parkville Victoria: University of Melbourne Library, 1986 contains biographical details
16 *Sydney Mail* 26 February 1898
17 *Strand* (New York) August 1915 quoted in McLaren *Mary Gaunt* p. xii
18 Quoted in McLaren *Mary Gaunt* p. xiv
19 Mary Gaunt *Alone in West Africa* quoted in McLaren *Mary Gaunt* p. xv; Death certificate Miller
20 ibid. p. xvi
21 *British Australasian* 17 September 1908
22 Quoted in McLaren *Mary Gaunt* p. 18
23 Information from Mrs Jill Marshall, Kerang, Victoria
24 Letter in possession of Mrs Jill Marshall
25 'An Australian Sick Nurse' *Town and Country Journal* 3 September 1887 contains information on Frances Gillam Holden's life
26 P. L. Hipsley *The early history of the Royal Alexandra Hospital for Children, Sydney 1880–1905* Sydney: Angus and Robertson, 1952, pp. 39–46
27 ibid. p. 39
28 *Town and Country Journal* op. cit.
29 *Bulletin* 24 September 1887
30 Quoted as an advertisement in Frances Gillam Holden *Her Father's Darling and other Child Pictures* Sydney: 1887, p. 93
31 Frances Gillam Holden *Woman's Ignorance and the World's Need, a plea for Physiology* Sydney: 1883
32 *Sydney Morning Herald* 28 August 1924
33 Ian F. McLaren *Grace Jennings Carmichael. From Croajingolong to London. An Annotated Bibliography* Parkville, Victoria: University of Melbourne Library, 1986 contains details of Jennings Carmichael's life
34 Grace Jennings Carmichael *Hospital Children. Sketches of Life and Character in the Children's Hospital, Melbourne* Melbourne: George Robertson, 1891
35 *Australian Woman's Mirror* 11 January 1927
36 *Argus* 16 April 1910
37 *All About Books* 15 June 1917
38 Mrs Harrison Lee *One of Australia's daughters* London: Ideal Publishing Co., 1900 contains details of Bessie Lee's life; Patricia Grimshaw 'Bessie Harrison Lee and the fight for voluntary motherhood' in Marilyn Lake and Farley Kelly *Double Time. Women in Victoria—150 years* Ringwood, Victoria: Penguin, 1985, pp. 139–147
39 Mrs Harrison Lee *Marriage and Heredity* 4th edn., Melbourne: Howard Printer, 1894

12 Women's Pages, Slightly Fanciful

1 *Illustrated Sydney News* 11 April 1891. The first sentence of this quotation (with 'Nearly' changed to 'Every') was reproduced in 'Women of Australasia' by Mrs Hirst Alexander in *Australasia* London: Kegan Paul, 1900. Mrs Hirst Alexander as Miss Hirst Browne was a journalist in Melbourne in the 1890s and a founder of the Lyceum Club.

2 *Bulletin* 6 January 1927

3 Catherine Spence *An autobiography* p. 56

4 Replies to letters to most major newspapers in Australia indicate that almost no records of staff in the nineteenth century have been kept. The *Sydney Morning Herald* has the best records with references to some staff in a card index in their archives section. The Latrobe Library holds some *Argus* and *Age* records but they contain very little on women in the nineteenth century. Some women are mentioned in R. B. Walker *The newspaper press in New South Wales* Sydney: Sydney University Press, 1976 and in his and J. Gibbney's card indexes held by the ADB

5 *Argus* 6 January 1894

6 *Sydney Morning Herald* 9 August 1890

7 Gavin Souter *Company of Heralds* Carlton, Victoria, Melbourne University Press, 1981, p. 83

8 *Town and Country Journal* 17 September 1870

9 Dymphna Cusack, T. Inglis Moore and Barrie Ovenden *Mary Gilmore: a Tribute* Sydney: Australasian Book Society, 1965

10 *Dawn* 1 August 1900; ADB Vol. 7

11 *Sydney Morning Herald* 25 June 1900

12 *Newcastle Morning Herald* 26 June 1900

13 Latrobe Library MS 10727 C. P. Smith 'Men who made "The Argus" and "The Australasian" 1846–1925'; *Sydney Morning Herald* 4 April 1935

14 Information on Mary Hannay Foott and her family from Gladys Cooney, Broadbeach Waters, Queensland; Celia Taylor, Rockingham, Western Australia; Bethia Ogden, Gloucestershire, England; Bethia Foott 'Mary Hannay Foott' *Bulletin* 1 July 1959; 'Mary Hannay Foott' *Bookfellow* 29 April 1899

15 Latrobe Library, MS6107, Letter M. H. Black, 18 August 1873

16 Information on life at Dundoo, Oxley Library OM 80–89, typescripts Foott, C. H., OM 81–37, original letter Brig. C. H. Foot, OM 72–14 MS 'Where the pelican builds'; Warrego and South West Queensland Historical Society; 'A collection of papers on the history relating to the Cunnamulla District' 1969–72

17 *Bulletin* op. cit.

18 *Queenslander* 25 May 1878, 1 June 1878, 20 July 1878, 27 July 1878, 3 August 1878, 7 September 1878, 5 October 1878, 16 November; *Brisbane Courier* 20 July 1878, 3 August 1878; 17 September 1932; *Bulletin* 24 July 1880, 22 April 1882

19 Oxley Library OM 72–14

20 *Bookfellow* op. cit.

21 *Bulletin* op. cit.

22 *Queenslander* 4 February 1888

23 *Bookfellow* op. cit.

24 *Maryborough Chronicle* 16 October 1918; *Herald* undated cutting ?October 1918 from Gladys Cooney

25 Agnes G. Murphy *One Woman's Wisdom* London: George Routledge, 1895, p. 76

26 ibid. p. 237

27 *British Australasian* 14 November 1895

28 Murphy *One Woman's Wisdom* p. 293

29 Agnes G. Murphy 'Social life in Victoria' in E. Jerome Dyer *Victoria and its resources*

Ballarat: n.d. pp. 26–8
30 Agnes G. Murphy *Melba* London: Chatto and Windus, 1909
31 ADB Vol. 9
32 Miss Moon's death is referred to in *Dawn* April 1900 as having occurred a few years before. (It is not clear whether she was the Miss Alice Moon referred to by Alice Henry as a women's rights advocate from England in her 'Marching towards citizenship' in *Centenary Gift Book*)
33 *Sydney Morning Herald* 23 May 1891
34 Information from books by Agnes Rose-Soley: *The call of the blood and other war verses* Sydney: Lyceum Club, 1914 and *Stray chords* Sydney: Tyrell's, 1923; H.J. Gibbney and Ann G. Smith (comps and eds) *A biographical register 1788–1939* [Canberra, ANU Bibliotech, 1987]
35 *Age* 3 September 1898
36 Latrobe Library MS 10727
37 *Age* 3 September 1898
38 Latrobe Library MS 10727
39 Address by Mrs Douglas Keep (Stella Allan's daughter) at Women's Australia Day ceremony, Melbourne 22 January 1976
40 *West Australian* 9 December 1938, 15 December 1943; West Australian Newspapers *Quarterly Bulletin* Vol. 2, No. 1, February 1963
41 Information from David Andrews, Chief Librarian, West Australian Newspapers; *Quarterly Bulletin* op. cit.
42 Mrs Leonard [Muriel] Matters *Australians who count in London and Who counts in Western Australia* London: Jas Truscott and Son, 1913
43 *Town and Country Journal* 29 November 1890

13 Newspaper Women and Social Ladies
1 Zara Aronson 'The early days' *Sydney Morning Herald* 4 April 1935
2 *Bulletin* 30 December 1926
3 ibid.
4 ibid.
5 ibid. 20 February 1892
6 W.E. Fitzhenry 'Some *Bulletin* books and their authors' in George Mackaness and Walter W. Stone *The Books of the* Bulletin *1880–1952* Sydney: Angus and Robertson, 1955
7 Mrs R. H. Todd *Looking back. Some early recollections of Mrs R. H. Todd* Sydney: Snelling Printing Works, 1938, pp. 11–12. Mrs Todd also recorded receiving help from journalists 'Miss Wright, afterwards Mrs Salmon, Miss Jones, Miss Darchy [D'Archy] and Mrs Fotheringhame'.
8 *British Australasian* 24 December 1896; NSW death records
9 Alfred Buchanan *The real Australia* London: T. Fisher Unwin, 1907, p. 108
10 *Bookfellow* 21 March 1907
11 Sheila Wigmore, Dolly Baverstock and Bill Baverstock 'Florence Baverstock — first president' Society of Women Writers *Ink* No. 2, Sydney: 1977; *Newspaper News* 1 October 1937 contain details of Florence Baverstock's life. Information from Fleur Harmsen, Snug, Tasmania
12 Latrobe Library MS 10727; *Bulletin* 15 September 1927. 'The Passing Show' by 'Oriel' which began on Saturday 15 August 1891 was a feature of the *Argus* for many years.
13 *Ink* No. 2
14 *Bulletin* 14 November 1896

15 ibid.
16 Florence Baverstock 'J. F. Archibald' Society of Women Writers *Ink* No. 1, Sydney, 1932
17 *Bulletin* 30 December 1926
18 *Ink* No. 2
19 Nancy Phelan *A kingdom by the sea* Sydney: ?1926; Nancy Phelan 'Louise Mack' *Australian* 18–19 April 1987; ADB Vol. 10 contain details of Louise Mack's life
20 *Cosmos* 31 October 1895
21 ibid.
22 ibid.
23 *Australian* op. cit.
24 *Sydney Morning Herald* 15 April 1901
25 *Bulletin* 24 January 1903. A review appeared in the *Sydney Morning Herald* 28 November 1902
26 *Sydney Morning.Herald* 30 November 1935
27 *Lone Hand* 1 December 1913
28 Writing written for the part of a newspaper devoted to fiction, criticism, light literature etc
29 *Lone Hand* op. cit.
30 *Bookfellow* 15 October 1915
31 ibid. 15 January 1915
32 *The Books of the Bulletin 1880–1952* p. 20
33 *Sydney Morning Herald* 30 November 1935; also 26 November 1935
34 *British Australasian* 1 October 1914; *Sydney Morning Herald* 7, 8 November 1939
35 Zara Aronson 'The early days'
36 [Conor O'Brien] *Macleod of 'The Bulletin'* by his wife, Sydney: Snelling Printing Works, 1931, p. 20
37 *Bookfellow* 21 March 1907
38 *Lone Hand* 1 April 1914; *British Australasian* 18 May 1911; Mrs Leonard [Muriel] W. Matters *Australians who count in London* London: Jas. Truscott and Son, 1913; Louise Brown et al. (ed.) *A book of South Australian women in the first hundred years* Adelaide: Rigby, 1936
39 *Bookfellow* 31 January 1907
40 Norman Lindsay *Bohemians of the Bulletin* Sydney: Angus and Robertson, 1965, pp. 28–9
41 *Bookfellow* 21 March 1907
42 *Bulletin* 12 July 1933. A memo in the *Sydney Morning Herald* archives dated 29 September 1899 indicates that Mrs Le Patourel was then social editor
43 *Sydney Morning Herald* 5 July 1933
44 Information on Theodosia Britton's life from Althea Farr, Double Bay, NSW
45 *Table Talk* 5 September 1901 and Lysbeth Cohen 'Zara Baar Aronson — writer and committee woman' *Australian Author* December 1986 contain details of Zara Aronson's life
46 Lysbeth Cohen 'Zara Baar Aronson'
47 *Table Talk*
48 *Sydney Morning Herald* 23 June 1936
49 *Lone Hand* 1 November 1915. This article by Bertram Stevens contains details of Ethel Turner's life
50 *Bookfellow* 25 March 1899
51 *Lone Hand* op. cit.
52 *Lone Hand* 2 December 1912 and Alison Alexander *Billabong's author* London: Angus

and Robertson, 1979 contain details of Mary Grant Bruce's life

14 Postscript
1 *Lone Hand* 1 November 1915
2 *Newspaper House News* July 1986
3 Henrietta G. McGowan and Margaret G. Cuthbertson *Woman's work* Melbourne: Thomas C. Lothian n.d. (?1905), p. 27
4 ibid. pp. 29–30
5 Alfred Buchanan *The real Australia* London: T. Fisher Unwin, 1907, pp. 108–9
6 *Bulletin* 18 April 1918
7 Valerie Lawson made this point in *Sun-Herald* 20 September 1987

Select Bibliography

This bibliography does not cover all the works referred to, particularly those used in relation to particular sections only. It seemed more useful to include the bibliographic details of these references in the notes. A great deal of research involved newspapers and periodicals. Specific references are included in the notes and text rather than a general listing of names of newspapers and periodicals.

Books

Adburgham, Alison *Women in Print, Writing Women and Women's Magazines from the Restoration to the Accession of Queen Victoria* London: George Allen and Unwin, 1972

Alford, Katrina *Production or reproduction. An economic history of women in Australia 1788–1850* Melbourne: Oxford University Press, 1984

Allen, Alexandra *Travelling ladies* London: Jupiter, 1980

Atkinson, Louisa *Excursions from Berrima and a trip to Monaro and Molonglo in the 1870's* Canberra: Mulini Press, 1980

Atkinson, Louisa *A Voice from the Country* Canberra: Mulini Press, 1978

Australian Dictionary of Biography Vols 1–10, Carlton, Victoria: Melbourne University Press, 1966–86 Douglas Pike (ed.) Vols 1–5; Bede Nairn (ed.) Vol. 6; Bede Nairn, Geoffrey Serle (eds.) Vols 7–10

Barker, A. W. *Dear Robertson. Letters to an Australian publisher* Sydney: Angus and Robertson, 1982

[Barton. Charlotte] *A Mother's Offering to her Children by a Lady long resident in New South Wales* Sydney: Gazette Office, 1841

Barton, G. B. *Literature in New South Wales* Sydney: Government Printer, 1866

Beilby, Raymond and Hadgraft, Cecil *Australian writers and their work* Melbourne: Oxford University Press, 1979

Bettison, Margaret and Summers, Anne *Her story. Australian women in print. 1788–1975* Sydney: Hale and Iremonger, 1980

Bevege, Margaret, James, Margaret and Shute, Carmel (eds) *Worth her salt*

British Library General Catalogue of Printed Books London: Clive Bingley, 1979

Brown, Louise (ed.) *A Book of South Australia: women in the first hundred years* Adelaide: Rigby for the Women's Centenary Council of South Australia, 1936

Browne, Spencer *A Journalist's Memories* Brisbane: Reed Press, 1927

Byrne, Desmond *Australian Writers* London: Richard Bentley, 1896

Cambridge, Ada *Thirty years in Australia* London: Methuen, 1903

Dutton, Geoffrey (ed.) *The Literature of Australia* Ringwood, Victoria: Penguin, 1964

Eldershaw, Flora (ed.) *Peaceful Army* Sydney: Women's Executive Committee 150th Anniversary Celebrations, 1938

Elliott, Brian and Mitchell, Adrian *Bards in the wilderness* Melbourne: Nelson, 1970

Ellis, Vivienne Rae *Louisa Anne Meredith. A Tigress in Exile* Hobart: Blubberhead Press, 1979

The English Catalogue of books 1853–1862 London: Sampson Low, 1864

Ewers, John Keith *Creative writing in Australia* Melbourne: Georgian House, 1962

Franklin, Miles *Laughter, Not for a Cage* Sydney: Angus and Robertson, 1956

Fraser, Frances and Palmer, Nettie *Centenary Gift Book* Melbourne: Robertson and Mullen, 1934

Fry, Eric (ed.) *Rebels and radicals* Sydney: Allen and Unwin, 1983

Gill, Thomas (comp.) *Bibliography of South Australia* Adelaide: Government Printer, 1886

Gillison, Joan *The history of the Lyceum Club* Melbourne: Lyceum Club, 1975

Giordano, Margaret and Norman, Don *Tasmanian Literary Landmarks* Hobart: Shearwater Press, 1984

Green, H. M. *A history of Australian literature* Sydney: Angus and Robertson, 1961

Greenof, Frank *History of magazine publishing in Australia* Sydney: K. G. Murray Publishing Co., 1947

Grieve, Norma and Grimshaw, Patricia (eds) *Australian women feminist perspectives* Melbourne: Oxford University Press, 1981

Hadgraft, Cecil *Australian literature: a critical account to 1955* Melbourne: Heinemann, 1960

Hergenham, Laurie *Unnatural lives* St Lucia, Queensland: University of Queensland Press, 1983

Hill, Georgiana *Women In English life* London: Richard Bentley, 1896

Kelly, Farley *Degrees of liberation* Melbourne: Women's Graduate Committee University of Melbourne, 1955

Kirkpatrick, Rod *Sworn to no master* Toowoomba: Darling Downs Institute Press, 1984

Lake, Joshua (ed.) *Childhood in bud and blossom* Melbourne: The Atlas Press, 1900

Lee, Sidney (ed.) *Dictionary of National Biography* London: Elder and Co., 1903

Lloyd, Clem *Profession: Journalist* Sydney: Hale and Iremonger, 1985

Loyau, George E. *Notable South Australians, or Colonists past and present* Adelaide: Carey Page and Co., 1885

Mackaness, George and Stone, Walter *The books of the Bulletin 1886–1952*

McLaren, Ian F. *Grace Jennings Carmichael. An annotated bibliography* Parkville, Victoria University of Melbourne Library, 1986

—— *Mary Gaunt. An annotated bibliography* Parkville, Victoria: University of Melbourne Library, 1986

Magery, Susan *Unbridling the tongues of women. A biography of Catherine Helen Spence* Sydney: Hale and Iremonger, 1986

Matters, Mrs Leonard [Muriel] *Australians who count in London and Who counts in Western Australia* London: Jas Truscott, 1913

Miller, E. Morris *Australian Literature A Bibliography to 1938* extended to 1950 Frederick T. Macartney ed., Sydney: Angus and Robertson, 1956

—— *Pressmen and Governors* Sydney: Sydney University Press, 1973

—— *Australian Literature from its beginnings to 1935* Sydney: Sydney University Press, 1975 (fac. ed.)

Moore, William *The story of Australian art* Sydney: Angus and Robertson, 1934

Ollif, Lorna *Louisa Lawson. Henry Lawson's Crusading Mother* Adelaide: Rigby, 1978

O'Malley, Ida Beatrice *Women in Subjection* London: Duckworth, 1933

Pierce, Peter (ed.) *Oxford literary guide to Australia* Melbourne: Oxford University Press, 1987

Pitt, George H. *The press in South Australia 1836–1850* Adelaide: Wakefield Press, 1946

Press, John (ed.) *Commonwealth literature* London: Heinemann, 1965

Richardson, Joanna *The courtesans* Cleveland: World Publishing, 1980

Roderick, Colin *An introduction to Australian fiction* Sydney: Angus and Robertson, 1950

Saxby, H. M. *A history of Australian children's literature 1841–1941* Sydney: Wentworth Books, 1969

Sladen, Douglas *Australian Ballads* London: Walter Scott, 1888

Souter, Gavin *Company of Heralds* Carlton: Melbourne University Press, 1981

Sowden, Will J. *An Australian Native's Standpoint* London: Macmillan, 1912
Spence, Catherine Helen *An Autobiography* Articles reprinted from the *Register* Adelaide: W. K. Thomas, 1910
——— *Handfasted* Preface and afterword by Helen Thomson, Ringwood, Victoria: Penguin, 1984
Steere, Francis G. *Bibliography of books dealing with Western Australia since 1827* Perth: Parliamentary Library, 1922
Stuart, Lurline *Nineteenth century Australian periodicals* Sydney: Hale and Iremonger, 1979
Teale, Ruth (ed.) *Colonial Eve* Melbourne: Oxford University Press, 1978
Turner, Henry Gyles and Sutherland *The development of Australian literature* London: Longmans, Green, 1898
Walker, R. B. *The Newspaper Press in New South Wales 1803–1920* Sydney: Sydney University Press, 1976
Walker, Shirley (ed.) *Who is she?* St Lucia: University of Queensland Press, 1953
Wilde, William H., Hooton, Joy and Andrews, Barry *Oxford Dictionary of Australian Literature* Melbourne: Oxford University Press, 1985
Women's Centenary Council *Records of the Pioneer Women of Victoria 1835–1860* Melbourne: Osboldstone, 1937
Young, Jeanne F. *Catherine Helen Spence* Melbourne: Lothian Publishing Co., 1937

Articles

Brunsdon, Fletcher C. 'Centenary of the "Sydney Morning Herald"' *RAHS Journal* Vol. XVII, Part II, 1931
Byrnes, John V. 'Catherine Martin and her critics' *Australian Letters* Vol. 3, No. 4, June 1961
Chisholm, A. R. 'Celeste de Chabrillan and the Gold Rush' *Meanjin Quarterly* 2, 1969
Gillison, Joan 'Two invincible ladies. L. Meredith and M. Gaunt' *Victorian Historical Journal* May 1980
Horner, J. C. 'The themes of four Tasmanian convict novels' *THRA Papers and Proceedings* Vol. 15, No. 1, June 1967
Kirk, Pauline 'Colonial Literature for Colonial Readers' *Australian Literary Studies* Vol. 5, No. 2, October 1971
Kramer, Leonie 'The Literary News, 1882–1883' *Australian Literary Studies* Vol. 7, No. 3, May 1976
Krimmer, Sally 'New light on Barbara Baynton' *Australian Literary Studies* Vol. 7, No. 4, October 1976
Lawson, Sylvia 'Edited, printed and published by women' *Nation* 25, October 1958
——— 'The mother of Henry Lawson' *Aussie* 15, July 1972
Manion, James 'History of Newspapers in North Queensland' *RHSQ Journal* Vol. 11, No. 4, 1983
Matthews, Brian 'Louisa, Henry, Gertie and the Drover's wife' *Australian Literary Studies* Vol. 9, No. 3, May 1980
Melville, Adam G. 'The book trade in Australia since 1861' *Library Association of Australasia Proceedings* October 1898
Miller, E. Morris 'Australia's first two novels' *THRA Papers and Proceedings* Vol. 6, No. 2, September 1957
——— 'First woman novelist' *Australasian Book News and Library Journal* March 1947
Niall, Brenda 'Images of Australian Colonial Children's books' *This Australia* Vol. 2, No. 1, 1982–83
Palmer, Nettie 'Who was Alice Henry?' *Australian Women's Digest* Vol. 1, No. 9, 1 April, 1945

Roe, Jill 'The scope of women's thought is necessarily less' *Australian Literary Studies* Vol. 5, No. 4, October 1972
[Sinnett, Frederick] 'The fiction fields of Australasia' *Journal of Australasia* September–October 1856
Spence, Catherine Helen 'A week in the future' *Centennial Magazine* 1889 (six issues)
Swann, Margaret 'Mrs. Meredith and Miss Atkinson, Writers and Naturalists', RAHS *Journal and Proceedings* Vol. XV, Part 1, 1929
Thomson, Helen 'Finding lost fictions' *Australian Book Review* June 1987
Turner, H. G. 'The beginnings of literature in Victoria' *Victorian Historical Magazine* Vol. IV, 1914–15
—— 'Some more Victorian Magazines' *Library Record of Australasia* Vol. 1, No. 3
Walker, R. B. 'Catherine Helen Spence. Unitarian Utopian' *Australian Literary Studies* Vol. 5, No. 1, May 1971
'Australian Pioneers [Louisa Atkinson]' *Sydney Morning Herald* 8 March 1911
'Catherine Spence: Pioneer journalist' *Australian Women's Weekly* 16 September 1950
'Mrs. Louisa A. Meredith' *Illustrated Sydney News* 4 June 1892
'Mrs. Louisa Ann[e] Meredith' RAHS *Journal and Proceedings* Vol. VII, Part IV, 1921
'Notes on Australian artists' RAHS *Journal* Vol. VII, Part III, 1921
'Some Australian women' *Illustrated Sydney News* 11,25 April 1891

Manuscripts
Allan, Stella, first exhibition of women's work, Melbourne, October–December 1907. Articles, Latrobe Library (LL) MS 10964
Age Wages of literary staff 1886–1937, LL, Box 1187/2, MS 9751
Cambridge, Ada, Letters to William P. Hurst, LL, Box 169/1
Couvreur, Jessie, Journal, Mitchell Library (ML), Mfm FM 4/447
Dexter, Caroline and William, LL, Box 1834/3, MS 11630
Foott, C. H., Oxley Library OM, 80–89, OM 81–37
Foott, Mary, Oxley Library OM, 72–14
Foott, Mary Hannay, Letter, LL, Box 168/1, MS 6107
Haddon, F. W., material, LL, Box 352/6 352/5, 377/1, 2, 3, Box 155/1, Box 155, 156, 157
Henry, Alice, 'Bibliography of Australian women writers' ML, QA 820.3H
Henry, Alice, Papers, National Library of Australia (NLA), MS 1066
Henry, Alice, Press cuttings on Alice Henry by Muriel Heagney, LL, MS 9106, Box 1163/1
Huybers, E. A., 'From birth to borderland' ML, MSS 1423
Kelly, Farley, 'The woman question in Melbourne 1880–1914' NLA McG 2025
Manning, A. W., Journal of *Earl Grey* 1839–40, NLA, MS 289
Sydney Morning Herald archival material
Smith, C. P. 'Men who made 'The Argus' and 'The Australasian' 1846–1925, LL, MS, 10727
Tucker, Maya V. 'The emergence and character of women's magazines in Australia 1880–1914' MS Thesis, University of Melbourne, August 1975
Turner, Ethel, Papers. Letters 1888–1941, ML, MSS 667

Index

Aberdeenshire, Scot. 92
Aborigines 18,20,41,43,54,57,58,59,60,77,
82,128,131,133–36,138,151,155
*An account of the state of agriculture and
grazing in New South Wales* 21,255
actress/writer 86,94–7
Adelaide, SA 18–19,28–31,79–80,86–9,
90–1,99–100,127,136,154–5,199,227,
234,239
Adelaide *Advertiser* 32,33,89
Adelaide *Chronicle* 83,239
Adelaide *Daily Telegraph* 31
Adelaide *Evening Post* 239
Adelaide *Observer* 28,31,32,33,88–9,90,
91,239,254
Adelaide *Register* 29,31,32,33,239,255
Adelaide University 154
Adey, Lucy Leman 6,8
Adey, Stephen 6,8
Adieux au monde 52
'Adrienne' see Chase, Muriel
*Adventures in Australia; or, the wanderings of
Captain Spencer in the bush and the wilds*
57–9
Adventures on a journey to New Holland 5
advertisements 66,80,164,165,167,168–9,
173,177,178,209,210,246,251
Aerschot, Belg. 237
Africa 59,60,193
Agnew, Sir James 147
Agnew, Dr J. W. 47,48
Aitken's Evenings at Home 22
Alcott, Louisa 83
Alexander, Mrs Hirst (née Browne) 157,
263,266
'All aboard: A tale for Christmas' 4,130–1
Allan, Edwin Frank 222
Allan, Stella 220–22,223
Anderson, Ethel 93–4
Anderson, Professor Francis 174,180
Anderson, Maybanke see Wolstenholme
Anderson, Wallace 199
Angaston, SA 87,88

Angaston House, North Adelaide (school)
87
Angus & Robertson 146
'Ann Cornstalk' 135
Annine: a novel 89
anonymous writing 1,11,18,20,29,30,41,
65–7,106,107,113,114,115,154; *see also*
pseudonyms
anthologies 101–5,142,156–9
Antrim, Ire. 225
Antwerp, Belg. 235,237
Archer, Ellinor 193
Archer, Lucy 189–90
Archibald, J. F. 228,231,232,233,234,238
Arena 181
Arnold's Library of Australian Authors 191
Aronson, Zara Baar 207,220,236,238,
243–6
artists/writers 2,17–8,27–8,35–40,44,55,
59,90,93–4,106–8,157,210,211
As the whirlwind passeth 193
Ashton, Eliza Ann 208–9
Ashton, Julian 208
Aspinall, Butler Cole 46
Aspinall, Clara 46
Athenaeum, London 49,56,106
Atkinson, James 20,21,40,255
Atkinson, (Caroline) Louisa 2–3,4,20,21,
23,27–8,31,40–44,106,126
Atlantic Monthly 146
'Auckland Marston' 91
'Aunt Mary' see Nanson, Janet and Chase,
Muriel
Australasian 32,38,46,49,128,137,138,144,
149,157,184,186,190,198,199,207,208,
209–10,210,231,238,241,242,243
Australasian Sketcher 210–11
'Australia Felix. Impressions of Victoria' 61
An Australian girl 154,154–55
An Australian girl in London 236
An Australian heroine 152
Australian Journal 147,150,200,202
Australian Journalists' Association 222,233

Australian Ladies' Annual 1878 101–04,149
Australian legendary tales. Folk-lore of the Noongahburrahs as told to the Piccaninnies 135–6
An Australian parsonage 127–8
Australian poets 1788–1888 105,157
Australian Woman's Magazine and Domestic Journal 4,172,173,196
'Australie' see Manning, Emily
'Australienne' see Holden, Frances Gillam
The Author's daughter 31
autobiography 28,29,30,32–3,34,63,106, 141,143,145,146,149,150,154,172,184, 186,187,193,201,202,214–5,256

Bairnsdale Advertiser 198
Baker, Hannah Newton 105
Balance of pain and other poems 114
Ballan, Vic. 143,144
Ballarat, Vic. 181,188,190,198,216,217
Balmain, NSW 23
Bangate station, NSW 134,135,136
Bank of Australia 14,16
Barbould, Mrs 22
Barker, Captain Sir George 62–3
Barker, Lady see Broome, Lady
Barney, Colonel George 89
Barney, Maria see Scott, Maria
Barton, Charlotte 2,11,12,20–3,40
Barton, George Bruce 21,40
Barton, George Burnett 18,41–2,182
Bathurst, NSW 35,225
Baverstock, Capt Archibald 233
Baverstock, Dolly 233
Baverstock, Florence 187,220,227,231–3, 234,238,267
Baverstock, William 233
Baxter, Annie 126,127,128
Baxter, Margaret Agnese 224
Baynes, William 98
Baynton, Barbara 3,126,138–43,237
Beaconsfield, Vic. 184
Bear-Crawford, Annette 186
Beatrice Melton's Discipline 87
The beauty of the British Alps; or, Love at first sight 6
Becke, Louis 158
Beechworth, Vic. 54,55,143
Belfast, Ire. 119
Belgium, 149,235,237
Bendigo, Vic. 75,104,143,258
Bengala: or, some time ago 26

Bennett, Samuel 210
Bentley, George 31,33
Berlin, Germ. 155,236
Berrima, NSW 21,40,41,43
Besant, Annie 177
'Billabong' series 248,249
Bird, Isabella 46,60–2,257
Birmingham, Eng. 2,27,34–5,37
Birmingham Journal 34
Bishop, Isabella (Mrs John) see Bird, Isabella
Bitter sweet — So is the world 95
Black, James 210,211
Blackburn, Lady 241
Blackwell, Anna 108–12,260
Blackwell, Dr Elizabeth 80,108,112
Blair, David 231,232
Blair, Florence see Baverstock, Florence
Blair, Lily (Mrs Percy Hunter) 231
Bloomer, Amelia 75,76
'bloomer' revolution 65,75,76,258
Bloomsbury, Lond. 240
Blue Mountains, NSW 40,41,43
Bode, Ettie E. 104–5
Bohemia 231
'Bohemian born' 154
'Bohemienne' see O'Ferrall, Nancy
Boldrewood, Rolf 128,134,138,150,244
Bonython, J. L. 89
A book of Queensland verse 101
A book of South Australia — women in the first hundred years 91,136,240,255
Bookfellow 142,145–6,157,211,230–1,238, 240,247
Boston, USA 83
Boulogne, Fr. 109,110
Bourke, NSW xi,92–3,211,259
Bourke, Sir Richard 97
Bow Bells 94,95,96,97
Bowen, Qld 123–5
Bowen Advocate 123
Bowen Mirror 123
Bowman, Anne 60
Boyd, William Carr ('Potjostler') 212
Boyle, Mary see Garland, Mary
Boyle, Edward Hugh 121,122
Bradford Girls' Grammar School, Yorks. 243
Braidwood, NSW 13,16,17,18
Bremer, Lady 20
Brereton, John Le Gay 114
Bright, Annie (Mrs C.) 182,234
Bright, Charles 182

Bright, John 149
Brighton, Vic. 84
Brisbane 100–1,151,159,207,211,212,213, 214,239
Brisbane Sun 125
Brisbane Telegraph 246
British Australasian 187,215,240
Britton, Alexander 242
Britton, Theodosia 220,242–3
The broad arrow: being passages from the history of Maida Gwynnham, a lifer 45,46, 48–9
Brodzsky, Maurice 240
A broken journey 193
Bronte, Charlotte 29,150
Broome, Sir Frederick 63,257
Broome, Lady (Barker) 62–3,257
A brother or lover? a sister or bride? and The lights of Hazelglen 89
Broughton, Bishop William 19,26
Borwne, Thomas A. see Boldrewood, Rolf
Browning, Robert 113
Bruce, Maj. George Evans 249
Bruce, Mary Gran 246,247,248–50
Bundaberg Mail 213
Brussels, Belg. 148,150–1,237
Buckle, Buckle, Bagster and Buchanan 14
Budd, Misses (school), Jolimont Vic. 242
Budd, Richard Hale (school), Melbourne 184
Buffalo 18
Bulletin 116,117–18,119,121–2,125,128, 136,137,138,140,167–8,181,182,187, 194–6,204,207,216,219,220,225,226, 227–31,232–3,234,237,238–40,241–2, 252
Bulletin Story Book 220
Bulwer, Edward Lytton 17
Bunce and Brothers, NY 36
Bunn, Anna Maria 1,2,11,13–18,254
Bunn, Capt. George 14
Bunn, William 13,14
Burke, Robert O'Hara and Wills 54,92,154
Burnett, Frances Hodgson 247
Burnett River district, Qld 151
bush as a subject 21,26,41–3,87,88,92–3, 105,126–33,137–41,152,155,162,212; see also gold-rushes
Bush friends in Tasmania. Last series 38,39,40
A bush honeymoon and other stories 137,138
Bush studies 138,140,141
'Bushwoman' see Palmer-Archer, Laura

Butler, R. L. 100
Butterfield, W. 213
Buvelot, Louis 84,210
Buzacott, C. H. 210,213
By creek and gully 156,158–9
Byrne, Desmond 144–5
Bystander 243

Caffyn, Kathleen 156,157,158,159,182
California 67–8,70,71,202
The call of the blood and other war verses 218,219
Calvert, James Snowden 43,256
Calvert, (Caroline) Louisa Waring see Atkinson, Louisa
Calvert, W. 77
Cambramatta and Woodleigh Farm 26
Cambridge, Ada 3,102,142–7,153,188, 199,247
Cameron, Mary Ann 208,225
Cameron, Mary Jean see Gilmore, Dame Mary
Canada 34,54,61,110,112,181
Carcoar, NSW 102,121–3
Carcoar Chronicle 121–2
Card, Mary 102
Carleton, Caroline 97,98–100,259–60
Carmichael, Evelin 102
Carmichael, Grace Jennings 183,188, 198–9,265
Carrington, Tom 209
Carrington, Mrs Tom 209–10
Cassell's Magazine 138,181,234,248,256
Cassell's Picturesque Australasia 190,191
Castella, Hubert de 53
Castilla, Ethel 237
Casterton, Vic. 225
Castlemaine Mail 242
Cavan station, Wee Jasper NSW 43
Centenary gift book 188
Centennial Magazine 33–4,113,114,191,260
Chabrillan, Celeste de 46,50–3,257
Chabrillan, Count Lionel 50,51,52,53
Chads, Ellen Augusta 172
Chambers's miscellany 126–7
Champion 186
Champion, Henry Hyde 181
Chandler, Alfred C. 89
Chapman and Hall 152
Character, or Jew and Gentile 9
Charles Eaton 20,22
Charters Towers New Eagle 159

Charters Towers Telegraph 125
Chartist movement 35
Chase, Muriel 224
Checkmated 86,104,259
Cheeseman, Clara E. 102
Chesholt, Margaret 102
Chesney, A. 172
Chicago, USA 187
Chicago Daily News 193
Childhood in bud and blossom 191,192
China 62,193
Chisholm, Caroline 45,188
Christmas 22,102,131,248
Christmas bells 89
'Cinderella' see Bruce, Mary Grant
Clacy, Ellen (Mrs Charles) 46,53–4,257
*Clara Morison — A tale of South Australia
during the gold fever* 29–30
Clarke, Mrs A. E. 172
Clarke, J. R. 41,43
Clarke, Lady (Janet) 189,199
Clarke, Marcus 46,150
Clarke, Sir William 198,199
Clear shining light 47,256
'Cleo' see Baverstock, Florence
Cleone: A tale of married life 9
*Cleone. Summer's sunset vision, the confession,
with other poems and stanzas* 6
Clisby, Charles 79
Clisby, Harriet 65,74,75,79–81,82,83–4,
258,259
Clyde, Constance 237
Cobbers 141
Cobden, Richard 109,149
Coleraine, Vic. 143
Colonial memories 63
*Colonist, or Journal of politics, commerce,
agriculture, literature, science and religion,
Sydney* 11,14–5
contributors x,4,29,32,33,34,86,87,90–1,
113,114,129,146,149,152,158,180,186,
187,198,210,211,215,218,220,224,225,
232,244,252
Convict once 151
convicts 1,5,9,12,26,45,46,47–8,49,52,54,
85,89,128,156
*Coo-ee: Tales of Australian life by Australian
ladies* 156–7,158,159
Cook, Capt. James 5
Coonamble, NSW 129,130,133,138–40
Cooper, Mrs 167
Co-operator 217

Cork, Ire. 14,15,92,119
Cornhill Magazine 31
Corowa, NSW 136
Cosmos 182,234,235
Country Press Association 243
Couvreur, Auguste 148,149
Couvreur, Jessie 3,102,104,142,147–51,
153,156,157,188
*Cowanda, the veteran's grant, an Australian
story* 43
Cowie, Bessie see Lee, Bessie
Creed, Louisa see Mack, Louisa
Creed, Percy 235
cremation 112,149,177
Croly, Mrs 33
Cross, Ada see Cambridge, Ada
Cross, Rev. George 143,146
Cross, Joseph 21
Cunningham, Sir Edward 186,231
Curlewis, Ethel see Turner, Ethel
Curlewis, Judge Herbert R. 248
Curlewis, Jean 248
Curnow, William L. 113–14,115,117,260
Curthoys, Mrs A. G. 223
Curtis Island, Qld 152,153
cycling 173,179
Cyclopaedia of Australasia 231

Daly, Dominic 127
Daly, Harriet W. 127
Daly, Victor 156
Dalysford, Vic. 200
'Dame Durden' see Turner, Ethel
Dampier, Kate 102
D'Archy, Susan 208,267
D'Arcy, W. Knox 158
D'Arenberg, Eva 239
Darling, Lady 13
Darling River, NSW 92–3,133
Darwin, NT 127
Dave's sweetheart 191
Dawbin, Annie see Baxter, Annie
Dawn 4,160,161,162–71,172,173,175,178,
182,196,230
Dawn Club 165–6,264
Day, Mrs Henry 156
Daybreak, NZ 178
Deadman's 190,191
*Debatable ground; or, the Carlillawarra
claimants* 43
Defoe, Daniel 49
Deniehy, Daniel Henry 107–8

Deniliquin, NSW 119
Denison, Lady 47
Dennis, C. J. 239
Derbyshire, Eng. 75
Devonshire, Eng. 9,23
Dexter, Caroline 65,74–9,80–2,84,258, 259
Dexter, William 75,77,78–9,82,84,258
Dick, Harriet Elphinstone 184
Dickens, Charles 3,138
Digging, squatting and pioneering life in the Northern Territory of South Australia 127
divorce reform 3,160,162,164,175
Doncaster Eng. 246
Donnelly, Annie C. 102
'Dora Falconer' see Lawson, Louisa
Dora's repentance 172
Doughty, Sir George 240
Doughty, Lady see Stone, Eugenia
Douglas, Captain Bloomfield 127
Drake-Brockman, Henrietta 136
Dreams in flower 235
Dredge, William Gilpin 116
dress reform 40,75,76,160
Dublin, Ire. 235
Duke and Duchess of York 238
Duffy, Charles Gavan 100
Dulwich Hill, NSW 174
Dumas, Alexandre 50,51,52,53
Dundoo station, Qld 211–12
'*Durable riches*', *or A voice from the Golden Land* 97–8
Durack, Elizabeth 136
Dyer, E. Jerome 215,231

earnings from writing 1–2,14,28,29–30,31, 32,33,34,36,38,56,86,90,91,112,115, 129,130,144,146,149,154,178,187,189, 191,193,228,243,246,247,249,252
Earth Spiritual 159
East Wellington, SA 90–1
Ebba 38
Echo 4,130,230
Edinburgh, Scot. 46,61,127
editors 5,12–13,64–84,95,118–25,160–71, 175–80,182,185,217,234; *see also* newspaper/magazine proprietors
education of writers 2,14,29,34,47,50,75, 90,98,107,113,116,120,123,133,138, 143,147,154,157,162,174,184,188,190, 194,200,210,218–9,234,236,239,241, 242,243,246,248; *see also* women's right

to education
Eurunderee, NSW 162
Eliot, George 113
Ella Norman; or, a woman's perils 46,54–6
Ellet, Mrs 82
Ellis, Rev. Dr. 122
Elliston, SA 90,91
Elmes, Frances F. 220
Emerson, E. S. 125
Empire 43,67–8,72,73,258
Emu 136
England 1,2,3,9,23,24–6,27,31,33,34–5, 40,41,46–8,54,63,64,71,75,80,83,84, 95,98,108–9,112,113,116,127,128,136, 138,141,142,144,146,149,152,155,157, 158,174,178,191,193,199,215,225,236, 237,238,240,241,246,249,250
The English Annual for 1836 10
Enoch's Point, Vic. 200
Essex, John Ridgwell 193
The Etiquette of Australia 243
Eton, Eng. 26
The Euahlayi Tribe 134–5,136
Evans (publisher) 20,22
Evans, Henry Congreve 89
Evans, Mary Sanger 176
Evans, Matilda Jane 3,85,86–9,188
Evans, William James 89
Evening News, Sydney 165
Evening Standard, Melbourne 238
Evening World, US 183,188
Everylady's Journal 240
Exeter, Eng. 23,47,48,50
The explorers and other poems 154
Eyre's Peninsula, S.A. 90,91

Fairfax family 108,117
Fairfax, James 4,109,110–12,260
Fairfax, John 12,43,109,260
Falkner, Emma 98,259
Falls, Alexander 119
Falls, Margaret 119
The Family at Misrule 178,248
fashions 167,169,173,205,207,208,244,245
Female Protestant Training School for Domestic Servants 90
Female Tatler, UK 64
'Feminine facts and fancies' 219,220
feminist/women's issues 3,9,10,27,28,33, 65–6,71–2,83,140–1,160,162,164–5, 167–70,173–80,183,184,186,187,189, 194,205,208,218,228,243,251,253; *see*

also women's suffrage
Fiction for family reading 95,96
Field, E. P. 203–4
Field, Catherine see Parker, K. Langloh
A fiery ordeal 150
Finlayson, John Harvey 32
The Fire-seeker 157
Fischer, Jane (Mrs Carl) 116–18,207,217, 243,245,261
Fisher, Mary Lucy (Lala) 158–9,188
Fisher, Unwin and Co. 235
Fitzhenry, W. E. 227,237
'flappers' 226,234,237,239
Florence 108,236
Flynn, John 119
Foott, Lt Arthur 213,214
Foott, Maj.-Gen. Cecil 213,214
Foott, Henrietta 85,91–4,126,259
Foott, Mary Hannay 94,188,207,210–14
For the term of her natural life: a tale of 1830 95
For the term of his natural life 46,150
Forbes, Joseph 22
foreign/overseas correspondents 108–12, 150–1,203,204,206,231–2,237
Forster, (Johann) Georg Adam 5
Forster, Johann Reinhold 5
Fotheringhame, Miss Josephine 264
Fotheringhame, Mrs Pattie 182,227,264, 267
Franc, Maud Jean see Evans, Matilda Jane
France 53,104,109,110–11,149,193,218
Frank Carey: a story of Victorian life 105
Franklin, Miles 155,187,251
Fraser, Charles Forbes 147,149
Frater, Alexander 138,140
free kindergarten movement 180,243
Freeman's Journal 217,224
French Geographical Society 149
Fricker, Edward 186
Fry, Elizabeth 224

Gadfly 239
Galveston, Texas 68
Galveston *Southern Age* 68,71
Galway, Ire. 100
Garland, Charles Launcelot 122–3
Garland, Mary (Boyle) 121–3
Garlick, T. B. 47–8
Garran, Dr Andrew 32
Gathered in 33

Gaunt, Admiral Sir Guy 189,190
Gaunt, Mary 183,188,189–93,265
Gawler Institute, SA 99,100
Geelong Ladies' College 116
Geer, Rev. G. T. 133
Geneva 83
Germany 5,6,44,109,155,243
Gertrude, the emigrant: a tale of colonial life 41–3
Gill, Henry Horatio 118
Gill, Sarah 118
Gill, Samuel Thomas 43
Gilmore, Dame Mary 93–4,208,224–5,233
Gipps, Lady 19,22
Gipps, Reginald 22
Gippsland, Vic. 77,78,184,187,198,199, 248,249,258
Girls together 235
Gladstone, Qld 89,152
Glasgow, Scot. 127,181,210
Glasgow Herald 210
Glenorchy, Tas. 130
Gloucestershire, Eng. 116
gold-rushes 26,29,45,46,50–2,53–4,54–5, 57,58,75,77,92,98,122,130,132,162, 190,191
Golden hours 113
Goldstein, Elsie 181
Goldstein, Vida 181,182,225
Good Health 182
Gordon, Adam Lindsay 158
Gordon & Gotch 80,81
Gough, Evelyn 181,185
'Gouli Gouli' see Mack, Louise
governesses/writers 2,20,29,35,55–6,86,90, 97,98,138,194,234; *see also* schoolteachers/writers
Gould, Ellen Julia 176
Grand Magazine, UK 240
Grandmama's Australian verse-book 102
Grass flowering 159
Greeley, Horace 205
Green, Fanny L. 204
Greig, Miss 164
Grimsby, Eng. 240
Grimstone, Mary 4,5–10,11,18,254
The Guardian, a tale 2,11,13,14,15–8
Guerard, Eugene von 210
Guerin, Bella 188–9
Gullett, Henry 186,207,208,209
Gullett, Lucinda (Lucy) 207–10,243
Gunn, Frances Hannah 18

Guy's Hospital 83,99

Halloran, Henry 188–9
Hall's vineyard 88
Hampden, Lady 117
Handfasted: a romance 33
Hannay, James 210
Happy Homes: A journal of pure literature for
  the household 180,181–2
Hare, Thomas 31
Harmsworth, Alfred 234,235,236,249
Harrison, Amy see Mack
Harrison, Launcelot H. 238
Harward, Nancy 152
Harwood, Ellen 91
'Hausfrau's Lucky Bag' 117,207
Headley, Lord 139,141
health and medical issues 79,81,82,83,167,
  172,177,181,182,183,194,195,196–7,
  198–9,200
Heney, Amy 209
Heney, Thomas 209,218
Henry, Alice 181,183–8,189,215,220,255,
  264,267
Her father's darling, and other child pictures
  196
Heron, Emily see Manning
Heyne, Therese see Huber
Hill, Cecilia H. W. 86,104–5,188,259
Hill, Fidelia S. T. (Mrs R. K.) 11,12,
  18–19,225
Hill, Frank 159
Hill, Thomas Padmore 104
Hindmarsh, Sir John 18
Hipsley, Dr P. L. 194
The history of Australasia 231
Hobart, Tas. 5–8,47,49,95,102,118,127,
  147,149,177,234
Hobart Colonial Advocate 7,8,254
Hobart Colonial Times 7
Hobart General Hospital 194
Hobart Southern Star 118
Hobart Town Chronicle 7
Hobart Town Courier 8
Hobart Town Magazine 18
Holden, Frances Gillam 3,167,172,173,
  177,183,194–7
Holland 235
Holman, Ada 216–17,234,236,237
Holman, W. A. 216
Home Queen 244
Hope, Florence 182

Hopkins, Francis 101–3
Horticultural Magazine 41
Hospital children, sketches of life and character
  in the Children's Hospital, Melbourne 198
Hospital for sick children, Glebe 194–6,265
Howe, Ann 12–13,118
Howe, George 12
Howe, Robert 12,13
Howitt, William 75,258
Huber, Ludwig Ferdinand 5
Huber, Thérèse 4,5,45,254
Hugh Lindsay's ghost 31
Hughenden, Qld 137
Human toll 141
Humanity and health 196
Hummer 224
'Humming Bee' see Gullett, Lucinda and
  Cameron, Mary Ann
Hunt, Leigh 35
Hunter, F. S. 172
Hunter, Mrs G. A. 199
Hunter, Governor John 193
Hunter, Mrs Percy see Blair, Lily
Huxley, Prof. Thomas 113
Huybers, Charlotte 147,149
Huybers, Edward 147,149,150,263

Ibsen's 'Doll's House' 218
'Icneoral' see Clarke, Mrs A. E.
Illabo, NSW 225
Illustrated London News 244
Illustrated Sydney News 4,95,114,115,
  128–9,131,132–3,147,150,203,207,
  230,234,246
Immomeena: An Australian comic opera 89
In an Australian city 182
In her earliest youth 150
The incredible journey 155
L'Indépendence Belge 149
Inman Valley, SA 79,82
Institute of Journalists, NSW 233
International Congress of Women 158
Interpreter 4,65,74,75,80–3
'Iota' see Caffyn, Kathleen
Ireland 2,13,14–15,16,17,54,92,97,100–1,
  119,137,157,214,234,235,250,254
Ironside, Adelaide 106–8,260
Irvine, Marie 239
'Isabel Massary' see Ramsay-Laye, Mrs E. P.
Isle of Skye, Scot. 153
Italiano Gazette 236
Italy 109,149,193,236,237

'Ixia' see Pelloe, Emily
Jandra station, NSW 92,93,211
Jane Eyre 29
Jersey, Lady 94
Johnson, William 26
Jolimont, Vic. 242
Jones, David Griffiths 119
Jones, Marion 220
Jones, Miss 267
Jones, Mrs D. G. 119
Journal of Australasia 255
journalists/journalism 4,6,28,29,30–1,
32–3,34,35,63,80,106–25,150–1,154,
155,158–9,164,167,171,173,182,183,
184–7,203–4,205–6,207–11,213,
214–27,228–50,251–3,266

*The kangaroo hunters; or, adventures in the
bush* 60
Kapunda, SA 99,239
Kapunda Herald 88,91
Keep, Mrs W. 182
Keese, Oline see Leakey, Caroline Woolmer
Kenna, Francis 125
Kidgell, Ada see Holman, Ada
King, Harriet (Mrs Phillip Parker) 20–1,255
Kirkham's find 191
Kirkland, Katherine 126–7
'Kodak' see O'Ferrall, Ernest
Kunyanga, SA 86
Kurrajong Heights, NSW 40,44
Kyneton, Vic. xi,119,147,261

*La Belle Assemblée, or Bell's court and
fashionable magazine* 9,10
'La Quenouille' see Foott, Mary Hannay
*Ladies Almanack 1858. The Southern Cross or
Australian Almanack and New Year's gift*
74,77–8
Ladies at work 204
Ladies Mercury 64
Lady Bridget of the Never-Never Land 152
Lady's Newsletter: A journal for women only
182
*A lady's visit to the gold diggings of Australia
1852–53* 53–4
Labor/socialist views 33,123–5,155,158–9,
181,185,186,187–8,189,215,224–5; see
also trade unions
'Lal Parklands' see Parker, Langloh
Lamond, Hector 122

Lancashire, Eng. 94–5
Landsborough, William 92
Lane, Anne 177
Lane, William 177,224
Lang, Andrew 136
Lang, Dr John Dunmore 15,106–7,108,260
Lang, Dr W. H. 136
Large, Dr William 119–20
Lasseter family 130
Launceston, Tas. 19,95,129
Lawrence, John 138
Lawson, Gertrude 167
Lawson, Henry 162
Lawson, Louisa 3,4,160–71,173,176,182,
205,208–9,230
Leader, Melbourne 91,246,248–9
leader-writers 32,107,108,115,203,204,
217,219,222,231
League of Nations 222
Leakey, Caroline Woolmer 45,46–50,188
Leakey, Emily 47
Leakey, James 47
Leathem, Charles 121
Leathem, Henry Vale 120
Leathem, John 121
Leathem, Marion 119–21
Lee, Bessie Harrison 3,183,200–2,265
Lee, Sarah (Mrs R. E.) 57–9
Leichhardt, Ludwig 43
Letters to Guy 63
Levy, Miss 182
Lewis, W. G. 34
Leyland, Capt Allen 237
Life and labor 187
Light, Maud 237
Light and shadows of Australian life 54
The lights of Sydney 248
Lily 75
Limerick, Ire. 13,17,137,254
Lindsay, Norman 236,240
Linger, Carl 99,100
Liston, Ellen 86,90–1,259
Literary News 196
Literature in New South Wales 18
A little bush maid 249
A little minx 144
Lloyd, George Alfred 130,133
Lloyd, Jessie 4,128–33,140,207,262
Lloyd, Walter 133
Lockett, Jeannie 225
Loftus, Lord 241
London 1,2,6,18,20,36,38,40,46,48,53,63,

64,75,76,84,86–7,88,95,98,108,113,
136,141,144,149,150,152,156–8,176,
183,192–3,199,215,219,224,225,232,
236,239,240
London *Daily Mail* 236,237,249
London *Daily Mirror* 236
London *Daily News* 53–4
London *Daily Telegraph* 191,193
London *Evening News* 237
London *Graphic* 206
London *Morning Chronicle* 210
London *Morning Herald* 7,8,254
London *Morning Post* 206
London *Observer* 84,158
London *Punch* 76
London *Times* 1,12,20,38,146,148,150–1,
186
Londonderry, Ire. 138
Lone Hand 125,133,135,136,138,236–7,
239,249
*Long Bay, by Bess of the Forest, the Lancashire
Lass* 85
Louisa Egerton, or Castle Herbert 7–9
'Lucinda Sharpe' see Lane, William
Lyceum Club, London 218,219; Melbourne
146,266; Sydney 218,219
Lynch, Andy 121
Lynch, William 84
Lyndhurst College, Glebe 75,82
'Lynette' see O'Brien, Conor
'Lyra Australia' see Holden, Frances
*Lyra Australis, or attempts to sing in a strange
land* 47
Lyttleton Times 221

Macarthur, Maria (Mrs Hannibal Hawkins)
20
McCarthy, Justin 152
Macdonnell, Donald 231
Macfaull, Charles 118
Macfaull, Elizabeth 118
McGowan, Henrietta 220,252
Mack, Amy 234,238
Mack, M. Louise 178,182,188,226,227,
234–7,238,244,246
Mackay, Catherine see Martin, Catherine
Mackenzie, Faith Compton 24,255
Mackinnon, Lachlan 231
Maclehose, James 15
Macleod, William 238
Macleod of "The Bulletin" 238
Macmillan (publisher) 33,38

McMillan, Angus 77
Macrae, Tommy 136
'Madame Carole' 79,80,81,258; see also
Dexter, Caroline
Maitland Mercury 119,208
Manley, Mrs de la Riviere 64
Manning, Arthur Wilcox 23
Manning, Emily 97,113–16,217
Manning, Sir William 113
Mansfield, Rev. Ralph 12,13
'Marcus Malcolm' see Holman, Ada
Margaret Falconer 95
Marian; or, The light of some one's home
86–7,88
A marked man 144,146,147
'Maroon Magazine' 151
Marra station, NSW 133,134
Marriage and heredity/and the social evil 200
A marriage ceremony 144–5
Married Women's Property Act 243
Marriott, Ida 188
Martens, Conrad 90
Martin, A. E. 239
Martin, Arthur Patchett 32,156,158
Martin, Catherine 142,147,153–5,188
Martin, E. A. 107
Martin, Harriette Anne 156,158,159
Martin, Letty H. 104
'Mary of Carcoar' see Garland, Mary
Mason, William 41,42
Massy, Annie Christie 123–5
Massy, John Eyre 123,125
Mates at Billabong 249
May, Phil 195,227,229
Maybanke College, Dulwich Hill 174,180
Medical College and Hospital for Women,
New York 83
Medland, Rev. James Gould 47
Melba, Dame Nellie 216
Melbourne 29,38,45,46,50,51,52–4,61,62,
65,66–7,74,77–9,80–1,83,84,92,95,98,
104,105,116,117,127,130,132,137,141,
143,144–5,146,150,156,157,172,179,
181,182,184,185,187,188,189,200,207,
209,210–11,214–15,222,227,231,233
238,240,242,244,248
Melbourne *Age* x,56,67,70,190,203,219,
220,231,246,248,249,266
Melbourne *Argus* x,29,30–1,36,53,71,146,
181,190,191,199,204–5,220–2,231,233,
238,242,243,266,267
Melbourne Children's Hospital 191,192,

198-9
The Melbourne cookery book 220
Melbourne Cup 102,103,187
Melbourne Herald 200
Melbourne Punch 207,210,214,215,216
Melbourne Shakespeare Society 248
Melbourne Review 32,101,102-4,145,149,
 156,196,259
Melbourne University 180,181,184,188,
 189,190
Melrose, Scott. 28
Memories of the past by a lady in Australia 127
A mere chance 145
Meredith, Charles 35
Meredith, George 151,152,247
Meredith, Louisa 2,27,28,34-40,45,46,
 102,126,188,256
Milan, It. 236
Miller, Dr Hubert Lindsay 191,192
Millett, Mrs Edward 127-8
Mills, Ethel 237
Mills, John Stuart 31
Mills & Boon 240
Minnie's Mission, an Australian temperance
 tale 88
'Mist' see Scott, Maria
The Mistress of Hawk's Crag 95
Mistress Quickly 95,96
Mitchell, David 90,113
Mitchell Library 90,113
Mogador, Celeste see Chabrillan, Celeste de
Molong Argus 120
Molong Express 119-21; Centenary Special
 1976, 120,261
'Montie' 90
Month 71,82
Monthly Packet of evening readings, England
 113,204
Moon, Miss (?Alice) 217,218,267
Moore, J. Sheridan 82
Moran, Cardinal 117
Mordialloc, Vic. 210
Morna Lee and other poems 212
Morris, Professor Edward Ellis 180,190
A mother's offering to her children 2,20,21-3
Mount Barker, SA 86,88,259
Mount Gambier Border Watch 154
Mount McDonald Miner 121,122
The moving finger 191
Mowle, Agnes 220
Mr Hogarth's will 31
'Mrs Alick Macleod' 155 see Martin,

Catherine
Mudgee, NSW 160,162
Mudgee Independent 162
Mudie, James 12
Mueller, Baron von 41
Muir, Marcie 20
Mullis, Grace Jennings see Carmichael,
 Grace Jennings
Mullis, Henry Francis 199
The mummy moves 193
Murphy, Agnes G. 188,214-16
Murray, Andrew 29
Murray, Anna Maria see Bunn, Anna Maria
Murray, Sir Brian 55,257
Murray, Elizabeth A. 46,54-6
Murray, Dr James 16,17,18
Murray, Robert W. F. L. 7
Murray, Sir Terence 16,18
Murray of Yarralumla 13,254
Murray's Home and Colonial Library 36,37
Murray-Prior, Thomas Lodge 151
Murrumbidgee River, NSW 35
musician/writer 116
The music makers 236
My Australian girlhood 152
My home in Tasmania during a residence of
 nine years 36-8,256
Myers, F. W. H. 154
'Myee' see Holman, Ada
Myra 43

Nanson, Janet 222-3,224
Nanson, John Leighton 222,223
'Nardoo' see Holman, Ada
Nation 100,101
National Council of Women 181,243
Native Companion 239
naturalists/writers 2,3,17,23,27-8,35,37,
 38-9,40-1,44,94,126
'New Australia', Paraguay 177,224,225
'new chums' 42
New Idea 225
New Orleans, US 71
New Orleans Picayune 68
New South Wales 5,13,15-18,21-6,35-6,
 40-4,72-3,92-3,97,102,107,108,
 119-22,128-33,134,136,138-40,
 160-2,193,241
'new woman' 28,157
New York, US 36,83,95,108,155,173
New York Herald 243
New York Tribune 205

New Zealand 61,63,102,127,176,177,178,
181,202,221–2,223,237,238
Newcastle Morning Herald 207,209
Newnham College, Camb. 218
newspaper/magazine proprietors 4,12,13,
64–84,118–25,160–71,173–81
Newstead, Darling Harbour 14,16
Nield, Dr J. 248
Nightingale, Florence 194,195
Nilkerloo station, SA 90
Nineteenth Century 225
Nisbet, Hume 158,215
Nixon, Anna Maria 47
Nixon, Dr Francis Russell 37,47
Norfolk, Eng. 143
Norfolk Island 5
Northcliffe, Lord see Harmsworth, Alfred
Northern Territory 43,127
Not all in vain 146
Not counting the cost 150
Notes and sketches of New South Wales during
a residence in that Colony from 1839 to
1845 35–6,37,45,46,256
Nottingham, Eng. 75,82
Nouvelle Revue 149
novels/novel writing 1,5,8–9,13,15–16,26,
29–30,33,38,41–3,47–50,50–3,55–6,
86–91,130,132,141,143–6,149–50,
152–3,155,157,191,193,205,206,219,
235–7,239–40,247–8,249–50
Nuriootpa, SA 87,157,172
nurses/writers 172,176,177,183,194–7,
198–9

O'Brien, Agnes Conor 227,238
Odin, Dr, Bishop of Texas 71
O'Doherty, Kevin Izod 100,101
O'Doherty, Mary Eva 97,100–1
O'Ferrall, Ernest 138
O'Ferrall, Nancy 138
O'Flaherty, Eliza see Winstanley, Eliza
O'Flaherty, Henry Charles 95
The old reef tree. Letters of Ishbel to her half-
brother Mark Latimer 155
Oldbury, NSW 21,40,43
One of Australia's daughters 201
One woman's wisdom 214–15
Orbost, Vic. 198,199
Osburn, Lucy 194,195
'Oriel' 231
'Oscar' see Grimstone, Mary L.
O'Shaughnessy, Edward 12

Osmond, Sophy 214
Over the Straits, a visit to Victoria 38
overseas writers 5,45–6,50–6,57–9,60; see
also visitors/writers

Pall Mall Gazette 156
Palmer-Archer, Laura Maude 128,137–8
Paraguay 177,224,225
Paris 46,50–2,53,75,100,108,109–10,110,
180,208,236
Parker, J. W. & Sons 29–30
Parker, K. Langloh 128,133–6,188
Parker, Langloh 134,136
Parkes, Henry 35,67,72,73
parliamentary reporters 204,221–2,223
Parramatta, NSW 20
Parthenon 246,248,249
Pastoral Times, Deniliquin NSW 119
Pastoralists' Review (Australasian) 102,136
Paterson, Walter 86
Patourel, Capt Henry Le 241
Patourel, Isabelle Le 220,226,241–2,243
Pease, Govenor, Texas, 71
Pelloe, Emily 223
The penance of Portia James 150
Penrith, NSW 14,24,26
Penshurst, NSW 194
People's Advocate and the New South Wales
Vindicator 107
People's Journal UK 10
Perricoote, NSW 102
Perry, Bishop Charles 143
Perry, Charles Stuart 98
Perry, Sarah Susannah 97–8,259
Perth, WA 57–8,63,127,222–4,244
Perth Daily News 133,223,251
Perth Gazette and Western Australian Journal
118
Perth Morning Herald 223
The picture of Sydney and Strangers' Guide in
New South Wales for 1838 15
Pioneers 91
Poems and recollections of the past 18,19
poets/poetry 7,18–9,35,38,47,85,97–101,
102,105,107,108–9,113,114,140,143,
145,146,154,158,159,162,172,196,
198–9,210,212–13,219,227–8,235
political journalists 73,221–2,223
Pope Pius IX 108
Port Arthur, Tas. 47–8
Port Denison Times and Bowen Advocate
123–5,261

Port Denison Times and Kennedy District Advertiser 123
Port Essington, NT 20,22,43
Port Macquarie, NSW 12,127
Port Melbourne, Vic. 80,83
Port Phillip Patriot and Morning Advertiser 7
Port Sorell, Tas. 36
Pread, Winthrop Mackworth 151–2
Praed, Rosa Campbell 3,142,147,151–3, 156,157,158,159,188,263
Prospect, SA 88
proportional representation 28,31,32,33,34, 187
prostitution 175,177,202,243
Prout, Alfred 212
Prout, John Skinner 57,58,59
Prout, Sylvester 212
pseudonyms x,32,33,34,41,46,48,64,85,86, 89,95,99,102,108,109,113,115,129,137, 138,147,148,154,155,156,157,162,163, 172,186,196,207,208,209,211,213,215, 216,218,222,227,228,231,232,239,240, 243,244,246–7,248; *see also* anonymous writing

Quarterly UK 36
Queen Adelaide 18
'Queen Bee' see Carrington, Mrs Tom
Queen Victoria 95,109
Queen's College, Ballarat, Vic. 181
Queensland x,3,43,89,100–1,123–5,137, 151–3,156,158–9,167,211–4,237
Queenslander 33,128,187,207,210,211,212, 213
Quin, Roderick 244
Quin, Tarella 237
Quintus Servinton 1
Quiz 89

Racing in the Never-Never 137,138
Ramsay-Laye, Mrs Elizabeth P. 45–6
Rawson, Mrs Lance 156
Rede, Mary Leman see Grimstone, Mary Leman
Rede, Leman Thomas 6
Rede, William Leman 6
religious/moral influences 1,23–6,32,40,41, 44,47,48–9,50,61,85,86–8,89–90, 91–2,97–8,106–7,132–3,143,172
Republican 162
Retribution 132
Review of Reviews 236,247

Rhymes without reason 89
Richardson, Henry Handel 251
Richmond, Vic. 183,184,200
Rio de Janeiro 18
Robbery under arms 150
Robe, SA 154
Robertson, George 49,130,146,263
Robson, Miss E. B. 176
Rockhampton, Qld 158,159,213
Rockhampton *Morning Bulletin* 158
Rocklea, Qld 211
The romance of a station 152
The romance of nature, or, The flower seasons illustrated 35
Rome 108
'Rose de Bohème' see Rose-Soley, Agnes
Rose-Soley, Agnes 217,218–220
Rose-Soley, John Fisher 219
Rosman, Alice Grant 199,239–40
Rosman, Alice Mary Bowyer 239
'Rosna' see Rosman, Alice Grant
Ross, Dr Andrew MP 120
Rowan, Ellis 94
Royal Geographical Society 62
Royal Society, Tas. 38
Ruskin, John 108

Saint James's Gazette 225
St Kilda, Vic. 52
St Omer, Braidwood, NSW 13,16,17
Sale, Vic. 248
Samoa 231
Sampson Low 86–7,88
San Francisco, US 67–8,70,71,100,219
San Francisco *Alta California* 67,68
San Francisco *Athenaeum* 67,68,71
San Francisco *Evening Bulletin* 67,68
San Francisco *Herald* 68
Sandes, John 231
'Sappho Smith' see Wildman, Alexina
Saturday Review London 56
Savery, Henry 1
school teachers/writers 29,30,75–7,86,87, 90–1,93,98,100,108,116,123,130,174, 181,184,188,210,211,212,213,225
Schurmann, Anna Maria 82
Scone, NSW 138
Scotland 2,28,33,46,61,123,127,153,181, 183–4,218
Scott, David Charles 89
Scott, Maria 85,89–90
Scott, Rose 89–90,176

Scottish Temperance Society 88
Selby, Elizabeth 85,259
Selkirk, Mrs Penelope 40
serial publication 3,28,31,33,38,40,43,46,
 86,88,90,91,95,132,144–5,150,154,172,
 202,213,236,251
'The settlers of Van Dieman's Land' 10
Seven little Australians 247,248
sex education 175,178,184
Shenton, Arthur 118
Shenton, Mercy 118
Shenton, W. K. 118
Shifting scenes of theatrical life 95
Shipley, A. E. 26,255
Short, Henry 248
'Sigma' see Nanson, Janet
The silent sea 154,155
'Silverleaf' see Lloyd, Jessie
Silverleaf Papers 4,129,131,140,207
Silverton, NSW 225
Singleton, Dr John 200
Sinnett, Frederick 30,31
Sister sorrow 152
Sketches of Australian life and scenery 105
Sketches of life in the bush: or, Ten years in the
 Interior 92,93,94
Sladen, Douglas 105,157,158
Smith, Elder & Co. 29,30,33
Smith, R. Kyffin 255
Smedley, William 78
Snodgrass, Colonel Kenneth 97
Snowdrop's message, and other tales 172
social columns 116,206,208,215,217,226,
 228,232–3,238,240,241–2
social issues/reform 2,3,28,30,34,115–16,
 162–71,173–81,186–7,191,194–7,
 198–9,200–2,224–5; see also feminist/
 women's issues
Social life in Sydney; or colonial experience: an
 Australian tale 46
Society of Women Writers, NSW 233,246,
 267
Some of my bush friends in Tasmania 38
'Song of Australia' 97,98,99–100,260
South Africa 5,63,110
South Australia 18–19,29–34,79,82,86–8,
 90–1,98–100,104–5,127,133–4,136,
 154–5,177,212,239
South Australian 29
South Australian lyrics 98,99
South Australian Christmas Annual 88
South Yarra, Vic. 78

Southern Cross 182,239
Southern Phonographic Harmonica 80
Sowden, Will 255
Spectator, London 150,220 or London
 Spectator. Journal of Literature and Art 4,64,
 65–73,75
Spence, Catherine 2,3,27,28–34,46,87,
 106,116,154,155,187,188,204,255
Spence, John Brodie 29,31
Spilsbury, James 14,15,17
Les squatters Australiens 53
Stead, W. T. 236
Steele Rudd's Magazine 159
Steele, William 247
'Stella' see Blackwell, Anna
Stephens, A. G. 140,141,167–8,212–13,
 235,236
Stephens, Brunton 151
Stevenson, Robert Louis 231
Stirling Castle 20,22
Stone, Eugenia 239,240
Storrie, Agnes 188
Stow, Catherine see Parker, K. Langloh
Stow, Percy Randolph 136
Stratford, Vic. 77,78
Strathalbyn, SA 105
Stray chords 219
Strzelecki, Count 77
Stuttgart Morgenblatt fur gebildte stande 5
subscribers and subscriptions 19,66,68,
 70–1,72,73,78,165,170,173,177,178,
 199,246
Sun: an Australian Illustrated Newspaper for
 the Home and Society 180–1,185
Sunningdale Park, SA 104
Surrey, Eng. 86,157
Sutherland, Alexander 32,182
Sutton Forest, NSW 21
Swansea, Tas. 35,36
Sworn to no master x,124
Sydney 5,11–12,14–16,18,21–5,35–7,
 40–1,65–6,70–1,75–6,78–9,82,93–4,
 95,100–7,109,113–15,116–17,130,136,
 140–1,159,162,165,174,179,181–2,188,
 194–6,207–9,217,225,227–30,232–3,
 234–5,237,238,241–6,252
Sydney Daily Telegraph 207,208,219,224,
 225,233,234,238,248
Sydney Dispatch 73
Sydney Evening News 165,225
Sydney Gazette and the New South Wales
 Advertiser 11,12–13,20,22–3,118

Sydney Girls' High School 234,235,236, 237,246
Sydney Mail 4,33,40–1,42,43,44,95,113, 116–17,128,135,144,190,196,206–7,217, 219,220,234,243,244,245
Sydney Morning Herald x,4,12,13,20,21–2, 31,32,36,40,41,43–4,65,67,68–70,73, 106,108,109–12,113,114,115–16, 116–17,119,140,153,156–7,165,205, 208,209,217,217–18,218–20,232,233, 238,241, 242–3,246,266
Sydney press 72–3
Sydney Punch 210
Sydney Quarterly Magazine 114,118–9,197
Sydney Sun 239
Sydney Sunday Times 217,234,246
Sydney University 180,238,242
Sydney University Review 196
Symmons, Davison (Peter) 231

Table Talk 182,240,243,246,249
Talbot, Susan 97
Tales for the bush 2,24–6,126
Tallis's Shakespeare Gallery 95
'Tasma' see Couvreur, Jessie
Tasmania 6–9,28,35,36–8,39,45,47–9, 100,129–30,132,134,137,147–9,156, 191
Tasmanian and Austral-Asiatic Review 9
Tasmanian friends and foes, feathered, furred and finned 38
Tasmanian News 118
Taylor, John 29
Tempted and tried: the story of two sisters, an Australian tale 202
Tender and true: a colonial tale 30
Teens 235,237
temperance 61,88,183,184,200,201,202, 243
Tennyson, Lord Alfred 113
Terembone station, NSW 129,130,132,133
Texas, USA 68,71
'Thalia' see Aronson, Zara
Theatre Magazine 159
Thirty years in Australia 145,146
Thomas, Margaret 156,157,158
Thomson, Catherine Hay 138,181,185,199, 256
The three Miss Kings 145
Three years in Melbourne 46
Thuman, J. A. 123–5
Tipperary, Ire. 157

Todd, E. (Mrs R. H.) 167,230
Todd, Dr Robert 230
Tom Hellicar's children 43
Tonga 231
Toorak, Vic. BB, 215,216
Town and Country Journal 106,107,113,128, 134,137,165,195,196,205–6,210,225, 234,244,246,247
Townsville Hospital, Qld 123,124,125
Tracked by bushrangers 172
Trade Union Woman 188
trade unions 165–6,187–8,215,224,225; see also Labor/socialist views
travel writing 5,38,57–62,193,231,232
Tressa's resolve 44
Tried as pure gold, and other tales 172
Trood, Thomas 12
Truth 97
'Tryphena' see Stone, Eugenia
Turner, Ethel 178,182,188,234,236,237, 244,246–8,251
Turner, Henry Gyles 32,82–3,86,104,156, 259
Turner, Lillian 188,237,246,248
Twain, Mark 247
Twamley, Louisa see Meredith, Louisa
Twenty straws 95–7
A twilight teaching and other poems 158
Typographical Association (NSW) 161, 165,166,205
Tyson, James 134,136

The uncounted cost 193
Uncle Piper of Piper's Hill 148,150
Under the gum tree 156
L'Union des Femmes, Geneva 83
University of Kiel 44,256
Unspoken thoughts 145
Up the Murray 144
Uphill work 31
United States 33,34,59,67–71,83,108,164, 183,187–8,193,202,205,240

'Vagabond' 181,264
Vagabond Annual 1877 149
Valentine, B. B. 243
Van Diemen's Land Co. 6,8
Venice, It. 149,155
Vermont Vale; or, home pictures in Australia 88
'Vesta' see Allan, Stella
Vickery, Bessie see Lee, Bessie Harrison

Victoria 3,29,38,50,52–3,54–6,61,77,92, 97,105,119,127,143–4,147,177,181, 190,191,200,214–16
Victorian Caledonian Society 210
'Victorian Girl' see Baverstock, Florence
Victorian Review 32
Vidal, Rev. Francis 23–4,26
Vidal, Mary 2,3,11,23–6,27,85,126,188
'Viola' 220
visitors/writers 3,5,45–6,47–60; *see also* overseas writers
'A voice from the country' 4,31,40–1,106
Volcanic gold and other tales 156
Les voleurs d'or 50,51,52,53,257
A voyage round the world in His Brittanic Majesty's sloop, Resolution 5

Waddy, Mr 86
Wagga NSW 120,211,213,224,225
Wagga Ladies Seminary 120
Walch, J. 38,48
The walkabouts of Wur-run-ah 136
Walker, Mrs Frank see McGowan, Henrietta
Wallace, Albert E. N. 243
Wallace, Theodosia see Britton, Theodosia
Wallaroo, SA 100
Wangaratta, Vic. 143
war correspondents 109–10,206,234,237
Ward, Lock and Co. 247
Waring, Charlotte see Barton, Charlotte
Warrnambool, Vic. 191
Warrawee Club 187
Watervale, SA 91
Watt, William 12
Watterston, David 186,187,198,210
Waukaringa, SA 154
Waverley, NSW 227,230
Webb, Beatrice 187
Weekes, Cora Anna 65–73,75,258
Weekes, George W. 67–8,69,73,75,258
Weisbaden, Ger. 243
Welch, Daniel Lovett 11
Wellington Evening Post 222
Wentworth, D'Arcy 35
Wentworth, William Charles 108
Werner, Alice 188
West Australian x,118,222–4,261
Western Australia 63,127–8,133,222–4
Western District, Vic. 61,127
Western Mail 222–3,244,246
Westminster Review 225

What is to be will be 95
The wheel of life: a domestic story of bush experience in Australia 130
Wheeler, Miss A. A. 220,242
Where the pelican builds and other poems 211,212
white Australia policy 125
Wigmore, Sheila 233
Wilcannia, NSW 133
Wild, Mrs. E. see Selby, Elizabeth
Wildman, Alexina Maude (Ina) 227–31, 232,235,237,238,252
Williams, Florence 184
Williamstown, Vic. 143,207
Willoughby, Howard 242
Wilson, Gwendoline 13,254
Windeyer, Margaret 176
The window 240
Windsor Magazine plus 247
Windsor, NSW 73
Winstanley, Eliza 85–6,94–7,259
Woden, ACT 16,17,18
Woggheeguy 136
Wolstenholme, Maybanke 3,4,173–80,182
Woman 249
Woman: a journal devoted to women in art, fashion, politics and literarture 182
Womanhood Suffrage League 176,177,208, 264
A woman's experiences in the Great War 237
Woman's love 7,8,9,10,254
Woman's Sphere 182
'Woman's Realm' 220–2
Woman's Voice 4,173,175–80
Woman's World 249
Woman's World: Australian magazine of literature and art 172–3,197
women police and warders 167,177,197
women typesetters 164–5,166,176,205
Women Writers' Club, Melbourne 146; Perth 224
Women's Budget 230
Women' Christian Temperance Union 200
women's columns and pages 4,115,116,117, 160,187,203–25,226–46,251,252
Women's Educational and Industrial Union 83
women's employment 3,31–2,71–2,160, 167,176,183,188,190,191,197,204–5, 217,224,252
Women's ignorance and the world's need 173, 196–7

Women's Industrial Guild 176
Women's Industries and Centenary Fair 217
Women's Literary Society 174;208,243
women's magazines 4,10,64–83,160–82,
  257,264
women's rights 75,160,161,162–4,170,174,
  187,194,196,202,205,258; see also
  feminist/women's issues
women's right to education 3,9,10,160,176,
  183,189,194,195,196,197,215,243
women's suffrage 3,84,140–1,160,165,167,
  170,174–6,181,182,183,185,186,187,
  188,202,217,224,228–30,251
Women's Work Exhibition 222
Women's World 146,197
Woollahra, NSW 94,241
Woolley, Professor John 113
Wolls, Dr William 41
Wordsworth, William 35
Worker Australian 122,125,159,224,225;
  Queensland 159
World, London 150

The world is round 235
World War I 141,189,193,213,218,219,
  234,235,237,238,249; World War II 193
Wright, Miss (Mrs Salmon) 267
Wright, Mrs E. P. see Hope, Florence
writing for children 2,11,20–3,57–60,182,
  222,224,227,238,246–7,248
Wytha Wytha: a tale of Australian life 105

Yackandandah, Vic. 143
Yarralumla, ACT 16
Yass, NSW 43
The yellow aster 157
Yonge, C. F. 113,187
Young, Jeanne 28
Young Australia 182,227,264
Young Ireland Movement 100,101
Yorkshire, Eng. 18,61,118,243

Zayda, a Spanish tale, in three cantos, and other
  poems, stanzas, and canzonets 6